LEADERSHIP FOR THE COMMON GOOD

John M. Bryson
Barbara C. Crosby

LEADERSHIP FOR THE COMMON GOOD

Tackling Public
Problems in a
Shared-Power
World

 Jossey-Bass Publishers
San Francisco

For sales outside the United States, contact Maxwell Macmillan
International Publishing Group, 866 Third Avenue, New York,
New York 10022.

Manufactured in the United States of America

The paper used in this book is acid-free and meets the
State of California requirements for recycled paper
(50 percent recycled waste, including 10 percent
postconsumer waste), which are the strictest guidelines
for recycled paper currently in use in the United States.

10% POST
CONSUMER
WASTE

Library of Congress Cataloging-in-Publication Data

Bryson, John M. (John Moore), date.
  Leadership for the common good : tackling public problems in a
shared-power world / John M. Bryson, Barbara C. Crosby.
    p.   cm.
  "A publication in the Jossey-Bass public administration series and
the Jossey-Bass nonprofit sector series."
  Includes bibliographical references and index.
  ISBN 1-55542-480-5
  1. Leadership.   2. Political leadership.   3. Common good.
4. Public administration. I. Crosby, Barbara C., date.
II. Title.   III. Series: Jossey-Bass public administration series.
IV. Series: Jossey-Bass nonprofit sector series.
JF1525.L4B79   1992
303.3'4 — dc20   92-19032
                                                    CIP

FIRST EDITION
HB Printing   10 9 8 7 6 5 4 3 2 1   *Code 9279*

A joint publication in

the
Jossey-Bass
Public Administration
Series

and

the
Jossey-Bass
Nonprofit Sector
Series

Contents

ix

Preface

We live in a world where no one is "in charge." No one organization or institution has the legitimacy, power, authority, or intelligence to act alone on important public issues and still make substantial headway against the problems that threaten us all. No one is in charge when it comes to the greenhouse effect, AIDS, homelessness, the federal deficit, declining inner cities, drug abuse, domestic violence, or a host of other public problems. Many organizations or institutions are involved, affected, or have a partial responsibility to act, and the information necessary to address public issues is incomplete and unevenly distributed among the involved organizations. As a result, we live in a "shared-power" world, a world in which organizations and institutions must share objectives, activities, resources, power, or authority in order to achieve collective gains or minimize losses (Bryson and Einsweiler, 1991; Trist, 1983; Reich, 1987b; Neustadt, 1990).

If we are to survive and prosper, and if our children and grandchildren — and their children and grandchildren — are to enjoy the benefits of our ability to make the world better, we must find ways to think and act more effectively in shared-power contexts. We must deepen our understanding of the interrelated phenomena of power, change, and leadership.

The Focus of This Book

This book addresses the question of how public leaders can inspire and mobilize others in a shared-power world to undertake collective action in pursuit of the common good. It presents a new, comprehensive approach to public leadership as a shared-power phenomenon that embraces many individuals, organizations, and institutions. It also suggests that sharing power to resolve public issues is a fortunate, rather than unfortunate, necessity, because it ensures that a diversity of voices and needs are heard and addressed. Also fortunately, while no one can give direct orders and dictate terms in a shared-power world with any assurance of compliance, there are effective indirect means available to leaders.

Public leadership, in our view, rests upon nine leadership abilities:

- Understanding the social, political, and economic "givens"
- Understanding the people involved, especially oneself
- Building teams
- Nurturing effective and humane organizations, interorganizational networks, and communities
- Creating and communicating meaning and effectively employing formal and informal forums as settings for creating and communicating meaning
- Making and implementing legislative, executive, and administrative policy decisions and effectively employing formal and informal arenas as settings for policy-making and implementation
- Sanctioning conduct — that is, enforcing constitutions, laws, and norms, and resolving residual conflicts — and effectively employing formal and informal courts as settings for sanctioning conduct

- Attending to the policy change cycle
- Putting it all together

This book is aimed at policy entrepreneurs and advocates of policy change who wish to be change agents and catalysts, reshapers of old arrangements and midwives of new ones. They may be leaders in government, nonprofit organizations, business, or communities, but they are alike in that they must be able to operate effectively across organizational or jurisdictional boundaries, understand power and shared-power arrangements, and raise and address issues so that the common good can be achieved.

Readers familiar with John Bryson's previous work on strategic planning (Bryson, 1988b; Bryson and Roering, 1988; Bryson and Einsweiler, 1988; Bryson, 1991) will see this book as a complement to that work. Strategic planning typically focuses on an organization and what it should do. Leadership clearly is involved; indeed, successful strategic planning requires effective leadership and followership. Public policy leadership, however, goes beyond strategic planning's organizational concerns to focus on the public problems that spill over any organization's boundaries. Collective action involving many organizations, governments, groups, or individuals typically is required to make valuable headway against these problems.

Leadership for the Common Good is based on the premise that successfully tackling public problems requires effective leadership. Effective public leadership will become more common, however, only if it is understood in its full complexity. This book presents the settings within which public leadership is exercised and articulates ways in which they can be developed and managed. It outlines a simple yet effective policy change process and offers clear advice for working through it. In describing the process, we focus principally on public policy change at local, state, and federal levels in the United States, although we believe the process can be adapted to most political contexts. However, we avoided focusing solely on governmental policies because the process of raising and resolving public problems requires effective action across public, private, and nonprofit organizations. We provide many examples of how the process works in practice, and we offer leaders and followers specific guidance for developing, evaluating, and implementing strategies for tackling major public issues and problems. In addition, the book ties our discussion of leadership and policy change to relevant research and literature so that readers can gain a fuller understanding of how and why the process applies to their needs, as well as where they can locate additional insights into the nature and requirements of policy change.

Most importantly, *Leadership for the Common Good* presents new ways of thinking about leadership. Until now, theories of leadership and power have been geared mainly to situations in which a single organization or institution is in charge, or to situations in which individuals, as opposed to organizations or institutions, must share power and authority — as, for example, in legislative bodies and boards of directors. Our shared-power approach allows leaders to be effective in those situations where responsibility must be assumed by many groups.

In a very real sense this book is also about planning, when planning is viewed as "the organization of hope" (Stephen Blum, quoted in Forester, 1989, p. 20). Planning, in other words, is what makes hope reasonable. However, the planning process in shared-power situations is quite different from the process many organizational theorists have recommended. Planning in shared-power situations hardly ever follows a rigidly structured sequence from developing problem definitions and solutions to adopting and implementing proposals. Serious difficulties arise when people try to impose this rigidly sequential approach on situations in which no one is in charge. Nonetheless, to be steadily effective, it is essential to have an organized approach of some sort. Therefore, the challenge is to instill political, technical, legal, and ethical rationality into these difficult situations; that is, the challenge is to link knowledge effectively to action (Friedmann, 1987). Therefore, we describe the kind of *procedural* rationality that can be used to effectively address *substantive* public problems, and we define the conditions and leadership actions that will support that rationality (March and Simon, 1958; Lynn, 1987; Benveniste, 1989; Stone, 1988).

Specifically, *Leadership for the Common Good* develops an integrated, comprehensive approach to public leadership; presents an effective orienting framework for the process of policy change, with special attention to the formulation, adoption, and implementation of public policies; and discusses the design and use of forums, arenas, and courts — the basic settings within which public leadership is exercised and policy change occurs.

Because we seek to develop a general framework and set of arguments, we do not emphasize the institutional details of the U.S. governmental system or of specific government agencies, nonprofit organizations, for-profit organizations, or the networks in which they operate. Instead, we present both a way of thinking about public leadership and guidelines for effective action that we think are useful in a variety of contexts. The details of institutional arrangements matter, however, and at key points, we advise readers to gain additional information that will help them exercise public leadership in their specific contexts.

Audience

We offer our concept of public leadership to people who are seeking to promote public policy change and community reform in a democratic context, even as we recognize that an understanding of how policy change really occurs can at least temporarily aid those who wish to thwart democratic action. Our model of public leadership opens important possibilities for democratic citizenship and change by drawing critical attention to what often has remained hidden or assumed, enumerating and naming access points for influencing public policy, and highlighting the moments of change in a shared-power world. Indeed, revealing the dynamics of shared power makes democratic change more likely, because wider awareness means many more people know how to get in on the action and forestall the abuses of power. As former Vice President Hubert Humphrey observed, "Democracy is based on the premise that extraordinary things are possible from ordinary people." Our hope is that this book ultimately will contribute to the continual regeneration of a democratic, just, free, and sustainable world.

The policy entrepreneurs and community activists for whom *Leadership for the Common Good* was written are likely to fall into three main groups. The first group consists of elected and appointed leaders — policy makers, managers, planners, and analysts in the executive, legislative, and judicial branches of the federal government; state governors, cabinet secretaries, legislators, and judges; county commissioners, administrators, and planners; city council members, city managers, administrators, and planners; school boards, superintendents, and principals; board members and managers of regional commissions and councils of governments; directors, executive directors, managers, and planners of nonprofit organizations involved in health, education, social services, economic development, and other fields; directors of associations; and board members, chief executive officers, public affairs directors, and strategic planners of for-profit corporations.

A second group comprises citizen activists and opinion leaders who wish to understand better how to initiate and effect successful policy changes. This group includes editors and reporters for print, visual, and audio communications media.

A third major audience consists of academics and students in the field of public leadership and policy change. Schools of public affairs, public administration, planning, and public policy offer courses on leadership and policy change, but rarely do those courses link theory and practical advice on public leadership. This book is intended to fill that gap.

Overview of the Contents

Chapter One introduces the idea of a shared-power world with no one in charge and contrasts two types of organization. These two types are the traditional hierarchical organization, in which someone is recognized as being in charge, and the lateral network of organizations and individuals, in which many people are partly responsible for acting on important public problems — and in which power must be shared if those problems are to be addressed effectively. The chapter also contrasts the rational planning model of the hierarchical organization with the political policy-making model of the shared-power world. The task of developing new appreciations of problems and potential solutions in a shared-power context is highlighted. Shared power and shared-power arrangements are defined and their causes and consequences discussed, leading to a call for public leadership. Finally, we introduce two cases of policy change that are used throughout the book to illustrate key points. One case involves civic reform brought about by the establishment and operation of a metropolitan government. The other concerns two competing social movements and the remaking of U.S. abortion policy.

Chapter Two presents our public leadership model in greater detail and outlines the key leadership tasks necessary to deal effectively with public problems in a shared-power world. Chapter Three defines the policy change process in shared-power settings. The process, or cycle, comprises seven phases played out as interconnected activities with shifting purposes and actors in shifting forums, arenas, and courts. Chapter Four discusses shared power and the design and use of forums, arenas, and courts — the settings within which public leadership must operate. The way forums, arenas, and courts are designed and used will affect dramatically how issues are framed and how public policies can deal with them. Our discussion of these settings is tied to a holistic concept of power.

Chapters Five through Eleven describe in detail how to work through the policy change cycle. Each chapter describes one phase of the cycle in terms of desired outcomes; benefits; roles of forums, arenas, and courts; and leadership guidelines. Chapters Five through Seven together consider the process of creating issues — which we define as linked problems and solutions — and placing them on the public agenda. Chapter Five covers the initial agreement to do something about an undesirable condition, or the "plan for planning." Chapter Six discusses the nature of public problems and presents a practical approach to formulating these problems so they can be addressed. Chapter Seven presents an effective way to develop solutions that can help to resolve the problems. This chapter also describes how the nature of issues affects the politics of doing something about them.

Chapter Eight discusses the process of proposal development. The characteristics of winning proposals are presented, as are the differences between "big win" and "small win" solutions. Chapter Nine covers proposal review and adoption. This phase requires a "coupling" of the following change cycle elements: a problem is recognized, a viable solution is available, the political climate is favorable, the barriers to effective action are down, and a decision is reached. Because political manipulation is involved, the chapter also covers agenda control, strategic voting, and the alteration of an issue's dimensions in order to build or break a coalition. Chapter Ten addresses the process of policy implementation, and Chapter Eleven concludes the detailed description of the policy change cycle with a discussion of policy maintenance, succession, and termination.

Our conclusion summarizes the two cases used to illustrate the change process and discusses the major lessons to be learned from them about leadership, policy change, and the design and use of forums, arenas, and courts. Chapter Twelve also guides readers on how to start addressing the important public problems with which they are specifically concerned.

We have also included five resource sections. Resource A shows how to construct cause-effect diagrams, and Resource B details the stakeholder analysis process. Resource C discusses the advantages of retreats to discuss policy and offers a retreat format. Resource D shows how to explore coalition formation options in relation to different problem definitions. And finally, Resource E discusses how "portfolio analyses" of stakeholders can be used to develop winning coalitions or to undermine opposition coalitions.

Leadership for the Common Good should provide much of the guidance public leaders need to formulate and address important public problems effectively. Our hope is that the information and processes supplied in this book will prompt many current and potential public leaders to further commit their time and attention to making the world a better place in which to live, love, dream, and work.

Minneapolis, Minnesota   John M. Bryson
September 1992   Barbara C. Crosby

Acknowledgments

In a sense, this book was begun shortly after we met in May 1970 in Augusta, Georgia. John was a VISTA volunteer working on several community organizing tasks and trying to improve the planning system of a community action agency, while Barbara was a reporter covering education and community affairs for the *Augusta Herald*. We quickly discovered a mutual interest in telling the public the stories of low-income people who were attempting to become effective public leaders. The conversations we began then, and have continued almost daily over the years, have helped each of us learn more about public leadership.

John is particularly grateful to Andre Delbecq, an important mentor and friend, currently professor, department of organizational analysis and management, and former dean, Leavey School of Business and Administration, Santa Clara University. Andre taught John what mentoring is all about: both helping others to discover and accept their embryonic leadership talents and nurturing people in ways that allow the talents to grow and flourish. Mentoring of this sort is a gift that cannot be returned, only passed on, and it is one important purpose of this book. What *can* be returned is heartfelt thanks. Thanks also are due to Andre for his ideas about how to approach major social change efforts. Those ideas are so much a part of John's worldview that he finds it hard to know how to offer thanks for them, except to note that this book would not have been written without Andre's instruction, encouragement, and friendship. Specific thanks are also due Andre for two long lunches important to the completion of this book. On both occasions John's enthusiasm for the project was waning, and Andre, in characteristic, sparkling displays of verbal persuasiveness, convinced John to persevere.

Other mentors for John must be thanked for their instruction. They include Fred Fisher, former city manager of State College, Pennsylvania, and now an international public management consultant; James Kimmey, Robert Durkin, and Joanne Masuret of the Wisconsin State Division of Health Policy and Planning (now part of the Department of Health); Jerome Kaufman, professor of urban and regional planning at the University of Wisconsin, Madison; and Robert Einsweiler, director of research at the Lincoln Land Institute in Cambridge, Massachusetts. John also thanks his father, James Bryson, and mother, Margaret Bryson, along with his sister and brother-in-law, Martha and Charles McIntyre, for the help they gave him in pursuing his educational and professional ambitions.

Special thanks are due to Colin Eden and Fran Ackermann of the University of Strathclyde in Glasgow, Scotland, who have challenged John to explore his public leadership concepts and skills in greater depth, taught him many of their own concepts and skills, and put his and their joint ideas to the test in some very difficult circumstances. In addition, for several years running they have taken him and Humphrey Institute colleague Charles Finn sailing aboard Colin's magnificent sloop *Inshalla* to show them both what the life of the mind was truly meant to be!

Barbara is especially grateful to those with whom she has worked over the last ten years at the Reflective Leadership Center at the Humphrey Institute of Public Affairs. Robert

Terry, the center's first director, has been an important mentor, a vital source of encouragement for Barbara's work, and a partner in working through the paradoxes of leadership. Sharon Anderson, the center's interim director, has been a courageous implementer of the center's leadership theories in practical settings. Lonnie Helgeson, with her special insights into intuitive leadership, has been both an intellectual partner and walking companion. Others who have contributed greatly to the center's efforts to advance leadership theory and practice are Linda McFarland, Pam Hudson, Shari Meerschaert, Marcia Cushmore, Nora Hall, Darryl Bussler, David O'Fallon, John Schneeweis, Gerri Perrault, Carrie Bassett, Bill Swenson, Kirk Milhone, Vicky Binner, Milne Kintner-Dee, and Rick Jackson. The leadership framework presented in Chapter Two has been greatly influenced by Barbara's collaboration with all of these people, especially Robert Terry.

A host of others have contributed to Barbara's learning about leadership and public affairs over the years. The support of her parents, Irving and Louise Crosby, enabled her to attend two excellent universities, where she delved into politics, governance, political philosophy, journalism, and practical research. Jeff Smoller, who preceded her as press secretary to Governor Patrick J. Lucey of Wisconsin, taught her the essentials of good media relations. Her colleagues at the Minnesota Project involved her in numerous public policy debates and in community development initiatives. One of those colleagues, Martha Greenwald, has offered a steady friendship through the long drafting of this book. Barbara also has benefited from being a part of Women Who Talk, a group of savvy women who, with great humor and love, keep alive the links among the professional, the personal, and the political.

Many people supplied their memories and documentation for the two case studies on metropolitan governance and abortion policy. Verne Johnson, Ann Duff, Robert Einsweiler, James Hetland, Thomas Anding, Clayton LeFevere, and Charles Ballentine were extremely helpful in the preparation of the metropolitan governance case. Robert McCoy and Betty Benjamin greatly assisted the development of the abortion policy case.

A number of people at the Humphrey Institute, in addition to those already mentioned, contributed to the book's preparation. Harlan Cleveland, emeritus professor and former dean of the Humphrey Institute, initiated a host of leadership-related educational and research activities at the institute, from which we both have benefited. He and Robert Einsweiler (a former institute professor) coined the "shared-power, no-one-in-charge world" characterization of our times and settings. That phrase has rolled around in our minds for some time and provided a focus for the discussions and inquiries that resulted in *Leadership for the Common Good.* G. Edward Schuh, the dean of the Humphrey Institute, has always been supportive of the project and was particularly helpful during its final six months by protecting John's writing time. Paul Light was an especially encouraging supporter who went over the entire manuscript. Charles Finn, Gayle Zoffer, Barbara Nelson, Harry Boyte, and the late Earl Craig also offered encouragement and insights. In addition, John Ellwood, now a professor at the Graduate School of Public Policy at the University of California, Berkeley, provided useful suggestions.

Colleagues elsewhere at the University of Minnesota also have been extremely helpful. These include Andrew Van de Ven, Stuart Albert, Rosita Albert, Sara Evans, Philip Bromiley, George Shapiro, and Richard Grefe. Colleagues at other institutions also have helped improve our ideas and manuscript. In particular, we would like to thank Robert Backoff, Kimberly Boal, Jeffrey Luke, Brint Milward, Paul Nutt, Festus Nze, Michael Patton, Hal Rainey, Peter Ring, Nancy Roberts, and especially Karl Weick, who first suggested that the forums, arenas, and courts idea deserved a book-length treatment. We are grateful to the many academic audiences who have listened to various aspects of our work and given us valuable feedback. And we would also like to thank our many students who have struggled with our ideas and presentations over the years and helped us improve both.

A number of public leadership practitioners have also helped improve our ideas and presentation. We would like to thank, in particular, John Wells and Joanne Musimeci of the

Minnesota Planning Agency; the Capitol Community Citizens of Madison, Wisconsin; David Riemer, director of administration for the city of Milwaukee; State Representative Beverly Stein of Portland, Oregon; and participants in our two-day public leadership seminars.

Parts of this book have appeared elsewhere. Parts of Chapter One were published in Bryson and Einsweiler (1991), and the discussion of big wins and small wins in Chapter Eight appeared in Bryson (1988a). We would like to thank the publishers for permission to use material that appeared previously.

Finally, we want to thank our children, John Kee Crosby Bryson and Jessica Ah-Reum Crosby Bryson, who keep reminding us that some things are more important than writing books. Of course, paying attention to their lives and needs has delayed completion of this manuscript in delightful ways. But we also must thank them for impressing on us daily the need for effective public leaders if their world — and their children's and their children's children's world — is to be safe, sane, just, free from want, and happy.

JMB
BCC

The Authors

John M. Bryson is professor of planning and public affairs at the Hubert H. Humphrey Institute of Public Affairs at the University of Minnesota. He also directs the Center for Information Technology and Group Decision Support, a research and service center established at the institute in 1991. From 1983 to 1989, he was associate director of the university's Strategic Management Research Center and was a visiting professor at the London Business School for the 1986–87 academic year. He received his B.A. degree (1969) in economics from Cornell University and three degrees from the University of Wisconsin, Madison: his M.A. degree (1972) in public policy and administration, his M.S. degree (1974) in urban and regional planning, and his Ph.D. degree (1978) in urban and regional planning.

Bryson's interests include public leadership, strategic planning, implementation, evaluation, and organizational design. His research explores ways to improve the theory and practice of policy change and planning, particularly through situationally sensitive approaches. He received the 1978 General Electric

Award for Outstanding Research in Strategic Planning. Bryson and William D. Roering received the award for best article in the 1987 volume of the *Journal of the American Planning Association,* and Bryson, Philip Bromiley, and Yoon Soo Jung received the Chester H. Rapkin Award for the best article in the 1989–90 volume of the *Journal of Planning Education and Research.*

Bryson has published numerous articles and book chapters. He is the author of *Strategic Planning for Public and Nonprofit Organizations* (1988), which was named the Best Book of 1988 by the American Society of Military Comptrollers, and of the audiocassette program *Getting Started with Strategic Planning* (1991). He is coeditor (with R. C. Einsweiler) of *Strategic Planning—Threats and Opportunities for Planners* (1988) and of *Shared Power: What Is It? How Does It Work? How Can We Make It Work Better?* (1991).

Bryson has served as a leadership and strategic planning consultant to a wide variety of public, nonprofit, and for-profit organizations. He also has been a regular presenter in many practitioner-oriented training programs, including the Pacific Program for State and Local Government and Nonprofit Executives, sponsored by the University of Oregon; the Legislative Staff Management Institute, sponsored by the National Conference of State Legislatures and the Humphrey Institute; the Michigan Political Leadership Program, sponsored by Michigan State University; and the management programs of the British Civil Service College.

Barbara C. Crosby is an associate of the Reflective Leadership Center at the Humphrey Institute of Public Affairs. She also is the University of Minnesota coordinator for the Hubert H. Humphrey Fellowship Program, which brings midcareer professionals, mainly from Asia, Africa, Latin America, and Central Europe, to the United States for a year of study and professional development. She earned her B.A. degree (1968) in political science from Vanderbilt University and her M.A. degree (1980) in journalism and mass communication from the University of Wisconsin, Madison. She is pursuing her Ph.D. degree in leadership studies at Union Institute.

Crosby has conducted numerous workshops, seminars, and courses on leadership and public policy, women in leadership, and organizational leadership. She has been a consultant for state agencies, professional groups, and community organizations. Her scholarly articles have appeared in *Planning Outlook, Journal of Planning Education and Research,* and *Social Policy.* Her current research interests focus on cross-cultural and transnational leadership.

Before becoming an associate of the Leadership Center, Crosby was on the staff of the Minnesota Project, a nonprofit organization engaged in policy research and community development assistance. She has been a speechwriter for Governor Rudy Perpich of Minnesota, a press secretary for Governor Patrick J. Lucey of Wisconsin, and a reporter or editor for a variety of daily, weekly, and community newspapers.

She is a former cochair of Minnesota Clergy and Laity Concerned and of the Minneapolis Communications Center. During the 1986–87 academic year she lived in England, along with John and their children, where she conducted research on the women leaders in that country.

Part One

Understanding Leadership
in Shared-Power Settings

This section defines and discusses the concepts of public leadership; public policy change; and forums, arenas, and courts as they are designed and used in a shared-power world.

In Chapter One, we discuss the meaning of shared power and articulate the characteristics of the shared-power world. We also describe the nature of political decision making—the characteristic method of raising and resolving issues when no one is in charge. We introduce the two cases that we draw on throughout the book to illustrate our argument. One is a civic reform involving the creation of regional government in the Twin Cities metropolitan area of Minnesota. The other involves two competing social movements and the continuing dispute over

1

U.S. abortion policy. We argue that the dynamics of a shared-power world place a premium on public leadership as a driving force for desirable policy change. In Chapter Two, we define public leadership as the inspiration and mobilization of others to undertake collective action in pursuit of the common good. It requires an understanding of the context, people, teams, and organizational and interorganizational networks, and it is visionary, political, and ethical. It is a collective enterprise and, when it works, a collective achievement.

Chapter Three presents an overview of a seven-phase policy change process, or cycle, in which policy change results from raising and resolving public issues in forums, arenas, and courts. A public issue is created when a public problem is linked with one or more solutions that have both costs and benefits for various stakeholders. The issue must first win a place on the public agenda — the list of items of concern to the public — and then it must win a place on the formal, or decision, agenda of government. Once a policy decision has been made, it must be implemented. Later, the policy must be maintained, succeeded by another policy, or terminated. In Chapter Four, we discuss in detail the design and use of forums, arenas, and courts, which are the characteristic shared-power settings in which public policy change occurs. The chapter elaborates our earlier discussion of the nature of power and presents a view of how public action and institutional arrangements are connected. We analyze the design elements that constitute forums, arenas, and courts and describe how these settings can be used to determine what is discussed and decided, and what is not.

The picture of policy change we present in this section is made up of many parts; but so is the world. Because there are many parts to the picture and because the final picture depends entirely on how the parts are assembled and organized, we have chosen to be guided by the words of Albert Einstein, who said, "Everything should be made as simple as possible, but not simpler" (quoted in Kingdon, 1984, p. 22).

Chapter 1

When No One
Is in Charge:
The Meaning of Shared Power

*The limits on [presidential] command suggest the structure
of our government. The Constitutional Convention of 1787
is supposed to have created a government of "separated powers." It did nothing of the sort. Rather, it created a government
of separated institutions* sharing *powers.*
— Richard E. Neustadt

*If there is no struggle there is no progress. . . . Power con-
cedes nothing without a demand. It never did and it never will.*
— Frederick Douglass

Every day U.S. citizens are confronted by newspaper and television headlines that shock and disturb them with declarations
of massive and seemingly intractable problems. The list appears
endless: crack babies; homeless people; AIDS victims; bruised
and battered victims of domestic violence, child abuse, and
crimes almost unthinkable a generation ago; teenagers with
problems we thought only adults had; families wiped out by cat-
astrophic illness; devastated inner-city neighborhoods; troubled
schools and training systems; small towns wiped out economically by plant closings; aging manufacturing and service industries; crumbling and outdated transportation and communication systems; a health care system that costs twice what it should

yet fails to cover tens of millions of people; inequities and disruptive tensions between genders, races, and classes; massive federal and state budget deficits; despoiled rain forests; a depleted ozone layer — and on and on.

We live in a world where public problems once thought extraordinary now seem routine — and they are piled one on top of the other. But what is truly disturbing is the nagging sense that we have lost our capacity to address these problems effectively. It is one thing to be faced with difficult problems, quite another to think they are insoluble. If nothing can be done, then pessimism, hopelessness, and despair follow.

This sense of ineffectiveness is caused in part by the fact that we live in a world where no one is "in charge" (Cleveland, 1973, 1985). No one organization or institution is in a position to find and implement solutions to the problems that confront us as a society. No one is "in charge" when it comes to helping the crack babies, the homeless, the substance abusers, the sick, and the disenfranchised. No one alone can decrease crime, restore economically ravaged inner cities and small towns, reduce government deficits, or reverse environmental damage. Instead, in order to marshal the legitimacy, power, authority, and knowledge required to tackle any major public issue, organizations and institutions must join forces in a "shared-power" world. In this world, organizations and institutions that share objectives must also partly share resources and authority in order to achieve their collective goals (Bryson and Einsweiler, 1991; Trist, 1983; Reich, 1987b; Neustadt, 1990).

People can become pessimistic about ever solving their problems when they are not altogether sure they know how to pursue desirable public policies in complicated shared-power settings. Nonetheless, if public leaders are to accept the challenge to make the world better, they must find ways to think and act more effectively in shared-power contexts. They must sharpen their understanding of how power, change, and leadership relate. They must view the shared-power world's demands for widely shared leadership as opportunities, not barriers. And they must discover how leaders can enhance their effectiveness when they cannot rely on command, but instead must use more in-

direct means. This book offers ways for public leaders to strive
for the best while avoiding the worst. It is a book about our
public hopes and dreams for a better world, and the way public leaders can make those hopes and dreams reasonable and
practicable.

Two Types of Organizations, Planning, and Decision Making

Let us examine two sharply different types of organizations,
planning, and decision making in order to clarify what we mean
by a shared-power world (see, for example, Morgan, 1986). On
the one hand, there is the traditional, hierarchical bureaucracy,
which fully encompasses a given problem area within its domain and engages in highly rational, expert-based planning and
decision making to resolve it. The organization is "in charge"
and efficiently and effectively makes short work of the problem
(Weber, 1947).

On the other hand, there are fluid and somewhat chaotic
networks of organizations with overlapping domains and conflicting authorities. The problem domain extends far beyond each
individual organization's domain, and even all their authority
combined may not match the boundaries of the public problems they face (see Figure 1.1). No one organization is in charge,
and yet many organizations are affected or have a partial responsibility to act. In such situations, just gaining rough agreement
on what the problems are is part of the battle. Then, in order
to coordinate actions and make progress against the problems,
the organizations involved must also engage in political, issue-
oriented, and therefore messy, planning and decision making.
Further, no matter what is done, the problems are not likely
to be "solved" as much as "re-solved" (Wildavsky, 1979), "dis-
solved" (Ackoff, 1981a; Alexander, 1982), "redefined" (Mitroff
and Featheringham, 1984), or "finished" (Eden, 1987).

Many leaders might wish that the ideal form of the in-
charge organization were more pervasive than it is in reality.
In this ideal form, expertise is rationally brought to bear on well-
understood and well-structured problems; efficient, ethical officials

Figure 1.1. Public Problems in a No-One-in-Charge World.

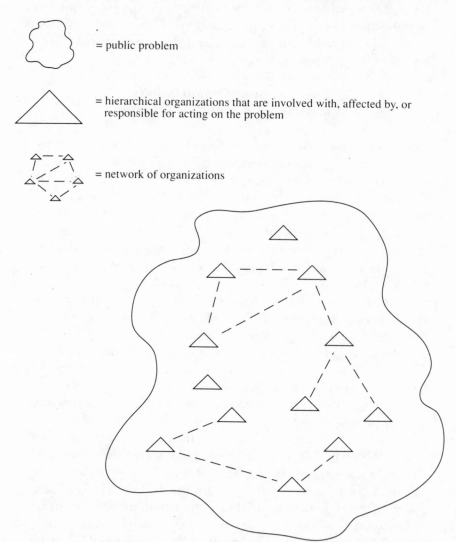

make wise and public-spirited decisions and the problems are solved. This kind of organization can be appealing. A well-managed driver and vehicle license bureau can be a marvel. The organization and staff of the National Park Service in most

U.S. national parks are typically professional, effective, and user-friendly. A municipal fire department that responds efficiently, expeditiously, and courageously to fires and other emergencies is exactly what is needed. Clearly, many situations call for organizations that correspond to this type—even while acknowledging that everyone has had frustrating, demeaning, and occasionally perverse encounters with typical bureaucracies and *petits fonctionnaires.*

In contrast, the second type of organization may not seem like an organization at all. Instead, confused and confusing networks of organizations—including all varieties of groups, associations, and institutions—grapple with inchoate issues and seek problem amelioration more than broad-scale advance. Needed technical expertise may not exist, or, if it does, may not be applied because of resource shortages or lack of agreement on what to do. The picture is not particularly comforting. On the other hand, it is often the reality, and those who want to tackle public issues must make the best of it. As Martin Krieger (personal communication, 1983; see also Krieger, 1981, 1987) has said, "We get into the public affairs business because we are Greeks at heart—we believe in Platonic ideals. Then, of course, we find out we live in a Roman world." However, having drawn a sharp distinction between the two types of organizations, we must emphasize that they are not inherently antithetical. Indeed, a key task in a shared-power world is to include existing hierarchical organizations in the networks that we create to respond to unwieldy problems and issues (Van de Ven, Emmett, and Koenig, 1974; Kiser and Ostrom, 1982; Garud and Van de Ven, 1989; Ostrom, 1990; Whetten and Bozeman, 1991).

The two types of organizations also have distinctly different approaches to policy change. Bureaucracy is associated with "rational planning" (Simon, 1947; Stuart, 1969), while the "issue network" (King, 1978), "policy network" (Milward, 1982), or "advocacy coalition" (Sabatier, 1988) is associated with political decision making (Braybrooke and Lindblom, 1963; Lindblom, 1965; Schultze, 1968; Wildavsky, 1979; Bryson, 1988b). The rational planning model, presented in Figure 1.2, begins with decision-making and problem-solving goals, from which

Figure 1.2. Rational Planning.

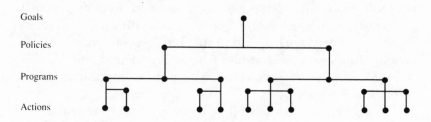

Goals

Policies

Programs

Actions

are deduced policies, programs, and actions to achieve the goals. If the actions are taken, the programs are implemented. If the programs are implemented, the goals are achieved, and the problems are solved. The model makes sense, and to some embodies the very essence of *technically* rational management. It rests on the assumption that there is consensus on the goals, policies, programs, and actions necessary to solve the problems. Moreover, it assumes consensus on what the problems are and how they should be defined. However, these assumptions do not hold in the fragmented, shared-power settings that characterize most important policy change environments.

The political decision-making model presented in Figure 1.3 contrasts sharply with the rational planning model, and its virtues have been articulated clearly and wisely by Lindblom, in particular, in a series of classic articles and books (1959, 1965, 1977; Braybrooke and Lindblom, 1963). This model is inductive, not deductive. It begins with issues, which almost by definition involve conflicts, not consensus. The conflicts may be over ends, means, timing, location, political advantage, and philosophy — and they may be severe. If the effort to resolve the issues produces policies and programs, they will be *politically* rational; that is, they will be acceptable to the involved or affected parties, or stakeholders. Over time, more general policies may be formulated to capture, shape, or interpret the policies and programs initially developed to deal with the issues. These various policies and programs are, in effect, treaties among the

Figure 1.3. Political Decision Making.

Most general
policies

More general
policies

Policies and
programs

Issue area

various stakeholders, and although they may not record a true consensus, at least they may represent a reasonable level of agreement (Pfeffer and Salancik, 1978; Trist, 1983; Sabatier, 1988). Moreover, the inductive movement from public issues to policy decisions can be quite slow. Public policies must usually be endorsed by politicians — those most directly involved in policy decisions — before they can be implemented, and politicians are likely to move cautiously, and often reluctantly, up the steps toward new policies. Their caution stems from three interconnected needs: the need to be sure the move is politically acceptable, technically workable, and legally and ethically defensible; the need to have the move endorsed by a coalition large enough to support and protect it; and the desire to keep as many options as possible open as long as possible.

In a shared-power world, the political decision-making model typically makes the most sense. It reminds leaders to make issues the heart of the policy change process and to frame the issues so that important public problems are addressed. Used effectively, the model can help political decision makers pursue and adopt solutions that contribute to the public good. A particular advantage of the model is that it does not presume consensus where consensus does not exist, yet it can illuminate the contours of consensus or agreement as it develops.

However, as with the two types of organization, we must emphasize that, while we have drawn a sharp distinction between the two approaches to decision making, they are not inherently antithetical. They may simply need to be sequenced properly. In the typical sequence, political decision making is necessary to determine the issues and the politically acceptable programs and policies that resolve them. Rational planning can then be used to recast that agreement in the form of technically workable goals, policies, programs, and actions.

For example, participants in many community-based strategic planning efforts are unclear about their goals, yet convinced that something must be done about problems in areas such as economic development, housing, government reform, and environmental protection. It is only as they grapple with the problems and possible solutions — the issues — that clear goals, policies, programs, and actions emerge. Alternatively, advocacy groups can use the rational planning strategy of starting with goals to highlight the differences between an existing situation and the situation or goals they desire. For example, the Bush administration's education challenge, *America 2000: An Education Strategy,* emphasizes the gap between what public education is and what it should be to achieve important national goals (U.S. Department of Education, 1991). The statement of goals is intended to prompt widespread political decision making as various organizations tackle the issues of translating these goals into practice within their jurisdictions.

Appreciating Problems and Solutions

Political decision making and rational planning in a shared-power context both involve what Vickers (1965) calls "acts of appreciation." Appreciation, in Vickers's usage, is a conceptual and perceptual process that merges judgments of what is *real* with judgments of what is *valuable.* The recognition and naming of a new problem involves a new *appreciation* of how a part of the world works, and what is wrong with it. This appreciation subsequently structures the extent of the problem domain, the development of directions, rules, and resources for addressing the problem, and the accommodation of stakeholder interests.

Typically, it is useful to categorize all problems in three descending levels: developmental, programming, and operational (Kraemer, 1973; Bryson, 1981; see also Ozbekhan, 1969; Jantsch, 1972, 1975). *Developmental* problems are the most complex because goals or policies for dealing with them are still unclear. The problems listed in this chapter's opening paragraph are all developmental. It is developmental problems that are addressed through acts of appreciation, in which the problem is named, defined to the extent possible, and articulated in terms of the values, norms, or goals that have been used to judge why it is a problem and that will guide subsequent efforts to deal with it (Ozbekhan, 1969; Jantsch, 1972).

Programming problems are created once developmental problems are understood and applicable values, norms, or goals articulated. Typically more tractable than developmental problems, programming problems are still quite difficult to approach because they involve multiple, conflicting, and often hard-to-define objectives. Programming problems are addressed through creating effective strategies embedded in policies and programs that can resolve the problems in light of desired values, norms, or goals.

Once strategies are set, problems become *operational;* the question becomes how the strategies can best be implemented. At this level, there are a limited number of objectives that are known or readily defined; agreement on what to do is relatively easy to achieve; and "right" or "correct" answers can usually be defined and articulated without much difficulty. Operational problems are addressed through development of specific budgets, priorities, schedules, regulations, standard operating procedures, and so on.

The rational planning model would suggest addressing problems in the order presented — namely, developmental problems first, in order to establish values, norms, or goals; programming problems second, to determine strategies to serve or achieve the goals; and operational problems third, to make sure the strategies are implemented. Often as not, however, in the real world of public policy-making, the process begins with an operational failure. The sewers do not have enough capacity, kids do not seem to be learning enough, or crime rates go up. These operational failures can lead to rehashing appropriate strategies and programming problems; rethinking appropriate and politically acceptable values, norms, or goals; or redefining the appreciation of the developmental problems. We will return to this three-level distinction in Chapter Three, where we discuss the policy change process in detail.

Our argument thus far is this: to make progress against major public problems in our shared-power world, public leaders can begin with political decision making or with rational planning. But at some point in the policy change process, they must create networks of organizations and groups that engage in issue-oriented political decision making aimed at developing widely shared appreciations of what the problems are and what can be done about them in terms of values, norms, or goals; strategies; and operational details. In effect, these networks will be shared-power arrangements, because no one group will be fully in charge.

What Do We Mean by Shared Power?

A network of organizations can effectively address important public problems only by sharing something, and this sharing can occur in several ways, each with its own level of commitment and loss of autonomy. These methods of sharing, going from least to most commitment and loss of autonomy, include sharing a common objective toward which participants work through informal coordination, sharing activities or resources to achieve a common objective, sharing power, and sharing authority.

This book focuses principally on sharing power. We do not discuss informal coordination (except as a means of policy formulation and implementation), since that level of sharing does not affect individual organizational accountability or responsibility, typically does not require major acts of leadership, and is unlikely to produce major progress on difficult public problems. Nor do we examine shared authority within an existing organization whose domain surrounds an important problem area. The metropolitan governance case discussed throughout this book resulted in an organization that, in a very real sense, is in charge of some problems. But we are principally concerned with the shared-power arrangements that produced that in-charge organization, rather than its subsequent operation.

We define *shared power,* following Giddens (1979, p. 90) and Bryson and Einsweiler (1991, p. 3), as *shared capabilities exercised in interaction between or among actors to further achievement of their separate and joint aims.* The actors can be individuals, groups, organizations, or institutions. For the sake of brevity, we refer to all these actors as organizations. The aims are the desire to achieve gains or avoid losses. Power sharing requires a common or mutual objective held by two or more organizations — whether or not the objective is explicitly stated, agreed upon, or even clearly understood. However, because shared-power situations are "mixed-motive" situations, authority is not merged. Participants reserve the right of "exit" (Hirschman, 1970), so that their other, unshared objectives are protected.

Viewed another way, shared-power relationships exist in the midrange of a continuum. At one end of the continuum are organizations that hardly relate to one another, or are adversaries, dealing with a problem domain that extends beyond their capabilities. At the other end are organizations merged into a new organization that contains a problem domain, pursues shared objectives, and operates cooperatively. In the midrange are coalitions of organizations that have characteristics of both extremes. As in a situation in which the problem outstrips organizational abilities, no one is fully in charge; but the organizations communicate directly and share objectives, as in a merged organization. In addition, although participant organizations hope for a win-win situation, as do those in a merged organization, they will settle for a reduced gain in exchange for a reduced loss, as would adversarial organizations. To borrow a concept from international relations literature, leaders can think of these midrange shared-power arrangements as "regimes" (Easton, 1965, pp. 190–211, 311–319; Young, 1982, 1986, 1989). In a widely cited work, Krasner (1983, p. 2) defines regimes as "sets of implicit or explicit principles, norms, rules, and decision-making procedures around which actors' expectations converge in a given area. . . . Principles are beliefs of fact, causation, or rectitude. Norms are standards of behavior defined in terms of rights and obligations. Rules are specific prescriptions or proscriptions for action. Decision-making procedures are prevailing practices for making and implementing collective choice."

Just as Krasner found the concept of regimes critical to understanding stability, change, and the creation of desirable outcomes in international relations, we found it helpful to understanding how interorganizational networks can tackle complex public problems. A regime essentially embodies ways of appreciating what problems are and what should be done about them. The most useful regimes are likely to be *regimes of mutual gain* that tap and serve people's deepest interests in, and desires for, a better world for themselves and those they care about (Reich, 1987b; Ostrom, 1990; Bellah and others, 1991). The next section will consider why shared-power arrangements, or regimes, are increasingly necessary.

Causes and Consequences of a Shared-Power World

Our shared-power world arises from a number of interconnected causes and produces many interconnected consequences. The result is a complex world system in which change is ubiquitous and not always beneficent (Bryson and Einsweiler, 1991). The challenge for public leaders is to guide change in desirable directions.

Causes

In the twentieth century, the human race entered an era in which it not only has the collective power to make the world better, but also the power to destroy it. This power has at least four causes — *technology, interconnectedness, public policy,* and *population growth.* Over the last several decades, "advanced" nations have used technological breakthroughs to build enough nuclear and chemical weaponry to destroy virtually every living thing. More recently, we have begun to see such unintended and seriously damaging side effects of economic "progress" as global warming and acid rain. Increased use of fossil fuels and certain aerosol sprays, clear-cut forestry, and slash-and-burn agriculture are also rebounding on us. Groundwater supplies are widely polluted as a result of extensive fertilizer and pesticide use, along with improper solid and hazardous waste disposal. Rachel Carson (1962) warned of these dangers years ago, yet in many ways environmental problems stemming from technology are worse than ever. Because the problems created by technology affect so many areas and interests, coping with them requires a shared-power approach.

Technology also contributes to the increased interconnectedness of systems and events (Wallerstein, 1974, 1980; Cleveland, 1985; Neustadt, 1990). Person-to-person communications can be virtually instantaneous anywhere in the world. The merger of computers and telecommunications has produced an increasingly integrated international economic and financial system. While technology has integrated the world, however, it has also made the world more hazardous. Events anywhere can have unexpected and dangerous consequences everywhere. Because of interconnectedness, many of the boundaries we once used to contain and order our world no longer make sense (Cleveland, 1985; Luke and Caiden, 1989; Luke, 1991). For instance, the distinction between domestic and international is becoming less important — witness the dependence of the U.S. economy on foreign trade and the tide of illegal immigration into the United States. Second, distinctions among federal, state, and local responsibilities are fading as more leaders and interest groups at each level become involved in issues at all levels. In many policy areas, we now have well-articulated "policy networks" (Milward, 1982, 1991) that bridge the previous distinctions. Third, traditional distinctions among the policy areas themselves are blurring. Educational reforms are pushed as a kind of industrial policy that will help U.S. firms cope with foreign competition. A strong economy is seen as a way to limit human service costs. And finally, boundaries between public, private, and nonprofit realms are eroding. The nation's health, education, and welfare are a public responsibility, yet increasingly, we rely on business and nonprofit organizations for these services. As distinctions and boundaries blur and areas of legitimate public interest grow, shared-power arrangements become more and more necessary.

Public policy also contributes directly to creation of a world in which sharing power is essential. Many of the previously mentioned distinctions have been embedded in public policy by constitutions, legislation defining state and national boundaries, or antitrust and tax laws. As readers of *The Federalist Papers* know, these distinctions have been created in part to avoid centralization of power and enhance democratic responsiveness and accountability. Similarly, most governmental organizations have their formal authority sharply constrained by statutes designed to limit the chances of unauthorized exercises of power (Rainey, 1991; Lowi and Ginsberg, 1990).

On the other hand, in order to make progress against many important public problems, these distinctions and constraints must be bridged — and often the bridges themselves are created by policy. For example, many different kinds of organizations and levels of government are statutorily involved in the U.S. food stamp program. Similarly, an incredible array of institutions, organizations, and individuals participate in implementing Medicare and Medicaid programs. Such sharing, of course, may not be easy; indeed, Huntington (1981) argues that — virtually by design — we in the United States have a "politics of disharmony."

Finally, dramatic population growth is placing increased pressures on all of the world's resources — natural, economic, social, and political. In 1650, the world's population was around 500 million. It then doubled between 1650 and 1850, and has quadrupled since then. In 1991, it was 5.363 billion — and growing at an annual rate of 1.7 percent. The world likely will have 6 billion people by the year 2000, an added 650 million people in just ten years!

People are a great resource, but they also come with needs that must be addressed through shared-power networks; otherwise, at the extreme, chaos, violence, and death may result. Conceivably, we could end up with the world described by the seventeenth-century political philosopher Thomas Hobbes in *Leviathan,* a world in which "there is always war of every one against every one." In this world, there would be "no arts; no letters; no society; and which is worst of all, continual fear and danger of violent death; and the life of man solitary, poor, nasty, brutish, and short" (Hobbes, 1962, p. 100). While there may not be a need for more *government* in today's world, there is certainly a need for more effective *governance* if the capacity of the world to respond to important public problems is not to be exceeded, and our worst fears of a Hobbesian world realized.

Consequences

The previous section has highlighted technology, interconnectedness, public policy, and population growth as forces that make power sharing necessary. The interaction of these forces produces several consequences that inform and characterize leadership and change in a shared-power, no-one-in-charge world (Bryson and Einsweiler, 1991).

Increased Complexity, Uncertainty, Turbulence, and Risk. As the world becomes increasingly interconnected and populous, it also becomes more complex. Increased complexity, in turn, produces increased uncertainty and, in extreme instances, turbulence — rapid and unpredictable change with bewildering, hard-to-define outcomes. This uncertainty and lack of clarity increases risk for public leaders and managers, because they are expected to make good decisions and take effective actions in situations they do not fully understand or control.

Public leaders and managers have three basic options for responding to complexity and risk. First, they can form shared-power arrangements aimed at reducing individual risk by sharing responsibility. Like most risk-reducing strategies — such as investing in blue-chip rather than high-growth stocks — this one precludes experiencing the lows by forsaking opportunities for the highs. Nevertheless, such strategies can be extremely valuable approaches to handling substantial risks. Second, public leaders and managers may use shared-power arrangements simply to manage complexity. For example, the use of policy networks (Milward, 1991), interorganizational or intergovernmental relations (Whetten and Bozeman, 1991; Anton, 1989), federations (Provan, 1983), public-private partnerships (Frieden and Sagalyn, 1991), or a variety of collaborations (Gray, 1989) are all shared-power strategies for managing complexity. Finally, public leaders and managers can change the way they view interconnectedness. A perception of risk and complexity may be more of a consequence of a particular worldview than of a changed reality (Luke, 1991). People in the United States have been taught to value autonomy and capacity for unilateral action. From this perspective, interconnectedness will always mean increased complexity and risk. It is possible, however, to value interconnectedness as a good in itself because it is a real reflection of our experiences. If we come to value interconnectedness, our sense of complexity and risk will decrease, and our sense of clarity and understanding will increase, as will our capacity to handle the complexity we actually do face.

The Blurring and Interpenetration of Previously Distinct Realms. Earlier, we noted that increased interconnectedness has blurred previously taken-for-granted distinctions between domestic and international venues; federal, state, and local responsibilities; different policy areas; and public, private, and nonprofit realms. Because of this change, managers can never take for granted the distinctions they think make a difference. New distinctions seem to be invented constantly, while old ones dissolve.

Fragmentation, Division, Separation, and the Concomitant Need for Integration. At the same time that technologies and common needs produce interconnectedness, our burgeoning numbers, philosophical differences, and traditional policies work to fragment and divide our world. As was mentioned earlier, sometimes the fragmentation is designed, as in the "separated institutions sharing power" embodied in the U.S. Constitution. The point to keep in mind is that division of any authority or responsibility creates the potential for a shared-power relationship to handle tasks that bridge the divisions. Leadership acumen is needed to ensure that such a relationship actually develops and produces public benefits.

Individual Versus Society and Competition Versus Cooperation.
Our shared-power world embraces enduring contrasts between
individuals and society on the one hand and between competition and cooperation on the other. In addition, individuals (or
individualism) are typically equated with competition, while society is equated with cooperation. Deep philosophical differences
divide those who value individuals most from those who value
society most (Friedmann, 1979, 1987; Mitnick, 1980). In the
world of practice, however, it is more difficult to generalize. An
organization may choose to compete in one situation and to
cooperate in another (Roberts, 1991), or it may cooperate internally to compete externally, or vice versa (Ouchi, 1984). The
world of practice demonstrates that shared-power arrangements
are not "either-or," but "both-and." That is, organizations which
share power typically do not meet as competitively as they would
in a pure competition, such as adversarial court proceedings,
nor as cooperatively as they would in a merger of authority.
Rather, they engage in "friendly" bargaining, which includes
both cooperating and competing, as they move toward a shared
objective.

Declining Capacity to Manage and to Govern. Technology, interconnectedness, certain public policies, and population growth
have reduced the capacity of single organizations, especially
governments, to manage and to govern. Our shared-power, no-
one-in-charge world is also a world of "weak regimes" (Janowitz,
1978). Shared-power arrangements typically are designed to increase governance and management capacity in this world that
is *functionally* interconnected but *structurally* divided, and in which
structural separations are often based on strongly held ideological beliefs. Such shared-power arrangements are not "easy" solutions to "easy" problems. Instead, they are usually difficult-
to-implement-and-manage responses to very thorny problems.

     Before we close this section, we should comment on a
potential critique of our view of the world. Marxists might find
naive our assertion that no one is in charge of most of the world's
problems. They might argue that global capitalism and its "logic
of action" (Karpik, 1977, p. 41), along with the owners of the

means of production, are in charge and that these owners make the policies to which the rest of us must respond.

We are sympathetic to that argument, though we are not Marxists. Business does occupy a privileged position in much of the world, and especially the United States (Lindblom, 1977). In the United States, for example, we basically allow markets to operate until they fail; then and only then do we usually think government intervention justified (Schultze, 1977; Weimer and Vining, 1989). Beyond that, rules embedded in social systems of action, such as capitalism, can allow coordination without overall design, planning, or conspiracy (McNeil, 1981); that is, the rules can produce coordination without a coordinator (Lindblom, 1977; Wildavsky, 1979). The result is that those already favored by the rules continue to dominate and accumulate the wealth produced by "The System," without necessarily directly coordinating their efforts and attacking the disadvantaged (Forester, 1989). When the game is power, those with the most power usually win (Edelman, 1964; Schattschneider, 1975).

But granting all that, what are public leaders and concerned citizens to do? To us, the response is that they must try to change the system, including its rules of operation and logic of action. Further, we think there are relatively independent sources of power that can be used to bring about this change. We think that the state is not simply a captive of "interests" such as big business, but has an independent power of its own (Carnoy, 1984; Evans, Rueschemeyer, and Skocpol, 1985). And we think that citizens can use various "free spaces" (Evans and Boyte, 1986) and existing or invented institutions to pursue a vision of the public interest that benefits most of us, and not just the privileged few (Boyte, 1989).

The Need for Leadership

Articulating opportunities and responsibilities for leaders in a shared-power world may at first seem like a paradoxical activity. After all, the very word *leader* summons images of someone in charge of a bureaucratic organization engaged in rational planning. However, just as there is a leadership image rooted in the in-charge organizational model, there is a leadership image rooted in the issue-networks model. This image calls for leaders who may or may not have positions of authority, but who inspire and motivate followers through persuasion, example, and empowerment, not through command and control (Burns, 1978; Kouzes and Posner, 1987; Bunch, 1987; Neustadt, 1990). Such leaders foster dialogue with their followers and the situations in which they find themselves, and they encourage collective action to address real problems. Further, they claim and make use of the powers they do have to push for changes in a world often resistant to their demands. As Frederick Douglass found, leaders must forcefully wield their own power if they expect to overcome entrenched power.

Of course, in reality, the distinctions between these two images of leadership are often blurred. The moment usually comes when an issues-network leader must make a decision and implement it using whatever powers and controls he or she has. Similarly, leaders who are formally in charge know they often must consult and compromise with other powerful people before acting. In shared-power situations, however, leadership that encourages the participation of others must be emphasized because only it has the power to inspire and mobilize those others. In the effort to tackle public problems, leadership and power must be consciously shared. As Bellah and others (1991, p. 271) argue, "The public lives through those institutions that cultivate a constituency of conscience and vision." Public leaders and their followers create and sustain these kinds of institutions and use them to change other institutions, so that a genuinely good society can result.

Two Cases

To better understand how public leadership and power can be employed and shared to tackle public problems effectively, we looked closely at several cases in which leaders and committed followers tried to find and implement solutions to difficult public problems. Two of these cases, in particular, are used throughout the book to illustrate key points. In both these cases, the existing ways in which issues and their social contexts were viewed became suspect, and new appreciations of what was problematic and what solutions might work were required. One case involves a major civic reform — the establishment of regional government in the Minneapolis–St. Paul metropolitan area of Minnesota — as a means of dealing with the disruptions and stress that accompanied major urban growth. The other focuses on the ethical, medical, legal, and political dilemmas highlighted by the struggles of two competing social movements over U.S. abortion policy.

Major change efforts fall into three categories: civic reforms, social movements, and revolutions. Civic reforms, while requiring complex supportive coalitions and new institutions, do not require deep social paradigm shifts — the central values of the change efforts are reinforced by most existing institutions. The creation of the Metropolitan Council for Minnesota's Twin Cities did not require a reconceptualization of government's functions and espoused operating values; it was, therefore a civic reform.

Some major changes do require paradigm shifts — that is, they seek new patterns of social relations wherein values that were secondary or latent will be articulated and elevated to primacy (Trist, 1983). Such change efforts must become social movements or revolutions in order to succeed. The difference, as Burns (1978) has pointed out, is that revolutions seek to destroy prevailing social and political structures, while social movements seriously challenge these structures without seeking their complete destruction and replacement. The effort to liberalize U.S. abortion laws became a central plank in the platform of the modern women's movement, a movement that challenged the prevailing values and institutional arrangements that enabled men to dominate women. Once the new values of women's equality gained a certain momentum, if not wide-scale institutionalization, a countervailing social movement, most visibly incarnated as the Moral Majority, rose to fight on behalf of an opposing social paradigm, in which sexuality was confined to marital relationships and the ideal marriage was a permanent union between a breadwinning man and a homemaking woman whose mission was to raise God-fearing children. Although both women's rights advocates and the Moral Majority sought fundamental change in U.S. social and political structures, they did not seek their actual destruction and replacement. These change efforts were social movements but not revolutions.

   We believe that the power dynamics of all three types of change efforts are essentially the same, with the possible exception of violent revolution. For the advocates of social movements or revolutions, however, the challenges are likely to be greater, the haul longer, and the use of violence more tempting than for the seekers of civic reform. Certainly, visionary leadership is more critical for social movements or revolutions. Movement or revolutionary leaders must vividly create and communicate images of very different behaviors and institutions than currently prevail. (Because this book focuses on the contemporary United States, we have not included detailed study of a major societal change carried out by revolution.) The following synopses introduce and summarize the Metropolitan Council and abortion policy cases.

Metropolitan Council

In the post–World War II era, the area surrounding the Twin Cities (Minneapolis and St. Paul) underwent the rapid growth characteristic of many other U.S. urban centers of the time. An expanding population found employment in expanding commercial and industrial enterprises. New housing proliferated as burgeoning highway construction made formerly rural areas accessible to urban commuters. By the 1960s, the growth was taxing suburban officials' abilities to provide the services and amenities their constituents demanded. Lacking adequate sewer systems, communities were plagued with overflowing septic tanks that polluted wells and waterways. Prime farmland and potential parkland were gobbled up by subdivisions, while school districts complained of crowded classrooms and strained budgets. Central city officials meanwhile were facing another, but related, set of problems. As the suburbs became attractive places to live, the central cities were losing middle- and upper-income families. Like other U.S. cities, Minneapolis and St. Paul increasingly became home to the poor, the elderly, and unskilled and semi-skilled workers. The cities' property tax bases were eroding, but demand for services was growing.

By the mid 1960s, several leaders in the Minneapolis–St. Paul area were suggesting that some form of metropolitan government might be needed to handle both sets of problems. Among these leaders was Verne Johnson, director of the Citizens League, a "good government" group of business and civic leaders initially organized to focus on Minneapolis. Under his direction, the league moved increasingly to a metropolitan focus and began comprehensive studies of metropolitan problems. Another leading advocate of the regional perspective was Ann Duff, an activist in the League of Women Voters, a member of the Citizens League, and a resident of a western Minneapolis suburb. She believed something had to be done to ensure that metropolitan communities had enough tax revenues to educate their young people and provide other basic services, such as health care and housing for people in need. Yet another early leader was Robert Einsweiler, head of planning for the Twin Cities Metropolitan Planning Commission (MPC). He realized that the MPC, which had merely advisory status, should be superseded by an entity with more real authority.

During the mid 1960s, Johnson, Duff, and Einsweiler joined other leading change advocates in organizing a plethora of study groups, breakfast meetings, and seminars that focused on regional problems and possible regional governance structures. By 1967, a consensus (skillfully orchestrated by the change advocates) had emerged. This consensus was organized around an appreciation of the region's developmental problems, whose existence challenged basic, widely shared values, norms, and goals relating to governance and quality of life. The problems were believed to be at least partly caused by an expanding population, urbanization, and an intergovernmental fragmentation pattern that made it difficult to provide basic services and maintain a satisfactory quality of life at reasonable cost. Therefore, the consensus was also organized around the belief that a *regional* solution was needed to achieve the goals of coordinated, cost-effective planning and coordination of services. Specifically, the consensus supported an elected metropolitan council, established by the Minnesota legislature, to guide regional development and oversee regional services.

At the legislature, the change advocates had supporters but also faced a formidable opponent, Gordon Rosenmeier. An extremely powerful rural senator, Rosenmeier controlled the senate committee that would consider metropolitan governance legislation. Representative William Frenzel and Senator Harmon Ogdahl introduced bills that would establish a "strong," elected metropolitan council with operating control over regional services. Rosenmeier and Representative Howard Albertson countered with bills that would create a "weak" council, appointed by the governor, that merely coordinated regional services. The Rosenmeier and Albertson bills became the heart of the 1967 law that created the Metropolitan Council.

Nevertheless, the new council had considerable potential for augmenting its power. For one thing, the governor appointed some of the most seasoned and respected regional governance advocates as original council members. Additionally, the council was authorized to review long-term comprehensive plans of the various Twin Cities governmental units. It also could suspend the plans of metropolitan agencies if they were inconsistent with the council's development policies. Moreover, the legislature directed the council to prepare reports (including legislative recommendations) on air and water pollution, parks and open space, sewage disposal, taxation, assessment practices, storm drainage, and consolidation of local services.

Since its creation, the council has used these built-in opportunities to develop its vision of the region's future and expand its control over regional policies and programs. It has also clashed with local officials and quasi-independent regional commissions responsible for transit and airports, but its first twelve to fifteen years were mainly expansive and successful. In the early 1980s, however, the council no longer had strong support in the legislature and the governor's office, federal dollars and incentives for regional programs were drying up, and the council began to lose its prestige and momentum. In 1991, a new governor, Arne Carlson, threatened to terminate the council if it could not reinvigorate itself. At the same time, Carlson appointed a respected local official as council chair, the legislature reestablished metropolitan affairs committees, and veteran council supporters offered ideas for council renewal — actions that augured well for the council's future.

Abortion Policy

In the late 1960s, restrictive U.S. abortion laws were challenged by an increasingly large group of civil libertarians, physicians, and feminists who believed women should be able to decide whether to carry their pregnancies to term. In 1962, public opinion had been stirred by the plight of Sherri Finkbine, an Arizona woman who had taken the drug thalidomide during the early stages of her pregnancy. Soon afterward, researchers associated the drug with birth defects. Considerable publicity attended Finkbine's unsuccessful effort to obtain an abortion in the United States and her subsequent trip to Sweden, where the operation was performed. A German measles epidemic a couple of years later also prompted some change in U.S. public opinion. Pregnant women who contracted the disease were in danger of giving birth to deformed babies but were barred from legal abortions because the women themselves were not in danger. Another important event was the formation of the Association for the Study of Abortion Laws in 1965, followed by the founding of the National Organization for Women (NOW) in 1966. Backed by women who were frustrated by women's second-class status in U.S. society, NOW initially sidestepped the abortion issue, but in 1967, adopted a call for abortion reform at its national convention.

Minnesota was a prime battleground for those who wanted to keep restrictive abortion laws and those who wanted to change them. A leading change advocate there was Robert McCoy, a flamboyant steel company salesman, who began operating an abortion information and referral service out of his home in a Minneapolis suburb. Another leader was Betty Benjamin, who,

like McCoy, was a member of the Minnesota Council for the
Legal Termination of Pregnancy. A social worker, Benjamin
had observed firsthand the plight of impoverished pregnant
women. She took to the speakers circuit to emphasize the social benefits of abortions and a woman's right to make her own
childbearing decisions.

Opposing Minnesota's abortion reformers was Minnesota
Citizens Concerned for Life (MCCL), founded in 1967 by a
small group of people including Dr. Fred Mecklenburg, a gy-
necologist from a Minneapolis suburb; his wife Marjory Mecklenburg; and Reverend William Hunt, from the Newman Center
at the University of Minnesota. These leaders contended that
the human fetus had a right to life that should be protected by
state law. MCCL would become a model for cooperation among
Catholic church officials, Catholic lay people, and non-Catholics
in the fight against legalized abortion (Sturdevant, 1978).

The Council for the Legal Termination of Pregnancy succeeded in having abortion reform bills introduced in the Minnesota legislature in 1967 and 1969, but the bills failed to pass,
even though, in 1969, the Minnesota Medical Association backed
the reform. Three other states — Colorado, North Carolina, and
California — did pass abortion reform bills in 1967, and by 1969,
seven more states had liberalized their laws and two had come
close to passing repeal. At the national level, reform gathered
considerable momentum. In 1968, Planned Parenthood, the
American Public Health Association, and the Presidential Advisory Council on the Status of Women endorsed repeal of restrictive abortion laws. National advocacy organizations were
also organized. In 1967, the Catholic church established a Family Life Division to coordinate a national offensive against abortion reform. In 1969, abortion rights activist Lawrence Lader
and others organized the First National Conference on Abortion Laws, the foundation for what would become the National
Association for the Repeal of Abortion Laws (NARAL). This
organization's name reflected a goal shift away from reform
toward total repeal, a shift caused by the reformers' realization
that, in practice, even liberal abortion laws deprived women
of real choice.

As the battle over abortion expanded, none of the combatants realized that the outcome would be greatly affected by an event near Augusta, Georgia, in 1969. As she later recounted the story, Norma McCorvey, a cashier in a traveling carnival, was gang-raped by three men. A few weeks later, after moving to Dallas, she learned she was pregnant. Divorced and already trying to raise one child on very little income, McCorvey sought a legal abortion but found she was not eligible because Texas law permitted abortion only to save a woman's life. McCorvey's physician put her in touch with Linda Coffee and Sarah Weddington, who were eager to challenge the Texas law in court. When McCorvey agreed to become their plaintiff, the two lawyers filed the case known as *Roe* v. *Wade* in U.S. District Court in April 1970. (Years later, McCorvey revealed that she had not been raped; her fabricated story allowed her to escape the social censure against pregnancy outside of marriage [Tribe, 1990].)

By the beginning of the 1970s, women's groups were holding local and national demonstrations demanding access to abortion. They protested at public buildings, medical association conventions, and legislative hearings. Although by now a few more states had passed abortion reform legislation, and four had approved repeal, the Midwest, in particular, remained a bastion of resistance. President Richard Nixon also endorsed the campaign against reform. The abortion debate rapidly became highly emotional and polarized. In Minnesota, for example, abortion opponents publicly equated abortion with murder and displayed pictures of dead fetuses. Robert McCoy countered with pictures of women who had died from illegal abortions. As a similar polarization prevailed wherever abortion legislation was under consideration, legislators became increasingly unable to apply traditional methods of compromise to the abortion issue.

More promising for the advocates of change was the trend in federal court decisions. For example, the district court considering *Roe* v. *Wade* ruled in 1970 that the Texas law was unconstitutional. At about the same time, Georgia's more liberal law was invalidated in *Doe* v. *Bolton*. Both cases were subsequently appealed to the U.S. Supreme Court, which issued its landmark rulings on them in 1973. In *Doe* v. *Bolton,* the court indicated it would not tolerate restrictions on abortion that did not apply to other medical procedures. In *Roe* v. *Wade,* the court emphatically endorsed a woman's right to choose abortion during the first trimester of pregnancy. Although these decisions did not satisfy those who sought a complete end to abortion restrictions, reform groups nevertheless hailed them as a solid victory. Reform opponents, meanwhile, began coalescing into a full-blown "right-to-life" movement aimed at overturning the decisions and enacting new restrictions. The movement was fueled by new national organizations and ultimately by alliance with Jerry Falwell's Moral Majority.

The two sides in the controversy thus have very different appreciations of the developmental problems that need to be addressed and the strategies to be applied. The group that puts the greatest value on freedom of choice for women and on women's health favors the strategy of legal abortion. The group that places the highest value on the life of the fetus promotes a strategy of outlawing, or severely restricting, abortion. The differing appreciations are embedded in the groups' differing concepts and language — pro-choice versus right-to-life, fetus versus baby, abortion versus murder, sex for recreation versus sex for reproduction.

The battle over abortion continues today in Congress, state legislatures, city councils, and the streets. The main change has been that abortion rights advocates have been mainly on the defensive since 1973. Organizational structures and strategies on both sides have varied in the intervening years, and both groups have had setbacks and successes. It is clear, however, that abortion rights advocates created fundamental change; today, abortion is widely available to women who can afford it, and public opinion polls show that a substantial majority of U.S. adults believe women should be able to decide whether or not to have an abortion in the early months of pregnancy.

Summary

Thus far, we have considered how different types of organizations and leadership can either limit or expand responses to a no-one-in-charge, shared-power world. We have discussed how appreciations of problems and solutions embody stability or change in the way values, norms, or goals are articulated and strategies to serve them are created and implemented. We have explored the meaning of shared power and emphasized the need for shared-power approaches to raising and resolving contemporary public problems. Finally, we have introduced two cases of policy change that we will use throughout as practical examples of our ideas.

Chapter 2

Leadership Tasks
in a Shared-Power World

*The essence of leadership in any polity is the recognition of real
need, the uncovering and exploiting of contradictions among
values and between values, the reorganization of institutions
where necessary, and the governance of change.*
— James MacGregor Burns

*[Leadership is] people taking the initiative, carrying things
through, having ideas and the imagination to get something
started, and exhibiting particular skills in different areas.*
— Charlotte Bunch

*Public leadership is the inspiration and mobilization of others
to undertake collective action in pursuit of the common good.*
— Barbara C. Crosby

Public leaders do not, indeed cannot, dictate outcomes and expect that they will happen automatically. Instead, these leaders
enable themselves and others to define or discover the common
good by grappling with public problems. To be effective in this
work, public leaders must understand the larger context, which
often includes the economy, the polity, and even the society as
a whole. They must attend to the people involved and to different levels of social organization from small groups to interorganizational networks. They must understand the policy change

cycle and be skillful in designing and using forums, arenas, and courts. However, before exploring these leadership tasks further, we should re-emphasize that in a world where shared power is more effective than individual power, the tasks of leadership must be widely shared. No one person can embody all the needed qualities or perform all the tasks. People will also pass into and out of leadership roles; a person may be a leader on one issue and a follower on others. This year's leader on a particular issue may even be next year's follower on that same issue.

Examples of the need for shared leadership have been evident on both sides of the abortion controversy. In Minnesota, the Council for the Legal Termination of Pregnancy had an array of leaders, each carrying out different leadership tasks. In addition to Robert McCoy, who provided abortion service information, and Betty Benjamin, who publicized the issue through her public speaking, leaders included Carolyn Qualle, McCoy's neighbor and a university student, who actually instigated the council; Maynard Pirsig, former dean of the University of Minnesota Law School, who drafted reform legislation; and Jeri Rasmussen, council secretary, who worked in the state Democratic Party organization and at the Minnesota legislature for abortion reform legislation. The council's anti-abortion counterpart, Minnesota Citizens Concerned for Life (MCCL), also had shared leadership. Founding leaders Marjorie and Fred Mecklenburg and Reverend William Hunt were joined later in the organization's life by David O'Steen, a Presbyterian schoolteacher who became MCCL executive director, and Nancy Koster, a publicist and spokesperson for the organization.

Shared leadership existed at the national level as well. The crusade for liberal abortion laws was led by Jewish and Protestant ministers, lawyers, physicians, NOW, Planned Parenthood, the American Public Health Association, and NARAL. The early campaign against abortion rights was led by Catholic clergy, the National Right to Life Committee, March for Life, People Expressing Concern for Everyone (PEACE), Prolife Nonviolent Action Project, American Citizens Concerned for Life, and the Right to Life Crusade.

Because it must be extensively shared, public leadership is an extraordinarily complex phenomenon; there is no "one-minute" leadership when it comes to public problems. Behavior in critical incidents certainly matters, but public leadership requires, above all, continuous, shared attention to the multiple dimensions of the process by which public policy is successfully challenged and changed. Before we discuss this process, however, we introduce eight public leadership tasks, or abilities, that we believe are essential to leaders engaged in policy change. A ninth task, attending to the policy change cycle, will be discussed in Chapter Three. The key tasks we will introduce here are:

- Understanding the social, political, and economic "givens"
- Understanding the people involved, especially oneself
- Building teams
- Nurturing effective and humane organizations, interorganizational networks, and communities
- Creating and communicating meaning
- Making and implementing legislative, executive, and administrative policy decisions
- Sanctioning conduct — that is, enforcing constitutions, laws, and norms, and resolving residual conflicts
- Putting it all together

Understanding the Social, Political, and Economic Givens

Leaders need an appreciation of social, political, and economic history, but at the same time, they must avoid being captured by that history (Neustadt and May, 1986; deLeon, 1988–89; Hunt, 1991). They must see history as the interplay of continuity, or stability, and change, and recognize how best to balance these forces in a given context. For example, advocates of regional governance for the Minneapolis–St. Paul area saw that economic and social shifts in the late 1950s and early 1960s opened the door for leadership that championed political change, but also emphasized the goal of preserving each community's desirable qualities. Moreover, they did not seek to supplant existing local government structures but rather to add a new structure that would give each community incentives and aid for acting in accord with a regional public interest. The advocates of liberalizing U.S. abortion laws both responded to and promoted a sea change in attitudes about sexuality and women's roles, a change greatly abetted by technological innovation in the form of the birth control pill. These change advocates initially emphasized continuity, seeking modification of abortion laws rather than outright repeal. They wanted to expand the definition and increase the importance of pregnant women's health and safety, as well as give women more choice in childbearing. It was only when they realized that reforming the laws produced little actual improvement in women's health, safety, and choice that most of them sought more radical change.

It is also important for leaders to recognize that social, political, and economic traditions shape people's ideas of who leaders are and what they do (Rosen, 1984; Higham, 1978), and that U.S. traditions, in particular, have produced some contradictory notions about leaders. People in the United States tend to admire the heroic, charismatic individual who can lead troops or organizations to great victories, yet at the same time, they distrust great concentrations of power and authority. Indeed, John Gardner (1965) suggests that U.S. citizens have been inoculated with an "antileadership vaccine." Thus, ironically, a major leadership challenge becomes countering the prevailing love-hate attitude toward leadership. The lesson for change advocates is twofold—share leadership widely and develop incentives to help sometimes reluctant citizens assume the roles of leaders and committed followers. In a shared-power world, the hero can appropriately be a team (Reich, 1987a) or even a community (Feinstein and Krippner, 1988).

Understanding the People Involved

Leaders who want to understand the people (including themselves) involved in major change must develop an appreciation of the rich diversity as well as the commonality among these people. This is the heart of personal leadership. Useful approaches range from formal assessments to informal storytelling.

Some instruments for formal assessments are the Myers-Briggs Type Indicator (Briggs and Myers, 1977), the Keirsey

Temperament Sorter (Keirsey and Bates, 1978, pp. 5-11), Quinn's competing values instrument (Quinn, 1988, p. 128), Hall and Thompson's grid matching leader-follower styles to value development (Hall and Thompson, 1980, p. 64), and Pearson's Self-Test (Pearson, 1986, Appendix). The Myers-Briggs and Keirsey instruments can help leaders and followers recognize their own strengths and blind spots, and understand and appreciate fellow leaders' and followers' diverse personality types. Hall and Thompson's grid and Quinn's competing values instrument clarify the styles that leaders and followers need to adopt if they wish to actualize certain values. Pearson's Self-Test helps leaders and followers understand where they are in their own "heroic" journeys; that is, the courageous quest to confront personal and societal demons.

One drawback of personality tests is that you can't always give them to those you want to recruit as leaders and followers. Furthermore, their reliability and validity is almost always open to question on one point or another. Fortunately, no one has to rely on paper-and-pencil tests to develop insights into oneself and others. Deep self-reflection may be the most effective tool, particularly when informed by observation and intuition, biographies and great literature, psychological studies, and the numerous studies and commentaries that help leaders appreciate how gender, race, and culture affect people's psyches and behaviors. Martin Luther King, Jr., for example, engaged in such reflection on his own values, experiences, and aspirations in order to guide his actions. To aid this reflection, leaders can write brief accounts of their leadership-followership histories; their economic and moral histories; and the people, events, and cultural forces that shaped their lives. They can consider their deepest values and truest dreams. Looking at what has shaped and guided them in the past clarifies who they are and what they want to achieve as leaders and followers. Two exercises of this type are included in the final chapter. From reflection, leaders can move to storytelling. Sharing histories with others allows leaders and followers to enrich their understanding of each other.

Understanding oneself and others can also develop the

strength of character that invigorates leadership. Such strength enables people to balance competing demands, develop spiritual depth, maintain a sense of humor, and find the courage to take risks, explore new territories, and pursue the unpopular cause — activities which, in turn, reinforce strength of character. Several authors — for example, Bly (1990), Bolen (1984, 1989), Greenleaf (1977), Murdock (1990), Palmer (1990), Pearson (1986), and Terry (forthcoming) — offer important insights for those who seek the inner strength to engage heroically with the world.

Building Teams

Public leaders must also be team leaders, and team leadership is basically facilitation and mentoring — what Schaef (1985, p. 128) describes as enabling "others to make their contributions while simultaneously making one's own." Team leaders naturally must focus on accomplishment of team goals or tasks, but they also must attend to individual team members' needs and consciously promote group cohesion (Johnson and Johnson, 1991). Team leaders will benefit from excelling in the following skills.

Communicating Effectively

The most essential team leadership skill is effective communicating — message sending and message receiving. To send spoken messages effectively, a leader should be complete, specific, consistent, personal, and credible, and should look directly at his or her audience. A message often must be repeated several times in several ways. To receive spoken messages effectively, a leader must be an "active" listener. He or she must look at the speaker, appear alert and interested, avoid interrupting, give verbal feedback, and when warranted, keep the speaker talking. Johnson and Johnson (1991) and Hunsaker and Hunsaker (1986) offer more detailed guidance on verbal communication. Written communication should be accurate, direct, and simple, yet vivid. A good guide for clear and concise writing is Strunk and White (1982).

Balancing Unity and Diversity

Team composition is important. Leaders must ensure that team members can coalesce around team goals, while contributing diverse perspectives, skills, and connections to accomplish those goals. Heterogeneous groups are more likely to generate multiple problem definitions and potential solutions (Johnson and Johnson, 1991; Delbecq, Van de Ven, and Gustafson, 1975). The solutions they adopt are more likely to be effective, integrative, all-gain, and widely accepted (Kanter, 1983; Susskind and Cruikshank, 1987). Leaders should especially try to recruit people who are strong in areas where the leaders are weak. Martin Luther King, Jr., succeeded, in part, because his leadership team included people like Ella Baker and David Abernathy, who had different but complementary leadership styles.

Defining Team Roles, Goals, and Norms

Once the team is together, leaders make their most critical contribution by ensuring that every member's role and the team goals are clearly defined (Johnson and Johnson, 1991). Goals should be set high enough to motivate the group but not so high as to be unachievable. Team goals should include sharing leadership functions and developing each member's leadership potential. Leaders should also help the team adopt basic norms, or guidelines, for working together. An easy way to do this is to have each member list "hope fors" and "hope nots" connected to the group's functioning. Using these lists, leaders can help the group define desirable and undesirable behaviors. Norms that can help teams function effectively include mutual respect, open and honest communication, resource sharing, and the use of consensus when feasible. Some roles, goals, and norms may be established before the team is formed, but it is important that the group decide for itself how to modify, supplement, or supplant these. Full-fledged goal setting and role clarification may be postponed until group members have worked together awhile, but "group norming" should happen early.

Establishing an Atmosphere of Trust

Building trust among team members requires time and contributions from each person, but leaders can lay the foundation. Kouzes and Posner (1987) have found that leaders build trust by:

- Making their values, ethics, and standards clear, and then living by them
- Keeping their commitments and promises
- Trusting those from whom they seek trust
- Going first
- Being open and sensitive to the needs of others
- Demonstrating competence

Fostering Group Creativity and Sound Decision Making

Team leaders can help groups be creative in defining problems and seeking solutions. They can also help groups to make sound decisions about policy through a combination of what Senge (1990) calls dialogue and discussion. Dialogue is a divergent strategy, through which team members explore complex issues from many points of view. They communicate their assumptions openly but suspend making judgments based on those assumptions. Discussion, by contrast, is a convergent strategy, through which team members evaluate alternatives and decide on the best course of action. Group problem solving is conflictual, so leaders must strive to keep the conflict constructive by showing respect for every team member, encouraging expression of feelings as well as ideas, and limiting criticism to ideas and positions rather than persons (Johnson and Johnson, 1991).

Leaders should also decide what amount of participation in decision making will produce the desired results. Vroom and Yetton (1973) have found that, in general, leaders should increase participation to the extent that information and acceptance from others is necessary to make a good decision that is actually implemented. Kouzes and Posner (1987) add that leaders should generally give people real choices as to how they carry out their tasks. This technique increases commitment to the tasks, especially if the choices are visible and difficult to abandon.

Obtaining Necessary Resources

An effective team must have adequate resources for accomplishing its task, and the team leader must help the team develop and implement strategies for acquiring what it needs. In addition to money, resources might include consulting and other services, meeting space, transportation, equipment, and even food.

Tailoring Direction and Support to Team Members

Leaders should vary the amount of direction and support they give followers according to the followers' competence and commitment (Hersey and Blanchard, 1988). As a team member becomes more adept in accomplishing a task, the leader should provide less direction; as the team member's commitment grows, the leader can supply less social and emotional support. Two-way feedback is an important part of this coaching and motivating process. A leader who wants to give effective feedback to a team member on his or her contributions should ask questions; pay attention to the answers; praise as well as criticize; focus on behaviors, not the person; share information and ideas, not advice; be specific; time the feedback well and gear it to the person's needs; and encourage the person to offer his or her own feedback (Hunsaker and Hunsaker, 1986).

Rewarding Achievement and Overcoming Adversity

Keeping in mind that people are likely to do that which is rewarded (Kerr, 1975), leaders should reward only the behavior they want, and be sure they are not rewarding unproductive behavior. Rewards can be as tangible as money and intangible as recognition. For instance, leaders should schedule celebrations to recognize small and large team accomplishments. It is easy to neglect celebrating when one thinks of more pressing group tasks, but leaders must remember that celebrations are a very effective way of rewarding desired behavior.

Because teams must weather adversity as well as success, leaders must also help team members learn from defeat and difficulty. They should nurture in themselves and others what Kobasa and Maddi (cited in Kouzes and Posner, 1987, pp. 65–69) call "psychological hardiness" — the ability to see stressful events as interesting, influenceable opportunities for development rather than as threatening difficulties to be avoided. Leaders in the abortion controversy — especially those advocating women's reproductive rights — had to be extremely hardy to withstand the charges leveled at them by their opponents. The "pro-choice" group battled on amidst cries of "baby killers"; their opponents, meanwhile, endured accusations that they were religious tyrants consigning women to back-alley abortionists.

Recognizing That Leaders and Followers Influence and Empower Each Other

Team leaders need to understand that leader-follower influence is two-way (Johnson and Johnson, 1991; Nicoll, 1984). For example, a leader might articulate a group's vision for working together, but followers probably contributed important elements of the vision. Followers also exercise their influence when they decide to accept or reject a vision. Johnson and Johnson (1991) point out that leaders can expect to receive encouragement and support from followers to the extent that the followers see the leaders as influential in the group's work. If followers do not give their leaders encouragement and support, the leaders know it is time to improve their persuasiveness or turn the leadership over to others. Effective leaders always remember that their power comes from their followers (Kouzes and Posner, 1987; Janeway, 1980; Jago, 1982). Followers meanwhile should empower themselves by rewarding desired leadership behavior (Milhone, 1987), resisting leaders' misuse of authority (Sennett, 1980), and using their collective power (reaching outside the group if necessary) to move into leadership roles themselves.

Nurturing Effective and Humane Organizations, Interorganizational Networks, and Communities

Often the work of a group or team is embedded in a larger organization, a network, or a community, making it necessary for leaders to learn how to operate effectively from various positions in these structures. Leaders who succeed in the key leadership task of nurturing effective and humane organizational structures will practice the following skills.

Attending to Organizational Purpose and Design

Leaders focus on organizational purpose and direction; they ensure that their organizations are designed with mission and philosophy in mind (Selznick, 1957; Bennis and Nanus, 1985; Hunt, 1991). Formal organizational mission and philosophy statements can be put together by a small group of founders, a representative team, or the entire membership. Involving more people is more time-consuming, but also increases the likelihood of widespread "buy-in" and allows everyone to contribute ideas. Effective leaders help organizational members translate these mission statements into inspiring visions of what the organization is striving to accomplish. The advocates of Minneapolis–St. Paul regional governance exemplified this advice as they established task forces and constructed overlapping networks precisely geared to helping participants develop shared meaning about public programs, general agreement about solutions, and pressure for legislative policy decisions and implementation.

Leaders who nurture effective and humane organizations foster cultures (see Schein, 1985) that support mission and philosophy. They align administrative arrangements, operating procedures, and membership or personnel policies with organizational values, and they build social support systems (Selznick, 1957). They use organizational designs that allow appropriate conflicts to surface, while they continually emphasize the organization's animating and unifying vision through organization-wide rituals, slogans, reports, and special events. They are willing to make critical, or nonroutine, decisions that represent irreversible commitments and increasingly institutionalize organizational missions and competencies (Selznick, 1957). Leaders must also be prepared to model the de-emphasis of values and commitments that conflict with new directions (Kouzes and Posner, 1987; Mangham, 1986). For example, they might conduct ceremonies or tell stories that consign old values to ancient history.

Fostering Organizational Integrity

In nurturing organizations that contribute to desirable policy change, public leaders must adopt practices and systems that promote what Wallace and White (1988) call "organizational integrity." Such leaders make a public commitment to ethical principles and then act on them. They involve the organization's stakeholders in ethical analysis and decision making, inculcate a sense of personal responsibility in followers, and reward ethical behavior.

Adapting to Organizational and Environmental Contingencies

Effective public leaders help their followers deal with complexities and uncertainties in the internal and external environments by providing direction, managing rewards carefully, and strengthening the links between individuals and their organizational unit and between units and the larger organization or network (J. G. Hunt, 1984).

Another tactic leaders can use to adapt to environmental demands is the judicious sequencing of decisions. Early in the Metropolitan Council's history, council leaders were under pressure from local communities, the legislature, and the federal government to deal quickly with regional sewer problems. Therefore, the council decided to deal with the issue itself, rather than follow its usual procedure of assigning the issue to advisory committees. Also, in order to avoid reopening wounds from previous battles over apportioning sewer system capacity and costs, the council tried to reach consensus in informal meetings. Because its leaders had recognized the need to make policy decisions at the right time, in the right order (Drake, 1987), the council was able to develop a sewage disposal plan for timely submission to the state legislature.

To ensure that their organizations respond effectively and rapidly to environmental shifts, leaders must continually monitor pertinent developments and trends, assess organizational performance, and be prepared to initiate organizational change (Bennis, 1987). Leaders should also understand how organizational needs vary as organizations progress from start-up to maturity (Selznick, 1957). Quinn (1988) has offered leaders an organizational "life cycles" model, which identifies the operating values leaders should emphasize at different life cycle stages. Bradley (1987) suggests that holistic organizational structures — that is, structures in which the whole is enfolded in all of the parts — are best able to adapt to environmental change because the parts are energized and empowered by their sense of being one with the whole organization.

Finally, leaders should aim for stable community relations (Selznick, 1949, 1957). Organizations — especially those with public policy missions — cannot afford to inadvertently violate community norms and expectations. The Metropolitan Council case offers an example of leaders adapting their policy-making to their political environment. Minnesotans traditionally have prized citizen participation in public affairs; therefore, regional governance advocates developed a highly participatory process for discussing the need for and shape of regional government. Both before and after the council's formation, leaders held seminars to which they invited representatives of diverse stakeholder groups. These seminars helped the leaders produce the consensus that was highly influential in persuading the legislature to create and strengthen the council. The council also followed the participatory model in appointing people from diverse groups (including council opponents) to serve on its many advisory committees.

Remembering That Management and Leadership Are Both Important

In order to motivate people in organizations to do their jobs well, leaders must be good managers or at least associate themselves with good managers (Behn, 1991; Hunt, 1991). Schriesheim, Tolliver, and Behling (1987, p. 55) contend that "effective leadership may account for only 10–15 percent of variability in unit performance" (although in nonroutine or crisis situations, leadership undoubtedly can account for more variance, both positive and negative). In their view, that leaves considerable scope for practicing good management techniques such as attending to details, establishing effective routines, making noncritical decisions, and coordinating with others.

Fostering Organizational Experimentation

Public leaders who are interested in accomplishing major change need experimental attitudes toward their organizations. In the course of their experiments to find suitable structures and methods, they must faithfully protect only those "few essential routines that serve the key values of the organization," and they must root out all others (Kouzes and Posner, 1987, p. 48). They must question assumptions, take risks, and be convinced that, even if they fail, what they learn will be worth the costs (Argyris, 1982; Kouzes and Posner, 1987; Drake, 1987; Behn, 1991). To develop flexible and adaptive organizations they must promote what Manz and Sims (1989) call "self-leadership" throughout the organization. This requires flattening hierarchies, educating people to think for themselves, and establishing open and constant internal and external communication channels (Kouzes and Posner, 1987).

Encouraging Collaboration, Building Teams, and Empowering Other Members of Their Groups or Organizations to Be Leaders Themselves

The leader who takes this approach nurtures collective leadership, increases the ranks of organizational leaders, and produces stronger, more capable, more committed followers. The indirect benefits are increased experimentation, creativity, and innovation.

Caring for Self and Others

Ultimately, successful leaders are "in love — in love with the people who do the work, with what their organizations produce, and with their customers" (Kouzes and Posner, 1987, p. 239). This does not mean, however, that organizational leaders must do all the caring themselves; instead, they should establish social networks, as Selznick (1957) suggests, that can share the tasks of caring.

Scheduling Organizational Celebrations

Celebrations are important ways of recognizing progress toward or achievement of organizational goals. Celebrations should emphasize key organizational values, be public, and have personal involvement of leaders (Kouzes and Posner, 1987).

Planning for Succession

Assuring the long-run survival of the organization includes planning for leadership succession. An organization's need for leadership does not end when current leaders step down. The expression, "The king (or queen) is dead, long live the king (or queen)" is an age-old recognition of the need for leadership continuity (see Bly, 1990). Future leaders must be mentored and grown if they are to assume additional responsibilities smoothly and adequately (Dalton and Thompson, 1986). In addition to training programs, an organization may need to develop specific policies aimed at facilitating leadership turnover (Taylor, 1987).

Nurturing Interorganizational Networks and Communities

To effectively address public problems in a shared-power world, leaders should build a sense of community — that is, a sense of relationship, mutual empowerment, and common purpose — within and beyond their organizations. Community may be tied to a place or be what Heifetz and Sinder (1988) and others have called a community of interest, an interorganizational network that often transcends geographic and political boundaries and is designed to address transorganizational problems (Trist, 1983). Leaders contribute to community building by facilitating communal problem definition and resolution, fostering democratic leader-follower relations (Kahn, 1982; Boyte, 1980), providing resources, and using their knowledge of group process to help people work together. Most importantly, Palmer (1990, p. 138) suggests, leaders build community by "making space for other people to act."

Creating and Communicating Meaning

Public leaders become visionary leaders when they play a vital role in interpreting current reality, fostering a collective group

mission, and shaping collective visions of the future. Furthermore, visionary leaders must not only understand their own and
others' internal worlds, they must also grasp the meaning of
related external worlds. As truth tellers and direction givers,
they help people make sense of experience, and they offer guidance for coping with the present and the future by answering
the questions, what's going on here, where are we heading, and
how will things look when we get there? They frame and shape
the perceived context for action (Smircich and Morgan, 1989),
and they "manage" important constituents' perceptions of public policy and its effects (Lynn, 1987; Neustadt, 1990). In order
to foster major change, they become skilled in the following
methods of creating and communicating new meanings.

Seizing Opportunities to Be Interpreters and Direction Givers in Areas of Uncertainty and Difficulty

Leadership opportunities expand in times of difficulty, confusion, and crisis, when old approaches clearly are not working,
and people are searching for meaningful accounts of what has
happened and what can be done about it (Boal and Bryson, 1987;
Kouzes and Posner, 1987). A sense of crisis definitely impelled
the efforts to establish regional governance for the Twin Cities
and their surrounding communities. Overflowing septic tanks,
overcrowded schools, vanishing farmland and open space, and
growing inner-city poverty constituted a powerful threat to citizens' desires for attractive, well-functioning communities. In
the abortion policy case, leadership opportunities rose from
changes in sexual mores, women's roles, and medical technology, changes that appeared to many to deprive old laws and
practices of their justification. Leaders like Robert McCoy, Betty
Benjamin, and the Mecklenburgs interpreted the clash between
new and old and provided direction for those who wanted to
resolve it.

Revealing and Naming Real Needs and Real Conditions

New meaning unfolds as leaders encourage people to see the
"real" situation and its portents. They find and communicate

a way to align experiences and feelings about a situation with behaviors that have consequences people care about (Boal and Bryson, 1987; Neustadt, 1990).

To illumine "real" conditions, leaders may use intuition or integrative thinking (Cleveland, 1985; Quinn, 1988). They formally or informally scan their environment and discern the patterns emerging from local conditions, or they accept patterns and issues identified by other people, such as pollsters. Simply articulating these patterns publicly and convincingly can be an act of revelation. Revealing new reality calls the old "consensus reality" (Pearson, 1986) into question. However, leaders cannot just delineate emerging patterns and issues; they must also explain them (Neustadt, 1990). They must relate what they see to their knowledge of societal systems (Maccoby, 1983) and to people's experience (Boal and Bryson, 1987). Going further, leaders alert followers to the need for action by their "uncovering and exploiting of contradictions in values and between values and practice" (Burns, 1978, p. 43). This is part of the unselling of old truths that is necessary before new perspectives can be accepted (Mangham, 1986). Awareness of contradictions may also convince followers that the relative emphasis among sets of competing values is dysfunctional and needs to be changed (Quinn, 1988).

Leaders seeking like-minded allies should be aware that people who study trends and issues are not the only revelatory leaders and that artists may also play this role. Guerrilla theatre helped reveal the absurd and outrageous side of U.S. policy in Vietnam. In the women's movement, it helped highlight women's second-class citizenship. Vaclav Havel's plays mocked the Communist regime in Czechoslovakia. Folksingers have long played truth-teller roles, from those who sang of Robin Hood in thirteenth-century England to Woody Guthrie, Bob Dylan, and Joan Baez in the twentieth-century United States.

It should be noted that commentators ranging from Machiavelli to Bailey (1988) have viewed leaders as the exact opposite of truth tellers. Leaders, they argue, must manipulate and even mislead the public in the service of worthwhile goals. We argue, however, that deception by leaders is problematic on practical as well as ethical grounds and must be carefully justified (Bok, 1978; Gutmann and Thompson, 1990).

Helping Followers Frame and Reframe Public Problems

In revealing and explaining real conditions, leaders are laying
the groundwork for framing and reframing public problems
(Stone, 1988). The *framing* process consists of naming and explaining the problem, opening the door to alternative solutions,
and suggesting outcomes. The *reframing* process involves breaking
with old ways of viewing an issue or a problem and developing
a new appreciation of it. Quinn suggests that the leaders most
able to do this are complex, holistic thinkers who engage in "action inquiry." These people have the "capacity to explore a developing situation while acting on the priority of highest apparent
importance, and if appropriate, simultaneously initiating reframing or restructuring" (1988, p. 7). As Trist says, "They learn
the art of walking through walls" (1983, p. 280).

Offering Compelling Visions of the Future

Leaders who effectively communicate meaning draw on past experience, present opportunities, scenarios of the future, fundamental values, and cultural traditions to articulate inspiring
visions of their organization's future (Kouzes and Posner, 1987;
Cleveland, 1985). These visions show how leaders' and followers'
needs, values, and dreams can be realized through their behavior
(Boal and Bryson, 1987). As Burns (1978, p. 18) suggests,
leaders help convert people's hopes and aspirations into "sanctioned *expectations.*" In recent years, this visionary work has been
powerfully evident in the leadership of Vaclav Havel during
Czechoslovakia's "velvet revolution" and of Nelson Mandela during South Africa's search for a post-apartheid society. Visionary leaders show followers what they have in common with each
other (Kouzes and Posner, 1987), and often with the larger society (Boyte, 1989). That is, visionary leaders emphasize the
"we" perspective (Kouzes and Posner, 1987).

      Leaders convey their visions through stories rooted in the
"shared history of a community" (Schneeweis, 1986, p. 8) yet
focused on the future. These stories link people's experience of
the present (cognitions), what they might do about the present

situation (behaviors), and what they might expect to happen as a result (consequences); in other words, the stories help people grasp desirable and potentially real futures (Brickman, 1978; Boal and Bryson, 1987). Effective stories are rich with metaphors that make sense of people's experience, are comprehensive yet open-ended, and impel people toward union or common ground (Terry, 1988). Finally, leaders transmit their own belief in their visionary stories through vivid, energetic, and optimistic language (Kouzes and Posner, 1987).

Championing, Though Not Necessarily Originating, New and Improved Ideas for Dealing with Public Problems

Astute leaders gather ideas from many sources (Burns, 1978; Neustadt, 1990; Meltsner, 1990). Within organizations and political communities, they foster an atmosphere in which innovative approaches flourish (Kouzes and Posner, 1987; Heifetz and Sinder, 1988). The best political leaders, says Burns, provide intellectual leadership by sorting out large public issues and by combining analytical ideas, data, and moral reasoning to clarify implications for political action and government reorganization. Acting in the mode of Schon's (1983) "reflective practitioner," they champion "improved" ideas, ones that have emerged from practice and been refined by critical reflection. Here, again, artists can be leaders by opening society to alternative ideas for handling public problems. For example, Irish musician Bob Geldof, through his Band Aid concerts and follow-up activities, persuaded many people that African hunger should be fought on a dual front, through both emergency aid and projects that foster stable indigenous food supplies.

Finally, leaders have to summon courage to overcome any fears they may have of the new, unpopular, and different. The best ideas often emerge from a dialogue between old and new perspectives, or as Boyte (1989) suggests, from the tension between the real and the ideal. Therefore, public leaders need to be cognitively complex "intuitive experimenters" (Quinn, 1988, p. 19). As Mikhail Gorbachev seems to have done (but perhaps did not do thoroughly enough), they may have to rend their own "cultural envelope" (Terry, 1988, p. 163) and accept "foreign" ways of seeing and doing.

Detailing Actions and Expected Consequences

Often actions and consequences are an integral part of leaders' visions, and become more detailed as implementation plans develop. Crises, however, can necessitate reversing this sequence. When old behaviors are not working and disaster is imminent, followers may wish leaders to prescribe new behaviors and may even be willing to try those behaviors without a full-blown vision of the outcome. To sustain a leader-follower relationship founded on crisis, however, a leader must soon link the recommended course of action to a "higher purpose" (Boal and Bryson, 1987, p. 17). Providing evidence of causal links between the new behaviors and desired outcomes is also critical.

Of the two cases investigated for this book, the abortion controversy involved the kind of crisis in which people feel the need to act immediately and ask questions about vision later. Women seeking safe abortions initially asked for abortion clinic telephone numbers and addresses, not for a comprehensive scheme to end unwanted pregnancies. In contrast, the metropolitan governance case followed the sequence of real needs leading to problem definition, to vision, to policies, and to detailed actions.

Understanding the Design and Use of Forums

Leaders must be adept in designing and using formal and informal forums — that is, the settings for the creation and communication of meaning. It is in forums that visions and policy ideas are articulated, discussed, and refined. We will discuss forums, arenas, and courts in detail in Chapter Four.

Making and Implementing Legislative,
Executive, and Administrative Decisions

Public leaders are also required to be political leaders, and as political leaders, they ultimately fail or succeed through their impact on the policy-making and implementation process of various arenas. The key to success, and the heart of political leadership, is understanding how intergroup power relationships shape policy-making and implementation outcomes. Specifically, political leaders must undertake the following responsibilities.

Mediating and Shaping Conflict Within and Among Constituencies

Conflict is necessary if people are to be offered real choices in various policy-making arenas (Burns, 1978), and political leaders must possess transactional skills for dealing with followers and other leaders who have conflicting agendas. They must bargain and negotiate, trading the things of value they control for others' support and developing gainful positions. Leaders should "use conflict deliberately to protect decision-making options and power, and even more, . . . use conflict to structure the political environment so as to maximize 'constructive' dissonance, thus allowing for more informed decision making" (Burns, 1978, p. 410). Constructive dissonance is maximized through systems of multiple access and advocacy, which link leaders with networks of leaders and followers that can be mobilized to support policy decisions. The trick is to not be immobilized by conflicting advice (Neustadt, 1990). Burns (1978, p. 39) emphasizes that leaders play a "marginal" role, avoiding complete assimilation by any one group in order to be able to deal with conflicts outside as well as inside their constituencies. "Their marginality supplies them with a double leverage, since in their status as leaders they are expected by their followers and other leaders to deviate, to innovate, and to mediate between the claims of their group and those of others." Burns sees this mediation process at work especially in legislative policy-making.

Understanding the Dynamics of Political Influence and How to Target Resources Appropriately

The first requirement for influencing political decision making may be knowing whom to influence. Who controls the agenda of policy-making bodies? Who chairs the key committee? Who can sway a bloc of votes? The next requirement is knowing how to influence. What forms of lobbying, vote trading, arm-twisting, and so on are acceptable? Should change advocates try to change the composition of the policy-making body? Should they use public opinion polls or voter surveys to persuade elected officials to vote for change? Will press conferences help? Given the available time, energy, and resources, how much should be devoted to election campaigns, how much to lunches with decision makers, how much to media relations, and how much to additional research that can bolster arguments for change? (Kaufman, 1986; Coplin and O'Leary, 1976).

Basically, political leaders manipulate the costs and benefits of actions, so supporters are more motivated to act in desired directions and opponents are less motivated to resist (Kaufman, 1986; Baron, 1987). Movement leaders on both sides of the abortion controversy have relied heavily on this technique to influence the promises and positions of candidates for public office. Their tools include endorsements, direct campaign assistance, and attack ads.

Avoiding Bureaucratic Imprisonment

Political leaders in government may find their ability to make and implement needed policy decisions severely constrained by the bureaucracies in which they serve. Those bureaucracies usually have intricate institutionalized rules and procedures and entrenched personnel that hamper any kind of change. Leaders committed to change must continually find ways to appeal over the heads of resistant bureaucrats to the broader public (Burns, 1978, p. 406). However, they must also enlist the bureaucrats in their cause, if possible, since the bureaucrats must be relied upon to carry out many policies.

Understanding the Design and Use of Arenas

Political leaders must be skilled in designing and using formal and informal arenas, the settings for legislative, executive, and administrative decision making. It is in arenas that the practical implications of visions emerging from forums are adopted, hammered into different shapes, or rejected.

Sanctioning Conduct — Enforcing Constitutions, Laws, and Norms and Resolving Residual Conflicts

Public leaders must also be ethical leaders. Acting in formal and informal courts, they must reinforce ethical principles, constitutions, laws, and norms and resolve conflicts about their application. The following leadership tasks are vital to exercising ethical, or judicial, leadership.

Educating Others About Ethics, Constitutions, and Laws

In court decisions, legal articles, and other public communications, leaders must emphasize the importance of acting ethically and upholding constitutions and laws, while explaining the basic principles involved (Tribe, 1985; Arkes, 1986). Basic principles — for example, due process and equal protection — undergird the legitimacy of court decisions and, therefore, their acceptance.

Applying Constitutions, Laws, and Norms to Specific Cases

Constitutions, especially the U.S. Constitution, are usually broad frameworks establishing basic organizational purposes, structures, and procedures. Laws, while much more narrowly drawn, still typically apply to broad classes of people or actions; moreover, they may emerge from the legislative process containing purposeful omissions and generalities that were necessary to obtain enough votes for passage (Posner, 1985). Therefore, both constitutions and laws require authoritative interpretation as they are applied to specific cases. In the U.S. judicial system, judges, jurors, and attorneys, and even interest groups filing amicus curiae briefs, all contribute to that authoritative interpretation. Outside the formal courts, leaders typically must apply norms, rather than laws.

Adapting Constitutions, Laws,
and Norms to Changing Times

Judicial principles endure even as the conditions that prompted them and the people who created them change dramatically. Sometimes public leaders are able to reshape the law to current needs in legislative, executive, or administrative arenas; often, however, as Neely (1981) suggests, leaders must ask formal courts to mandate a change because vested interests that tend to oppose change hold sway over the executive and legislative branches. In the area of constitutional law, in particular, the courts — as the "keepers" of constitutions — are usually the most legitimate venues for reinterpreting those constitutions in light of societal changes.

Resolving Conflicts Among Constitutions, Laws, and Norms

Ethical leaders working through the courts must find legitimate bases for deciding among conflicting principles. In the abortion controversy, several leaders focused on judicial enforcement and reconciliation of constitutions, laws, and norms. By initiating the case that ultimately became *Roe* v. *Wade,* Sarah Weddington and Linda Coffee helped educate women about laws and constitutional principles affecting their reproductive options, even as the two lawyers sought to change the laws. For its part, the U.S. Supreme Court agreed, in effect, to review Texas abortion laws in light of changing medical practices, the evolving constitutional principle of privacy, the common law, and what Justice Harry Blackmun — writing the decision — called "the profound problems of the present day." The decision in *Roe* v. *Wade* both reinterpreted and reinforced constitutional principles and, by overturning a state law, began the process of resolving conflicts between laws and the Constitution. The court was also responding to a conflict between restrictive abortion laws and changing social norms, although it did not directly admit this. Norms were changing in favor of more sexual and reproductive freedom for women, while the laws still embodied a punitive attitude toward women who sought to terminate unwanted pregnancies.

President Reagan subsequently focused on the design of courts in order to resist change, using abortion stance as a litmus test for Supreme Court appointments. President Bush did not publicly use such a test when searching for replacements for retiring justices William Brennan and Thurgood Marshall, but he was quite clear about his personal anti-abortion stance, knew the backgrounds of his nominees, David Souter and Clarence Thomas, and had reason to assume that they were likely to allow additional restrictions on abortion.

Understanding the Design and Use of Formal and Informal Courts

Leaders must be skilled in the design and use of formal and informal courts, the settings for enforcing ethical principles, constitutions, and laws and for resolving residual conflicts. Courts provide the ultimate social sanctions for conduct mandated or promoted through policy-making arenas.

Putting It All Together

The tasks of leadership in a shared-power world are complex and many (Bass, 1990). No single person or group can perform them all; that is why leadership must be shared. Effective public leadership is a collective phenomenon, and a collective achievement. Over the course of a policy change cycle, public leaders must put together the elements we have described in such a way that some important part of the world is made noticeably better. At its best, public leadership can facilitate construction and maintenance of a regime that effectively encourages individuals and groups to organize their actions in such a way that public problems are continuously raised and resolved and the common good is served.

Although leaders sometimes require formal authority, they are often able to act without it. Conversely, people in positions of authority often fail utterly at leadership, either by ignoring the tasks we have described here or by violating laws or ethical principles (Posner, 1985; Tribe, 1985). Instead of circumventing law or opinion, public leaders must inspire others to action by proving to them that the action is in their own interest, when that interest is rightly understood and informed by virtue, as Alexis de Tocqueville and James Madison might have said. In a shared-power world, such a call to action is likely to be effective only when based on widely accepted ethical underpinnings.

Implicit in our argument until now has been the assumption that effective public leaders are systems thinkers (Neustadt, 1990; Senge, 1990; Hunt, 1991) with a deep appreciation of the connectedness of things. They understand people, groups, organizations, institutions, and communities as separate entities and as parts of interorganizational networks. They understand policy change cycles. They are skilled in communicating meaning, making and implementing policies, and sanctioning conduct. They understand people, groups, organizations, interorganizational networks, communities, and their interconnections. And they know how to make a difference. They know when, where, how, and why to intervene with whom and what. And, finally, they are systems thinkers because they know how to put all this knowledge together to achieve their goals of change in public policy.

Summary

This chapter has focused on eight essential public leadership tasks in a shared-power world. These tasks center on understanding environmental "givens"; understanding participants' needs and organizations' and communities' cultures, structures, and processes; knowing how to achieve desired results from communicating, policy-making, and reconciling new and traditional ethical principles; and practicing systems thinking.

Our next objective is to discuss in depth the ninth element of public leadership—attending to the policy change cycle and the opportunities and challenges it offers public leaders. All of the elements of public leadership must be put together effectively *across a policy change cycle* if important issues are to be raised and resolved in politically acceptable, technically workable, and ethically and legally justifiable ways.

Chapter 3

How Innovation Happens: The Policy Change Cycle

For all that moveth doth in Change delight.
— Edmund Spenser,
The Faerie Queene

History is one damn thing after another.
— Robert Sherrill

The general process whereby leaders and followers tackle public problems in a shared-power, no-one-in-charge world can be described as a *policy change cycle* — the term is adapted from the title of May and Wildavsky (1978) — which is depicted in Figure 3.1. We use the word *policy* as a generic shorthand for policies, plans, programs, projects, budgets, and procedures — that is, for all the concepts and activities that are used to resolve problems. We must also emphasize that most public decision making occurs "off cycle" in the course of normal day-to-day bureaucratic operations (Jones, 1982, pp. 39–41; Waste, 1989, p. 39). Off-cycle policy and decision making are not part of the public agenda because day-to-day bureaucratic decision making,

Figure 3.1. The Policy Change Cycle.

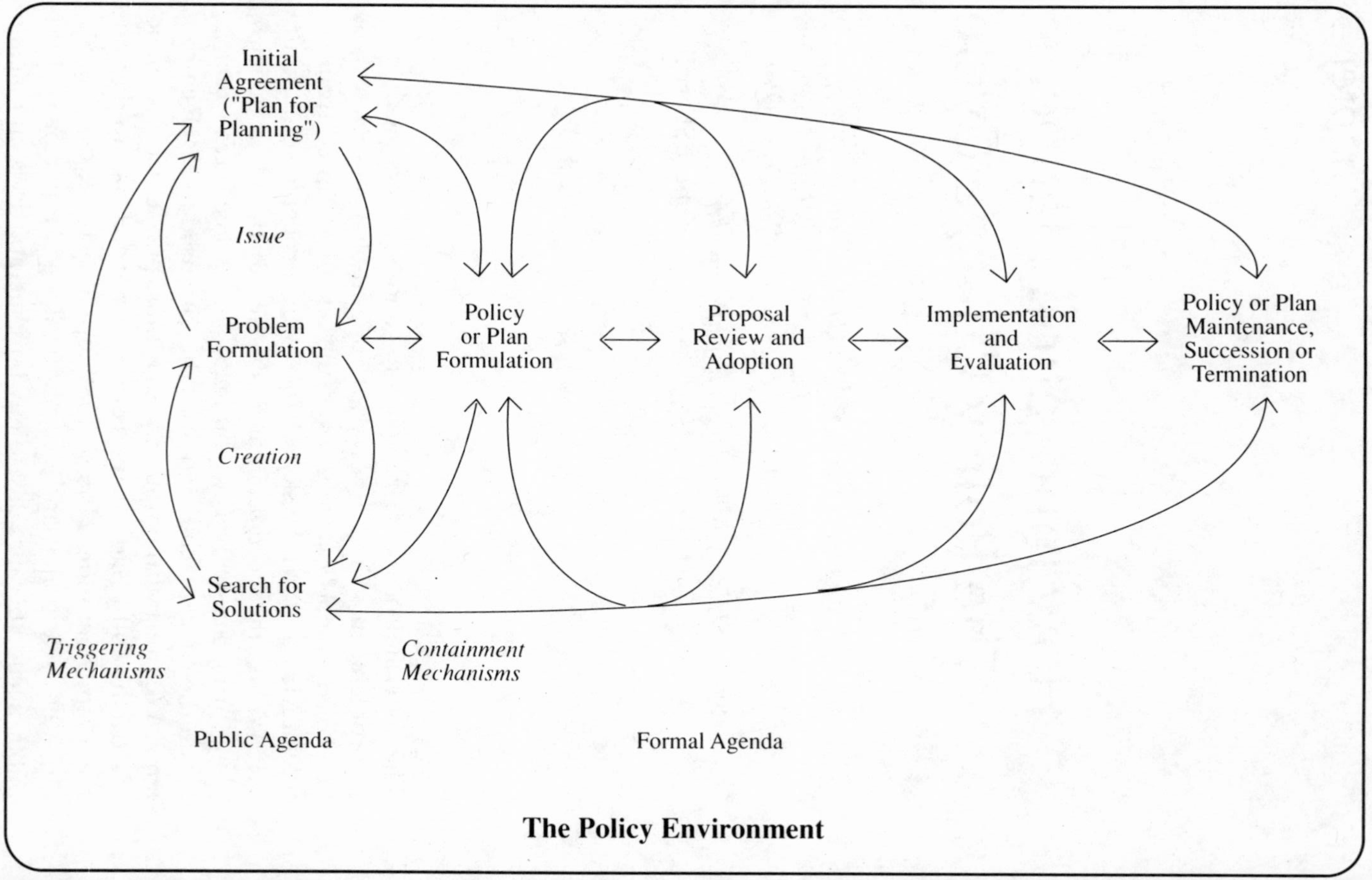

Initial
Agreement
("Plan for
Planning")

Policy or Plan
Formulation

Proposal
Review and
Adoption

Implementation
and
Evaluation

Policy or Plan
Maintenance,
Succession or
Termination

Issue

Problem
Formulation

Creation

Search for
Solutions

*Containment
Mechanisms*

*Triggering
Mechanisms*

Public Agenda

Formal Agenda

The Policy Environment

while it may have widespread indirect effects, does not directly
affect most people, and, therefore, few take an interest in it.
It is usually routine, incremental, and based on formulas, rules
of thumb, or past practice. For example, off-cycle civic decision making might include building and fire code enforcement,
water billing, garbage collection scheduling, city employee pen-
sion investment decisions, and scheduling of personal holidays.

Nonroutine policy-making, on the other hand, usually
occurs "on cycle" as leaders and their various kinds of organizations act on public issues within sets, or structures, of rules,
resources, and transformation procedures. These actions, in
turn, either reinforce or modify the structures, which, in turn
again, shape subsequent actions (Giddens, 1979, 1984). Thus,
the change process itself may alter underlying structures in such
a way that new meanings, actions, or consequences are made
possible. Indeed, the desire to create these new possibilities is
typically the reason for policy change (Lynn, 1987).

The policy change cycle can also be viewed as a set of
interconnected "games" played by reasonably structured and stable rules. The play, however, is often designed to change the
rules. When the rules of the policy game change, meanings, actions, or consequences are also likely to change (Long, 1958;
Schattschneider, 1975; Bardach, 1977; Kiser and Ostrom, 1982;
Lynn, 1987; Ostrom, 1990). The international headlines of the
recent past emphasize what dramatic and fundamental changes
in the rules can occur in a relatively short time. Who would
have guessed in the mid to late 1980s that the Soviet empire
would distintegrate, that we would see the hammer and sickle
lowered over the Kremlin for the last time on the last day of
1991, and that the Communist party would give up its monopoly of power in so many erstwhile communist countries? Who
would have guessed that South Africa's apartheid policies would
begin to be dismantled, Nelson Mandela freed, and the African National Congress party legalized?

On the domestic scene in the mid 1980s, hardly anyone
was worried about ozone depletion or the ethics of conceiving
babies to provide human transplant tissue. The idea that black
men would be elected governor of Virginia and mayor of New

York City by 1990 might have seemed outlandish. And anyone voicing the idea that the defense budget would soon be radically and voluntarily reduced by a Republican president, the
secretary of defense, the chairman of the Joint Chiefs of Staff,
and Congress might have been taken aside and asked solicitously
about her or his mental health.

Turning to the cases prepared for this book, it was hard
to imagine in the 1960s that a woman's right to choose abortion (if she could pay for it) would be taken almost for granted
in the 1980s, or that two U.S. presidents would make their personal opposition to abortion an important consideration in their
choice of Supreme Court nominees. Participants in the early
debates over Minneapolis–St. Paul's regionwide problems would
have been surprised to know that the Metropolitan Council, ten
years after its creation, would be generally unquestioned in its
exercise of broad regional authority. Change is unstoppable,
as both Edmund Spenser and Robert Sherrill saw. Yet people
require both changes — to meet their new needs — and continuity —
to avoid losing what they still value. The world of public policy
is in constant motion, but it also has regularities.

Organized Anarchies, or Anarchy Within Structure

The continual demand for new policies not only creates ubiquitous change but also an anarchic quality in much of the world.
Governmental authority is questioned around the globe. Free
association and voluntary cooperation among individuals across
organizational boundaries and national frontiers is an important value for a large fraction of the world's people. The dream
of life, liberty, and the pursuit of happiness embodied in the
Declaration of Independence and the U.S. Constitution may
turn out to have been the United States' most important import and export. When collective action is needed to address
important problems, however, citizens' individual quests for life,
liberty, and happiness can lead to considerable confusion, disorder, and stress — in short, to some of the consequences of a
shared-power, no-one-in-charge world.

Nevertheless, if much of any public leader's environment
is anarchic, it is also an *organized anarchy,* a term coined by

Cohen, March, and Olsen (1972) to capture the disorder, confusion, ambiguity, and randomness that accompany much decision making in large organizations. The term applies, perhaps with even more force, to the shared-power, interorganizational, interinstitutional environment where no one is in complete charge, and many are partly in charge. For example, Kingdon (1984) uses the same concept to make sense of policy-making at the U.S. federal level, while Lynn (1987) uses it to inform his discussion of U.S. federal executives' management of public policies.

Some characteristics of organized anarchies, especially ones engaged in public policy-making and implementation are offered by Cohen, March, and Olsen (1972); March and Olsen (1979); Pfeffer (1981); and Kingdon (1984), who emphasize the "anarchic," as opposed to the "organized," qualities.

- Goals and preferences are fairly consistent, at least for a time, within social actors — for example, individuals, organizations, and coalitions — but inconsistent and pluralistic across organizations and coalitions.
- The positions of interest groups and the composition of coalitions can change, sometimes quickly.
- Conflict is seen as legitimate and is expected as part of the free play of the political marketplace. Struggle, conflict, and winners and losers result.
- Information is used and withheld strategically.
- Within a social group, actors hold consistent, often ideological, sets of beliefs about connections between actions and outcomes. Across a set of groups, however, there may be considerable disagreement about action-outcome relationships.
- The decision process often appears disorderly because of the clash of shifting coalitions and interest groups.
- Decisions result from the negotiation, bargaining, and interplay among coalitions and interest groups — indicating that these groups find it necessary to share power.

Despite this evidence of anarchy, there are obvious points of stability and predictability in the public policy change process.

Indeed, shared-power arrangements typically are designed to provide some of this stability. The basic organizing features of the policy change process are the various rules, resources, and transformation procedures that structure and legitimate specific actions. Within a single organization, these organizing features constitute what Downs (1967, pp. 167–168) calls the "structured depths," and range from the organization's charter or purpose — the fundamental source of its legitimacy — at the deepest level, through more malleable rules and resources, to its actions. For the United States as a whole, these structured depths begin with a common language, the population's major demographic and socio-economic characteristics, the Constitution, and ideologies that emphasize democracy, equality, liberalism, and individualism (Huntington, 1981; Kammen, 1986). Above this deepest level are various ideas, rules, modes, media, and methods that are drawn on to create and guide action within sets of often hierarchically organized forums, arenas, and courts.

Of particular importance in policy-making are the reasonably predictable "routines of politics" (Sharkansky, 1970; Bromiley and Marcus, 1987), which include various standard operating procedures and predictable behavior patterns, along with regularized decision and action points. These routines make formal change not only possible but likely. They include professional norms, the inertia that propels day-to-day bureaucratic decision making (Allison, 1971), and "accepted practices" — norms that emerge from discussions, comparisons, and contrasts among similarly situated actors. They also include the formal requirements of public policy-making, such as annual budget cycles, legislative renewals, and regular reports and addresses.

Our own view, based more on experience and observation than any scientific study, is that policy-making is most anarchic at the federal level, less so at the state level, and least anarchic at the level of cities and counties, interorganizational networks, and communities of place or interest. Smaller scale makes situations more comprehensible intellectually and manageable processually. Local governments, single interorganizational networks, and communities of place or interest generally are smaller and have a correspondingly increased ability to understand and manage the policy change process. However, even though policy change efforts rarely follow a rigid lock-step sequence in any organization, large or small, it is often possible to predict some of what will happen at particular decision and action points. For example, winning proposals can have predictable characteristics. And politicians can be expected to want to take credit and save face; they need to be able to point to action on important problems. Their need to promote themselves can become a strong incentive for them to promote change (Mayhew, 1974).

In sum, our shared-power world is not as anarchic as it may at first seem. It has many predictable features that, when understood and used properly, can make desirable change more likely. Furthermore, even its anarchy is necessary, because that is what opens up innumerable chances for leaders to take advantage of both the routines of politics and the opportunities for accomplishments that are nonroutine and extraordinary.

What Is Public Policy?

Politics and policy are intimately entwined. Easton (1965, p. 21) defines politics as "the authoritative allocation of values." The "allocations" are embodied in policies. Gerston (1983, p. 6) emphasizes the substantive aspects of policy when he defines public policy as "the combination of basic decisions, commitments, and actions made by those who hold or affect government positions of authority." Lynn (1987, p. 30), on the other hand, emphasizes the symbolic aspects when he says, "Public policy can be said to comprise the meanings or interpretations ascribed by various affected publics to identifiable sequences of governmental actions based on perceived or anticipated consequences of those actions." For our purposes, it is important to include both substantive and symbolic aspects. We therefore define public policy as *substantive decisions, commitments, and actions made by those who hold or affect government positions of authority, as they are interpreted by various stakeholders.* Thus, public policy is what affected people think it is, based on what the substantive content symbolizes to them. People's perceptions here are absolutely critical because they are politically consequential—even when they are at odds with the "facts" as seen by reasonably objective observers (Lynn, 1987).

Public policies may go by various names in different circumstances; they may be called policies, plans, programs, projects, decisions, actions, budgets, rules, or regulations. Moreover, they can emerge deliberately or be "resultants" of mutual adjustment among partisans (Lindblom, 1959; Mintzberg and Waters, 1985). In other words, public policies sometimes are decided upon, and at other times simply "emerge" or "happen."

The Policy Change Cycle

The partly structured anarchy that we call the policy change cycle is a way of thinking about how policy formulation, adoption, implementation, perseverence, and change occur in a shared-power world. Although we will emphasize the cycle as it applies to public policies, we think the process we describe is typical of "on-cycle" change in large organizations and interorganizational networks (Quinn, 1980; Trist, 1983). However, the particular change setting does matter a great deal, and we will be discussing the situational factors that affect how the process might unfold or be guided in particular circumstances.

The policy change cycle is represented in Figure 3.1 as a seven-phase process. At first glance the process may appear orderly, sequential, and rational. However, policy change is typically "messy" in practice. Therefore, the process is not a precise causal model (Sabatier, 1991), but rather an orienting framework to assist thought and action. It contains a set of repeating and intersecting loops that highlight the frequency and pervasiveness of feedback throughout the cycle. In addition, it is clear that the process actually can, and often does, start almost anywhere in the cycle—at the beginning, end, or somewhere in between.

The seven phases of the policy change cycle are:

1. Initiating and agreeing on a preliminary strategy for policy change
2. Identifying problems that probably can be solved

3.   Searching for solutions to identified problems
4.   Developing policies that incorporate desirable solutions to
     the problems
5.   Reviewing and adopting the policies
6.   Implementing and evaluating the policies
7.   Maintaining, changing, or terminating the policies

The remainder of this chapter will be a relatively ideal-
ized discussion of these phases. Subsequent chapters will develop a more complex picture.

The first three phases together constitute *issue creation,* in
which a public problem and at least one solution—with pros
and cons from the standpoint of various stakeholders—gains a
place on the public agenda. By *stakeholder* we mean any person, group, or organization that is affected by the causes or consequences of an issue. An issue is on the public agenda when
it has become a subject of discussion among a fairly broad cross
section of a community of place or of interest. Typically, in order
to win a place on that agenda stakeholders develop a new appreciation of the nature and importance of a problem and its
potential solution, or solutions. Usually, the three phases are
highly interactive. Various agreements are struck as problem
formulations and solutions are tried out and assessed in an effort
by different actors to push or block policy change. Sometimes
efforts to create and place an issue on the public agenda are successful, sometimes not. If they are unsuccessful, the issue remains a "nonissue" as far as the general community is concerned
(Bachrach and Baratz, 1963; Crenson, 1971; Gaventa, 1980).

Issues—linked problems and solutions—drive the political decision-making, or policy-making, process. Unfortunately,
all too often in this process, the real problems and the best solutions get "lost," if ever they were "found." Instead, vaguely
specified problems search for possible policy options; policy advocates try to find problems their solutions might solve; and politicians seek both problems and solutions that might advance their
careers, further some group's goals, or be in the public interest.
The result can resemble a "garbage can" (Kingdon, 1984; Cohen, March, and Olsen, 1972). Politically acceptable agreements

may be reached—pulled out of the garbage, as it were—but whether desirable public purposes are served is often an open question. As Will Rogers once said, "I don't tell jokes; I just watch Congress and report the facts."

　　Let us be clear: our purpose in outlining the policy change cycle is not to deny the obvious virtues of political bargaining, negotiation, and decision making. Rather, our purpose is to emphasize that the advocates of change should be clear, at least in their own minds, about the problems they wish to solve and the solutions that will effectively address those problems. An advocate group that is not clear on these points cannot expect to get what it wants (Schultze, 1968; Susskind and Cruikshank, 1987). Issue framing is a prime leadership responsibility, because the way an issue is framed will have a powerful impact both on the politics that surround it and on stakeholders' perceptions of the meaning of the proposed solutions (Lowi, 1964, 1972; Peterson, 1981; Waste, 1989; Sabatier, 1991). The public's interpretation of the impact of the solutions will result either in the activation or acquiescence of interest groups that can powerfully influence subsequent steps in the process (Wilson, 1967, 1980, 1986; Edelman, 1964, 1971, 1977).

Phase One: Initiating and Agreeing on a Preliminary Strategy for Policy Change

The purpose of the first phase of the public policy change cycle is to develop an understanding among an initial group of key decision makers or opinion leaders about the need to respond to an undesirable condition and to develop a basic response strategy. The support and commitment of these people is vital if the change process is to succeed. In addition, decision makers or opinion leaders from multiple affected organizations typically should be involved if their groups will have to adopt and implement the resulting public policies.

　　Initiating strategy is a critical leadership role, which can be played by one person or a group. One of the initiators' first tasks is to identify the key decision makers or opinion leaders.

The next task is to identify which stakeholders — persons, groups, or organizations — should be involved. The initial strategy will be negotiated with at least some of these critical constituencies. Initiators use visionary leadership in order to create shared meaning among these people and to persuade them to join the change effort. Initiators must convince them that the effort is important, possibly urgent, in some way dependent on their participation, likely to produce desirable changes, and frequently, in their personal as well as the public interest.

The agreement itself should highlight the purpose and worth of the effort and should outline a "plan for planning." Subsequent agreements are likely to be struck along the way as an array of possible problem definitions and solutions becomes clear. The ultimate result may be a detailed agreement that fully articulates the need to respond; the stakeholders whose support or acquiescence are necessary to build a winning coalition; the general strategy and specific steps to be followed, at least early on; a shared sense of the optimal design, use, and sequencing of necessary or desirable forums, arenas, and courts; the preferred form and timing of early reports; the role, function, and membership of any group or committee empowered to oversee or guide the effort and of any planning team; and the commitments of resources necessary to begin the endeavor.

A "triggering mechanism" (Cobb and Elder, 1983, p. 84) typically prompts the initiation of an agreement among key actors that something must be done. Typical triggering mechanisms (discussed in more detail in Chapter Six) include changes in important indicators, such as unemployment rates, crime rates, or school achievement test scores; focusing events, like oil spills, strikes, or plane crashes; crises, including perceived failures in schooling, health care, or crime control; and manipulation of powerful symbols, such as the flag, the "free enterprise system," or the family. Such triggers may also lead to modification of initial agreements — for example, a decision to include more affected parties or more concerns. A triggering event for the national effort to liberalize abortion laws was Sherri Finkbine's fight to obtain an abortion because she feared that she would give birth to a baby deformed by thalidomide. The German measles epidemic that put many pregnant women at risk of delivering deformed babies was another trigger.

Phase Two: Problem Identification

In this phase, participants engage in diagnosis to gain a clearer understanding of a problem that probably can be solved. They also determine directions for subsequent action (Nutt, 1992). In general, success in major change efforts hinges more on shared agreement about the precise nature of the problem and the need for a solution than it does on the technical feasibility of proposed solutions (Kingdon, 1984; Morris and Hough, 1986; Bryson, Bromiley, and Jung, 1990). Diagnosis is tied, at least in part, to whatever triggered attention to the problem. Performance gaps in key indicators, for example, often lead to diagnostic action. The subsequent direction setting takes one of four different forms, depending on whether the chosen response is to overcome specified problems; to achieve goals or targets that are presumed to indicate a healthy system; to reframe the problem in such a way that effective action becomes more likely; or to adopt, adapt, and implement ready-made solutions from elsewhere (Nutt, 1992).

Reframing is clearly apparent in the abortion case. What probably turned the tide for liberalizing efforts was the growing perception that the abortion issue concerned women's rights at least as much as, if not more than, unwanted pregnancies. The increased medical safety of abortion made it a technically feasible solution, but reframing the problem really led to the change effort's eventual success. Reframing efforts also undergird the more recent success of attempts to sharply circumscribe abortion. Framing the issue around the "right to life" of the fetus, rather than women's rights, has inspired large and powerful groups of abortion foes.

An effective problem identification phase establishes a firm basis for addressing stakeholder, user, client, or implementer needs in later phases. It also helps the planning team figure out where to look for possible solutions. As we mentioned earlier, in the absence of a clear understanding of the problems, it is unlikely that people will find or recognize good solutions. Indeed, if you do not know what the problems are, any solution will do; and if such a solution is adopted, it is unlikely that it will address what anyone thinks is a real problem. Worse yet, it will solve the wrong problem or aggravate the problem it was supposed to solve (Bryson, 1984; Wildavsky, 1979).

Phase Three: Search for Solutions

The purpose of this policy change phase is to search for solutions that respond to identified problems or needs. There are three basic approaches (Nutt, 1990): adapting solutions already known to the planning team; searching for solutions that might exist but are beyond the planning team's present knowledge; or developing new and innovative solutions. Beyond identifying or developing solutions, the team must capture enough public attention to place the problem and its potential solution — the issue — on the public agenda, thus making the issue a legitimate candidate for public action (Cobb and Elder, 1983; Hilgartner and Bosk, 1988; Waste, 1989). Once on the public agenda, the issue will be able, in subsequent phases of the cycle, to claim the attention of affected parties who can influence the formulation, adoption, and implementation of specific policies.

The first three phases of the policy change cycle are particularly clear in the metropolitan governance case. After agreeing that Minneapolis–St. Paul had a regional governance problem, several leaders began backing specific solutions, such as a council of governments, a federation of area municipal officials, or a multiservice district under the jurisdiction of a coordinating agency. These ideas were evaluated and refined in studies by the Citizens League and the League of Minnesota Municipalities and in informal strategy sessions attended by leading change advocates. The ideas also were discussed at invitation-only seminars sponsored by the Upper Midwest Research and Development Council. The agreement on the problem and the possible solutions resulted in an issue that could be taken to the public at large. Eventually, a strong consensus developed in favor of one particular solution, creating an elected metropolitan council.

Phase Four: Proposal Development

In this phase, policies — including plans, programs, budgets, projects, decisions, and rules — are developed for review and adoption in phase five. Therefore, design is a crucial activity in phase four (Alexander, 1982; Bobrow and Dryzek, 1987; deLeon, 1988, 1988–89; Linder and Peters, 1989; Schneider and Ingram, 1990; Sabatier, 1991), and in major change efforts, can include the design of a new regime. Both policies and regimes must be designed to address real problems in ways that are technically feasible, politically and economically acceptable, and legally and ethically responsible (Kingdon, 1984; Benveniste, 1989).

While bargaining and negotiation are common in the fourth phase, so can be a quiet, collegial informality in which elected officials, policy analysts, planners, and interest group advocates try out alternative policies on one another, speak persuasively of their options' relative merits, and generally engage in the give-and-take of successful design sessions. It is here that change advocates need political leadership skills, especially the skill of attending carefully to the goals and concerns of all affected parties in order to construct a coalition large enough and strong enough to adopt the proposal in the fifth phase and to protect it during implementation. Also, the atmosphere surrounding fourth-phase activities contrasts dramatically with the klieg lights and television cameras of the official meetings of city councils, state legislatures, or Congress that will surround the proposal in the fifth phase. If a proposed policy has not reached the point at which official decision makers can comfortably say yes to it under the glare of thousand-watt bulbs and the scrutiny of journalists, it will be sent back for further work, or buried indefinitely. The phase-four design process helps ensure that official, fifth-phase adoption sessions will produce desired outcomes. Savvy political leaders know that adoption sessions are not the time for unexpected embarrassments or difficulties that may force people to say and do things they will regret and that foreclose, for the present, the most beneficial and cost-effective policies. Indeed, politics in the United States relies on elaborate "politeness rituals" to maintain friendly relations among all parties, avoid embarrassment, and discourage unnecessary costs and enmities (March, 1981). As Lord Acton observed, "In politics, there are no permanent friends and no permanent enemies." You never know when you may need today's "enemy" on your side. A careful design process helps public leaders avoid making unnecessary enemies.

Once numerous alternative solutions for the Minneapolis-St. Paul regional governance problem had been proffered, a small committee of advocates began drafting a bill to create an elected metropolitan council that would oversee regional services. The committee included Verne Johnson, representatives of business groups, an attorney for suburban governments, an editorial writer for the *Minneapolis Star Tribune,* and Representative William Frenzel, who would later sponsor the bill in the state legislature. This group hammered out its proposal with relatively little publicity, and although the legislature eventually approved a competing proposal, Frenzel's bill — distilled as it was from the growing consensus among change advocates — ensured that the legislature would pass some kind of metropolitan governance legislation.

Leaders must be aware that in the fourth and subsequent stages in the process innumerable structural and strategic containment mechanisms can limit or constrain action. The same structures — ideas, rules, modes, media, methods, and resources — that are used to guide planning can also rule out actions. In addition, there are various stratagems that can be used to limit effective policy formulation, adoption, and implementation. These include attacking or undermining proponents of change; defusing, downgrading, blurring, or redefining the issue; controlling agendas; and strategic voting (Cobb and Elder, 1983; Riker, 1986). For example, efforts to bring right-to-life and pro-choice groups together to agree on proposals related to abortion, maternal and child health, and medical research have often been sabotaged by the participants' tendency to attack their opponents and the opponents' position, while refusing to reformulate their own positions in light of the offered proposals.

Phase Five: Proposal Review and Adoption

In this phase, change advocates seek an official decision to adopt and implement favored policies. The first task is to place the proposed policy on the formal, or decision, agenda of government, a task that exercises advocates' technical understanding of the formal machinery of government policy-making. There are two keys to success in the review and adoption phase — conducting the informal reviews of phase four and paying careful attention to the interests and concerns of all affected parties. More than in the previous phase, bargaining, negotiation, and often compromise over policy specifics are likely to dominate.

In the legislative battles over creation of the Metropolitan Council, bargaining and negotiation revolved around two main proposals — one for an elected council with operating authority over mass transit, sewage disposal, and mosquito control; and one for a weaker, appointed council that would only plan and coordinate metropolitan services. The proposal that became law more closely resembled the appointed-council proposal, but it also included compromise provisions — such as one granting the council limited taxing power — that appealed to the supporters of a stronger council. In the abortion controversy, the proposal adoption and review phase has been highly conflictual, in large part because debates have been over ideologies not amenable to compromise. Once women's rights advocates decided to press for outright repeal of abortion laws, the ideological clash became even sharper. It was only when the federal courts added their massive weight to the women's rights position that local and state legislators abandoned restrictive abortion laws.

Crucial to policy adoption is what Benveniste (1989, p. 27) calls "the multiplier effect." The multiplier effect kicks in when stakeholders begin to perceive that a policy has a high probability of adoption. As that perception spreads, many stakeholders who were on the fence, or even against the proposed policy, join the supporting coalition. On the other hand, that same perception may cause opposition to harden. Thus, perceptions about a policy's technical and political feasibility affect the likelihood of its adoption and implementation. Further, the timing and substance of proponents' and opponents' actions can influence these perceptions dramatically (Benveniste, 1989, pp. 130–155). Crises can also turn on the multiplier effect, as perceived costs and benefits shift. In the midst of crisis, advocates of change can come to be seen as system saviors, promising benefits to many, rather than as self-interested partisans whose proposed changes will benefit only themselves and place undue burdens on others (Wilson, 1967; Bryson, 1981).

Once policies or plans are officially adopted, opposition becomes a rearguard or guerrilla activity — witness the tactics of anti-abortion forces in the immediate wake of *Roe* v. *Wade*. The burden of proof shifts from the initiators of change to the opposers of change (Wilson, 1967).

Phase Six: Implementation and Evaluation

In the next-to-last phase of the policy change cycle, formally adopted solutions are incorporated throughout a system, and their effects assessed. Ideally, changes will be implemented at an optimal pace and real problems or needs will be addressed to the satisfaction of key stakeholders. A new regime may be created.

Successful implementation doesn't just happen; it requires careful planning and management, ongoing problem solving, and sufficient incentives and resources, including people. The original leaders of the change effort may have to play new roles and allow new leaders to emerge. For example, one of the original advocates of the Metropolitan Council, Minneapolis lawyer James Hetland, was appointed as first council chair. His new leadership role required that he shift his attention from building consensus on the need for the council to shaping policies and procedures that would give it as much clout as possible under the enabling legislation. Often implementation involves a whole new set of actors, so considerable communication, education, and guidance may be necessary to get everyone "on board." Successful implementation is unlikely unless adopted policies are clear, workable, and politically acceptable to implementers. Further, completely new processes, mechanisms, or structures may be needed to resolve implementation difficulties. Finally, it is important to work quickly to avoid unnecessary or undesirable competition with new priorities (Mazmanian and Sabatier, 1983; Benveniste, 1989). There are two basic approaches to implementation: direct and staged. In direct implementation, changes are simultaneously implemented at all applicable sites in the network or system. In staged implementation, changes are tried out in selected locations first.

Successful evaluation also does not just happen. Like implementation, it must be planned and supported if it is to inform judgments about program performance. Two kinds of evaluation are desirable in this phase of the change cycle: *formative* evaluations, which facilitate learning and program improvement while implementation is under way, and *summative* evaluations, which assess whether or not desired outcomes have been achieved once implementation is complete (Scriven, 1967; Bryson and Cullen, 1984; Patton, 1982, 1986, 1987).

Implementers typically view formative evaluations as more "friendly," because, at their best, they are designed to facilitate implementation by providing useful administrative, fiscal, and organizational feedback and advice, in addition to information that reports directly on the "treatments" being tried. In order for these evaluations to be useful, however, key decision makers from implementing organizations must be involved in evaluation design; administrative, fiscal, and organizational measures must be included; several alternative solutions must be examined in order to assess comparative strengths and weaknesses; and understandable and wise recommendations based on evaluation results must be offered. For example, during major construction projects, formative evaluations are conducted by inspectors representing the architects, independent testing laboratories, the firm managing the construction contract, and the owners, who visit the site daily to gather information to guide subsequent decision making and implementation.

Summative evaluations, however, are often threatening to implementers, particularly those who are committed to the adopted policies, because these evaluations tend to be more thoroughly scientific than formative ones and can produce damning evidence that desired outcomes either have not been produced or were not worth the cost. Professional egos, jobs, and even whole organizations and programs may be on the line. The fact that summative evaluations typically are performed by outsiders can make them even more threatening, because the evaluators and their sponsors may have a different stake in the outcome than the implementers. Nonetheless, summative evaluations can add valuable information to public debates over the wisdom of specific policies. For example, declining achievement test scores in U.S. public schools have prompted much of the debate over the ideal goals and organization of public education. Studies of the impact of liberalizing U.S. abortion laws are another example. Those conducted by the Alan Guttmacher Institute, showed that in the decade after *Roe* v. *Wade* millions of U.S. women had obtained legal abortions and that deaths from illegal abortions were much less frequent. But a Guttmacher Institute study also indicated that efforts to make abortion only a last-resort method of birth control were not working.

Phase Seven: Policy Maintenance, Succession, or Termination

In this phase, public leaders review implemented policies to decide whether to continue, modify, or eliminate them. This review requires leaders to decide what is important, including appropriate indicators of success and failure. It also entails using existing opportunities — often present in the routines of politics — to review and rethink policies, or else creating new opportunities to do so. In the abortion case, the judicial process has allowed U.S. Supreme Court judges to review and modify *Roe* v. *Wade*. At the Metropolitan Council, the appointment of a new chair has often provided an occasion to review the council's operations.

What is done with existing policies depends on whether they resolve public problems and whether the associated costs and benefits are acceptable (Wilson, 1973, p. 330). If policies are to be maintained or modified only slightly, advocates must marshal supportive evidence and maintain constituency support.

If new policies or major modifications are desired, a whole new pass through the policy change cycle will be required. The reformulated problem and new solution will have to be placed on the public agenda so that appropriate policy decisions can be made.

A Hierarchy of Process

Another useful way of viewing the phases of the policy change cycle is to divide them into levels that represent different versions of the "game of politics." Each level typically involves different participants, addressing different kinds of problems, using different rules and resources, in different settings, with different rhetorics, which together have a significant impact on the character of the action and outcomes of the game (Schattschneider, 1975, pp. 47–48; Kiser and Ostrom, 1982; Throgmorton, 1991).

Lynn (1987, pp. 59–64) describes three such levels of the public policy-making process: "high," "middle," and what he calls the "low" and we call the "operational" level. Lynn argues that the participants at each level must answer a different question. At the high level, the question is whether or not there is a public problem that requires government action and, if there is, what the purpose of that action should be. In terms of the policy change cycle, the high-level activity is principally one of issue creation. This activity, as we discussed in Chapter One and earlier in this chapter, involves the articulation and appreciation of developmental problems in terms of the values, norms, or goals used to judge why the problem is a problem and to guide efforts to address it.

In the middle level, the question is what strategies or policies should be pursued to achieve the agreed-upon purpose. These are programming problems. In addition, government action that is desired must be defined further. The answers to the question should encompass the policy mechanisms that will be employed — for example, taxes, subsidies, vouchers, insurance, regulation, or government service — and the parts of the government that will be responsible for action. Participants at this level must also decide how statutory roles and financial, personnel, and other resources should be allocated among implementing agencies or organizations. In terms of the policy change cycle, middle-level action moves the process into the proposal development and policy review and adoption phases.

The operational level emphasizes the details of policies — or plans, programs, budgets, rules, and projects. Exactly what will the instruments of action look like; how will they be organized and managed; and what procedures, regulations, and guidance will be followed? Operational-level action takes policy change into the implementation stage.

The highest level of the policy process centers on the philosophies, ideologies, values, and fundamental justifications that support public action and government responsibility. As Lynn notes, "Debate focuses on the right thing to do, on philosophies of government and the fundamental responsibilities of our institutions, on what kind of nation and society we should be, on social justice and our basic principles" (1987, p. 62). Debates of this sort are often heated and ideological. They can involve the highest executive, legislative, and judicial leaders of government, heads of interest groups and political parties, and the media. In addition, high-ranking appointed political executives whose departments are affected by the answers reached in the high level also become involved, unless they are explicitly kept out by higher-ranking officials. The process is typically played in the open and involves skillful formulation and use of symbols and interpretive schemes. It requires an understanding of public opinion, political influence, and broad-scale political strategy.

In the abortion controversy, those who opposed as well as those who endorsed restrictive abortion laws devoted considerable energy to the high level. They emphasized fundamental philosophical stances such as human equality and respect for life. They called upon religious sanctions. They argued over constitutional guarantees of personal liberty and privacy. They debated the state's interest in and responsibility for protecting a fetus and its responsibility for guaranteeing that poor women have access to abortion. Presidents, members of Congress, Supreme Court justices, state and local officials, political candidates, the shapers of party platforms, and religious leaders all have been drawn into the fray.

The debate over governance of the Minneapolis–St. Paul metropolitan area was not carried on at such a high ideological pitch. Nevertheless, the opponents of regional governance emphasized their fear that it would usurp local government autonomy, which is greatly valued in a society that resists centralized power. Meanwhile, council supporters argued from the premise that state government had a responsibility to protect citizens, businesses, and communities from severe harm resulting from uncontrolled development. Leaders of citizen organizations and business groups, the governor, local officials, and state legislators were very visibly involved in the policy discussion.

The middle-level process takes over once the broad purposes and justifications for public action have been set. More specific actions, responsibilities, rules, and resources are discussed and assigned. Most of the political news reported in the media concerns middle-level action, or inaction. Lynn argued that this middle level of the policy process is "the predominant one for departmental executives, and the bread-and-butter game for legislators" (1987, p. 63). The predominant participants, in other words, are positionally lower than the participants in the high level. Lynn adds: "Debate is about results (that is, the effectiveness and efficiency of governmental actions), about the fairness, appropriateness, and consequences of distribution, about administrative competence, and about costs. Debate is often fueled by organized groups usually acting out of self-interest. Sharp controversies and disagreements are likely to break out, but they are usually less emotional than high-game controversies. Reasoning will have a larger place in the controversies, and compromises will be easier to reach" (1987, p. 63). The middle level in the regional governance case was played out as state legislators debated how independent the Metropolitan Council should be from state government—for example, whether council members should be elected or appointed. It was also at this level that legislators debated what mechanisms the council would use to guide or control development. The middle-level debate in the abortion controversy swirled around issues like public funding for abortion services and pregnant teenagers' freedom to choose abortion.

Success in the middle level depends on leaders' having effective working relationships and relatively constant interaction with key participants. It requires a good understanding of the substantive and political issues connected to legislation, programs, and budgets. And it requires skill in the strategy, tactics, and timing of persuasion, negotiation, and bargaining to identify and create potential trade-offs and politically attractive compromises (Lynn, 1987; Roberts and King, 1991).

The operational level usually involves lower-level appointed officials and technical specialists and professionals associated with executive branch agencies, legislative staffs, and interest groups. These experts concern themselves with the specifics of organization, management, personnel, finance and accounting, costs, legal sufficiency, purchasing and procurement, and contract monitoring associated with policy implementation. At this level, an appreciation of politics is useful, but an understanding of substance is crucial (Lynn, 1987). The original members and staff of the Metropolitan Council operated at this level as they established advisory groups, set research priorities, and nurtured relationships with local officials and other regional bodies. The advocates of women's right to choose abortion operated here when they began establishing abortion clinics in the wake of *Roe* v. *Wade,* and had to deal with local zoning requirements, secure financing, and meet local health regulations.

Summary

This chapter has outlined the policy change cycle, a phase-based orienting framework designed to help leaders think about and structure their strategies and actions to address public problems. The process can begin anywhere in the cycle, but it is often helpful for key leaders to begin with an initial agreement to do something about an undesirable condition, which may sometimes be a consequence of previously adopted policies. This agreement is followed by more detailed problem identification and a search for solutions. As awareness of the problem and possible solutions spreads, an issue is created that may gain a prominent place on the public agenda. Once on the agenda, more formal policy designs may be made, with an eye toward government adoption of a policy. Once a policy is adopted, implementation and evaluation follow. Later, policies may be reviewed to determine whether they should be maintained, changed, or terminated.

It is also helpful to view the policy change cycle as being played out over a series of levels, with each level typically involving a different set of participants, rules and resources, and settings.

Chapter 4

Settings for Exercising Leadership: Forums, Arenas, and Courts

All the world's a stage,
And all the men and women merely players.
—William Shakespeare

If you let me set the constraints,
I'll let you make the decision.
—Herbert Simon

We could even say that institutions are socially organized
forms of paying attention or attending, or they can also,
unfortunately, be socially organized forms of distraction.
—Robert Bellah and others

To effectively maneuver through the cycle of policy change in a shared-power world, public leaders must be skilled in the design and use of forums, arenas, and courts, the principle shared-power settings in which the policy process occurs. Because the design and use of forums, arenas, and courts can be extremely complex, they open up innumerable opportunities for leadership that may result in desired change. In forums, visionary leadership inspires powerful formulations of issues and creates winning proposals. In arenas, political leadership shows people how to work together to produce and implement desired policy decisions. And in courts, judicial, or ethical, leadership resolves residual disputes and enforces constitutions, laws, and norms. Our understanding of how these shared-power settings operate, interact, and change begins with a holistic concept of power that illuminates the connections between public action and social structure. After discussing this model of power, we describe the essential elements and dynamics of each setting.

Public Action and the Dimensions of Power

Basing our findings partly on the work of Giddens (1979, 1985), we identify three basic kinds of public action: communication; policy-making and implementation; and the sanctioning of conduct, or, more broadly, the resolution of residual conflicts and the enforcement of the system's underlying norms. Each of these kinds of action is shaped, and biased, by three different dimensions of power (Lukes, 1974), presented in Exhibit 4.1.

The *first dimension* of power is emphasized by the pluralists (for example, Dahl, 1961), who argue that the power of public actors in the United States varies with issues, that there are several bases of power — such as wealth, status, knowledge, and skill — and that there is some substitutability among power bases. In other words, winners and losers vary by issue — all of us are "merely players" — and society, therefore, is pluralist rather than elitist. The pluralists focus on observable behavior — that is, communication, policy-making and implementation, and sanctioning; key issues; observable conflict; and interests, defined as policy preferences revealed by political participation.

In its *second dimension,* power is exercised more subtly, through manipulation of the vehicles of bias that affect decision and action. As Bachrach and Baratz (1962, p. 949) note, "To the extent that a person or group — consciously or unconsciously — reinforces barriers to the public airing of policy conflicts, that person has power." Various ideas, rules, modes, media, and methods — including "organization" in the general sense — are the principal barriers that bias attention toward some matters and away from others (Bachrach and Baratz, 1963, 1970; Schattschneider, 1975; Forester, 1989; Healey and others, 1988). These same barriers can also be described as asymmetrically

Exhibit 4.1. The Three Dimensions of Power.

Interaction	The First Dimension of Power
	Focus on: behavior (communication, policy-making and implementation, and sanctioning of conduct) key issues observable (overt) conflict (subjective) interests, seen as policy preferences revealed by political participation
Ideas, rules, modes, media, or methods (also: rules, resources, and transformation relations)	The Second Dimension of Power (Qualified critique of behavioral focus) **Focus on:** policy decision making and non-decision making issues and potential issues observable (overt or covert) conflict (subjective) interests seen as policy preferences or grievances ideas, rules, modes, media, or methods that influence transformation of a set of potential decisions, issues, conflicts, and policy preferences into those actually considered and those not considered.
Deep structure	The Third Dimension of Power (Critique of behavioral focus) **Focus on:** policy-making and control over political agendas (not necessarily through decisions) issues and potential issues observable (overt or covert) and latent conflict subjective and "real" interests collective basis for a set of potential decisions, issues, conflicts, and policy preferences that people might consider

Adapted in part from Lukes (1974, p. 25) and Clegg (1989, p. 214).

distributed rules, resources, and transformation relations (such as control over agendas) that create decision and "nondecision" categories, and "live" issues versus what must remain, at least for a time, "potential" issues. In other words, built-in organizational bias has the effect of creating precepts that "rule out" certain behaviors — which, therefore, will not be observed (Bryson and Einsweiler, 1982; Bryson and Crosby, 1989). This chapter's epigraph from Herbert Simon draws attention to power's second dimension.

The *third dimension* reveals an even subtler exercise of power, the shaping of felt needs, rights, and responsibilities. These are rooted in "deep," or "bedrock," social, political, and economic structures. These structures provide the "generative rules and resources" that allow human relationships, organizations, and coalitions within and among organizations to exist in the first place (Giddens, 1979, pp. 89–91). They also provide the basis for a potential set of issues, conflicts, and policy preferences and decisions — all rooted in consciously or unconsciously felt needs — that public actors *might* address. However, it is the vehicles of bias — ideas, rules, modes, media, and methods — of the second dimension that influence the transformation of that potential set into the actual set of issues, conflicts, and policy preferences and decisions addressed in the first dimension. The vehicles of bias also determine which items remain in the second dimension as potential issues, covert conflicts, grievances, or nondecisions (Bryson and Einsweiler, 1982; Bryson and Crosby, 1989). Figure 4.1 illustrates how this process works.

The three-dimensional view of power reveals how the biases embedded in rules, resources, and transformation relations can severely distort communication, policy-making and implementation, and adjudication, so that some matters of importance are considered, while others are not (Clegg, 1981). The chapter epigraph from Bellah and others (1991, p. 256) captures in brief this idea that society's institutions — as embodiments of bias ultimately based on the social bedrock — lead us to attend to some things while they distract us from others.

Action in particular consciously and unconsciously repro-

Figure 4.1. Dividing What Is Possible into What Is Seen and Not Seen.

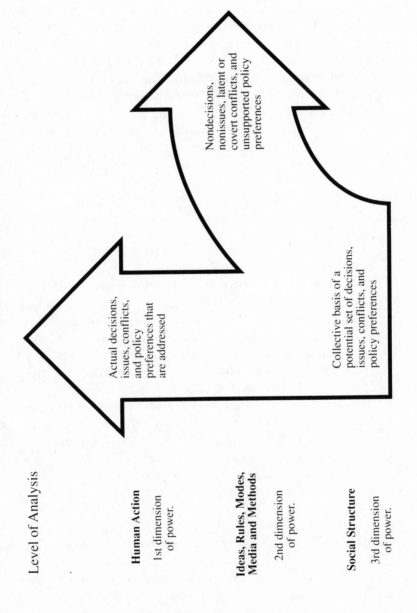

Level of Analysis

Human Action

1st dimension
of power.

**Ideas, Rules, Modes,
Media and Methods**

2nd dimension
of power.

Social Structure

3rd dimension
of power.

Actual decisions,
issues, conflicts,
and policy
preferences that
are addressed

Nondecisions,
nonissues, latent or
covert conflicts, and
unsupported policy
preferences

Collective basis of a
potential set of decisions,
issues, conflicts, and
policy preferences

duces these biases. For example, in the controversy over the meaning and function of a metropolitan council, no public leader even considered actions that would amend the U.S. Constitution to change the nature of our compound republic; establish a metropolitan state; abolish all individual local governments; or abandon democracy, individualism, equality, and capitalism in the Twin Cities region. These possible actions were simply not seen. The actions that were seen, by those who favored the council, were those that allowed the council to fit in with existing bedrock social structures and become a more or less permanent fixture of the metropolitan social and political landscape.

The Connections Between
Public Action and Social Structure

Within and among organizations, action is linked to the three dimensions of power primarily through the design and use of forums, arenas, and courts. In these shared-power settings, people interactively draw on third-dimension social structures or relationships and second-dimension organizational and interorganizational rules, resources, and transformation relations to produce instrumental effects such as discussion papers, policy statements, or action plans. While producing instrumental effects, they also reproduce organizational and interorganizational structures, including social relationships and the vehicles of bias that influence outcomes. However, as these structures are reproduced, they are also modified, in an "ongoing strengthening, altering, or weakening of those social relations without which the production of desired results ([for example], plans, reports, recommendations) would not be possible" (Forester, 1989, p. 71; see also Giddens, 1979, pp. 49–130). In other words, people draw on structures to *create* action, which subsequently *recreates,* yet also reshapes, the structures that permitted the action in the first place.

Our view of forums, arenas, and courts highlights the central role played by ideas, rules, modes, media, and methods in governing both continuity and change in structures, and therefore the production and reproduction — or "structuration" — of social systems (Giddens, 1979, pp. 66–73), from small groups to entire societies. The vehicles of bias that mediate change can also be viewed as a dynamic bond between the two main traditions of social analysis. The first tradition focuses on patterned regularities in social interaction. In this view, structures exist only insofar as they are actively created by actors. The second focuses on structures as prescribed frameworks of constraint. Here, structures are givens, and actors are assumed to learn, work within, and adapt to the structures. The distinction between the two traditions dissolves when we recognize "the duality of structures," in which structures are both the medium and outcome of human action (Giddens, 1979, p. 77). Figure 4.2 depicts how structuration occurs through the interaction of the three dimensions of power and in relation to the two views of society. (Giddens [1979, pp. 88–94] argues, a bit ambiguously, that there are only two dimensions of power, one corresponding to each view of society. The three-dimensional view emphasized here clarifies the overlapping elements of Giddens' model.)

An appreciation of structuration implies that today's public leaders can have their greatest influence over action and outcomes by focusing on the second dimension of power—that is, by strengthening, weakening, or altering the ideas, rules, modes, media, and methods that divide what is theoretically conceivable into what is actually possible and what is not. This is leadership by indirection. Instead of dictating directly what people should do or not do, or directly controlling the social bedrock, leaders must influence the way action and structure are created and recreated. The relevant image is not one of the in-charge leader, but of the visionary, political, and ethical leader who is also a guide, persuader, facilitator, coach, and team player.

The world of public policy has become a shared-power world precisely because public leaders are rarely able to prescribe actions and dictate terms to other actors. Similarly, these leaders are unlikely to be able to make significant changes in the underlying social bedrock. On the other hand, leaders may be able to have a significant influence on the ideas, rules, modes, media, and methods that link bedrock social structure to action—

Figure 4.2. The Three-Dimensional View of Power
in Relation to the Two Main Traditions of Social Analysis.

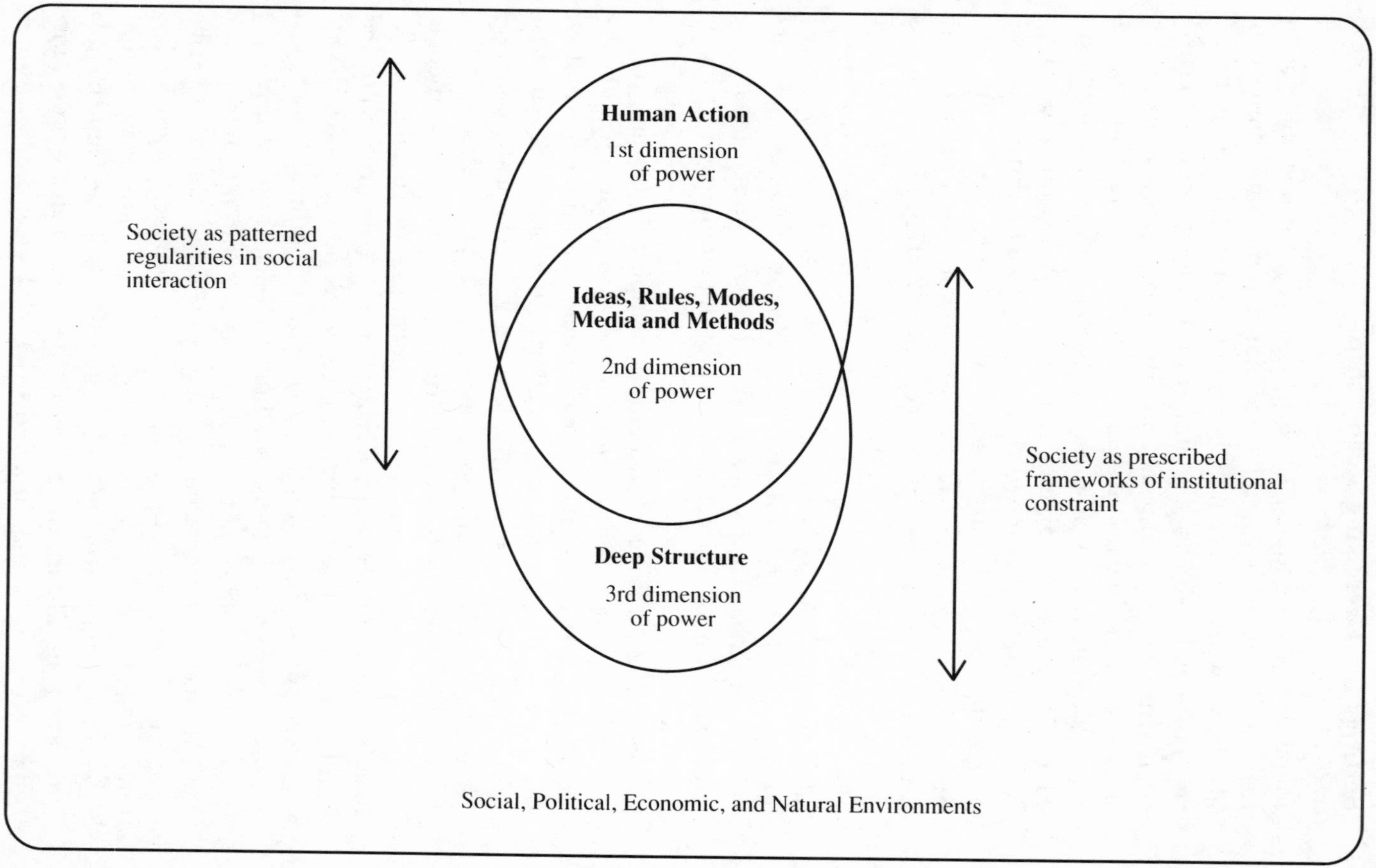

Human Action
1st dimension
of power

**Ideas, Rules, Modes,
Media and Methods**
2nd dimension
of power

Deep Structure
3rd dimension
of power

Society as patterned
regularities in social
interaction

Society as prescribed
frameworks of institutional
constraint

Social, Political, Economic, and Natural Environments

perhaps, in part, simply because others may not pay as much attention to these matters. This influence will have a major impact on what is up for discussion, decision, and control — and what will remain in a public policy never-never land. In other words, in order to raise and resolve public problems constructively, leaders must attend to human interaction, institutional arrangements, and the ways human interaction and social structures are linked through ideas, rules, modes, media, and methods.

Civic leaders and elected officials in and around Minneapolis–St. Paul, for example, recognized that existing institutional arrangements didn't encompass the problems threatening their communities. The existing organizations tended to be only city- or countywide; so to change the perception of what was possible, these public leaders began by altering rules and resources. The Citizens League in Minneapolis changed its membership rules to include people from all over the metropolitan area, local League of Women Voters chapters established a formal affiliation with each other, and advocates of metropolitan governance convened meetings and established task forces that linked people and organizations from across the Twin Cities region. Women's rights advocates were also changing ideas of what was possible when they challenged laws that severely constrained women's choices about pregnancy. They also changed social norms that associated abortion with immoral sexuality and thus hampered open discussion.

Public leaders in both these cases often demonstrated an intuitive understanding of the importance of focusing on the second dimension of power, and specifically on ideas, rules, modes, media, and methods as the main levers of power in a shared-power world. We hope to extend such intuitive insight by elaborating a holistic concept of power in which the design and use of forums, arenas, and courts is an important key to using these levers of power to promote or retard desirable social change.

A Holistic Concept of Power

When leaders understand how three of their essential skills — communicating, policy-making and implementation, and adjudicating—interact with each other and relate to the three dimensions of power, they have a holistic concept of power that can be put to practical use. To begin with, communication, policy-making and implementation, and adjudication are so important because they are the three basic types of social action, and each of these basic social actions is an aspect of particular social practices (Giddens, 1979, 1984). Social practices are the regular dynamics we described when discussing the two traditions of social analysis; they are produced by the patterned interaction of human actors who are both empowered and influenced by rules and resources in specific situations. We call the social practice that results in the communication of meaning *the design and use of forums;* the social practice that results in policy-making and implementation *the design and use of arenas;* and the social practice that results in the normative regulation of conduct *the design and use of courts* (see Figure 4.3). (Incidentally, we must note that in naming the second type of social action, we preferred "policy-making and implementation" to Giddens' term, "exercise of power." In Giddens' model of social life, it is clear, at least to us, that what he calls the exercise of power can be meaningful only if it incorporates or comprehends the other two basic types of social action.)

Although the design and use of forums, the design and use of arenas, and the design and use of courts are analytically separable, in reality these basic social practices are in constant interaction. Thus, if one is to understand policy-making and implementation, one must also understand the communication of meaning and the normative regulation of conduct. In addition, as the social practices interact with each other, they also draw upon all three dimensions of power in order to split a society's potential decisions, issues, conflicts, and policy preferences into those that will be considered and those that will not. Of course, the emphasis on each practice will vary greatly in different situations.

The leader who can locate the pertinent forums, arenas, and courts and understand and explain their operation in relation to each dimension of power has a holistic and practical grasp of the power that is the capacity to affect and effect change.

Figure 4.3. The Triple Three-Dimensional View of Power.

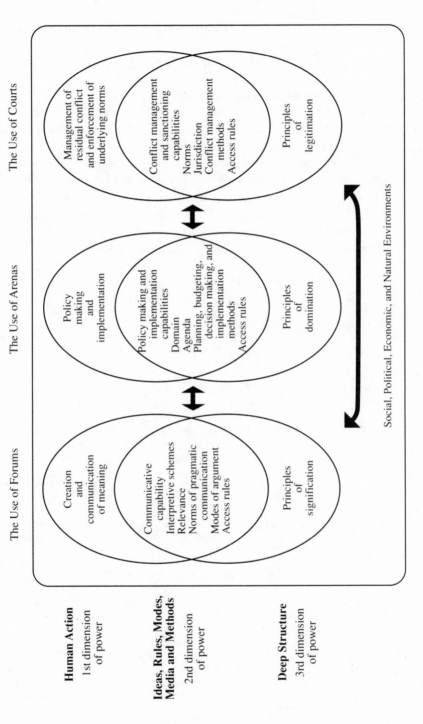

The Design and Use of Forums

In today's society, forums abound. For example, there are discussion groups and brainstorming sessions; formal debates, public hearings, task forces, and conferences; newspapers, television, and radio; plays and other forms of dramatization; and popular and professional journals. Forums may be place-bound — for example, public hearings — or non–place-bound — for example, newspaper, television, and radio (see Exhibit 4.2).

Verne Johnson, Ann Duff, Robert Einsweiler, and other metropolitan governance advocates organized multiple forums in the mid 1960s to understand and delineate the problems affect-

Exhibit 4.2. The Design and Use of Forums.

Definition	A practice of linking speakers and audiences wherein meaning is created and communicated through discussion, debate, or deliberation.
Examples	Task forces, discussion groups, brainstorming sessions, public hearings, formal debates, newspapers, television, radio, plays, conferences, professional journals.
Policy-related role	Maintenance or change of symbolic orders and modes of discourse, especially through distribution and redistribution of access to the communication of meaning.
Structural properties	A speaker and audience (of at least one) along with a minimum set of common linguistic rules and resources.
Action	The use of symbols to create shared meaning and values among participants. Characteristic activity is discussion, debate, or deliberation.
Ideas, rules, modes, media, and methods	Communicative capability, interpretive schemes, and ways of deciding among interpretive schemes — for example, relevance, norms of pragmatic communication (speaking comprehensibly, sincerely, in context, truthfully), modes of argument, access determinants.
Effect or outcome	A potential list of decisions, issues, conflicts, or policy preferences available for discussion. In addition, a forum mediates the transformation of that list into an actual list of decisions, issues, conflicts, or policy preferences to be discussed and not to be discussed.

ing the Twin Cities metropolitan area and to develop solutions. Johnson's Citizens League organized task forces that produced study after study. Duff chaired the newly created Council of Metropolitan Area Leagues of Women Voters, which studied and discussed area problems like water pollution.

Beginning in 1962, the Metropolitan Planning Commission (MPC) undertook the Joint Program for Landuse and Transportation Planning, funded in part by the national government. Einsweiler and his staff organized forums that brought together representatives of Minneapolis and St. Paul; state, local, and federal highway officials; housing officials; and MPC staff to discuss public problems resulting from Twin Cities urban growth. Those discussions led to several reports demonstrating that essentials of high-quality urban living such as affordable housing and reliable transportation would be in short supply if current development patterns and practices continued. By late 1965, Joint Program participants were able to focus on recommendations for minimizing the problems they had identified. In this final stage, the program participants worked in large forums with an Elected Officials Review Committee (consisting of about 300 elected metropolitan-area officials) and the Citizen Advisory Committee (comprising about 100 people).

Other groups sponsoring forums on metropolitan problems were the Upper Midwest Research and Development Council, chambers of commerce, and local officials' organizations. Because many participants in one group's forums often were invited to other groups' forums, the forums facilitated networking. Eventually most of the forum sponsors formed a coalition that advocated specific action in the legislative arena. Another important forum was the Minneapolis evening newspaper. In the fall of 1965, Ted Kolderie, an editorial writer for the paper, wrote a series of articles emphasizing the local governments' inability to cope with problems of rapid growth. He also reported a growing consensus in the Twin Cities that "some kind of area-wide agency" should be established to handle "genuinely area-wide problems — [for example], sewage disposal, water supply, transit, major roads, air pollution, planning, mosquito control, airports, and perhaps regional parks" (Kolderie, 1965).

The advocates of women's right to choose abortion also

organized numerous new forums and took advantage of existing ones. They held rallies, conducted workshops, spoke to church groups, held press conferences, and gave interviews to reporters. They held state and national conferences of their own organizations and spoke out at the conferences of Planned Parenthood, NOW, and other groups. The mass media offered prime forums for these change advocates, particularly those who had a flair for sensational statements or actions. Robert McCoy's open and probably illegal operation of an abortion referral service was news. So was the arrest of Patricia Maginnis, leader of California's Society for Humane Abortion — first, for handing out phone numbers and addresses of abortion clinics in Mexico, and, later, for holding workshops on self-abortion techniques. In New York City, a former contraceptive salesman named Bill Baird attracted media coverage as he agitated for abortion reform and defied state law by dispensing contraceptives from a van. Lawrence Lader, a New Yorker who had become committed to abortion reform as a result of writing about the life of birth control advocate Margaret Sanger, traveled across the country to "stir as much controversy and debate as possible while bringing the facts to the public" (Lader, 1973). Prominent and not-so-prominent women announced at public meetings that they had had abortions.

Those who sought to retain restrictive abortion laws likewise held rallies, workshops, meetings, and press conferences, and gave speeches and interviews. Following *Roe* v. *Wade*, "right-to-life" activist Nelly Gray organized March for Life, which sponsored mass demonstrations on Capitol Hill each year on the anniversary of the decision. (In response, women's rights advocates have often held simultaneous counterdemonstrations to celebrate the decision and renew their commitment to their cause.) "Right-to-life" activists have also attracted news coverage through sensational activities. In recent years, groups like the Lambs of Christ and Randall Terry's Operation Rescue have gained media attention by demonstrating at and sometimes invading clinics that provide abortions or abortion counseling. Advocates from both sides of the abortion controversy have published articles, research studies, and books; rented billboards; and produced films. They've passed out leaflets at political conventions, on street corners, and in the case of "right-to-life" groups, in church parking lots.

The use of forums links speakers and audiences through discussion, debate, and deliberation in order to create and communicate meaning (see Exhibit 4.2). Forums are the principal settings within which the appreciations of developmental problems, and their potential solutions, are either maintained or changed. Forums distribute and redistribute access to the creation and communication of meaning, and thereby help maintain or change symbolic orders and modes of discourse.

How this happens becomes clearer when forums are viewed through the three dimensions of power. In the first dimension (action), people use symbols to discuss, debate, and deliberate various issues. Their goal is to create shared meaning, and perhaps shared values, in the minds of the relevant publics around a policy issue. As the abortion controversy developed, for example, in the 1960s, supporters and opponents of less restrictive laws used every available forum — from the mails, to television, to legislative chambers — to persuade voters and lawmakers to accept their interpretation, or meaning, of abortion.

The third dimension of power appears in forums as basic signification principles, or bedrock signification structures. These principles require a speaker and audience (of at least one), at least a partly shared set of common linguistic rules and resources, and one or more shared worldviews. For example, most of the participants in the metropolitan governance and abortion policy forums spoke English and believed in representative, democratic government and in citizen action.

In forums, the most important second-dimension ideas, rules, modes, media, and methods used to link desired outcomes with deep structure are communicative capability, interpretive schemes, relevance, norms of pragmatic communication, modes of argument, and access rules. *Communicative capability* is simply the capacity to create and communicate meaning. That capability may include, for example, rhetorical skill, the ability to catch the interest of print and electronic media, or the potential to pull together a supportive, chanting crowd on a moment's notice. Organizers of the forums that laid the foundation for establishing the Metropolitan Council clearly had strong communicative capacity. Johnson, Duff, Einsweiler, and others had long experience in organizing task forces and committees and producing and publicizing reports at critical junctures. Their status as leaders in recognized organizations also gave them increased access to mass media.

Interpretive schemes (Schutz, 1967) are intersubjective organizing frameworks that people use to structure cognitions, interpretations, or understandings of events in ways that are meaningful. They embody the desired values and interests that underlie communication (Bolan, 1980; Bartunek, 1988; Wildavsky, 1987), and they include beliefs, expectations, and rules through which we interpret our personal experience and social knowledge. Interpretation of new experiences or knowledge is thus based on our understanding of our own and others' cumulative experience. An individual's set of interpretive schemes is structured by a set of relevances determined by his or her concerns (Schutz, 1967; Bernstein, 1976; Throgmorton, 1991). For example, U.S. women relied on their own actual or anticipated experience as mothers to interpret Sherri Finkbine's 1962 fight to obtain an abortion. They added certain values, such as reverence for life or the desire to give birth to healthy children, to this experience. And many of them concluded that Finkbine and others in her situation should be able to decide whether or not to have an abortion. They reasoned that a woman who gives birth to a child with severe birth defects must care for it, but if she knows in advance that the child will be deformed, she should be able to decide whether to carry the fetus to term. Other women decided that reverence for all stages and forms of human life required laws prohibiting abortion except to save a woman's life.

Inside forums, competing, conflicting, or contradictory interpretive schemes must be at least partially mediated as a necessary condition for the emergence of concerted action. Norms of relevance and of pragmatic communication, as well as modes of argumentation and access rules, play crucial roles in mediating among incompatible interpretive schemes. In the abortion controversy forums, the two main competing interpretive schemes were women's right to decide and the fetus's right to live. In the forums leading to creation of the Metropolitan Council, five interpretive schemes dominated the discussion. One of these schemes saw the metropolitan area as one economic unit, or one community. The believers in this interpretation argued that the major problems of any single Twin Cities community could not be solved without attention to all the communities in the seven-county region. A second interpretive scheme suggested that, in a democracy, government must be accountable to the people, or to some representative elected body. Many council advocates pointed out that the Twin Cities already had regional government in the form of various single-purpose districts, agencies, and compacts. The problem was that these entities were largely independent, and their policy-making was hidden from public view.

A third scheme was adopted by the suburban mayors who feared the state legislature would respond to regional problems by creating more independent service districts like the one already in charge of airports and sewage disposal. Their belief was that more government was not the answer, and they tended to promote county cooperation, or a slightly strengthened Metropolitan Planning Commission, as the solution to area problems. Yet another belief was that local government is best. Government should be kept as close to the people as possible; the bigger and more removed government becomes, the more it endangers citizens' rights and infringes upon their freedom. In keeping with this theme, those who wanted a stronger regional governance mechanism promoted their proposals as a way of strengthening local government and protecting it from the whims of state and national government. The fifth interpretive scheme emphasized government and market failures. Its adherents emphasized that market-driven growth in Minneapolis–St. Paul after World War II had some undesirable side effects. Most of these people were not against the market or against growth, but rather against disorderly, disruptive growth that excessively burdened public services and threatened the Twin Cities' quality of life. Additionally, it was clear to these people that local governments, separately or together, were unable to deal with regional problems, especially sewage disposal.

As we have noted, there is a personal aspect to relevance, but there also is a clearly social aspect to relevance as well, since public issue forums are usually not open to discussion of every topic. Instead, discussion must be germane to the occasion. For example, in legislative hearings related to abortion or the Metropolitan Council, the focus typically had to be on an actual law that might be passed.

In addition, people presume that *norms of pragmatic communication* will be met in communicative interactions (Habermas, 1979; Forester, 1989). Forester (p. 36), drawing on the work of Habermas, suggests these norms lead to four practical criteria for judging speech aimed at influencing subsequent action: "In every interaction, speakers may be expected to speak more or less (1) comprehensibly, (2) sincerely, (3) appropriately or legitimately in the context at hand, and (4) accurately. In every interaction, too, a listener's subsequent action depends in part on how these same four criteria are satisfied." When these criteria are violated, listeners feel confusion, distrust, lack of consent and disbelief (Forester, 1989, p. 147), or, alternatively, "puzzlement, mistrust, anger and disbelief" (Forester, 1980, p. 280).

Generally spokespersons for groups advocating new Twin Cities governance arrangements were likely to be viewed as having legitimate and sincere concerns for metropolitan problems by virtue of their organizational affiliation and status. Moreover, their description of these problems probably matched the experience of their listeners who were living with the problems. However, it is easy to see that participants in the U.S. abortion debates — especially the "right-to-life" advocates — have violated the norms of pragmatic communication. By hurling epithets like "murderer" and "baby killer" at women's rights advocates, "right-to-life" activists have ensured that many of their opponents will feel personally attacked. Such communication is untruthful and illegitimate from the women's rights standpoint and fosters extreme distrust of the opposing camp. Compromise and grounds for common action are thus foreclosed.

Argumentation is another important aspect of mediating

differing interpretive schemes aimed at the creation of shared meaning and values in forums. Dunn (1981, 40–43), drawing on the work of Toulmin (1958) and Freeley (1976), contends that policy arguments — those related to decisions, issues, conflicts, or policy preferences — have several elements. These include policy-relevant information; a policy claim, which is the conclusion of a policy argument; a warrant, which is an assumption permitting the move from information to claim; and the backing for the warrant, which consists of additional supporting assumptions or arguments, often based on scientific laws, the authority of experts, or ethical or moral principles. Policy arguments also include a rebuttal — or second conclusion — assumption, or argument that indicates the conditions under which the original claim is unacceptable or in need of modification; and a qualifier, which expresses the degree to which the arguer is certain about the policy claim. The design and use of forums influences which information will be offered; which claims, along with which rebuttals, will be accepted — based on which warrants and backing; and how much weight will be given to the qualifiers (see Bozeman, 1986; Landsbergen and Bozeman, 1987; Bozeman and Landsbergen, 1989; Throgmorton, 1991).

These elements of argumentation can be traced in the operation of legislative forums in the abortion liberalization campaign. Legislators were interested in information about need based on the experience of local women and physicians. They also wanted to know the likely effects of change, the dollar costs, and the political benefits and liabilities. Advocates claimed that their proposed policy would improve the situation of many citizens and that the continuation of existing laws harmed great numbers of women, sometimes fatally. The warrant for the advocates' argument was that it was logical to assume women were using back-street abortionists because of existing law and would stop using them if the law were liberalized. Backing for the warrant was available in testimony from physicians, legal experts, and clergy. Rebuttals were offered by opponents who disputed many elements of the change advocates' argument. The reformers then had to qualify their arguments with the recognition that outcomes brought about by more liberal abortion laws could not be predicted with complete certainty. Perhaps the most important mode of argumentation connected to forums for debating the Metropolitan Council was the plethora of reports issued by the sponsoring organizations. These reports contained a wealth of policy-relevant information supporting policy claims. They also often included alternative ways of viewing the problems and solutions, but they cumulatively steered policy makers and interested citizens toward consensus and decision.

Finally, rules governing *access* to participation in forums strongly influence who speaks what, where, when, why, and how, and who listens. In so doing, these rules strongly influence which decisions, conflicts, issues, and policy preferences get discussed and which do not. For example, having the senior people talk first may inhibit discussion by junior people. Forcing people to talk about the issue at hand may make it difficult to redefine the issue. But the most powerful rules are those that limit attendance at a discussion. For example, holding meetings in places, or at times, or at a cost that makes attendance by interested parties difficult or impossible can alter resulting debates by altering the set of participants.

Early advocates of more liberal abortion laws found their access to the mass media limited by the unwritten rules of newsworthiness. Reports or statements advocating change were not considered newsworthy, and wide coverage came only when the issue was personalized in Sherri Finkbine's plight or connected to sensational or controversial activities. In legislative forums, access was constrained by time limits and the democratic norms that encourage testimony by representatives of both sides of an issue. Access to the forums debating the need for new governance mechanisms in Minneapolis–St. Paul was by invitation, and forum organizers focused on a relatively elite group of people, which included business leaders, planners, Citizens League members, and local officials. The organizers also involved legislators, either by inviting them to the forums or sending them copies of the reports generated by the forums. Therefore, the debate about regional governance was carried out essentially by people whose jobs compelled them to attend to regional issues or whose responsibilities left them time for civic activities. One probable result was that forum participants reached consensus on general direction more easily than if more diverse groups had been included.

Most societies use rules governing access to establish hierarchies of forums, reserving those near the top for global discussions of big issues. The editorial pages of the *New York Times* and the *Washington Post,* for example, are not open to everyone, nor is membership on the presidential, gubernatorial, mayoral, United Way, or Chamber of Commerce task forces and commissions charged with identifying relevant problems and solutions. Access rules thus manage what gets defined as an important public problem and what does not. Fortunately, however, public leaders and followers in the United States are allowed great freedom to use existing forums or to establish new ones when they are needed. Freedom of speech, assembly, and the press are built into the Constitution, and U.S. citizens jealously guard those freedoms.

In sum, there are two general outcomes of the way forums are designed and used. The first outcome is the identification of the structural, or collective, basis for a *potential* list of decisions, issues, conflicts, and policy preferences that might be debated. The second outcome is the transformation of that list into the *actual* items that will be addressed and those that will not be addressed.

The Design and Use of Arenas

In 1967, the council partisans in the metropolitan governance debate focused their energies on the legislative arena — in this case, the Minnesota legislature. They urged the legislature to create an elected metropolitan council that would guide regional development and oversee regional services. Before the *Roe* v. *Wade* decision, the champions of women's reproductive rights urged state legislators to liberalize or repeal restrictive abortion laws. After *Roe v. Wade,* the most significant abortion policy arena became Congress, as those who opposed the ruling sought to overturn it via constitutional amendment. Nevertheless, skirmishes continued at state, county, and even city levels.

There are arenas that are primarily political and those that are principally economic. Both types distribute and redistribute access to participation in policy-making and implementation, and thereby help maintain or change political and economic relations. Examples of political arenas are legislatures; city councils; corporate executive committees and boards of directors; and the decision-making mechanisms of public bureaucracies, nonprofit organizations, and interorganizational networks.

The market is the basic form of economic arena. Deciding what to leave inside and what to leave outside markets is a crucial determinant of subsequent economic patterns in most societies (Lindblom, 1977; Wildavsky, 1979; Giddens, 1984; Williamson, 1985). Arenas may also be place-bound — for example, legislatures — or non-place-bound — for example, mail-order markets.

The first dimension of power is manifested in an arena when people interact as they use their capabilities to obtain desired outcomes, which are the preferred policies and their implementation (see Exhibit 4.3). Policy-making in arenas characteristically involves the establishment of rules, laws, norms, principles, policies, standards, or prices that apply generally to a specified population or category of actions. In addition, plans, programs, budgets, or particular recommended actions may be adopted.

The third dimension of power, or the deep structure, in policy-making and implementation is shaped by aspects and principles of "domination." These principles are embodied in, or rationalized by, unequal distributions of resources within institutional frameworks — for example, social position, authority, skills, intelligence, status, or money. These are often referred to as the "bases of power" (French and Raven, 1968). Unequal resources generate unequal individual or group capacities to make and implement policies. There must be a policy maker and at least one other participant, and the policy maker must be able to affect a shared resource base that renders policy-making necessary and possible. The vehicles of bias (the second dimension of power) used to link action with deep structure include

Exhibit 4.3. The Design and Use of Arenas.

Definition	Participation by actors in a delimited domain of activity as part of the process of policy-making.
Examples	Corporate executive committees, city councils, cartels, markets, faculty senates, boards of directors, legislatures.
Policy-related role	Maintenance or change of political and economic relations, especially through distribution and redistribution of access to the exercise of power.
Structural properties	A policy maker and at least one other participant in an institutional framework of asymmetrically distributed resources. The policy maker must be able to affect a shared resource base that makes policy-making necessary and possible.
Action	The use of actors' interacting capabilities to secure outcomes through the agency of others. Characteristic activity is policy-making that establishes rules, laws, norms, principles, policies, standards, plans, or prices of general application to a specified population or category of actions.
Ideas, rules, modes, media, and methods	Capabilities and means of mediating among capabilities—for example, domains; agendas; permitted methods of planning, budgeting, decision making, and implementation; access rules.
Outcomes	Structural basis for a set of potential nondecisions and decisions about policy, and transformation of that set into actual nondecisions and decisions.

capabilities; domains; agendas; planning, budgeting, decision making, and implementation methods; and rules governing access to participation in the arenas.

The *capabilities* that a leader has available to influence a sequence of policy-related interactions depend on the rules and resources he or she can use and mobilize. They range from verbal skill, to the ability to hire and fire, to computer literacy, to the threat of physical violence. Capability refers, in other words, to one's *potential* to affect outcomes through drawing on rules, resources, and transformation relations that offer any kind of advantage. Policy-making and implementation refer to the *actual* application of some or all of these advantages. Different capabilities of differing actors will strongly influence which decisions, issues, conflicts, and policy preferences count in particular arenas and which do not.

In the legislative arena, legislators themselves have the greatest potential to directly affect outcomes. Some, however, by virtue of personal skills or positions have considerably more potential than others. In the 1967 Minnesota legislature, an extremely powerful rural senator, Gordon Rosenmeier, was able to thwart fellow legislators William Frenzel and Harmon Ogdahl, who sponsored bills reflecting the consensus for an elected council developed in the forums. Rosenmeier introduced a bill to create an appointed council that merely coordinated regional services, and because he controlled the committee to which the council legislation was assigned, his bill became the heart of the law that was eventually passed.

Domains, agendas, and planning, budgeting, decision making, and implementation methods are the means by which differing or conflicting capabilities in arenas are at least partially mediated. A domain is the spatial and substantive extent of an arena's policy-making and implementation authority. Planning, budgeting, decision making, and implementation methods are the rules used to govern the process of putting together policies, plans, and budgets; making decisions; and implementing them. Therefore, the selection of methods constitutes one of the most important actions in any arena, because different methods will favor different actors' capabilities and purposes (Pfeffer, 1981; Friend, Laffin, and Norris, 1981; Riker, 1986). Further, rules governing *access* to participation in arenas strongly influence which persons, groups, organizations, and capabilities are admitted to an arena, and thus also influence which items will be considered in the process of policy-making and implementation and which will not.

The state legislature's domain in the Metropolitan Council case included the Twin Cities geographic area and the authority to establish governing structures for that area, within the framework of the Minnesota constitution and other applicable laws. Perhaps the most important legislative method in the case was the use of the committee system to debate and vote on policy proposals. The committee system allowed Senator Rosenmeier to exert considerable control over the substance of the legislation. Groups involved in the abortion controversy became very savvy about the planning, budgeting, and policy-making process in local, state, and federal legislatures and executive branches. Since lobbying was a permitted method of influencing decisions about abortion laws and abortion funding, both supporters and opponents of women's reproductive rights lobbied members of legislatures and executive offices intensely. Those who wanted highly restrictive abortion laws, however, sometimes overstepped the bounds of acceptable pressure and alienated legislators who had previously sided with them.

Because time is a limited resource, *agendas* are a crucial mediator among competing capabilities. Agendas can be systemic or public agendas, which consist of both general and recurring problems, or they can be formal agendas, which consist of problems under current serious consideration by authoritative policy makers (Cobb and Elder, 1972). Only capabilities applicable to dealing with agenda items become relevant. Furthermore, the nature of the agenda item and its order on the agenda can differentially favor the relevant capabilities of competing actors or coalitions (Riker, 1986). Agendas are composed of *issues,* which are points of controversy between two or more actors over procedural or substantive matters involving the distribution of positions or resources (see Cobb and Elder, 1975)— or, in our terms, a public problem accompanied by at least one solution that has pros and cons from the standpoint of various stakeholders. Complicated agenda rules can benefit the group that has considerably more political connections and financial resources than its opponents. Agenda rules can also permit some public decisions to be made with only a minimum of public scrutiny.

In order to claim a place on the legislative formal agenda, the advocates of metropolitan governance developed a compelling integrated picture of public problems and proposed solutions backed by considerable consensus among interested groups. They emphasized the urgency of the problems and highlighted the likelihood that the national government would impose its own partial solution if state government failed to act. Rules permitting testimony and lobbying by outside groups allowed the advocates access to legislative deliberations. Especially influential were business leaders who testified and lobbied on behalf of creating the Metropolitan Council.

Rules governing *access* to participation in arenas strongly influence who decides what, where, when, why, and how. Access may be based on formal rules, position, precedent, reputation, financial resources, rhetorical skill, or some other criterion. But regardless of the particular rules, the mere inclusion of some people and exclusion of others can be expected to affect what gets onto the formal agenda and, subsequently, which decisions get made on which issues and preferences.

Legislative reapportionment in 1966, by changing legislative actors, ensured that advocates of metropolitan governance would get at least some of what they wanted. In the early 1960s, when rural legislators were firmly in charge, the legislature went into gridlock over every proposed solution to metropolitan problems. The reapportionment aligned representation more closely with population, thus increasing the number of metropolitan-area legislators and loosening the domination of rural politicians. To ensure important access, participants on both sides of the abortion controversy have sought direct influence over who sits in legislatures and executive offices. They have organized political action committees and endorsed candidates for Congress, the Presidency, state legislatures, governor's offices, and even city and county offices.

Most societies use rules governing access to establish hierarchies of arenas, reserving more global policy-making for those nearer the top. Procedures for appealing policy decisions to higher-level arenas also are usually established. Both the rules of access and of appeal are basic methods of political management, allowing those further up the hierarchy to exercise greater power than those below. In the Metropolitan Council case, local governments on their own could not establish regional agencies or binding cooperative arrangements. The state legislature had to authorize such structures. Similarly, in the abortion controversy, local and state legislatures could not call a national constitutional convention to consider a human life amendment. Only Congress had that authority, although it could be forced to exercise it if requested to do so by three-fourths of the state legislatures.

To summarize, the design and use of arenas in concrete situations does two things. First, it establishes the structural, or collective, basis for a set of *potential* policies, plans, programs, decisions, budgets, and implementation actions. Secondly, it transforms that list into the *actual* matters that will be dealt with and those that will not.

The Minnesota legislature considered basically two sets of potential policies and implementation actions for creating new institutional arrangements to govern metropolitan development. One set would create an elected council with operating control over regional services. The other would create an appointed council that would coordinate metropolitan services. The set actually adopted through legislation combined elements of both sets, built in opportunities for further strengthening of the council, and gave the council limited taxing power. The council was also authorized to review long-term comprehensive plans of the various Twin Cities governmental units if the plans had an area-wide or multicommunity effect or a substantial effect on metropolitan development. The council could also suspend those plans if they were inconsistent with council development policies. Additionally, the legislature directed the council to prepare reports (including legislative recommendations) on air and water pollution, parks and open space, sewage disposal, taxation, assessment practices, storm drainage, and consolidation of local services.

The opponents of restrictive abortion laws were able to place their proposals for reform or repeal on the agendas of state legislatures in the late 1960s and 1970s. Fifteen legislatures passed reform bills and four approved repeal. After 1973, the set of potential abortion policies, programs, and other decisions considered in state and local arenas was strongly shaped by the U.S. Supreme Court's decision in *Roe* v. *Wade*. Most state legislatures overturned or ceased enforcing old laws, while some local and state legislators and executives passed laws or issued regulations designed to test the decision's limits. Since 1973, Congress has considered proposals to add a human life amendment to the Constitution and to cut off public funding to any program that might support abortion. The attack on public funding of abortion services and related programs has generally succeeded, but the human life amendment campaign has fizzled.

The Design and Use of Courts

Courts are used to judge or evaluate decisions or conduct in relation to laws or norms, usually in order to settle disputes. They are associated with the organization of laws (or norms, principles, policies, rules, standards, criteria, or decisions) and modes of sanctioning or adjudicating — that is, ways of allowing some conduct and not others. Courts distribute and redistribute access to legitimacy, and therefore help maintain or change laws or other modes of adjudicating conduct (see Exhibit 4.4.).

Exhibit 4.4. The Design and Use of Courts.

Definition	A practice of judging or evaluating policies or conduct in relation to laws or norms, usually in order to settle disputes.
Examples	Court of public opinion, professional licensing bodies, deans' offices, formal courts — for example, the Supreme Court, military tribunals, traffic courts.
Policy-related role	Maintenance or change of laws and other modes of sanctioning conduct, especially through distribution and redistribution of access to legitimacy.
Structural properties	Two disputants and a third party to resolve their dispute, plus at least partially shared norms.
Action	Moral evaluation and sanctioning of conduct, and especially conflict management and dispute resolution.
Ideas, rules, modes, media, and methods	Conflict management and sanctioning capabilities, along with differing norms as mediated by jurisdiction, conflict management methods, access rules.
Outcomes	Structural basis for potentially permitted policy decisions and modes of conduct and the transformation of that set into actual policy decisions and modes of conduct that are permitted and those that are not.

Courts may be formal or informal. Formal courts include the Supreme Court, military tribunals, local traffic courts, and ecclesiastical courts. The most important informal court is the "court of public opinion." Courts that fall between the formal courts and the informal court of public opinion include regulatory agencies hearing differing views before issuing or changing regulations, professional licensing bodies conducting disciplinary hearings, deans' offices resolving disputes between college departments or individual professors, referees conducting binding arbitration, special court-appointed masters dealing with individual cases as part of a class-action settlement, and a host of "alternative dispute resolution" mechanisms. In each example, the emphasis is on conflict management through judging or evaluating policy decisions or conduct in relation to laws or norms; it is not on communication or policy-making, though each of these is present. Courts may or may not be confined to particular places. The court of public opinion, for example, is not a place-bound construct.

The principal activity (first dimension of power) in courts is moral evaluation and sanctioning of conduct, especially through conflict management. The disputes handled are typically "residual" — they are left over after arenas have established policies and made decisions, or for some reason, the political or economic arenas cannot deal with them. The activity of courts either affirms or modifies policies and/or the underlying norms in the system. The deep structure (third dimension of power) of courts is two disputants plus a third party to help them resolve their dispute, along with at least partially shared norms, or principles of legitimation, to govern resolution of the dispute. Action and structure are linked through the mediation of conflict management and sanctioning capabilities, norms, jurisdiction, conflict resolution methods, and access rules (second dimension of power).

Conflict management and sanctioning capabilities are vital tools that leaders bring to courts in varying degrees. For example, the Metropolitan Council is responsible for Minneapolis–St. Paul regional governance, yet within the region many other governing units exercise authority over limited areas. Partly because of these domain overlaps it has been necessary for various public

bodies and officials to resolve conflicts over whose policies will
prevail. In some cases, the council itself has played this court
role. In others, the formal court system, the legislature, or the
state attorney general has handled the conflict. In other words,
differing actors have had differing capabilities to resolve conflicts
over domain. In the abortion controversy, the federal courts
and particularly the U.S. Supreme Court had sanctioning capabilities that could overrule the decisions of local, state, and federal arenas and also of lower courts. The court of public opinion also placed powerful sanctions on women's sexual conduct
and their decisions about abortion.

   Norms are the standards against which, or with which,
conflicts are addressed. These norms may be formal — for example, legal due process rules — or informal — for example, widely
applied standards of etiquette or fairness. In resolving disputes
over development controls, Minnesota courts have reconciled
the conflict between personal property rights and government
authority by permitting local governments to enact reasonable
development controls as long as due process is observed. In
deciding whether women should have access to abortion, federal courts relied on the principle of "constitutionality" — that
is, they asked whether restrictive abortion laws conflicted with
constitutional guarantees. Indeed, the U.S. Constitution is the
ultimate norm controlling the resolution of almost all U.S. public
conflicts.

   Jurisdiction denotes the spatial and substantive extent of
a court's authority to interpret and apply norms to resolve
conflicts. For example, the Metropolitan Council had review
power over local governments' federal grant applications and
used this jurisdiction to resolve conflicts between local government authority and metropolitan authority.

   Conflict management methods significantly affect the outcomes
of the conflict management process, since they favor some decisions and modes of conduct and rule out others (see, for example, Filley, 1975; Fisher and Ury, 1981). Furthermore, since
methods of conflict resolution differ in the extent to which they
invoke specific norms, they differ in their efficacy as methods
of social control. The selection of methods, therefore, is one of

a leader's most important actions in any court setting, since different methods will favor different objectives. Standard methods include use of a go-between, mediation, arbitration, and the substitution of law and office for consent, which has become the conventional courtroom method in the United States. These methods differ in the extent to which they rely on consent or coercion, on the one hand, and nondichotomous or dichotomous solutions, on the other. In nondichotomous solutions, each party gets something. In dichotomous solutions, the "winner takes all" (Shapiro, 1975, pp. 223–233; Shapiro, 1981.)

The question of consent arises because of the basic structure of courts—namely, the use of a triad for conflict resolution. As soon as the third party decides in favor of one of the disputants, a two-against-one situation can develop that has no logic at all for the loser, who may, therefore, have to be coerced to accept the verdict. The need for coercion diminishes when the disputants can agree on the norms that should govern the settlement and the selection of the third party. By agreeing to both norms and judge, the eventual loser has gone a long way toward consenting to the judgment. Furthermore, chances for consent are also enhanced to the extent that both parties can agree on a nondichotomous solution.

Using a go-between comes closest to the ideal of consenting to a judge and certain norms and to a nondichotomous solution. Both parties consent to the go-between and all solutions offered and accepted are those of the disputants themselves. A mediator also operates with the consent of both parties, but plays a more active advisory role. Arbitration differs from mediation in that the arbitrator typically is expected to create his or her own solution to the conflict instead of merely advising the disputants. Furthermore, the arbitrator usually works within a fixed set of legal norms in the shape of laws or, more typically, contracts. There is an important distinction, however, between voluntary and binding arbitration. The former more closely resembles mediation, while the latter resembles "the substitution of law and office for consent" (Shapiro, 1975, p. 325). Metropolitan Council staff have acted as both mediators and arbitrators in various dispute areas.

However, as organizations and societies become more complex there is a tendency to substitute preexisting law — or policies, regulations, and rules — for unique norms fashioned for unique situations, and to substitute "office" for the third party chosen by two disputants. In the extreme case, both the applicable law and the judge are imposed on a defendant. The substitution of law and office for consent aggravates the basic contradiction in social logic of using a triad to resolve the conflict of a dyad. The consent of the loser may still be gained, however, if he or she feels the judge and the applicable law are just and not prejudiced in favor of the opponent. The difficulty is that most laws in most situations are not neutral because they tend to favor some classes of people and not others. They have the built-in organizational bias we described earlier in this chapter. Furthermore, the judge as an organizational or governmental representative is likely to interject a third set of objectives quite independent of the two disputants' objectives. A persistent crisis of legitimacy can develop as the social logic and the norms of the courts are continuously challenged (Shapiro, 1975; Habermas, 1973; Heydebrand, 1977a, 1977b, 1981; Stone, 1988).

The substitution of law and office for consent also increases the likelihood of dichotomous, imposed solutions, which work well only if the parties do not need to have further interactions with one another. To maintain relations between the parties, some mutually agreeable conflict management method is needed — a circumstance that rules out dichotomous, imposed solutions except as a last resort or as a tool to force negotiations.

Formal courts deal with these difficulties in several ways. The first is simply to avoid dichotomous solutions, principally by converting disputes over something that is indivisible — such as injury, trespass, or breach of contract — into something that is divisible — usually money — and by converting disputes over legal right or wrong into disputes over the "balancing of equities" (Shapiro, 1975, p. 228). Indeed, the U.S. Supreme Court attempted such a balancing in *Roe* v. *Wade*. After finding that the right of personal privacy "is broad enough to encompass a woman's decision whether or not to terminate her pregnancy," the court also declared that this right conflicts with three important state interests — the health of its citizens, maintenance of medical standards, and the protection of potential life. "At some point in pregnancy," the court continued, "these respective interests become sufficiently compelling to sustain regulation of the factors that govern the abortion decision." The court went on to outline when and how states might regulate abortion based on these interests. Even so, those who wanted to restrict abortions were unhappy with this decision, since it removed most restrictions from first-trimester abortions. The women's rights supporters meanwhile proclaimed the decision as a clearcut victory.

Courts also can channel the bulk of legal conflict into negotiations between the disputants, who are threatened with eventual formal court action if the negotiations fail. The mediation or arbitration procedures for such negotiations are often built into legally binding contracts between the parties (Williamson, 1985). Another solution to the legitimacy crisis is giving the losing party several channels of appeal. The Metropolitan Council, for example, has the authority to overrule local land use plans that conflict with council policies, but local governments can appeal council decisions to the state courts. Finally, courts usually rely on the parties themselves to enforce the terms of any settlement. They typically have limited capability to monitor compliance with their rulings, and they reintervene to ensure compliance only at the request of one of the parties (Shapiro, 1975).

Finally, rules governing *access* to participation in courts strongly influence which residual conflicts will be resolved according to which norms, and therefore which actions — and especially which decisions and policy preferences — will be allowed and which will not. Access may be based on evidence of rule violation, demonstrated injury, formal rules (including rules of appeal), position, precedent, custom, financial resources, or some other criterion. Access rules also are used by virtually all societies to establish hierarchies of courts, reserving the most fundamental pronouncements to those at the top. When the Metropolitan Council acts as a court to resolve conflicts between its own and local authority, local officials and citizens advocating the supremacy of local authority have access to the court, but it is naturally outweighed by the access of the council members themselves and their staff. A similar imbalance of access occurs when the council acts as a court to resolve conflicts between its own authority and that of other regional agencies. Lawyers Linda Coffee and Sarah Weddington would not have been able to challenge Texas abortion law in court if they had not been representing a woman who could claim actual harm from the law. Moreover, they had access to a federal court only because they could plausibly argue that the law violated a right guaranteed by the Constitution.

In sum, like the design and use of forums and arenas, the design and use of courts has two main results. First is the creation of a *potential* list of residual conflicts that might be raised and resolved and actions that might be condoned or disapproved. Second is the transformation of that list into the *actual* conflicts that are addressed and the actions that are morally sanctioned and those that are not.

The creation and operation of the Metropolitan Council, for example, led to conflicts with existing government authorities. Subsequent court decisions (sometimes by the council itself) specified the limits of local government and regional agency autonomy. In the abortion controversy, federal courts have been called upon to resolve an array of conflicts related to a woman's freedom to have an abortion. The U.S. Supreme Court in *Roe* v. *Wade* and subsequent decisions has ruled on many of those conflicts—for example, whether a teenage girl's right to privacy outweighs her parents' right to be consulted in her decisions. In one of the most controversial and central conflicts—the assertion that a fetus has a right to life that can override a woman's right to choose abortion—the Supreme Court has not made a definitive ruling. In *Roe* v. *Wade,* it simply noted the "wide divergence of thinking" on the question of when life begins, summarized legal precedent, and concluded that "the unborn have never been recognized as persons in the whole sense." Although the court subsequently has seemed willing to give more weight to the state's interest in protecting a fetus, it still has not endorsed fetal rights.

It is important for public leaders to be aware that courts have a role beyond the management of particular residual disputes. They also serve as general social control mechanisms, principally because conflict management almost invariably relies on norms held by society at large, or in the case of intraorganizational conflict resolution, by the organization itself or by comparable organizations. The use of such norms to resolve disputes reproduces social control based on those norms. The link between courts and general social control becomes even stronger when law and office are substituted for consent, since judging is an extension of sovereignty in which the judge is charged with enforcing constitutions, legislation, or precedents instead of norms originated by the disputants (Shapiro, 1975). Once again, the logic of the triad is severely questioned, unless the law is seen as neutral in its intent and effects and the judge is seen as independent of political authority. However, neither of these circumstances is likely to prevail.

Social control also results from using formal courts because these courts make supplementary laws. When judges and court-appointed administrators apply general rules — typically developed by others — to specific cases, they invariably add details that become precedents. Judges thereby become agents of social control for more distant authorities. Courts also develop their own rules to manipulate factual issues to achieve policy goals. Presumptions, burdens of proof, and per se rules are typically open to such manipulation. For example, the Metropolitan Council had authority to develop regional plans, but it was formal courts that developed criteria for deciding whether those plans conflicted with individual rights. Those criteria included reasonableness, thorough analysis, and open public debate. Another fundamental contradiction, therefore, is between judges as independent, neutral third parties and judges as lawmakers who should be accountable to some portion of society. Because no sovereign power is likely to tolerate a fully independent judiciary, the contradiction is unresolvable in many cases, and judging in all societies tends to be associated with sovereignty, because of its social control and lawmaking potential (Shapiro, 1975).

Appeal procedures are also a method of hierarchical social

control. The availability of appeal helps stabilize a system by
not overstraining the logic and structure of the triad. In other
words, the possibility of appeal tells the loser he or she has access to another triad and thus need not contemplate changing
the system. Procedures for moving through the appeals hierarchy also allow judicial and political authorities time to explore
the implications of basic legal changes that may be mandated
by "final" rulings of the highest courts. The use of appeal procedures thus allows central political authorities to do two things:
monitor lower court operations to enforce compliance and unifor-
mity throughout the legal system, and prepare for changes as
they work their way through the system. Since the chain of appeal typically ends with the chief political authorities, appeal
may thus be seen as a means of centralizing political control
and change.

Implications for Change in a Shared-Power World

Several implications can be drawn from our discussion of power
and the design and use of forums, arenas, and courts. The first,
and perhaps distressing, conclusion is that social relationships
are complicated, particularly in shared-power situations. Furthermore, what one sees on the surface is not the only activity
going on — and very well may not be the most important activity, since it is the underlying ideas, rules, modes, media,
methods, and bedrock social structure which strongly influence
what becomes observable action.

The second conclusion, however, is that the very complexity of social life makes change more possible. The principle
social practices we use to foster discussions, make policies and
implement them, and resolve residual disputes and enforce the
underlying norms in the system are the design and use of forums, arenas, and courts — and specific uses of forums, arenas,
and courts almost always can be designed to some extent. The
constituting elements of forums, arenas, and courts are numerous, and therefore, the design elements are many. As a result,
numerous moments for change are highlighted, points of access identified, and methods of intervention clarified. Leaders

must pay attention to these elements because they are the basic levers of change in situations where no one is in charge.

Third, leaders can have their greatest influence over actions and outcomes by strengthening, weakening, or altering the vehicles of bias that divide what is theoretically possible into what is actually done and what is not (see Lindblom, 1980). Figuring out what to do in particular circumstances requires attention to both social interaction and institutional arrangements and to the ways they are linked through the design and use of forums, arenas, and courts. Differing designs alter the stock of rules, resources, and transformation relations available to underpin action. Therefore, attention to the design and use of forums, arenas, and courts allows public leaders to achieve indirectly what they cannot hope to achieve directly.

Key Steps in Tackling Public Problems

The leadership opportunities and challenges connected with each phase of the policy change cycle will be presented in detail in Part Two. The chapters in this section offer public leaders conceptual clarity about the immediate purposes of each phase, give them the means to achieve those purposes, and illustrate the settings within which each phase is likely to be played out.

As we noted in Chapter Three, the policy change cycle should not be viewed as a linear, lock-step model. In practice, it typically falls somewhere in between a rigid sequence of steps and near chaos. Therefore, flexibility is required to apply the model to a particular situation. The degree of chaos may be greatest at the federal level; less at the state, big city, and big county level; and least at the level of medium and small cities and counties, single interorganizational networks, and relatively small communities of place or interest — even though those communities may cross many organizational and governmental jurisdictions. Usually, however, and particularly at lower levels, there are reasonably predictable outlines of action, filled with short- and long-term strategies, maneuvers, and recyclings. The policy change cycle framework provides a conceptual overview of these actions through which important issues gain a place on the public agenda and are effectively addressed.

Chapters Five through Seven focus on issue creation. An issue is created when an important problem is on the public agenda and is linked to at least one solution that has pros and cons from the standpoints of various stakeholders. Chapter Five covers the initial agreement phase, when key leaders agree to do something about an undesirable condition. Chapter Six focuses on defining the problem to be addressed, and Chapter Seven discusses methods of searching for solutions that can become policies. Chapter Eight discusses how to develop a winning policy proposal, while Chapter Nine covers the review and adoption of policy proposals. Implementation and evaluation are the focus of Chapter Ten. Chapter Eleven completes the cycle by illustrating policy maintenance, succession, or termination. Each of these chapters also discusses the desired outcomes of the phase, the benefits of the process, and specific leadership guidelines. Chapter Twelve presents our guidelines for getting started on a policy change effort.

Public leaders who attend to the leadership tasks outlined in these chapters should be well on their way to developing politically acceptable, technically workable, and legally and ethically acceptable responses to important public problems. In the process, we hope to make it clear that all of us can be collectively in charge of our futures.

Chapter 5

Forging an
Initial Agreement to Act

It must be considered that there is nothing more difficult to carry out, nor more doubtful of success, nor more dangerous to handle, than to initiate a new order of things. For the reformer has enemies in all those who profit by the old order and only lukewarm defenders in all those who would benefit by the new order, this lukewarmness arising partly from fear of their adversaries, who have the laws in their favor; and partly from the incredulity of mankind, who do not truly believe in anything new until they have had actual experience of it.
— Niccolo Machiavelli

Never doubt that a small group of thoughtful, committed citizens can change the world; indeed, it is the only thing that ever has.
— Margaret Mead

In the first phase of the policy change cycle, an initial group of key decision makers, opinion leaders, or committed citizens agrees on the need to respond to an undesirable condition and develops a basic response strategy. As the number of people involved with the change effort expands, additional agreements are likely to be necessary. This phase is one of the most important in any policy change cycle, and may be one of the most time-consuming, since much thought and effort are typically necessary to develop agreements that bind actors together and commit them to positive change.

      This first phase and the next two — or frequently, the next three — phases in the change cycle often form continuous loops, as the momentum for change builds and as what happens in one phase informs what happens in the others. The phases must be linked in this fashion to generate action and to place an issue on the public agenda. Moving an issue to the public agenda principally involves bringing about changes in the public's perceptions so that a situation which was not viewed as a solvable problem begins to be seen as an area in which action is possible. In order for this problem to become an issue, a viable solution must be available (Kingdon, 1984). Phase one political agreements are negotiated in order to forge ahead with the development of an issue that can capture public attention. These agreements are likely to be facilitated by political changes such as shifts in public opinion, pressure group campaigns, election results, partisan or ideological shifts in policy bodies, or changes in the leadership of relevant organizations (Kingdon, 1984). The phase two problem formulations develop perceptions and definitions likely to generate action. In phase three, change advocates seek a viable policy prescription for addressing the problem. The three phases together comprise the issue creation process, and they clearly must be thought of as interdependent. Issue creation is high-level politics that involves important elites and opinion leaders (Lynn, 1987; Sabatier, 1991) in order to compete strongly for some of the limited carrying capacity available at any time on the public agenda (Hilgartner and Bosk, 1988). Sometimes issue creation involves the fourth phase as well, when a detailed policy change proposal may be necessary to galvanize action.

      While the initial phases are closely linked, they must also be pulled apart, at least conceptually, to prevent premature closure, which could cause the wrong problems to be solved, produce solutions that perpetuate the problems, or create new problems. Pulling the steps apart helps leaders avoid policy blindness. Yet another reason to keep the phases conceptually separate is that policy change efforts often do not "begin at the beginning" with initial agreements to act. Sometimes they begin with suggested problem formulations that must be subsequently linked to viable solutions and to agreements with other decision makers. At other times, these change efforts begin with solutions that must search for important problems and a hospitable political environment. Indeed, each of the first three phases — as well as the last phase — is a likely starting point for policy change. For conceptual clarity, however, our presentation begins with the initial agreement phase.

The emphasis in the initial agreement phase is on the design and use of boundary-crossing forums and informal arenas — although in major change efforts, formal arenas may need to authorize the initiation of significant policy change actions. The most important components of forums are interpretive schemes, symbols, communication patterns, arguments, and access rules. In particular, change advocates must demonstrate that the proposed policy change is in the public interest (Stone, 1988). The cases studied for this book indicate that a series of initial agreements made in forums is usually part of a major change effort. Additionally, agreements by some people to seek change may be accompanied by agreements among others to resist change. The cases also reveal that the seeds of possible solutions are often present in the initial agreements, emphasizing the interconnectedness of the first three phases.

In their attempts to develop a regional approach to problems besetting the Minneapolis–St. Paul area in the 1960s, several community leaders first developed separate agreements within their organizations to do something about the undesirable consequences of suburban growth. In 1962, for example, the Metropolitan Planning Commission (MPC), acting with federal encouragement, authorized a Joint Program for Landuse and Transportation Planning to be overseen by a committee of representatives from Minneapolis and St. Paul, the highway departments of the seven metro-area counties, the Minnesota Highway Department, the U.S. Bureau of Public Roads, and the U.S. Housing and Home Finance Agency. Robert Einsweiler, head of planning at MPC, coordinated the program, and planners and engineers from the participating organizations did the research and other staff work. The Joint Program committee was also assisted by a technical and a citizen advisory committee. The program issued several reports demonstrating that such essentials of high-quality urban living as affordable housing and reliable transportation would become scarce in the Minneapolis–St. Paul area if current development patterns and practices continued. In late 1965, when the Joint Program had completed most of its research, participants focused on recommendations for minimizing the problems caused by rapid suburban growth. In this final stage, the program participants worked with the 300-member metropolitan-area Elected Officials Review Committee and with the 100-member citizen advisory committee.

About the time that the Joint Program began, area chapters of the League of Women Voters established the Council of Metropolitan Area Leagues of Women Voters (CMAL) to engage local leagues in the study of metropolitan-area problems. CMAL leaders recognized the need for cooperation among cities and suburbs, particularly for resolving environmental threats caused by metropolitan development. Verne Johnson's Citizens League had also adopted a metropolitan focus by this time and had issued numerous studies that highlighted the interconnections among various regional problems.

As the Joint Program was finishing its work, the Citizens League began advocating various metropolitan governance mechanisms, as did individual elected officials who spoke in public forums. Meanwhile, a Minneapolis banker named Dennis Dunne initiated a concerted effort to build business support for a new metropolitan government structure. In his role as chairman of the legislative committee of the Minneapolis Chamber of Commerce, he persuaded the St. Paul Chamber of Commerce to join the Minneapolis chamber in sponsoring a meeting among representatives of the Upper Midwest Research and Development Council (UMRDC), the two city chambers of commerce, and suburban chambers. The meeting produced an agreement to establish a fifteen-member urban action committee, chaired by Dunne and assigned the task of developing recommendations on metropolitan government.

In early 1966, MPC members and staff met with Verne Johnson, two suburban mayors who were championing competing regional governance concepts, and several other people to discuss the metropolitan governance mechanisms that had been proposed in the public forums described in Chapter Four. Those at the meeting agreed that the suggestions should be studied in depth and a proposal made to the legislature. Meanwhile Johnson; Art Naftalin, the Minneapolis mayor; Tom Anding, the director of UMRDC; Ted Kolderie of the *Minneapolis Star Tribune;* and other main players in the regional governance discussion had been holding informal strategy sessions. This group decided that UMRDC was an ideal vehicle for expanding the metropolitan governance discussion beyond the circles traditionally interested in government reform. In particular, UMRDC's board of prestigious business leaders offered the potential for additional business community involvement. UMRDC agreed to host discussion sessions in the spring of 1966; the invited participants included corporate executives, legislators, local officials, and a few interested citizens like Ann Duff, who had become CMAL chair. However, one group, county officials, decided to resist the move toward metropolitan governance. In the fall of 1965, they organized the Metropolitan Inter-County Council to urge that metropolitan-area counties be allowed to handle metropolitan problems through cooperation.

The beginning of the effort to establish metropolitan governance in the Minneapolis–St. Paul area demonstrates how the initial agreement phase of the policy change cycle overlaps the problem formulation and search for solutions phases. It also illustrates how several initial agreements were made to respond to the consequences of rapid suburban growth. First were the agreements within the Citizens League, CMAL, and MPC. These organizations agreed that an array of problems, ranging from overflowing septic tanks to crowded classrooms and highways, had to be attacked together and at the regional level. Their initial solutions were studies and reports. There also was the agreement to establish an urban action committee consisting of business and civic leaders from Minneapolis, St. Paul, and the suburbs. The problems to be attacked remained the same, but in agreeing to develop recommendations on metropolitan government, this group focused on a more specific initial solution. The group convened by MPC in early 1966 focused on the same problems, but its agreed-upon solution was the development of a legislative proposal. Finally, UMRDC agreed to host discussion sessions on the major metropolitan reorganization proposals. After these initial agreements, metropolitan governance advocates were able to focus more intensely on problem identification and the search for specific solutions.

Seeking to reduce unwanted pregnancies and combat the dangers of back-street abortions, many people came together in the late 1960s and early 1970s to advocate the liberalization of U.S. abortion laws. Their initial agreements brought many new state and national organizations into existence. Likewise, those who opposed liberalization often agreed to start new groups dedicated to making abortion laws as restrictive as possible.

In Minnesota, for example, the two main opposing organizations — both founded in 1967 — were the Council for the Legal Termination of Pregnancy (later Minnesotans Organized for the Repeal of Abortion Laws) and Minnesota Citizens Concerned for Life (MCCL). Also created specifically to challenge Minnesota's abortion laws was the Women's Abortion Action League, a feminist group that held demonstrations and was generally more militant than the Council for the Legal Termination of Pregnancy. In addition, feminist organizations such as the Minnesota Women's Political Caucus and the state chapter of the National Organization for Women (NOW) agreed to support abortion reform as part of their efforts to improve women's social and economic status. By the early 1970s, the Minnesota Medical Association, the state Democratic party, the Methodist church, and the American Lutheran Church Council had endorsed abortion reform. Parallel development occured in many other states, and the formation of some groups was no doubt influenced by reform activity elsewhere — for instance, California and New York were early hotbeds of reform efforts. Minnesota, meanwhile, provided a model for the opposition, as Minnesota Citizens Concerned for Life became more and more successful.

Abortion reform activities at the state level were encouraged by national organizations at the same time as these activities contributed to initiatives by national organizations. The American Civil Liberties Union and the American Law Institute were two national organizations that decided to champion liberal abortion laws in the early 1960s. In 1965, a national organization called the Association for the Study of Abortion Laws was formed, and in 1967, NOW adopted a call for abortion reform at its national convention. The next year Planned Parenthood, the American Public Health Association, and the Presidential Advisory Council on the Status of Women endorsed repeal of restrictive abortion laws. Participants in the first National Conference on Abortion Laws in 1969 laid the foundation for what was to become the National Association for Repeal of Abortion Laws and, later, the National Abortion Rights Action League (NARAL). According to its statement of purpose, NARAL was "dedicated to the elimination of all laws and practices that would compel any woman to bear a child against her will." However, a couple of years before this, the national opposition had begun to coalesce when the Catholic church organized the Family Life Division to coordinate a national counteroffensive against abortion reform. Also important was the 1970 agreement between Norma McCorvey, or Jane Roe, and her lawyers, Linda Coffee and Sarah Weddington, to challenge Texas abortion laws in court. McCorvey's suit would eventually result in the U.S. Supreme Court's 1973 *Roe* v. *Wade* decision allowing pregnant women and their physicians to choose abortion during the first trimester of pregnancy.

In the abortion reform campaign, initial agreements were aimed at the twin problems of unwanted pregnancies and unsafe abortions. State-level reform groups, such as Minnesota's Council for the Legal Termination of Pregnancy, focused on changing their respective states' laws. National organizations advocated more liberal abortion laws throughout the country. While both state and national groups tended to focus on solutions that could be achieved in legislative arenas, Norma McCorvey's lawyers pursued a solution that was dependent on the courts.

Desired Outcomes

The change efforts of abortion reform in the United States and metropolitan governance in the Twin Cities were aimed at problematic conditions that could not be resolved by any one person or organization. Thus from the outset, change advocates faced the likelihood that they would have difficulty obtaining intended results and that a number of unpredictable, and sometimes undesirable, outcomes would occur. Difficulties and undesirable outcomes, however, can be diminished through careful planning aimed at obtaining the key desired outcomes. Considered first are those outcomes desired from the initial agreement. Ideally, this phase of the policy change cycle will produce agreement among the initial group of change advocates that will clarify the need to respond; the organizations, groups, or persons who should be involved or informed in an effort to build a winning coalition; the general strategy and specific steps to be followed for the time being; a shared sense of the design, use, and sequencing of necessary or desirable forums, arenas, and courts; and the form and timing of early reports. In addition, a coordinating committee and a planning team should probably be formed, and the necessary resources to begin the endeavor must be committed.

The Need to Respond

Convincing others that they need to respond to an undesirable condition is a leadership task. Leaders focus attention on the condition. Using interpretive schemes, they emphasize how the condition violates or threatens deeply held values of existing or potential followers, they indicate that change is possible, and they offer compelling visions of a better social life once the undesirable condition is alleviated. Leaders reveal and name felt needs and conditions. They provide evidence that the time is right for change and indicate the general direction of actions that can produce that change. In other words, leaders make both the undesirable conditions and the possibility of a better future *real* by linking interpretive schemes, actions, and consequences (Boal and Bryson, 1987). Opportunities to initiate change with some chance of success don't happen everyday; leaders must seize opportunities when they come, offering convincing visions of the future, articulating interpretive schemes that link values to outcomes, giving clear direction, and detailing actions and consequences.

In the regional governance case, studies by the Citizens League, CMAL, and governmental planners revealed clearly what otherwise would have been perceived only dimly. Whether these groups looked at sewers, transit, parks and open space, or the tax base, the results showed that metropolitan communities were in trouble and that their fates were interconnected. Ted Kolderie's newspaper articles also helped reveal the dimensions of the metropolitan governance crisis. The studies and articles helped many people see how their experiences with community problems fit into a larger picture. These people also gained an understanding of the consequences of their own behaviors, a key step in making the situation real. They began to perceive the contradictions between certain values that they held — for instance, between their desire for new, spacious housing and their desire for unpolluted waterways. They began to shift their emphasis from one set of values — freedom to build and innovate — to a competing set — control and regulation in the common interest.

The people who initially challenged restrictive abortion laws built the momentum for response by focusing on the individual women who had been harmed or were now endangered by the laws. They talked about the women who had died at the hands of illegal abortionists. They talked about the women who had reason to fear birth defects. They talked about the women whose pregnancies resulted from rape or incest, those whose pregnancies endangered their physical or mental health, and those who could not afford to raise another child. These women could be just about any woman, they emphasized. They argued that abortions performed in sanitary facilities by qualified people were a safe and humane alternative to forcing these women to carry their pregnancies to term. They argued that times were changing; women deserved and were demanding control over their lives.

The Organizations and Individuals Who Should Be Involved

The support and the commitment of key decision makers are vital to the potential success of any policy change effort (Hage and Dewar, 1973; Kingdon, 1984; Lynn, 1987; Sabatier, 1991). These decision makers and opinion leaders supply important information about who should be involved, when key decision points will occur, and what arguments are likely to be persuasive when. They can also provide critical resources such as legitimacy, staff assignments, budgets, and meeting spaces. A well-articulated initial agreement provides a clear definition of the initial network of involved organizations and individuals and the process by which the network is to be maintained. Key actors gain a sense of the other actors who must be involved, the nature of the communication channels among them, and the timing and content of the messages and resources that are likely to flow across those channels. The tasks of creating, learning about, using, and expanding or contracting this network are central to the process of coalition formation.

The promoters of regional governance for the Minneapolis–St. Paul area were masterful network builders. Their network included officials from the suburbs and the inner cities, representatives of good-government groups and governmental agencies, business leaders, a legislator, and a capable journalist. The initial groups of abortion reformers and their opponents had a more grass-roots flavor, because they wanted to build a mass membership, but they also recruited people with legal or medical backgrounds who could be persuasive in abortion debates.

The General Strategy and Specific Steps

A good initial agreement will include a "best guess" about the general sequence, purpose, and content of steps in the policy change effort. The outline must ensure that the steps are tied to key organizational and interorganizational decision points, such as elections, budget cycles, and the rhythms of legislative sessions. Time in organizations and social change cycles is not linear; it is junctural (Leo Jakobson, personal communication,

1987; Bryson and Roering, 1988, 1989; Neustadt and May, 1986; Neustadt, 1990), and the most important junctions are decision points.

The Shared Sense of the Design, Use, and Sequencing of Necessary or Appropriate Forums, Arenas, and Courts

The basic settings within which the policy change effort will unfold are forums for discussion, arenas for policy decisions and implementation, and courts to manage residual disputes and enforce underlying norms. Leaders are likely to have their most profound impacts on outcomes through their design and use of these settings. Taking time in advance to think carefully about the settings within which desired changes will, or must, unfold is critical. Exercising a deliberate choice, where possible, of forums, arenas, and courts, and their constituting elements, is the most important lever for change that leaders have at their disposal. The regional governance advocates were very skilled in designing forums and linking them to decisions in arenas. Since the advocates of liberalized abortion laws did not initially have strong support from elected officials and civic leaders, they benefited from choosing to focus on courts as well as forums and arenas. They saw a possibility of obtaining favorable decisions from the courts, which would force resistant arenas to decide on policies that supported change.

Form and Timing of Early Reports

As part of the initial agreement phase, leaders must figure out how to develop an audience for change and secure the commitments necessary to produce change. Various kinds of reports are probably necessary to build this audience and these commitments. The reports must be prepared and presented in ways that are tailored to intended audiences and in ways that produce desired actions when they are needed. In both the metropolitan governance and abortion policy cases, change advocates had to plan, even if only informally, when and how to put their proposals before state legislatures and when particular research or position papers should be issued.

The Coordinating Committee and Planning Team

A good agreement provides one or more mechanisms, such as a coordinating committee or task force, for buffering, consulting, bargaining and negotiating, or problem solving among the organizations and persons involved in, or affected by, the change effort. Without such mechanisms, conflicts are likely to stymie or even destroy the effort (Bryson and Delbecq, 1979; Trist, 1983; Susskind and Cruikshank, 1987; Carpenter and Kennedy, 1988; Gray, 1989). With these mechanisms, leaders have a valuable way to detect errors and make needed midcourse corrections. A coordinating committee is also a useful sounding board for ideas and a vehicle for "reality testing."

In addition, a planning team is almost always necessary, for at least two reasons (Bryson and Roering, 1988). First, no one person is likely to have the information necessary to bring about successful change. And second, a team is necessary for political reasons — that is, to provide the initial representational and ideational basis for a winning coalition. In complex, multiparty situations, the planning team — which may include coordinating committee members — in all likelihood will facilitate the coordinating committee's decision making. The team, itself a forum and an informal arena, gathers information, advises, and produces recommendations for committee action. These committees and teams can evolve over time. For example, a coordinating committee might start as an informal breakfast group focusing mainly on a short-term goal such as organizing a conference. In effect, the coordinating committee at this stage is its own planning team. Later, the committee might become the nucleus of a formal organization.

Resources

A good initial agreement will provide for the flow of necessary resources. Typically, money is not the most important resource in policy change efforts; the time and attention of key decision makers and opinion leaders, along with enough staff time to provide needed support, are more essential to success. For example, consider the following statistics: decision makers and managers generally have no more than nine minutes for any one task

(Mintzberg, 1973). The 1977 Obey Commission Report estimated that, on average, members of the U.S. House of Representatives have only eleven minutes of free time each day in which to read and think. The average married couple spends four minutes a day in meaningful conversation together, and only thirty seconds in meaningful conversation with their children (Bryson, 1989b). Clearly, the management of attention is of fundamental importance when it comes to promoting policy change (Bryson, 1988b; Bellah and others, 1991). The initial agreement should ensure that key decision makers will devote enough time to the process to provide reasonable assurances of success. In addition, staff time will be needed to gather information and provide logistical and clerical support. The numbers of people needed will vary with the magnitude of the envisioned changes.

To revert to the story metaphor we developed in Chapter Three, a good initial agreement will name the actors, outline the plot that is about to unfold, designate the stages on which it will be played, demarcate specific acts and scenes, describe the general character of the story and the themes to be followed, and suggest how the endeavor will be underwritten. The metaphor is appropriate as well as useful, given how dramatic many change efforts become, but it is also important to realize how difficult the metaphor is to apply in situations where no one is in charge (Allison, 1969; Mangham and Overington, 1987). In particular, the initial agreement is likely to point out that there will not be a single "director," but many, and much of the "story" will be made up as events unfold unpredictably and perhaps dangerously. As leaders direct these dramatic processes, they must be prepared for their well-made plays to change suddenly into improvisational theater, or even theater of the absurd! An initial agreement that has delineated themes, actors, and plots will help leaders know when it is time for key decision makers to rewrite their scripts, for a happier ending.

Benefits of the Process

A number of significant benefits flow from a good initial agreement (Bryson, 1988b; see also Delbecq, 1977). The first benefit is simply that, once an agreement is reached, the worth of responding to some problematic condition becomes more likely to be recognized by many of the affected parties, leading to reasonably broad sponsorship of the policy change mission and to legitimacy. Broad sponsorship dispels suspicion that the change effort is a power play by a single advocacy group with narrow interests, and encourages a belief that the results of the effort will be objective and in the general public interest. Broad sponsorship at an early stage also makes it easier for additional groups to "sign on" at a later stage. In the metropolitan governance case, the early agreements ensured sponsorship by several government agencies, elected officials, and civic organizations. They also made it natural and logical for business leaders to become strongly involved later in the reform effort. In the abortion controversy, initial liberalization efforts brought together clergy, civil libertarians, family-planning advocates, and feminists. National organizations, such as NOW, Planned Parenthood, and the American Public Health Association, joined the effort later.

Legitimacy justifies the occasions, content, and timing of the discussions in the remaining phases of the process. Such discussions — particularly when they involve making decisions that cross levels and functions within an organization and cross the boundaries of multiple organizations — do not occur without prompting. And they will not be prompted unless they are legitimated, or authorized (Whetten and Bozeman, 1991). Authorization is a tremendous resource to discussion planners, because it gives them considerable control over the design and use of discussion forums, the information that is provided, the way topics are framed, and the agenda (Bryson and Crosby, 1989). Since authorization must usually come from several sources if it is to be meaningful, discussion planning is typically crossorganizational, rather than under the control of one particular organization. However, this can be an advantage to leaders, because organizations usually represent institutionalized responses to particular problem definitions; therefore, little reconceptualization of problems and solutions will occur unless these organizations find their thinking challenged in settings that they do not control (Sabatier, 1988). Such reconceptualization is often necessary before a range of organizations can discover a shared interest in doing something about a problematic condition. A shared sense of common interest enhances the possibilities of forming a coalition large enough to make major headway against the condition (Stone, 1988; Boyte, 1989).

In the metropolitan governance case, the early sponsorship of the Citizens League, CMAL, and MPC lent legitimacy to the crossorganizational forums convened later by UMRDC to discuss metropolitan governance. Conversely, abortion reform advocates were not able to draw legitimacy from preexisting institutional sponsors. They had to create new organizations that could draw legitimacy from many individuals' concern for women's welfare.

Implicit or explicit in any initial agreement will be some sense of the "givens," or assumptions, on which the initial change effort will be based. These may include agreements concerning key actors and organizations, credible data sources, early problem definitions, the boundaries of acceptable change, and so forth. It is important, however, to keep in mind two alternate points. First, if everything about a problematic situation *must* be taken as a given, there is no point in undertaking a change effort. And second, in a situation where no one is in charge, the "givenness" of *all* the givens is probably doubtful. The advocates of regional governance for the Twin Cities took the existence of local governments as given, and they expected those governments to retain considerable autonomy under any new system. Initially, those who opposed restrictive abortion laws took as given the right of state legislatures to determine the conditions under which a woman could choose abortion. Later, many of these reformers opposed state regulation of abortion beyond ensuring the procedure's medical safety.

Another implicit or explicit feature of any initial agreement — and a benefit of the process — is likely to be some sense of policy change directions and possibilities. For example, Nutt (1992) argues that responses to undesirable conditions can include efforts to overcome specific problems; to achieve goals or targets that are presumed to indicate a healthy system; to reframe or redefine the problem in such a way that effective action becomes

more likely; or to adopt, adapt, and implement ready-made solutions from elsewhere. More precise specification of desired
responses is likely in later stages, but some shared sense of the
expected policy change directions and possibilities is necessary
to convince key actors to become part of the change effort. The
organizers of the Joint Program for Landuse and Transportation Planning clearly had a sense that a regional approach was
required for problems affecting communities in the Minneapolis–
St. Paul area. This approach was signaled by the composition
of the coordinating committee, the citizen advisory committee,
and later the Elected Officials Review Committee. In the abortion policy case, members of the Council for the Legal Termination of Pregnancy had a clear solution in mind from the beginning: they wanted to change Minnesota's abortion statute.

Finally, a good initial agreement signifies the beginnings
of extensive and intensive political support from key decision
makers and opinion leaders who function both within and across
organizations at various levels and at different points in the
process. As we observed earlier, for a policy change effort to
succeed, a coalition must develop that is large enough and strong
enough to formulate and implement policies, plans, or programs
that deal effectively with important issues, and that is able to
protect these solutions during implementation. Such coalitions
do not come together quickly. Instead, they form around important ideas that emerge over time from the ongoing discussions, consultations, mutual education, and reconceptualizations
that are at the heart of any policy change effort (Schon, 1971;
Kingdon, 1984; Lynn, 1987; Bryson, Van de Ven, and Roering, 1987; Stone, 1988; Boyte, 1989; Bellah and others, 1991).
In the metropolitan governance case, the early agreements were
the foundation of a coalition that included suburban and inner-
city officials, good-government advocates, and business leaders—
a coalition that state legislators could not ignore. The initial
agreements to fight for abortion law reform provided the base
for future support by feminist, religious, and public health organizations. This coalition, however, was not strong enough
to obtain desired policy changes in more than a fifth of state
legislatures before the Supreme Court's *Roe* v. *Wade* ruling.

Developing an Initial Agreement

So far we have covered the purpose, desired outcomes, and benefits of the first phase of a policy change effort. Now we can go into more depth on the process of developing an initial agreement. This process is simple and straightforward in concept — and typically, very difficult, roundabout, and time-consuming in practice. It usually proceeds through the following stages:

- Introducing the idea of policy change
- Developing an understanding of what that change might mean in practice
- Developing a commitment to the change effort
- Reaching an actual agreement

The more numerous the decision makers, the more divergent their interests, the less they know about possible changes and the reasons for undertaking them, the more time-consuming and indirect the route to agreement will be. Nonetheless, as in the cases described in this book, an initial agreement — or sometimes a series of agreements — must be reached before the change effort can begin in earnest.

A key ingredient in the process is leadership. It takes involved, committed, and courageous people to make policy change happen. In each of the cases we have looked at, policy change happened because there were leaders and key decision makers who initiated and championed the process. These champions were of two different types. Some emphasized particular solutions that they wished to push in response to the problematic situations. Champions of this sort are often referred to as "policy entrepreneurs" (Roberts and King, 1989, 1991; Kingdon, 1984), and they share many of the same characteristics ascribed to business entrepreneurs. They have a vision that embodies specific solutions to what they perceive to be important problems; they are willing to make substantial investments of their time, and often their money, in hopes of a substantial "reward"; they typically face difficult odds in getting their favored solutions adopted and implemented; and they must overcome hostile entrenched interests (Bardach, 1987; Milward and Laird, 1990). For example, the odds were against abortion reformers as they sought to change the laws of all fifty states while facing legislatures that were heavily male and also conservative on family and sexuality issues. The reformers also battled opposition entrenched in the Catholic church.

Other champions do not have preconceived notions about desirable solutions. Instead, they are committed to the process of policy change in a particular problem area because they believe that "something must be done" and that a policy change effort is likely to produce desirable solutions. They might be called "process champions," because they are similar to the process champions often found in successful strategic planning efforts (Bryson and Roering, 1988, 1989; see also Roberts and King, 1991). Process champions, also, are willing to make substantial investments of their resources in hopes of a significant reward. Citizens League president Verne Johnson, for example, was dedicated to doing something about the connection between urban decay in Minneapolis and rapid suburban growth. Initially, he and other league members simply agreed that Minneapolis could not solve its problems alone. As the league continued its study process, it became the champion of some form of regional government but did not champion a specific form until very late in the proposal development process.

Both kinds of champions play a crucial role in linking problems, solutions, and politics. They may get involved for any number of reasons (Kingdon, 1984) — to do something about a problem or to push a solution, or both; to further the values, interests, and groups they favor; to promote their personal interests; to protect their "turf"; to gain material rewards; to achieve electoral benefits; or simply to enjoy the thrill of the "game." Regardless of why they are in the policy change game, however, champions are unlikely to be effective unless they can draw an audience for their views. They may develop this audience because of their expertise or their roles as group representatives, opinion leaders, or decision makers. They also typically need good political connections; communication, bargaining, and negotiation skills; and energy and persistence (Kingdon, 1984;

Bardach, 1987; Roberts and King, 1989, 1991). It is important for leaders to realize that champions and initiators are not always the same people. For example, in the Minnesota abortion reform campaign, Carolyn Qualle initiated the Council for the Legal Termination of Pregnancy, but other council members became more visible champions of the cause.

In addition to champions and initiators, a policy change effort requires some person, organization, or group of organizations to sponsor the process. Sponsoring is different from championing, although sponsors and champions may be the same people. Sponsorship provides legitimacy (Trist, 1983) and access to resources; championship provides desire, energy, and commitment to follow through. A coordinating committee or task force often serves as the legitimizing, sponsoring body. For example, the Metropolitan Planning Commission sponsored and thus legitimized the Joint Program on Landuse and Transportation Planning, while Robert Einsweiler was the process champion who made sure that committees were convened and research was undertaken and published.

Early sponsors may be quite different from later ones. Joseph Robbie, who was executive secretary of the Minnesota Municipal Commission, argued for creation of a multifunctional metropolitan service district for the Minneapolis–St. Paul area several years before the Citizens League, CMAL, and MPC became strong sponsors of regional governance. The effort to liberalize abortion laws had early sponsorship from the American Law Institute, which, in 1962, issued a model penal code lifting many restrictions on abortion, but sponsorship later shifted to prominent feminists and their organizations. The Catholic church was an early sponsor of opposition to liberal abortion laws that has remained a strong sponsor, whereas conservative Protestant groups such as the Moral Majority became prominent sponsors only after the *Roe* v. *Wade* decision.

Leadership Guidelines

In the initial agreement phase, public leaders will pay most attention to the design and use of forums. At the same time, they should identify arenas and courts that they will ultimately seek to influence. As a consequence, some key decision makers are likely to be included in the forums used in this step. Alternatively, leaders may decide in this phase to pursue change in the courts instead of waiting for policy decisions in the arenas. In any event, the development of effective initial agreements is likely to be time-consuming and complicated; however, it is also crucial. To be effective in this phase, leaders should focus on the following guidelines.

Initiate and Champion the Process of Policy Change

An individual or group may play one or both of these two roles, but successful policy change is unlikely unless both are played reasonably well. Effective sponsorship is also necessary, but that is likely to come later. Here we are simply talking about the initial sources of deep caring, commitment, courage, energy, intelligence, and imagination for undertaking a change effort.

This is a good point for those who are considering becoming involved in a change effort to review the discussion of personal leadership in Chapter Two. It is a time for potential leaders to ask themselves such questions as: Why do I feel compelled to work on this emerging problem, difficulty, or challenge? What can I give to this change effort — skills, time, money? What personal difficulties or weaknesses are likely to hamper my work? How do I assess the other people involved? How will I protect myself from burnout? What are the essential beliefs and values that will keep me going in tough times? Chapter Twelve contains two exercises to help leaders answer these questions.

Focus on Building Effective Teams and Establishing an Organizational Base

Leaders might begin by reviewing the sections on team and organizational leadership in Chapter Two and remembering especially the need for shared leadership. The initial team may simply be an informal group that comes together out of a shared sense of urgency, but this group must consider how to involve current organizations or how to create new ones to champion change. It must decide what further teams — such as coordinating committees — must be assembled, and how to involve major stakeholder groups in these teams.

Get Key Stakeholders Involved

A stakeholder in policy change efforts is any person, group, or organization that is affected by the causes or consequences of an issue. This is an extremely broad definition of a stakeholder — or public, or constituency — yet it seems wise to be inclusive rather than exclusive. The reason is that the fluidity and the ease of access in most shared-power, no-one-in-charge situations allow people to identify themselves as stakeholders, even if others do not. Inclusivity allows change advocates to be forewarned, and therefore forearmed. Of course, the question of who the *key* stakeholders are is one that must be decided after the initiators of change have identified the *potential* stakeholders and discussed the effects they might have on the change effort.

There are several categories of actors who are routinely involved in policy change efforts. Typical categories include members of elected policy bodies — such as legislatures, county boards, and city councils; elected chief executives and their staffs; heads of administrative agencies and the civil servants who work for them; representatives of the courts; members of interested groups — including business and nonprofit organizations, professional associations, and lobbying and advocacy groups; important opinion leaders — including policy experts and journalists; existing or potential implementers; representatives of political parties; spokespeople from research organizations; and individual citizens (Kingdon, 1984; Sabatier, 1988; Anderson, 1990; Goggin and others, 1990). Each actor brings to the process particular capabilities rooted in his or her roles and access to different rules, resources, and transformation relations. As Lindblom (1980, p. 45) observes, "A political system is at the core a system of rules specifying the different roles to be played. . . . [The rules] specify who is eligible to play each role and how persons are to be chosen for them. They also specify what each player is to be allowed to do or prohibited from doing in the role."

It can be extremely helpful to perform a stakeholder analysis, which is outlined here and described in more detail in Resource B. A complete stakeholder analysis will answer six questions:

1. Who are the stakeholders?
2. What are the goals, expectations, or criteria each stakeholder uses to judge what the stakeholder should want in a problem area and how the stakeholder should evaluate any solution?
3. How well does the status quo meet each stakeholder's goals, expectations, or criteria? In order to answer this question, some preliminary research into the nature and impact of the status quo may be necessary.
4. How important is each stakeholder to the success of the policy change effort?
5. How can each stakeholder influence the policy change effort?
6. What is needed from each stakeholder to initiate and complete a successful policy change effort?

To answer the first question, change initiators can put together a "stakeholder map." In the metropolitan governance case, such a map might have looked like the one in Figure 5.1. This stakeholder map graphically illustrates several important points about policy change efforts. First, the number of stakeholders is likely to be large. Therefore, leaders may need an explicit strategy for keeping track of the stakeholders and for gathering appropriate intelligence regarding their membership, interests, and activities. Second, leaders should make special note that future generations are always stakeholders in public policies. All citizens and their governments have an obligation to leave the world as well off as they found it — if not better. It is important in this era of special interests to keep this public trust in mind; stewardship, citizenship, leadership, and followership should go hand in hand. As the Iroquois Great Law of Peace said, "In our every deliberation, we must consider the impact of our decisions on the next seven generations." The alternative is to validate Yehudi Menuhin's remark, "We are the worst ancestors any people could

Figure 5.1. Stakeholder Map at the Beginning of the Metropolitan Governance Change Effort.

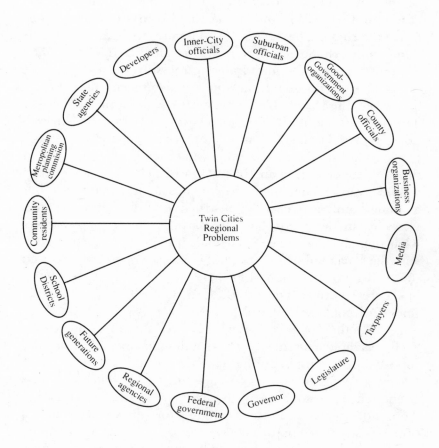

possibly have." Fortunately, it is usually necessary for advocates of winning policy proposals to show that their proposed solutions are somehow in the public interest (Stone, 1988). The map also provides clues about possible or likely forums, arenas, and courts that may be, or will be, the settings for the change effort.

The people who can gain access to these settings, along with their rule- and resource-governed interaction patterns, will determine which issues are raised and resolved. A stakeholder map can help the initiators of change think systematically about the design and use of forums, arenas, and courts in order to improve the chances for success. And finally, the search for additional policy change champions will be facilitated because they are most likely to be found among the stakeholders.

The second step in the analysis is to specify the interest, or "stake," the stakeholders have in the general problem area. This interest should be formulated as a set of goals, expectations, or criteria that the stakeholders are thought to use — either explicitly or implicitly — to judge what they think they want in the problem definition and in any solution. Initiators of change should always make their own estimates about this interest, but at some point, it may prove instructive to use surveys, interviews, group discussions, or third parties to ask the stakeholders what their interests are. Stakeholders may well be concerned with the broad public interest, but it also is wise to keep in mind the realistic observation of former Speaker of the U.S. House of Representatives Thomas P. "Tip" O'Neill, who frequently said, "All politics are local."

The third step is to judge how well the status quo meets each stakeholder's criteria. These judgments need not be very sophisticated. Simply noting whether the status quo performs poorly, adequately, or very well against stakeholder interests is enough to prompt useful discussion and strategic insights. Topics of discussion should include strengths and weaknesses of the existing system (or nonsystem); overlaps, gaps, conflicts, and contradictions among the interests; the nature of existing and potential stakeholder coalitions; and the opportunities and threats to those coalitions. To carry out the fourth step of the stakeholder analysis, change initiators rank the stakeholders according to their importance to the change effort. The order, which will vary with different problem definitions and proposed solutions, will give the initiators an idea of which stakeholders demand the most attention.

Completion of these four steps should force change initiators to place themselves in the shoes of others, especially outsiders, and to make a fairly objective assessment of the chances that the change effort will succeed. It should be clear, at this point, whether stakeholders already have enough interest in doing something about the public problem, whether stakeholders need to see the problem as more important, or whether political changes are necessary, including changes in elected officials, partisan distributions in elected bodies, pressure group activity, or public opinion.

Two additional stakeholder analysis steps are also likely to prove useful. First, change initiators can discuss exactly how the various stakeholders can influence the policy change effort. What rules, resources, and relationships — whether social, economic, or political — can stakeholders draw on to either help or hinder the change effort? Second, what will be needed from each stakeholder in order to initiate and complete a successful change effort? The strategic question here is: exactly how can the proponents of policy change gather enough support from enough key individual stakeholders and stakeholder groups to create a coalition that is large enough and strong enough to adopt policy changes and to protect them during implementation? When the analysis has gone this far, change initiators must decide whether to circulate it outside their group. It is primarily an input to other steps in the process, so there may be no good reason for more public discussion of it.

In the metropolitan governance case, something like a formal stakeholder analysis occurred. The protagonists did not actually construct a stakeholder map, but they did make lists of the key actors and discussed their interests and positions in relation to possible problem definitions and policy proposals. The use of maps might have facilitated those discussions. Stakeholder analyses and maps also might have helped leaders in the abortion controversy pursue their policy change aims by helping them understand more clearly the implications or consequences of their actions.

Form a Policy Change Coordinating Committee or Task Force

If few people, groups, or organizations are involved, minor resource commitments are necessary, and the situation is simple, a coordinating committee, or task force, probably will not be needed. But if many parties are involved, significant resource commitments are necessary, and the situation is complex, a coordinating committee probably should be appointed. Such a committee may be advisory to official policy decision makers, or it may have some formal power and authority granted from higher-level authorities or from constituent organizations (Trist, 1983). And, as mentioned, this committee is useful as a mechanism for consulting, negotiating, problem solving, or buffering among organizations or people. The committee probably will adopt its own initial agreement, although it may be necessary to work out agreements first with various groups and factions represented on the committee. Committee decisions should be recorded in writing and probably circulated to key stakeholders.

However, change initiators must be careful not to form such a group too early. It is easier to include someone later, after the committee is formed, than it is to drop a troublesome participant who is already a member. Be sure to consult with trusted advisers before inviting people to participate. Initiators should also keep in mind that there is a big difference between giving people seats on a committee and consulting with them as part of the process. People can supply a great deal of information and advice — and legitimacy for the process — without actually being committee members. Unless membership on the committee is limited, the committee may balloon and become unmanageable and unproductive.

The coordinating committee probably should include representatives of key stakeholder groups, top-level decision makers, technical and professional opinion leaders, process experts, and critics. It may be desirable to include more than one representative of each key stakeholder group in order to provide a more accurate picture of stakeholder preferences, interests, and concerns. Remember, however, that there is a trade-off between a broadly representative committee, which may be large, and an effective group, which typically numbers no more than nine to twelve. On occasion, two groups may be necessary — a large, representative, and legitimizing body, and a smaller executive committee that engages in more extensive discussions, makes recommendations to the larger group, and is empowered to make decisions on behalf of the larger group when necessary, subject to that group's subsequent ratification. The representative body may also authorize establishment of smaller representative bodies to explore specific issue areas. If one of these groups is to exist for a long period, its membership should be rotated to keep new ideas flowing and widen involvement in the process.

Initiators of change will not necessarily be asking for a major commitment of time from committee members, particularly those on the larger body, at this point in the process, although later they often need to call on many members to become more extensively involved. Membership on the executive committee implies a significant commitment of time and attention at some point, and this committee's meetings, in particular, should be structured so that everyone's time is used productively.

Promote Effective Policy-Making

The policy change process is likely to flow more smoothly if the coordinating committee and any other policy board that is involved are effective policy-making bodies. Indeed, the process may break down completely if it is not overseen by a such a group. Effective policy-making bodies (Carver, 1990; Houle, 1989; Van de Ven, Emmett, and Koenig, 1974):

- Focus most of their attention on their policy-making role.
- Have a mission statement that clearly states their purposes as a policy-making body.
- Establish a set of policy objectives in the areas they oversee.
- Concentrate their resources to be more effective as policy makers.
- Control staff primarily through the questions they ask; the general form of these questions is: how does this recommendation — whether a proposal, strategy, or budget — serve our purposes, values, or policies?
- Have staff help them become better policy makers.
- Rely on various media (press announcements, newsletters,

television, and so forth) to transmit information to key stakeholders and the general public.
- Hold periodic retreats to develop policies, plans, strategies,
  and programs for subsequent years.

Few public or nonprofit organizations, communities, or
other jurisdictions are governed by effective policy-making bodies. Because of this absence of effective arenas, issues that bridge
organizational or jurisdictional boundaries and require shared-
power decision making and solutions can be extraordinarily
difficult to raise and resolve. Therefore, a major focus for change
initiators may be developing effective policy-making bodies that
encompass the problem area. For example, the aim of reformers
in the Metropolitan Council case was to produce an effective
policy-making body for the Minneapolis–St. Paul region to overcome the deficiencies of MPC, which had no teeth. They succeeded by networking with organizations that did have effective policy-making groups.

A coordinating committee should be headed by someone
with enough standing and credibility to assure that the effort
is given visibility and legitimacy. Ideally, this person should be
trusted by all or most parties to the change effort, thus enhanc-
ing prospects for a strong and powerful coalition. The committee can be an existing group, such as a city council, or the board
of directors of an umbrella organization, such as the United
Way, or it can be created for the occasion. There can even be,
in effect, several coordinating committees, operating simultaneously or in different phases. Coordination for the regional governance change effort was provided by the Joint Program coordinating committee, Dennis Dunne's urban action committee,
and an informal strategy group.

Assemble a Planning Team
to Carry Out Needed Staff Work

This team — possibly a subset of the coordinating committee —
should include planners, change advocates, and change agents,
but also helpful critics, so that difficulties are recognized and

dealt with expeditiously. It is also possible to have a project-specific planning team, such as the one that planned UMRDC's metropolitan governance forums. In practice, if the problem to be addressed is small, few resources are needed, few organizations are involved, and the situation is relatively easy to handle, a team may not be needed. A single skilled and committed planner, perhaps with the assistance of a few resource people, probably will suffice. On the other hand, if the problem is large and difficult, substantial resources are needed, many organizations are involved, and the situation is complex, a team probably will be necessary. Most team members may not need to work full-time on the effort, except for brief periods, but their presence on the team allows many different skills to be brought to bear at appropriate times.

Whether the team does much of the planning itself, or facilitates planning and decision making by key decision makers, will depend on several factors. If team members possess most of the information needed to prepare policy proposals, and if they hold positions of substantial power, then they may prepare the proposals themselves. In this situation the planners themselves are the key decision makers. On the other hand, if key decision makers possess much of the necessary information, and if the planners themselves are not powerful by virtue of their position or person, then these planners will serve primarily as facilitators. In our experience, planners can typically be of most use as facilitators of crossboundary planning, policy-making, and decision making (Bryson and Crosby, 1989). At the same time, planners must have at least some substantive knowledge of the topic areas under discussion to be good facilitators. A blend of process skill and content knowledge thus is required of policy change planning teams (Howe and Kaufman, 1979; Benveniste, 1989), but the specific proportions of skill and knowledge will vary by situation.

Once change initiators decide that a planning team is needed, they can turn their attention to procedures that will make the team more effective. First, they should ensure that the team is headed by a statesperson who commands respect from essential stakeholders. Second, the team leaders must recruit skilled, committed team members. If leaders have the resources, they may be able to use special hiring, transferring, or compensating procedures. If people cannot see how they can be helped by participating, they are not likely to join voluntarily. If the assignment is temporary, people must be assured they can return to their old jobs — or even better ones — when the effort is completed. Third, well-defined and satisfactory working relationships must be negotiated among team members and supervisors. Fourth, arrangements must be made for the team to meet frequently and communicate effectively. Teams may have many volunteer members. The Citizens League, CMAL, the Council for the Legal Termination of Pregnancy, and MCCL were mainly volunteer organizations. Personnel hiring, transfer, and compensation procedures may not be an issue for volunteers, but good working relationships and effective communications are very important. Frequent praise and other forms of positive reinforcement, such as celebrations of successes and inspirational talks, are also likely to be vital.

Obtain the Necessary Resources to Begin the Endeavor

Two resources in particular will be necessary — financial resources and key decision makers' attention. Financial resources are obtained from monies controlled by key decision makers or else raised for the specific purpose. In many policy change efforts initiated by "outsiders," the initial resource commitments come out of the pockets, or "hides," of change advocates. The advocates of liberal abortion laws, for example, tended to be outsiders whose greatest resource was personal zeal translated into commitment of time and energy. As they formed organizations, they were able to raise money from members and donors. In the Metropolitan Council case, on the other hand, the Metropolitan Planning Commission received a large federal grant to undertake the Joint Program. Ultimately, the most important, and typically scarce, resources are the attention and involvement of key decision makers. These people must perceive the change effort as truly important before they will commit enough of their time and attention to make success a reasonable prospect.

Take Time for Vision Work

Leaders must ensure that the change effort teams and organizations begin developing an animating vision that vividly describes what the world is like now and what it will be like if the change effort succeeds. Of the visionary leadership skills noted in Chapter Two, perhaps the most important is helping people frame and reframe public issues. Since issues in large measure drive politics and the possibilities for successful issue resolution, the interpretive scheme used to frame an issue can have an enormous impact on outcomes. Abortion reform advocates were able to achieve at least partial success because they reframed abortion as an issue of maternal health and women's rights rather than an issue of sexual morality. Thus, they were able to change the interpretive scheme used to think about abortion and to place women's rights and choices within the American tradition of personal liberty. A useful tool for exploring the causes and consequences of alternative issue framings is the cause-effect diagram, described in Resource A.

In framing issues, leaders must keep track of and figure out how to use such policy change triggers as changes in important indicators, focusing events, crises, and the manipulation of powerful symbols. The reciprocity between issue framings and triggers can either constrain or increase leaders' abilities to influence the way an issue is framed and the politics that subsequently surround it. If initial discussions show a preferable way to frame the issue, then leaders can search for policy change triggers that will reinforce that interpretation, and can underplay triggers that favor alternative framings. (We will have more to say about issue framing in Chapters Six and Seven.)

Identify Appropriate Forums, Arenas, and Courts

In this guideline, we will concentrate on forums, typically the most important settings for the initiation of policy change. The great advantage of using forums is the relative ease with which they may be created and their openness to design. Advocates of policy change might first introduce their ideas and visions in informal forums, which can be as simple as conversations among neighbors or brainstorming breakfast meetings. At some point, as agreement becomes more solid and requires more stakeholder involvement, more formal visioning and planning sessions will be needed. Retreats or short conferences are often a good idea. A suggested outline for a policy retreat can be found in Resource C. Guidelines for staging a conference can be found in Emery and Emery (1978), Trist (1983), Gray (1989), and Nadler and Nadler (1987).

Before retreats, conferences, or formal discussion sessions are held, some preliminary work to identify and specify the problem more clearly and to search for possible solutions may be necessary in order to create enough of an issue to mobilize action among a wider circle of participants (cf. Kahn, 1982). Change advocates in the Metropolitan Council case, such as the Citizens League, the League of Women Voters, and MPC, generated study after study as they sought to forge broader initial agreements. Ted Kolderie's articles in the *Minneapolis Star Tribune* also helped lay the groundwork for agreement. Sometimes, it is also possible to take advantage of studies done by other groups.

Even at these early stages, change advocates should be thinking ahead to arenas and courts that are likely to be important to the policy change effort. They should sketch out possible paths the change effort might take in order to identify relevant arenas and courts. If changes will involve public agencies, legislatures, and civil or administrative courts, conversations should be held with trusted informants concerning the best ways to approach these bodies and the important procedures or mechanics that should be kept in mind. Some background reading may also be helpful. Good basic overviews of U.S. national government may be found in Lowi and Ginsberg (1992), of state and local government in Dye (1991) and Waste (1989). Rainey (1991) and Perry (1989) are quite useful on public organizations, Wise (1991) should be consulted on how legislatures work, and Shapiro (1981), Neely (1981), and Posner (1985) on courts.

It is also important for change advocates to outline a media strategy for the entire change process. Detail can be added to the strategy throughout the process, as needed, but the following actions should be taken in phase one.

- Identify mass media that reach the general public as well as the decision makers whose public support will be valuable.
- Identify alternative media — for example, neighborhood newspapers, public radio, professional journals — that reach specialized audiences, since most audiences may be characterized as cognitive misers (Sabatier, 1991; Nelson, 1984).
- Decide whether and how to create new media.
- Compile, in useful form, media addresses, telephone numbers, publication dates, deadlines, newscast schedules, format requirements, the names of reporters interested in the general problem area, and the names of editors or news directors who may make decisions about when and how to cover the change effort.
- Anticipate reports, speeches, and other activities and decide how they should be publicized. Options include press releases, photographs, articles for in-house publications, audiotapes, and videotapes.
- Decide which interpretive schemes should be emphasized in initial public utterances and reports.
- Determine what resources will be needed.
- Identify supporters who are especially knowledgeable, articulate, and possibly attention-getting as potential spokespersons.
- Decide whether to publicize an initial agreement, through press releases and public ceremonies, for example. Doing so makes sense when the agreement includes enough advocates, especially well-known and respected ones, to signal the effort's importance and potential success.
- Even if a decision is made not to publicize initial agreements, be prepared for the effort to become public.

Decide Whether a Detailed, Jointly Negotiated Initial Agreement Is Needed

An informal understanding may suffice when there are only a few individuals or groups involved in the early stages of mobilizing action, few resources are needed, or the situation is relatively straightforward. However, a detailed, jointly negotiated agreement is likely to be needed as the number of groups increases, significant resource commitments become necessary, or the situation grows more complex. Formal contracts are unlikely to be needed, but initiators should prepare a written memorandum that outlines the initial agreement. The agreement might also be summarized in a chart with supporting text and distributed to all coordinating committee and planning team members. If outside consultants are used, formal contracts with them probably are desirable.

Understand That the End of the First Phase May Be the First Major Decision Point in the Process

If the condition to be addressed is big, the number of people who must be involved large, and the situation complex, then it makes sense to go ahead with the change effort as soon as agreement is reached. If agreement is not reached, either the effort can go on anyway — with little likelihood of quick success — or this first phase can be repeated until an effective agreement is worked out. The initiators may want to try again, wait for an appropriate policy change trigger, wait for political changes to produce more receptivity to action, engage in further problem formulation or solution search activities, or focus on areas in which key decision makers can reach agreement. In relatively simple situations, the first major decision points are likely to be reached later.

Summary

The initial agreement is essentially an understanding among at least some key stakeholders that something should be done to promote policy change in a particular area of interest. The agreement should cover the desired outcomes; the worth of the effort — that is, the need to respond to an undesirable condition; the organizations or persons who should be involved; the expected sequence of steps, activities, and decision points; a shared sense of the design and use of forums, arenas, and courts; the form and timing of initial reports; the role, functions, and membership of the coordinating committee and of the planning team; and the commitment of necessary resources to begin the effort.

An effective initial agreement helps change advocates raise and address issues through discussions, policy decisions, and the sanctioning of conduct so that an effective political coalition can develop. Otherwise, issues, answers, and politics are likely to flow randomly through shared-power spaces, disconnected from the actors, energy, decisions, rules, and resources necessary for effective action (Kingdon, 1984). The world is unlikely to be improved in any important way when this "garbage can" model of public policy choice is left to its own devices. Public leadership is necessary to turn the policy change process from a garbage can into a process, or game, in which many people win and the public interest is served.

The game-like quality of the policy change cycle can be likened in some ways to chess, in which one must understand the purpose of the game, the rules, and the function of each piece, as well as one's opponent. One also must have an excellent strategic sense, think many moves ahead, and know what it takes to win (Behn, 1983). Perhaps the best description of this way of thinking comes from one of novelist Amy Tan's characters (1989, pp. 95–96):

> I studied each chess piece, trying to absorb the power each contained.
>
> I learned about opening moves and why it's important to control the center early on; the shortest distance between two points is straight down the middle. I learned about the middle game and why tactics between two adversaries are like clashing ideas; the one who plays better has the clearest plans for both attacking and getting out of traps. I learned why it is essential in the endgame to have foresight, a mathematical understanding of all possible moves, and patience; all weaknesses and advantages become evident to a strong adversary and are obscured to a tiring opponent. I discovered that for the whole game one must gather invisible strengths and see the endgame before the game begins.

The policy change cycle is far more complicated than chess, and the desirable conclusion is one in which everyone

benefits. Nonetheless, the imagery is helpful, for more often than
not public leaders encounter clever opponents who design their
own strategies in order to oppose important policy changes. Wise
and equally clever public leadership is needed to overcome determined opposition and to pursue virtuous ends. Because of
the complicated nature of policy change in shared-power settings, many agreements among many different parties may need
to be struck in order to move the action along. Various problem formulation and solution search efforts may be needed before the various actors can strike an argreement that is likely
to result in a powerful coalition that can back policy changes
all the way through implementation.

Chapter 6

Developing an Effective Problem Definition to Guide Action

It is not difficult to tally preferences in this era of instantaneous electronic polling and of sophisticated marketing techniques for discovering what people want and how much they want it. It is a considerable challenge, however, to engage the public in rethinking how certain problems are defined, alternative solutions envisioned, and responsibilities for action allocated.

— Robert B. Reich

The world is made of stories, not atoms.

— Muriel Rukeyser

The aim of this book is to help leaders and committed followers tackle public problems effectively and responsibly — especially complex, messy problems that are very difficult to address and yet must be addressed if we are to advance as a nation and civilization. Leaders exercise extraordinary power over policy change processes when they help people to see new problems, or to see old problems in new ways. As Kingdon (1984, p. 121) notes, to do either is "a major conceptual and political accomplishment" — because the way a problem is formulated will have a powerful impact on the way it is addressed, including whether it is addressed at all. Thus, the purpose of the problem formulation phase of the policy change cycle is to develop widespread

157

awareness and appreciation of an important public problem, along with a sense that it can be solved, and to specify further directions for the rest of the cycle in such a way that solutions adopted in a later stage are likely to be technically workable, politically acceptable, and legally and ethically defensible.

How Leaders Identify Public Problems

To call something a "problem" implies that there "is an undesirable situation which may be solvable by some agent, although probably with some difficulty" (Agre, 1982, p. 122). Based in large part on Agre's work, we argue that public problems have five distinguishing characteristics:

- They are difficulties or conditions affecting geographic communities or communities of interest (where community boundaries typically will cross horizontal organizational and governmental boundaries).
- Members of those communities, or at least key representatives, are aware of the problems.
- The problems are important—that is, nontrivial and more than an annoyance.
- In principle, they are actionable.
- The consequences of not dealing with them are serious.

The first characteristic—community impact—is what makes a problem "public." Such problems affect many people and require some sort of public action, governmental or not. The stage is thus set for the exercise of public leadership. However, leaders must recognize that a problem without a potential solution is not a public problem; it is simply a difficulty or condition that we must live with (Banfield, 1970, 1974; Kingdon, 1984). Wildavsky (1979, p. 42) also argues that "a difficulty is a problem only if something can be done about it." We do not talk about the "immortality problem," because as far as we know there is no feasible way for us to become immortal in our earthly form. We can talk, however, about the problems of the frail or indigent elderly, because we can imagine ways society can make life more agreeable for these people. Similarly, bad weather, terminal illnesses, persistent global poverty and famine, and human imperfectibility will remain simply part of the "human condition" until we can do something about them.

Moreover, public problems tend to be more than merely difficult; they are what Rittel and Webber (1973, pp. 160–167) call "wicked." Most public problems are wicked in the sense that:

- They have no definitive formulations, and there are many different ways to frame them. Some ways may be better than others, but the criteria used to determine what constitutes a "better" problem definition are themselves likely to be disputed.

- The problems are not solved once and for all but are resolved again and again. For example, problems of poverty, gender, race, war, and peace are never solved conclusively, but reemerge, in the same or different forms, with great frequency.

- The solutions to the problems are not true or false, but good or bad. Different stakeholders will use different, often fundamentally conflicting, expectations or criteria to judge the worth of solutions.

- Typically, the full consequences of any solution cannot be known immediately—and may never be known. Sometimes a solution solves a different problem than it was intended to solve, exacerbates the original problem, or causes a new problem.

- One-shot solutions don't work. These problems require a solution process that permits midcourse corrections and even the substitution of new solutions for the original ones.

- Each of the problems is unique. While there are often numerous similarities between the current problem and previous ones, there will always be additional features, which may be of such overriding importance that they outweigh apparent commonalities with prior problems (Neustadt and May, 1986).

- The problems can be symptoms of other problems. Wicked problems are messy; that is, they are an interconnected set of problems (Ackoff, 1981a). It is often difficult to know which part of the mess to attack. Further, problems formulated too generally may appear too difficult to solve, while problems that are too narrowly defined may prompt solutions that are not cures, but merely address symptoms of a more serious disease.

- The problems can be explained in many ways, and in large measure, the choice of explanation will determine the solutions chosen. For example, there are many ways to describe or define the U.S. drug problem, but President Bush and his former "drug czar" William Bennett decided to declare a "war on drugs." The resultant strategies focused on military aid to South American countries and beefed-up criminal justice policies and actions in the United States to punish drug users and dealers, with some additional attention to drug education and rehabilitation. The financing for this "war" came from a reallocation of funds away from precisely those social services that reasonable observers argue get at the actual causes of the drug problem by helping individuals and families move toward economic opportunity and security.

- Leaders have no inherent right to be wrong. If one constructs a careful scientific experiment and one's hypothesis is not supported, it is still a triumph for science. Human knowledge has been advanced. Leaders, on the other hand, are theorists who often pay, or exact, a high price for being wrong. They bear responsibility for the consequences of their actions, and if people don't like the consequences, the leaders may be punished. More importantly, the people who are affected by public leaders' actions can be hurt by those actions. Leaders in shared-power situations have a responsibility both to seek reasonable gains *and* to minimize losses for the people they lead.

No one said it would be easy to address public problems. Indeed, the very use of the word *problem* may be optimistic, because it implies the possibility of a solution (Neustadt and May, 1986). *Crises, threats, intractable issues,* or *severe difficulties* may be better terms in particular circumstances (Agre, 1982). On the other hand, a key leadership task may be to frame or reframe situations that deserve these more sobering terms, so that they can legitimately be called by less threatening names (Jackson and Dutton, 1988; Dutton, 1990). For example, although leaders might find the term *problem* optimistic, many people find it oppressive; it induces a kind of pessimism and paralysis. The terms *challenge* or *opportunity* may be better because they can induce optimism and action (Dutton, 1990). It may also be helpful to remember that — according to *The Oxford Dictionary of English Etymology* — the etymological meaning of *problem* is simply something "put forth" to be worked on or handled in some way.

Through problem reframing, a public that might otherwise be paralyzed can be galvanized to take effective action. Recall President Franklin D. Roosevelt's famous statement on March 4, 1933, in the midst of the Great Depression: "We have nothing to fear but fear itself." That sentence uttered with force, confidence, and courage helped turn a terrible crisis into a situation that people felt empowered to solve. The Hundred Days that followed, with their remarkable series of legislative acts and executive decisions, helped lead to a degree of real recovery. As a kind of shorthand, we will continue using the terms *problem* and *solution*. In particular situations, however, and with particular audiences, public leaders should be aware that other descriptors may be more apt.

The Sources of Public Problems

Public problems occur in any polity when vocal and powerful people discern a significant gap between what they believe is happening, or will happen in the future, and what they think can or should be done about it. This gap can be caused by changes in economic, social, and political conditions. Some recent changes that have highlighted perceived gaps in the United States are changes in the status of women and of racial and ethnic groups, changes in the role of government, the transition to a service economy, the increased numbers of women and children in poverty, and a thriving drug culture. The gap may also be caused by the success or failure of previous policies. For example, one can argue that, since the end of World War II, the mortgage interest deduction feature of the federal income tax laws has been either a resounding success or a disastrous failure. On the success side, millions of people have been helped to own their own homes in neighborhoods of their choice. On the failure side, the deduction may have stimulated overproduction of suburban housing, sucked central cities dry of middle-class residents and new housing construction, aggravated metropolitan transportation problems, and contributed to serious urban physical and social decay. Further, since housing doesn't directly contribute to the nation's productive capacity once it is built, one might also argue that the mortgage interest deduction has diverted savings from more productive investments in industrial plant and equipment (de Neufville and Barton, 1987).

The most important and powerful tool for helping people perceive a gap between what is and what can or should be is situation framing, the very basis of problem definition. As we noted in Chapter Four, people use interpretive schemes to make sense of the world. These schemes include beliefs, expectations, and rules that enable us to interpret our personal experience and the social knowledge we receive. Problem definitions are both a consequence and source of these schemes.

The most important interpretive schemes for defining public problems are stories deeply rooted in culture (Hilgartner and Bosk, 1988; Mandelbaum, 1991; Maynard-Moody, 1991). These stories help us constitute our world, and the most powerful ones are widely shared and believed "myths" (de Neufville and Barton, 1987; Innes, 1990). *Webster's Seventh New Collegiate Dictionary* defines a myth as "a usually traditional story of ostensibly historical events that serves to unfold part of the world view of a people or explain a practice, belief, or natural phenomenon." De Neufville and Barton (1987) argue that myths provide analogies that simplify complex realities. Myths also contain a moral component and provide a clear picture of good and evil and appropriate object lessons. Widely shared myths provide shared rationales for perceiving and behaving in certain ways. And, because myths take a dramatic form and tap deeply seated values, they generate strong emotional responses that can prompt public action. While new versions of old myths, or even new myths, may be created over time, many themes remain almost timeless in a particular culture, because they are created or recreated out of the culture's fairly stable repertoire of images, symbols, characters, and action styles (see also Swidler, 1986).

In his *Tales of a New America,* Reich (1987b) outlines four "morality tales," or myths, that have profoundly affected the way people in the United States have defined problems and acceptable solutions. One myth revolves around "the mob at the gates," barbarians and tyrants that might overrun the country and destroy its freedoms and the "American Way of Life." The hordes might be Nazis, Communists, illegal immigrants, or South American drug lords. The Bush Administration's "war on drugs" can thus be interpreted as defending U.S. citizens from "the mob." The Moral Majority and other opponents of women's reproductive rights are trying to evoke this myth when they suggest that a menacing group of anti-family sexual libertines are undermining traditional American families and values.

Another myth stars "the triumphant individual," and puts forth the idea that with hard work and courage anyone can make it in the United States. Horatio Alger, "Rocky," Ronald Reagan, Lee Iacocca, Chris Evert, Madonna, and Barbara Jordan come to mind. Obscured from view are the millions who, realistically, stand no chance at all of making it to the top. To some extent, advocates of liberal abortion laws appealed to the power of this myth by arguing that restrictive abortion laws limited women's opportunities to succeed and infringed on their entitlements to life, liberty, and the pursuit of happiness.

The third myth presents a picture of "the benevolent community" and highlights the country's tradition of civic improvement, philanthropy, and local boosterism. Presidents Ronald Reagan and George Bush drew on this myth when they argued, either naively or disingenuously, that the private sector and volunteer efforts would fill any gaps created by federal budget cuts in social services. The advocates of metropolitan governance for the Minneapolis–St. Paul area relied on this myth and tried to expand it. They emphasized local communities' traditions of reliable public services and amenities, and tried to build an image of a new regional community that could preserve those traditions.

The final myth describes "the rot at the top." U.S. citizens as a group are quite willing to believe there is corruption, decadence, and irresponsibility in high places and, indeed, a conspiracy against the public. They are not surprised, only saddened and angered, by the defense procurement scandals and the influence peddling at the Department of Housing and Urban Development in the Reagan years. Tragically, the myth also prevents people even from searching for tales of civic virtue, although they are to be found at the top of most organizations.

The power of these four myths is such that facts *and* fancy, vision *and* blindness, problems *and* solutions can all be bundled up into simple stories that are easily communicated and that prompt almost unthinking public action or inaction. The message for public leaders is that they must understand their culture's most important myths and the power of these myths to highlight *and* hide, enable *and* constrain. Leaders must also learn how to draw on those basic myths and to help create new ones in order to produce problem definitions that lead to virtuous public action. While the way situations are framed has the most impact on leaders' and the public's perception that a problem exists, other factors also contribute to developing problem definitions. These include categorization, value judgments, indicator warning signals, troubling comparisons, triggering events, and feedback (Kingdon, 1984).

Categorization

Problem framing inevitably leads to, and flows out of, the question of which category "contains" the problem. Analysis cannot proceed, nor action be mobilized, until a public problem has been placed in the proper category, and that category will dramatically affect how people see the problem and who is empowered to deal with it. For example, does abortion come under the category of women's rights and well-being, the regulation of medical procedures, sexual morality, the application of sacred teachings to a secular world, or fetal rights? Did the problem of overflowing septic tanks in the Minneapolis–St. Paul area center on developers' rights, environmental protection, communal health and safety, or government's responsibility for pursuing the common good? Is the "drug problem" one of crime, health, education, employment, or poverty? The category will determine which aspects of the problem are highlighted, which solutions are emphasized, and whose jurisdiction is involved.

As another example, the sit-in strikes for union recognition at Ford's River Rouge plant in the 1930s were first defined as a problem of trespass by Ford management and the local law enforcement authorities. Brutal attacks on the strikers by Ford's Pinkerton guards and the local police were authorized on these grounds. The situation changed fundamentally, however, when John L. Lewis, president of the United Mine Workers, arrived on the scene and said, "A man's right to a job transcends the right of private property." The workers' spirits soared, and their resolve was strengthened by the sense that what they were doing was legitimate, not illegal. Public opinion turned against Ford's tactics; the strike succeeded, and Ford was rapidly unionized.

Value Judgments

Values tell people what is worthwhile and important. When faced with a complex, problematic situation, an individual's first step is simply to determine his or her interests, aims, purposes, or goals. Do these interests involve freedom, justice, equity, economic efficiency or growth, physical safety, environmental quality, or something else? Once people know what they value, they can develop strategies that maintain and uphold those values. The importance of values is clarified by Easton's (1965, p. 21) classic statement that "politics is the authoritative allocation of values." Politics thus defines which values will be supported and which will not, which public actions will be justified and which will not. Not all values are equal; some are bigger, more important, and more worthwhile than others (Stone, 1988), and politics determines which is which. Politics makes a difference because values make a difference.

The effort to liberalize U.S. abortion laws was driven explicitly by the values of freedom and equity. Reform advocates argued that women, and especially poor women, would never have the freedom men have unless they were able to choose whether and when to become pregnant and whether to carry a pregnancy to term. Civic leaders who backed metropolitan governance valued the freedom of entrepreneurs to establish new businesses and open subdivisions, but they valued more the stability of well-functioning, interdependent communities that could provide a sound long-term base for economic growth.

Warning Signals from Indicators

Categories and values are embodied in various indicators people use to assess the health of systems, signal the existence of problems, and gauge the problems' size and trace their development (Kingdon, 1984; Innes, 1990). Literally thousands of indicators are monitored routinely by various organizations and people around the world. For example, in the United States, measures of gross domestic product; employment and unemployment; personal income and spending; business income, spending, and profits; inflation; and foreign trade, along with many others, depict the health of the economy. Embodied in the most influential indicators are negotiated agreements about what problems the indicators measure and what solutions might address those problems (Stone, 1988; Innes, 1990). In the case of the economy, for example, national decision makers tend to believe that fiscal and monetary policy changes are the best options for stimulating or restraining the economy, and the indicators they use are designed to assess when such changes are needed.

Because of the importance of indicators in stimulating public perception that a problem exists, public leaders and change initiators may spend a great deal of time constructing a particular indicator and getting others to agree on its worth. For example, in late 1991, the United States switched to using gross domestic product (GDP) to assess the health of the economy, rather than gross national product (GNP), an indicator that had been used for decades. However, it had taken years for public and private economists to get the Commerce Department to agree that GDP provided a more accurate and more easily calculable picture of the economy than did GNP (Meyers, 1991). Another example is provided by the Carter administration, which was extremely concerned about international human rights violations. Consequently, the administration put a great deal of energy into constructing indicators of human rights abuses that could be used to influence U.S. foreign policy (de Neufville, 1986). Metropolitan governance advocates for the Minneapolis–St. Paul region studied indicators such as average commuting times, housing prices, declining inner-city property values, and numbers of polluted wells and waterways to prompt greater awareness of problems caused by rapid metropolitan development. Both advocates and opponents of liberal abortion laws have used reports on the numbers of women seeking and obtaining abortions to convince the general public that abortion laws need to be changed.

Troubling Comparisons

Once indicators are established, comparisons become possible, and one of the standard routines of politics is to compare how one group or program is doing in relation to others (Sharkansky, 1970). Cities, states, and nations compare themselves with similar cities, states, and nations; income, racial, and ethnic groups compare themselves with other groups. Comparisons can spur action or redefinition of a problem. In 1957, when the Russians launched a satellite — *Sputnik* — ahead of the United States, the U.S. undertook a phenomenal set of initiatives to "catch up." Space-related spending increased dramatically, as did spending on math and science education. Current comparisons that show the United States falling further behind Japan and many other nations on various child care, education, health, and economic indicators can be expected to prompt either positive public action or a redefinition of ourselves as something other than "the greatest nation on Earth."

Triggering Events

Warning signals and worrisome comparisons may not be enough to prompt action. Sometimes a dramatic event, crisis or disaster, a powerful symbol, or the personal experience of a key leader is necessary to focus public attention on a problem (Kingdon, 1984). For example, several sensational airplane crashes in the 1980s roused public concern, finally prompting the airlines and the Federal Aviation Administration to improve airline maintenance and increase safety checks. The explosion of the space shuttle *Challenger* in 1986 led to deep soul-searching about goals and analysis of the strategies, equipment, and management of the U.S. space program. Ultimately, *Challenger* became a symbol of renewed commitment to a major U.S. role in space. As another example, the passage of Proposition 13 in California became a powerful symbol of citizen resistance to higher taxes. The assassination of President John F. Kennedy became a symbol that led directly to the passage of the Civil Rights Acts of 1964 and 1965 and a host of Great Society social programs. As noted previously, Sherri Finkbine's fight to obtain an abortion and a German measles epidemic focused public attention on the effects of restrictive abortion laws. Ted Kolderie's series of newspaper articles on metropolitan problems made Twin Cities residents more aware of each problem and the problems' interconnectedness. As Neustadt (1990, p. 86) observes, "Events provide the emphasis required for attention."

Finally, action often happens simply because some occurrence makes key decision makers *care* about a particular problem area. Poverty in the United States rose on the national agenda because John F. Kennedy made a 1960 campaign stop in West Virginia, where he was stunned by the poverty he saw. Similarly, drug abuse rose on the national agenda because First Lady Nancy Reagan cared about the problem.

Feedback

Feedback about existing programs is another important source of information about the existence, or nonexistence, of a problem (Kingdon, 1984). Feedback can come from systematic monitoring and evaluation studies, complaints and casework, the news media, and day-to-day administration of programs. If feedback indicates that stated policies or goals are not being met, costs are getting out of hand, or unanticipated and undesirable consequences are occurring, chances are that decision makers will decide that a problem exists. For example, feedback on the effects of state abortion law reforms led many of those who had supported reform to advocate total repeal of abortion laws.

To summarize, public problems occur when vocal and powerful people see a gap between what exists and what they think can or should be done about it. The gap is not necessarily between some ideal and reality; more often, it is simply a gap between reality and what people think they can reasonably have (Wildavsky, 1979). The way situations are framed in the first place has the most powerful — and yet often very subtle — impact on how problems are defined. Beyond that, categorization, value judgments, indicators, comparisons, focusing events, and feedback will also influence what is and is not considered a problem. In addition, it is important to keep in mind that different purposes are served by different problem formulations (Volkema, 1986). Some formulations define the problem and delineate a solution. Some set the boundaries of the feasible solution set. Some simply get a group working on a problem area. And some are intended to protect or advance the interests of the people who propose them.

Desired Outcomes

Several desirable outcomes may be sought by change advocates as part of the problem formulation process. First and foremost, of course, is clear and apt identification of the nature and range of the problems for which solutions might be sought, since the nature of the problems addressed is more important than the availability of technical solutions in determining the success of any change effort (Utterback, 1974; Morris and Hough, 1986). Typically, key decision makers must be convinced there is a problem before they are willing to authorize solutions. Furthermore, political mobilization will develop most readily from the belief that there are real problems to be solved. People are not as likely to rally around some particular policy proposal in the absence of a shared sense that the proposal is a solution to real problems.

In the metropolitan governance case, studies by the Joint Program for Landuse and Transportation Planning, the Citizens League, and the Council of Metropolitan Area Leagues (CMAL) clearly defined the range of interconnected problems that might be solved by some form of metropolitan government. In the abortion controversy, problem definition was at once more complicated and simpler. It was more complicated because many of those who opposed restrictive abortion laws saw the underlying problem not as the unavailability of safe, legal abortions but as unwanted pregnancies. Initially, however, the groups that fought for more liberal abortion laws focused on the harm caused to women by highly restrictive laws. The problem definition was simpler in that it prompted a simple focus on laws that made abortion illegal under most circumstances. Somewhat later, as access to abortion became a very visible part of the feminist cause, the problem was made more general and was focused on women's need to control their own destinies.

Meanwhile, reform opponents focused on the vulnerable fetus. The problem for them became the lack of protection for the "unborn child" in the womb. To be sure, some supporters of fetal rights — a prominent example being Marjory Mecklenburg — have expanded their problem formulation to include a concern for the quality of life after birth. In its mission statement, Mecklenburg's American Citizens Concerned for Life pledged to address "the specific issues of increased legal protection for human life, alternatives to abortion, adolescent pregnancy, maternal and child health, death, dying, and problems of the elderly, health care for the poor, respect for the handicapped, and domestic and world hunger." For the most part, however, the movement favoring the reinstatement of restrictive abortion laws has focused more narrowly on threats to the developing fetus, with some attention to end-of-life concerns, such as treatment of vegetative patients on life-support systems.

The second desirable outcome for problem formulation

efforts is that they should identify differences among affected parties. Stakeholders and constituencies can vary greatly in their problems, needs, interests, and emotions. These differences must be considered if policy change efforts are to succeed. Change advocates must practice a fundamental marketing principle — namely, that since it is impossible to be all things to all people, one must be something very special to some people. Technically workable, politically acceptable, and legally and morally defensible policy changes are unlikely, unless important differences among stakeholders are taken into account. A good stakeholder analysis should identify many of the similarities and differences among stakeholder groups.

The stakeholders in the metropolitan governance case, for example, had many different interests and goals. State legislators wanted to win elections and avoid the difficult task of reorganizing regional services themselves. The governor wanted to keep the region's voters and powerful business groups happy. Local officials wanted leeway in regulating local development and providing services. Federal officials wanted a regional review of federal grant applications. Developers needed reassurance that solutions to metropolitan problems wouldn't halt residential and commercial construction. Homeowners wanted assurances that their communities would have affordable services, adequate open space, reliable roads, unpolluted rivers and lakes, and stable or growing property values. Finally, business people wanted a regional infrastructure that supported long-term economic growth. Abortion reform advocates focused first and foremost on women's desire to make their own reproductive decisions, but other stakeholders with differing desires had to be considered also. Doctors wanted to make their own decisions about medical procedures, various religious groups wanted to act on religious principles, and state legislators wanted to be reelected.

As a third desirable outcome, criteria for measuring the satisfaction of affected organizations or persons should be developed. It is important to be able to identify the degree to which stakeholders think their problems or needs have been satisfactorily addressed. These criteria may change over the course of a policy change effort, and they may never be made public, but the initiators, sponsors, and champions of change must be reasonably clear in their own minds about which criteria must be met in order to form a winning coalition. Again, a good stakeholder analysis can provide much of this information. For example, advocates of liberal abortion laws might set endorsement by a state medical association as a criterion for meeting doctors' concerns. They might see religious denominations' adopting statements that outline how women might responsibly choose abortion as a signal that denominational groups have been satisfied.

The fourth result that should be sought is the identification of the feelings and attitudes of affected parties. Too often planners and policy analysts make the mistake of assuming that dry facts and figures are the real motivators of change. Politicians and community organizers know differently. Emotion is the real motivator behind policy change, a connection that most problem identification or needs assessment efforts completely overlook. Identification of stakeholders' feelings corrects this shortcoming. Minnesota state legislators considering metropolitan governance could have understandably felt threatened by the creation of an elected regional body that would represent an area larger than a legislative district. The advocates of establishing a strong metropolitan council needed to take these feelings into consideration. Efforts to liberalize abortion laws obviously tapped strong emotions in several stakeholder groups. Women, in particular, could be expected to be angry that state laws severely restricted their access to safe abortions. Some women, on the other hand, saw abortion as morally repugnant, if not tantamount to murder. They and the men who agreed with them could be expected to passionately defend restrictive abortion laws.

Finally, as a last outcome, the coordinating committee should agree on who will have to respond to which problems. Problems rarely correspond to preexisting organizational domains; therefore, change advocates must agree about what existing organizations will do and about which new organizations are needed. A temporary organization of some sort — such as a task force, formal or informal committee, or special-purpose grouping of organizations — is likely to be necessary in order to consider the problems holistically and to ensure that causes, rather than mere symptoms, are addressed (Trist, 1983).

When the coordinating committee has agreed on the specific desired outcomes of the problem formulation process, it should develop a written problem statement, unless there are compelling reasons not to do so. These statements, of course, can take many forms, depending on the circumstances. They can be formal reports, needs assessment documents, or press releases, for example. The group might also draw on reports compiled by the news media or other organizations. The statement and relevant supporting documentation should be published and widely distributed unless, again, there are compelling reasons not to do so. These materials provide a focus for stakeholders' subsequent action and involvement and also instill a measure of accountability in the process. At the very least, the problem statement might serve as a trial balloon to help leaders gauge public interest in pursuing a policy change (Benveniste, 1989).

The advocates of metropolitan governance for the Minneapolis–St. Paul area did not fashion one comprehensive problem formulation statement, but in effect, the reports issued by the Citizens League, CMAL, the Joint Program on Landuse and Transportation Planning, and the Minnesota League of Municipalities, plus Ted Kolderie's articles, constituted the statement. By the mid 1960s, an informal coordinating committee including Citizens League director Verne Johnson; Clayton LeFevere, an attorney who had represented a number of suburban governments; Minneapolis mayor Art Naftalin; Ted Kolderie; UMRDC executive director Thomas Anding; law professor James Hetland; and Minneapolis lawyer David Graven began holding strategy sessions on how to design a governmental mechanism for responding to the problems outlined in the reports.

In the abortion controversy, problem formulation statements, often connected with proposed solutions, have been contained in the writings, reports, and press releases of both supporters and opponents of legal abortion. In this policy debate, formal organizations coordinated efforts to find and enact solutions. Examples at the state level are the Council for the Legal Termination of Pregnancy and Minnesota Citizens Concerned for Life; examples of national-level organizations are the Association for the Study of Abortion Laws and the National Right to Life Committee.

Benefits of the Process

A number of benefits flow from successful problem formulation efforts. The first benefit is simply the recognition and appreciation of problems or needs. A recent study of fifty-eight cases of major change efforts (Bryson, Bromiley, and Jung, 1990) indicated that a more extensive problem identification effort resulted in significantly higher goal achievement from the standpoint of the organization most responsible for the change efforts. In contrast, effort expended on searching for solutions did not significantly increase goal achievement. Moreover, the way leaders frame a problem predetermines much of the solution (Cartwright, 1973). Indeed, once leaders know exactly what the problem is, relatively little effort may be needed to find good solutions.

Second, extensive and careful problem formulation efforts provide a basis for effectively addressing real stakeholder, client, user, or implementer concerns, and the problem statements provide a rallying point. It becomes a symbol of hope for those who can see their own interests served by action on the problems, and as the late urban designer Kevin Lynch noted, "Hope is the engine of public action."

Third, in the absence of extensive and careful problem formulation efforts, leaders never really know whether they are addressing hearsay or suspicions, vested interests, or a widely shared sense of real needs. Without careful problem formulations, disputes are likely to erupt over the nature of the problems, making successful policy change unlikely. Moreover, resolution of disputes over problems can occur only if the evidence used to formulate the problems is collected and analyzed in such a way that key actors believe the results are objective and "unmassaged."

Fourth, problem formulation efforts by change advocates provide a need-centered basis for user and implementer involvement in later phases of the policy change cycle. If formulation efforts are left to professional "experts," three serious difficulties are likely. First, the resulting problem statements are unlikely to match real user or implementer problems or needs, and second, experts are likely to bend problem statements to match known solutions. Either way, a policy change effort that is successful from any standpoint other than that of the professional experts is unlikely. And third, problems framed in the language of technical experts are likely to put users on the defensive, unsure how to respond without difficulty and embarrassment. Conversely, if problem formulations are in the words of the users and implementers, these groups are more likely to be active, supportive, and effective participants in the policy change efforts (Eden and Huxham, 1986).

Fifth, successful problem formulation efforts will provide detailed criteria for, first, the selection of technical experts to be involved in the search for solutions and, second, the search for solutions itself. Technical expertise is typically tied to issues or to linked problems and solutions. Left to their own devices, technical experts have an uncanny knack for finding problems connected to solutions over which the experts have substantial control. Public leaders who wish to avoid being trapped by this all-too-human foible make sure problem formulation efforts involve key stakeholders, particularly the ultimate clients, users, or customers for potential changes. Furthermore, the likelihood that different stakeholders will use different criteria to make judgments concerning problems and solutions is information technical experts *must* keep in mind if solutions that are politically acceptable — not just technically workable — are to be found (Kartez, 1989; Throgmorton, 1991).

Finally, a statement of the problems develops a useful tension among stakeholders and an implied threat of what can occur if the change effort is not pursued further (Dalton, 1970). Problem formulation efforts can activate stakeholder expectations of success, and these expectations can become a self-fulfilling prophecy when stakeholders become involved to make sure their expectations are met, and when key decision makers and opinion leaders respond because they are concerned about adverse consequences if they do not.

Leadership Guidelines

In the problem formulation phase of policy change, visionary leadership skills continue to be especially important, as leaders focus on creation and communication of shared problem definitions and appreciations that can inspire and motivate subsequent action. Leadership guidelines for this phase fall into three groups: problem formulation; report preparation, review, and dissemination; and caveats.

Problem Formulation

Be Sure the Emphasis in This Phase Is on the Design and Use of Forums, with a Secondary Emphasis on the Design and Use of Arenas. Fact-finding, discussion, and the creation of meaning are the principal activities in the problem formulation step. Because meanings established here will guide subsequent activities, positive collective action is most likely to emerge from shared meanings established through discussion in forums that bridge organizational boundaries.

For example, during this phase of the Metropolitan Council case, committees established by the Citizens League and League of Women Voters produced studies analyzing such problem areas as sewers, transit, parks and open space, water pollution, and the tax base. Ted Kolderie's articles in the *Minneapolis Star Tribune* illumined the areawide nature of many problems, including sewage disposal, water supply, transit, major roads, air pollution, planning, mosquito control, airports, and parks. Reports from the Metropolitan Planning Commission and the Joint Program for Landuse and Transportation Planning warned that problems such as congested highways would become much worse if current development patterns continued. A Citizens League report also highlighted the inadequacies of existing metropolitan service districts. A League of Municipalities study suggested that disparities in local tax revenues might be dealt with regionally. These studies and news reports conveyed the meaning that these problems were regional and interconnected and that they would only get worse if nothing were done. Leading change advocates made public speeches that also employed the regional interpretive scheme to define the problem and suggest solutions. In formulating the regional governance problem, change advocates also began exercising political leadership by paying attention to arenas. As we described earlier, many of the forums were carefully designed to include an array of government officials and citizens who would be important in arenas later. Change advocates who looked ahead to action in the legislative arena also realized that legislators were an important audience for their discussions and reports, and in some instances, invited legislators to attend their forums.

Be Sure This Step Emphasizes Problems or Needs, Not Solutions. Leaders must constantly ask themselves and the others involved whether they are focusing on problems or whether they have become the captive of particular solutions. Because there is tremendous pressure to converge quickly—probably too quickly—on a specific solution (Nutt, 1984), it may take strength and courage to follow this guideline. Leaders must keep in mind that effort expended on problem identification is an important determinant of success.

In the abortion case, for example, a group of people became increasingly concerned about the damage done to women because they lacked full control over their reproductive capacity. In various forums—organizational meetings, demonstrations, news media, and speeches to church and school groups—these change advocates linked problem formulations and solutions, and the problem was quickly narrowed to restrictive abortion laws. Thus, the solution was obvious—liberalize those laws. Change advocates then focused on legislative arenas, with some attention to overturning the laws through the federal courts. There was no prolonged search for solutions other than abortion to unwanted pregnancies. Had such a search occurred, there might have been less divisiveness and more progress in reducing unwanted pregnancies.

This does not mean, however, that advocates of liberalizing abortion laws completely ignored the broader problem. For example, the Council for the Legal Termination of Pregnancy and its successor organization, Minnesotans Organized for the Repeal of Abortion Laws, collected and disseminated data and horror stories on unwanted pregnancies and back-street abortions. The group also supplied data on the safety of legal abortion. This information evoked meanings that were critical rationales for changing restrictive abortion laws. One important meaning was that abortion in medical clinics was safe. This allowed change advocates to argue that — in a society that ostracized pregnant unmarried women — it was unfair to deprive women of a safe procedure and thereby force them — often because of social or economic pressures, rape or incest, or fear of birth defects or damage to their own health — to either bear babies or resort to back-street abortionists. Another important message was that abortion could be a moral choice for women. Women should be able to control their reproductive capacity because of its critical impact on their life prospects. This meaning became the basis for rallying women's rights advocates in support of abortion reform and for attempting to overturn restrictive abortion laws through the courts by appealing to personal rights.

During problem formulation it is important for leaders to identify specific behaviors, exchanges, or transactions "on the ground" on the part of the recipients or targets of policy change as either problematic or desirable. In other words, effective leaders start at the *end* of the chain of policy delivery linkages, not at the *beginning*. In shared-power, no-one-in-charge situations, leaders are far more likely to effect useful policy change if they "map backward" from desired behavior to proposed policy changes than if they "map forward" (Elmore, 1982). More on this distinction will be found in Chapter Ten.

Despite the need to emphasize problems rather than solutions in this phase, it is important to remember that problem formulation is typically a product of negotiation and consensus, in which desirable and acceptable problem definitions emerge as a product of discussions concerning potential courses of action, or solutions (Eden and Sims, 1978; Eden and Radford, 1990). Problem formulation, therefore, cannot be completely divorced from the search for solutions. Indeed, it may be necessary to explore several solution options before an effective and final problem definition can be formulated. In addition, problem formulation can continue to be refined even after solutions are under consideration.

Focus on Interpretive Schemes That Frame Problems in Such a Way That They Can Be Solved. The way a problem is framed structures stakeholders' views of and interest in the problems, the debates surrounding possible solutions, and the coalitions that develop to support or oppose those solutions. Therefore, leaders must articulate the view of the world that lies behind problem definition and make sure that world view is one that will draw significant support from key stakeholders. The world view a leader should seek is one that will call up widely shared concepts of what constitutes the public interest (Stone, 1988). Further, it will clarify how the problematic situation violates a widely shared vision of how society ought to be, and it will tap people's deeply held values and aspirations in such a way that they will see the problem as a challenge to be overcome and an opportunity to call upon their best selves to realize the kind of world they seek to create.

   As noted earlier, the advocates of regional governance in the Twin Cities conjured up a vision of a thriving regional community that continued traditions of progressive government, an attractive natural environment, and economic vitality. At the same time, they were careful to emphasize that they were not trying to centralize power at the regional level. They argued that regional governance mechanisms would help local communities have more control over their destinies. Viewing the Minneapolis–St. Paul area as one community implied that the area's towns and cities should not be engaged in a life or death competition but should cooperate for mutual benefit. By reframing abortion as an issue of personal liberty and safety, those who supported women's access to abortion also tapped a powerful U.S. tradition, and they became part of wider feminist efforts to fully claim that tradition for women. This view also offered a solution to the problem of who decides which women can have abortions, since it led logically to giving women themselves the ultimate choice in the matter.

As part of the process of exploring the explicit or implicit interpretive schemes that might illuminate a problem area, leaders should consider developing stakeholder maps — as described in Resource D — for each major formulation of the problem area, including those definitions put forward by seeming opponents. These maps will clarify the intensity with which various stakeholders will support or oppose action based on different problem definitions. The committees convened as part of the Joint Program for Landuse and Transportation Planning allowed different stakeholder groups to understand what metropolitan problems looked like from others' perspectives. Federal highway officials, for example, probably saw the situation primarily as a road-building problem. For local officials, it might have looked like a zoning problem. Housing officials, no doubt, were mainly concerned about the area's housing problem. In the committee meetings, they could begin to understand the contours of a comprehensive problem formulation that took all these perspectives into account.

Determine If a Two-Step Problem Identification Process Is Desirable. In the first step, change advocates conduct exploratory research in order to get a feel for possible problems or needs, while in the second step they undertake detailed research into identified problem areas (Delbecq, Van de Ven, and Gustafson, 1975). The sooner in the policy change process such problem identification efforts are undertaken, the greater the impact the policy change advocacy group can have on the way the problem is framed. The further along one is in the change process, the more likely it is that problem definitions and the politics that surround them will become fixed and hard to change.

Exploratory research includes the following four steps:

1.   Identify affected organizations or persons by using, for example, simple brainstorming or the snow card technique (described in Resource B).

2. Develop a research strategy for gaining access to key organizations, persons, or other information sources, and for gaining necessary information from them.
3. Use exploratory techniques for engaging key information sources — for example, on-site observation (Jorgensen, 1989), unstructured interviews, focus group discussions (Krueger, 1988; D. L. Morgan, 1988; Stewart and Shamdasani, 1990), the nominal group technique (Delbecq, Van de Ven, and Gustafson, 1975), and the snow card technique (Bryson, 1988b). Literature reviews may also be quite useful.
4. Attend to the following problem formulation factors, which affect stakeholder responses to problem identifications or needs assessments: situation framing, interpretive schemes, stories, gaps, categories, values, indicators, comparisons, triggering events, and feedback. Discuss these factors and note similarities and differences across groups, as well as any missing items that might significantly affect problem formulation.

Throughout the exploratory research process, leaders should make an effort to collect people's "stories." They are more likely to discover the real problems by examining story components than by asking directly, What's the problem? To study these stories, leaders should construct a timeline of key events, and constantly ask the journalist's questions — what, when, where, who, how, and why. Constructing an "issue history" in this way helps guarantee that the right problem gets solved in the right way. It helps the advocates of change understand relevant trends and specifics that can sharpen their definitions. As time allows, advocates should explore other aspects of relevant history — in particular, the history underlying important presumptions, the history in the heads of other people, and the history of relevant organizations or institutions (Neustadt and May, 1986). This may seem like a lot of work, but recall the adage that those who forget history will relive it; or the words of Mark Twain, "History may not repeat itself, but it rhymes a lot."

Exploratory research sets the stage for more detailed research, which includes these four steps:

1. Identify affected organizations or persons.
2. Develop a research strategy for securing desired information from these sources.
3. Use structured techniques to engage key information sources — for example, survey research (Fink and Kosecoff, 1985; Lavrakas, 1987; Fowler, 1988; Frey, 1989), structured interviews (McCracken, 1988), structured group meetings (Delbecq, Van de Ven, and Gustafson, 1975), and detailed analysis of existing or collected literature and data (Stewart, 1984).
4. Analyze and discuss the findings of this more detailed research activity, including similarities and differences across groups and the possible or likely prompts to further action by these groups (Miles and Huberman, 1984). In particular, focus on whether there appears to be a problem important enough — from the standpoints of key stakeholders — to make policy change necessary and its implementation likely.

In the cases studied for this book, change advocates conducted extensive research, both exploratory and detailed. The Metropolitan Council case offers the best example of a coordinated research strategy that focused on a wide range of stakeholders, ranging from taxpayers, to business groups, to commuters, to inner-city dwellers. In the abortion case, there was extensive research by the various state and national groups seeking liberal abortion laws, but no unified research strategy. Some groups studied state laws; others collected data — sometimes systematically, sometimes loosely — on pregnancies, illegal abortions, and the safety of abortions performed in clinical settings. Still others studied judicial and theological precedents. Attention mainly was directed to one undifferentiated stakeholder group — women.

Report Preparation, Review, and Dissemination

Prepare a Preliminary Report That Outlines the Problems and the Recommendations for Next Steps for Review by the Planning

Team, Coordinating Committee, and Involved Organizations or Persons. In preparing this report, it is important not to define problems too broadly, because then it may be difficult to develop targeted solutions; too narrowly, because then problem symptoms are likely to be identified, not underlying causes; or too rigidly, because often a calculated degree of vagueness is necessary in order to obtain agreement to move to solutions, and because room for revision allows for responses to unforeseen situational changes. As noted earlier, recommendations for next steps are likely to include one or more of the following directions (Nutt, 1992): to overcome specified problems; to achieve goals or targets that are presumed to indicate a healthy system; to adopt, adapt, and implement ready-made solutions from elsewhere; or to reframe the problem in such a way that effective action becomes more likely.

Several techniques are available to remedy tendencies to define problems too broadly, too narrowly, or too rigidly. Weick (1984) urges people working on complex social issues to break them down into manageable problems that are amenable to "small win" strategies or solutions, although Ackoff (1974) and Senge (1990) insist that these problems must still be treated as a system, or real headway will not occur. Instead, symptoms will be treated, not root causes. Volkema (1987) advocates adoption of problem statements that reflect the complexity of the problem. He argues further that problem definitions should highlight the purposes to be served by addressing the problem, so that the range of solutions generated in response to each problem statement will be expanded (Volkema, 1983). Dror (1987) reminds problem formulators to be clear about what they can and cannot know. Finally, Argyris (1982), Neustadt and May (1986), and Senge (1990) recommend conscious checking of assumptions and interpretations in order to be sure one is not mentally trapped. Advocates of metropolitan governance for the Twin Cities, in keeping with Ackoff's and Senge's advice, treated their problems as a system; they made a host of problems manageable by taking a regional approach that embraced and connected them all. This approach made the outlines of a general solution clear, without creating an immediate need to decide on the details of solving individual problems, such as inadequate sewerage.

Use a Normative Process to Review and Modify the Draft Problem Formulation Document. Drafts typically should be reviewed by planning team members; key decision makers, including the coordinating committee; relevant governing boards; and other selected stakeholders. Review meetings need to be structured so that the strengths of the document are recognized and modifications that would improve on those strengths are identified. Review sessions can be structured around the following six-step agenda (Barry, 1986; Bryson, 1988b).

1. Overview of the document
2. General discussion of the document and reactions to it
3. Brainstormed list of strengths
4. Brainstormed list of weaknesses
5. Brainstormed list of modifications that would improve on the strengths and minimize or overcome weaknesses
6. Agreement on next steps to complete the document

This agenda embodies a "SWIM Analysis," which ensures that any particular proposal, recommendation, or budget is really "in the swim of things" by highlighting strengths, weaknesses, and modifications (SWIM) that would improve the document (J. Erickson, personal communication, 1990). The virtue of this normative process is that it forces reviewers to acknowledge strengths and to suggest helpful modifications. Left to their own devices, too often reviewers focus only on weaknesses and leave planners with few suggestions for improving a document's workability, acceptability, and defensibility (Delbecq, Van de Ven, and Gustafson, 1975) with the result that coalition formation efforts become stymied. A SWIM analysis is advisable anytime documents that will become part of the official record are prepared.

Refer Identified Problems Not Directly Connected to the Policy Change Mission to Appropriate Organizations or Persons for Resolution. People's problems are unlikely to match up neatly with the boundaries of existing organizations or networks of organizations. Planners should anticipate the need to alert noninvolved organizations to the existence of problems that the planners have uncovered but that are in others' bailiwicks. Planners should also anticipate that these organizations may not be altogether happy to have these problems brought to their attention. Thus, some intelligence gathering on how best to transmit this information may be in order.

Prepare and Distribute a Final Report That Outlines the Problems to Be Addressed. Include as many of the following sections as are necessary for clarity and thoroughness.

- Title page, indicating content and sponsorship of the study
- Executive summary, highlighting problems or needs and recommendations
- Table of contents
- Statement of purpose and sponsorship, along with brief historical background
- Review of relevant literature
- Study design and methodology, including brief description of research staff and their qualifications
- Data sources, including people, organizations, and data banks
- Data analysis
- Findings
- Conclusions and recommendations for further action
- Appendices

Leaders should be aware that different versions of the report may be necessary for different audiences.

Set a Media Strategy to Generate Sustained Attention to the Problem. Leaders can try to interest reporters, editors, or news directors in doing a series of reports on the problem. Interested journalists will need to be supplied with background data, human interest angles, promising leads, and so on. Leaders may also need to seek publicity for the forums in which the problem will be discussed. Additionally, the publication of preliminary and final problem formulation reports may count as a significant news event for which coverage should be sought.

Caveats

Keep in Mind That the Term* Problem *Can Be Problematic. Use language that empowers people to take responsible action to improve their situations. If *problem* induces a sense of oppression and defeat, use some other term, such as *challenge* or *opportunity*. In order to use these other terms, however, visionary leadership is necessary to articulate the challenges or opportunities in terms of inclusive and motivating interpretive schemes widely shared by existing or potential participants in the change effort. Further, it is important that these schemes not lead automatically to particular solutions that may not be wise.

Remember That This Phase — Like Every Other Phase — Can Be Overdone As Well As Underdone. The precise manner in which and extent to which problems are identified and needs assessed is not as important as the clarity with which they are documented and understood.

Do Not Promise Stakeholders, Clients, Users, or Implementers That All of Their Problems Will Be Solved. Such promises, whether explicit or implied, might gain participation in the problem formulation phase, but will almost certainly doom policy change efforts to failure later on when those expectations are not met and frustration ensues.

Remember That Particular Activities Will Recur and Expand as the Situation Becomes More Difficult Politically or Technically. It is likely that more detailed research will be necessary; greater involvement of affected organizations or persons will be required; greater assurances that problems have been objectively identified will be required; more extensive review of the prelimi-

nary report will be necessary; and broader distribution and discussion of the final report will be required. In the most technically and politically difficult situations, however, there is a limit
to how much additional agreement leaders can achieve through
more extensive problem formulation efforts. In such situations,
a decision must be made — perhaps more than once — on whether
it is worthwhile to engage in further formulation efforts as a
means of bolstering the supporting coalition. Sometimes the
choice must be simply to forge ahead in the face of implacable
opposition (Bryson and Delbecq, 1979).

***Understand That This Phase May Culminate in the Second Major
Decision Point.*** In simple situations, the initial agreement, problem formulation, search for solutions, proposal development,
and proposal review and adoption phases may all be, in effect,
a single phase with differential emphases culminating in a single decision point — namely, adoption of the proposed changes.
In difficult situations, however, leaders need to keep in mind
the need to break the process down into workable steps with
more than one decision point.

Summary

The metropolitan governance and abortion policy cases are fairly
typical of policy change efforts in that much of the problem formulation work proceeded without an explicit strategy. An explicit problem exploration and identification process is desirable,
however, because of the profound impact problem formulation
has on the prospects for subsequent action. The purpose of this
second phase, therefore, is to identify and frame problems in
such a way that solutions can be found that are technically workable, that can garner the support of a winning coalition in subsequent phases, and that are legally and ethically defensible.

Typically, a conscious research strategy is needed in order
to develop such problem framings. The strategy we propose involves two basic steps, exploratory research and detailed research. Each step should be informed by careful attention to

stakeholder analyses, the interpretive schemes explicitly or implicitly tied to alternative problem formulations, and the consequences of these interpretive schemes and problem formulations for stakeholder interests and involvements. The way a problem is framed will structure how the various parties view their interests, the debates surrounding possible solutions, and the coalitions that develop in support of, and in opposition to, those solutions.

Chapter 7

Searching for
Solutions in Forums

Whatever the locus of action, from national government down to precinct, whether in an executive body or a legislative committee, some participants are almost sure to start with favorite, long-developed schemes. Their inclination will be to ignore whatever seems not to fit and to define the problem as one calling for solutions they have handy.
— Richard E. Neustadt and Ernest R. May

In American politics, the sine qua non of innovative policy is controversy.
— Richard E. Neustadt

The search for solutions phase of the policy change cycle has two main purposes: finding or creating solutions that effectively address the problem identified in the previous phase, and capturing enough public attention to place the problem and its potential solutions — the issue, in other words — on the public agenda. A successful search for solutions is an important component of the issue creation process, since a problem is likely to be placed on the public agenda only if it is associated with at least one potential solution. In this phase, public leaders continue the work of constructing and communicating collective visions for improving the world. In effect, they are facilitating the construction of alternative scenarios for moving from the

189

problem-laden present, through the implementation of certain strategies, to a relatively problem-free future. A key task in this phase is to make sure that whatever solutions are forwarded respond to the problem as defined in the prior phase. As Neustadt and May remind us, there is a powerful tendency for solutions to be advocated that do not actually address important public problems, but instead favor the knowledge and interests of particular actors.

Desired Outcomes

The second phase turned a condition into a problem; this third phase turns a problem into an issue, which we have defined as a problem with at least one solution attached to it that has pros and cons from the standpoints of various stakeholders. Creating an issue is the first desirable outcome. A second important outcome is development of conceptual frameworks for understanding problems and solutions. People are sense-making animals and need such frameworks in order to guide and justify their actions. Further, in a culture that glorifies rationality, it is important for leaders to provide decision makers and opinion leaders with understandable and defensible reasons for their decisions and actions (Dunn, 1982; Sabatier, 1991).

As a third outcome, a successful search identifies the components necessary for a high-quality solution. These components can then be assembled into a viable policy proposal in the next phase. Since "off-the-shelf" solutions to major problems are unlikely, every truly desirable solution probably will be specially tailored to particular circumstances. As Kingdon (1984, p. 131) notes, creative activity in this phase "usually involves recombination of old elements rather than fresh invention of new ones. . . . Change turns out to be recombination more than invention." Fourth, a well-executed solution search should result in saving time and money through use of appropriate networks of expertise and efficient use of people's time and other resources. Fifth, an effective search enhances the quality, legitimacy, and prestige of the policy change endeavor. Finally, after completion of this phase, the issue should be clearly in place on the public agenda. Development of a substantial public audience for addressing the problem with one or more viable solutions builds pressure for effective action in subsequent steps.

By the time they reached this phase, metropolitan governance advocates had formulated a regional problem that encompassed existing or potential crises in public services, tax revenues, transportation, open space, and other areas. Then, different groups engaged in different solution searches. The Joint Program for Landuse and Transportation Planning took a planner's approach in which the participants looked at alternative future development patterns for the Minneapolis–St. Paul area. Using information about the effects of each pattern, they chose one that could be the basis of a metropolitan development guide. Other groups and individuals looked for governance mechanisms that could oversee regional services, reduce competition among local communities, and ensure that development contributed to regional well-being.

One solution tried in other parts of the country and most vocally supported in this instance by Stanley W. Olson, mayor of the Minneapolis suburb of Richfield, was a council of governments (COG). These councils usually consisted of municipal and county officials and representatives of single-purpose districts in a metropolitan area. Their main drawback was their advisory nature. The Metropolitan Planning Commission was essentially a thirty-member COG and was widely regarded as unwieldy, unresponsive, and dominated by its staff. Another suburban mayor, Milton Honsey of New Hope, advocated a federation of area municipal officials, modeled on a system used in the Toronto area. The federation would be a state agency that would supervise areawide departments of mass transit, roads, traffic, airports, libraries, parks, air pollution control, and tax assessment. Minneapolis mayor Art Naftalin suggested a multiservice district under the jurisdiction of a coordinating agency. The Minneapolis Chamber of Commerce urban action committee chaired by Dennis Dunne supported an elected metropolitan-area services council to handle planning, mosquito control, transit, sewers, and a zoo.

As these solutions were circulated and discussed in a variety of forums, a Citizens League committee went to work on a report analyzing the solutions. Issued in November 1966, the report summarized metropolitan problems, the inadequacies of existing governmental structures for dealing with those problems, and the solutions that were advocated by various groups. The committee emphasized that the proposed solutions "revealed a substantial degree of agreement on several points, including the fact that a metropolitan governmental organization must be established by the 1967 Legislature" (Citizens League, 1966). A thousand copies of the report were distributed to government, civic, business, and labor leaders in the Twin Cities area.

Also in November 1966, the Upper Midwest Research and Development Council invited a "cross-section of people representing the state legislature, government, business, citizens associations, and labor" (Vance, 1977, p. 64) to a seminar on metropolitan reorganization. The council tried to include everyone who had a well-considered proposal for dealing with regional problems. As a starting point for discussion, the council commissioned Ted Kolderie to prepare a background report outlining the need for better metropolitan governance and the general direction of proposed changes. The report began with an emphasis on existing governmental fragmentation. Altogether, Kolderie noted, there were nearly 300 units of local government in the Twin Cities area, including counties, municipalities, townships, boroughs, and school and other special districts. The seminar attracted "much publicity" and seemed to increase the momentum for action by the 1967 legislature (Vance, 1977).

In January 1967, the Metropolitan Planning Commission (MPC) issued a position paper calling for an elected metropolitan government that would provide metropolitan services and have taxation and development powers. MPC would be abolished and its staff would become the new agency's planning department. MPC chairman Kenneth Kumm appeared before a committee of the Minnesota house of representatives to support the proposal. During February, both the Citizens League and the Metropolitan Section of the League of Minnesota Municipalities issued reports calling for an elected metropolitan council. The Citizens League also put together a chart outlining the major proposals for a metropolitan government framework and demonstrating the existence of broad agreement. In its February report, the league forcefully presented all the major arguments for establishing a metropolitan government of the sort endorsed in the MPC position paper. Although the council that was being recommended would take over the functions of existing agencies — such as the Mosquito Control District and the Minneapolis–St. Paul Sanitary District — and be authorized to take on other regional functions — such as solid waste disposal — the report emphasized that the council would have no "major new powers" and would "exercise only those powers and responsibilities specifically granted by the Legislature" (Citizens League, 1967, p. 16). All local units of government would remain intact and the council would handle only those functions that the local units could not handle.

The problem and solutions developed by regional governance advocates reinforced the regional community interpretive scheme. Reports issued in the search for solutions phase provided plenty of reasons for acting in accord with this scheme. Additionally, this phase produced a clear sense that any viable proposal for dealing with the regional problem would have to include a new regional body that had more authority and power over regional development and services than the old MPC. The proposal would have to specify the composition of the body and include specific directives for dealing with the various components of the regional problem.

Frequent meetings among representatives of the groups included in the change effort ensured that information was shared and that reports were well-timed and mutually reinforcing. The extensive public discussion of various solutions by mayors, business representatives, and members of the Citizens League and MPC indicated that the search was being carried out by credible people and that a variety of viewpoints was considered. At the end of the phase, the regional governance issue was not only on the public agenda, but lay squarely at the door of the state legislature.

The searches for solutions in the abortion controversy have been less tidy but often more creative and radical, as befits a social movement. They have drawn on experts in law, medicine, and religion; state and national groups have provided forums for information sharing and cooperation. Those who argued that women should have access to safe, legal abortions tried to alter restrictive state abortion laws, first seeing reform as the answer and later arguing for repeal. They also operated abortion information and referral services. They found physicians who would perform safe abortions illegally. They handed out contraceptives, and some taught self-abortion techniques. Those who wanted to protect the developing fetus, on the other hand, tried in the post–*Roe* v. *Wade* era to pass constitutional amendments, enact new restrictive laws, cut off public funds for abortion services and fetal research, overturn *Roe* v. *Wade,* block access to abortion clinics, and place strong religious sanctions on women's abortion decisions.

From the standpoint of the two main contending camps at least, the pros and cons of favored solutions have been well articulated in public forums. The two camps have articulated opposing issue frameworks, one emphasizing women's freedom and equality and the other the sacredness of life and conservative family values. Within these frameworks, problems and solutions were linked in ways that rationalized decisions and actions. For those who fought for safe, legal abortions in the years preceding *Roe* v. *Wade,* it was clear that any proposal for dealing with the abortion problem should make abortion legal and give pregnant women the right to choose between pregnancy and abortion. For their opponents, any proposal should protect fetal life and allow abortions only under very limited circumstances. Large numbers of people were galvanized by the visions of both camps, and they demanded that elected officials help those visions materialize. What has not been so well articulated in the searches for solutions is the spectrum of opinion and ambivalence within various stakeholder groups such as physicians, feminists, Catholic women, and poor women. The two major competing positions have been clear, but within those two frameworks there has still been considerable room for doubt, second thoughts, and not a little anguish. Thus, the basis for a different formulation of the problem and a different result to the solution search continues to exist.

As conducted, the searches for solutions have allowed each main camp to claim moral high ground and build legitimacy in the eyes of its supporters. On the other hand, the searches have not produced solutions that could accommodate more than one point of view.

Benefits of the Process

A number of benefits flow from a well-done search for possible solutions (see also Delbecq, Van de Ven, and Gustafson, 1975). The first is avoiding the usual organizational tendency to engage in searches that are simplistic, short, and shallow (March and Simon, 1958; Cyert and March, 1963; Nutt, 1984). A good search also overcomes the tendency to latch on to the first solution that comes anywhere close to addressing the problem — search behavior that Simon (1957) calls "satisficing." When an organization is short on resources, a truncated search and satisficing may be perfectly rational, but when more resources are available, such behavior is not rational. Even when resources are scarce, a well-executed search makes sense, since it can save time and money through tapping existing knowledge, models, and expertise; it can prevent planners from reinventing the wheel.

Large organizations tend to be provincial, spending most of their time talking to themselves and to selected, already familiar others. They rely on existing channels of communication, especially those within their dominant coalition, and they tend to rely on existing networks for boundary spanning. They also try hard to buffer their core technologies (Thompson, 1967), the important patterns of practice and behavior that are typically central to existing, institutionalized solutions to previously defined problems. In such circumstances, the discovery of new ideas, particularly of radically different ones, is accidental. A consciously designed, managed, and normatively based search process is therefore necessary in order to increase the likelihood of discovery or invention of new solutions to new, or even old, problems. Consider an analogy: if you see someone walking down the street talking to himself or herself at a high rate of speed and at high volume, what do you think? You suspect

mental illness. Similarly, when you see an organization spending most of its time talking to itself, you should suspect some
sort of organizational pathology. Normatively based, professional intervention is called for in both cases.

In a no-one-in-charge world, where lots of organizations
are satisficing, the possibilities for attaching a good solution to
a problem may approach randomness (Kingdon, 1984). Solutions will always be floating around. The question is whether
a technically, politically, legally, and ethically workable solution can be attached to the problem that needs to be addressed.
In such situations, leaders have to be particularly astute in linking problems to wise solutions.

A second major benefit is that rationales are provided for
adopted solutions. Political interests matter, but when it comes
to policy change, so do ideas and argumentation (Stone, 1988).
A good solution search indicates how best to link interests, ideas,
and arguments so that successful policy change becomes more
likely. A good solution search also identifies the major pros and
cons of solutions. Such an analysis will allow advocates and decision makers to make wiser choices in subsequent stages. Further, as change advocates explore solution options, they will begin to see the first clear indications of the resources that will
be needed to address the problems. And a good search demysti-
fies the difficulties of addressing problems by bringing the planning team and others in contact with existing knowledge, models,
and expertise. If the search brings to light previous success stories of comparable change, planners have some reassurance that
their policy changes may work.

Another benefit of this phase is the reconceptualization
almost always necessary for a major change (Dalton, 1970; Bartunek and Moch, 1987; Bartunek, 1988; Reich, 1987b). Consider one of our favorite stories—the building of the Panama
Canal. John Stevens, who was in charge of the United States'
attempt to build the canal, backed completely revamped canal
plans, because he had acquired new information as part of his
solution search. The earlier French attempt to build a *sea-level*
canal through a mountain range covered by rain forests and
infested with yellow fever–carrying mosquitoes had resulted in

20,000 deaths, the financial ruin of the construction company, and the collapse of the French government. The successful U.S. attempt was based on a series of tropical rain–fed step locks and an understanding of how to control the mosquitoes that caused yellow fever.

Finally, a well-executed search enhances the boundary spanning ability, knowledge, and communication capabilities of the participants, as they talk to people they would not ordinarily have encountered, in places they would not ordinarily have searched. Finally, as problems are linked to well thought-out and politically acceptable solutions, the advocacy base for policy change is enlarged. The *issue* is on the public agenda and moving forcefully toward the formal agenda of government for action.

Identifying Types of Issues

Once an issue is on the public agenda, the nature of the issue, in large part, determines the politics that surround it (Peterson, 1981; Wilson, 1986; Waste, 1989). Issues drive political decision making and almost invariably involve conflict and controversy; this is especially true when major changes are involved. (There are, of course, a few exceptions, such as legislation to combat child abuse, which Nelson [1984] describes as a "valence" issue; that is, one around which little, if any, opposition forms.)

Two typologies are especially useful for explaining and predicting the politics likely to surround particular policy proposals, or proposed solutions to public problems. The first was developed by Wilson (1986). He argues that important distinctions must be drawn between changes to old policies and the adoption of new ones, and between the costs and benefits associated with different policies. A new policy requires a change in public opinion in order to establish its legitimacy and to place it on the public agenda. An existing policy, on the other hand, may not require much change in public opinion, depending on the extent to which the unrevised policy effectively addressed the problem and the extent to which the public is willing to accept the costs and benefits associated with the changes. Wilson goes on to draw a distinction between how widely benefits from a proposed policy are distributed, on the one hand, and how widely the costs are dispersed, on the other. When the two dimensions are dichotomized and matched, a fourfold categorization of politics results: majoritarian politics, client politics, interest group politics; and entrepreneurial politics.

Majoritarian politics can be expected when both costs and benefits of proposed policies are widely distributed, and an appeal to popular majorities is necessary for the policies to be adopted. Majoritarian politics thus tend to evoke less conflict than the other types, because there is less incentive for organized interests to engage in conflict. The politics of Social Security in general can be characterized as majoritarian and relatively conflict-free at present, although there was a great deal of conflict at the time the system was established in 1935.

Client politics occur when perceived benefits are highly concentrated on an identifiable group, but perceived costs are distributed widely. This type of politics can become highly conflictual as the visibility of the benefits rises while their legitimacy falls in the estimation of those asked to pay for them. "Pork-barrel" policies are the classic example of policies that lead to client politics, because they allocate some favor or benefit to a narrow constituency while the costs are borne widely. Public works projects that give roads, parks, schools, airports, dams, or bridges to localities while the costs are covered by state or national taxpayers are typical pork barrels.

Wilson points out that the benefits sought from client politics may not always be monetary. For example, "certain groups may enjoy special protections from the government or have their values specially honored" (Wilson, 1986, p. 420). Veterans, for example, receive symbolic rewards on Memorial Day from government officials. Wilson goes on to note that interest group politics arise from policies that will "confer benefits on one relatively small, identifiable group and impose costs on a different equally identifiable group." Interest group politics are typically more conflictual than majoritarian politics and are dominated by interest group activity: "Each side sees the policy as hurting or helping it. Each side is small enough to make it worthwhile

and relatively easy to get organized, raise money, and hire lobby-
ists and lawyers. Though many issues of this type involve money
costs and benefits, that need not always be the case" (see also
Moe, 1980).

Finally, entrepreneurial politics can be expected when "society as a whole or some large part of it will benefit (or is led
to believe it will benefit) from a policy that imposes a substantial cost on some small, identifiable segment of society" (Wilson, 1986, p. 420). Policy entrepreneurs are crucial to adoption of such policies because they must persuade policy makers
that a policy actually will benefit a very large, dispersed group
and that the concentrated costs are merited. Alternatively, the
actual benefits may be targeted to a small client group—and
thus, there may be some duplicity on the part of the entrepreneur—but the perception is that they are widespread.

There are some difficulties with Wilson's typology, as
Waste (1989, pp. 84–85) points out. In particular, it is often hard
to categorize a policy neatly as one type rather than another.
Further, "in the real world issues tend to move around, back
and forth, among classifications," and not always because rational actors make calculations of perceived costs and benefits
as Wilson presumes. Movement may occur, for example, when
someone radically redefines the issue or escalates the conflict
associated with it, or when some event alters how people perceive the issue and their stake in it.

Advocates of liberalizing abortion laws, for example, practiced entrepreneurial politics when they defined legal abortion
as every woman's right. The losers would be back-street abortionists, people whose religious beliefs forbid abortion, and the
upholders of a conservative family morality. However, advocates who went on to support the right of access to abortion
moved toward client politics, since guaranteeing access mainly
meant providing public funds to help poor women pay for abortions. As advocates of creating metropolitan governance in the
Minneapolis–St. Paul area moved away from efforts to deal
piecemeal with regional problems, they also moved away from
solutions with a client or interest group orientation. These old
solutions that had pitted suburbs against each other and the big

cities benefited a small group of commercial developers, and harmed many area citizens. As change advocates searched for solutions that would control developers and produce widespread regional benefits, they and their solutions became entrepreneurial.

Waste (1989, pp. 72–126), drawing on the work of Peterson (1981), as well as Wilson (1986), has developed a second extremely useful typology. His typology, presented in Figure 7.1, was developed specifically for city politics, but appears to be more generally applicable. Waste, too, assumes that, in general, issues and policies—that is, proposed solutions to problems—determine politics. While his typology does not highlight the effect of perceived costs and benefits on issue politics as well as Wilson's, his typology does clarify further the level of conflict likely to surround particular policy proposals.

The vertical dimension of Waste's typology consists of a distinction between city residents and those same residents plus nonlocals. However, for our purposes, it seems more reasonable to distinguish between people who belong to a community of place or interest—which may or may not be a city—who can be thought of as local, and people who belong to a larger supra-local group. Either version of the distinction is important, because perceived costs and benefits may vary considerably depending upon who is doing the perceiving and where the costs and benefits are concentrated. The horizontal dimension consists of five major policy types: autonomous, pork barrel, routine, redistributive, and intrusive. Within each type, the differentiation between local and supra-local results in a distinction between selective and collective policies. Movement from left to right across policy types produces heightened levels of conflict. Further, there are low and high ranges of conflict within each policy type.

The first policy type, what Waste (1989, pp. 86–87) calls "autonomous" policy-making, is basically the "housekeeping" functions of government. Examples include "such issues as staffing and logistics for police, fire protection, sanitation, and public works, [and] procedural matters relating to the training or conduct of municipal employees." Typically, these issues evoke little or no public scrutiny or conflict. Decisions about

Figure 7.1. Policy Conflict Typology.

	Autonomous	Pork-barrel	Routine	Redistributive	Intrusive
Supra-local	Collective allocational	Collective goods	Collective mixed goods	Collective social welfare	Collective bads
Local	Selective allocational	Selective goods	Selective mixed goods	Selective social welfare	Selective bads

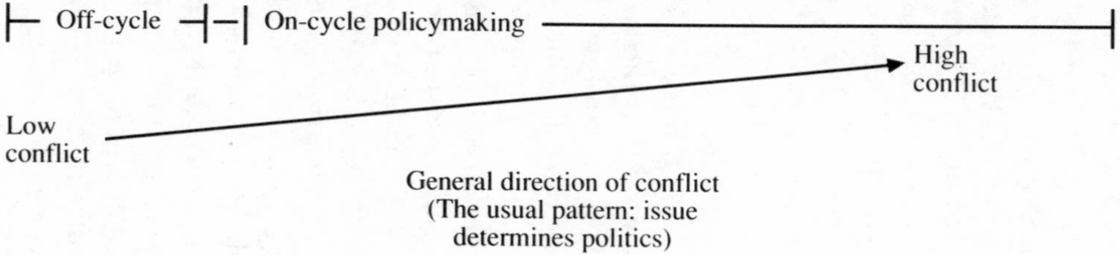

Off-cycle — On-cycle policymaking

Low conflict

High conflict

General direction of conflict
(The usual pattern: issue determines politics)

Source: Adapted slightly from R. J. Waste, *The Ecology of City Policymaking*, New York, Oxford University Press, 1989. Reprinted by permission.

them are made "off-cycle" (Jones, 1982), and they never get on
the public agenda; instead, they are hidden from view and handled
bureaucratically. Jones (p. 39) argues that "most public decisions are made off the policy cycle. . . . They remain hidden
from public view, not because anyone is trying to hide them,
but because not very many people are very interested. Off-cycle
policies generally affect very few people directly (although their
indirect impact may be considerable)." Because autonomous policies concern the allocation of time, staff, finances and other
resources, Waste refers to them as "selective allocational" policies at the local level, and "collective allocational" policies at the
supra-local level. These policies often are needed for the actual
implementation of a broad problem solution. Those who shaped
proposals for establishing the Metropolitan Council, for example, anticipated that the council itself would develop and adopt
policies for most staffing, for office space, and for budgeting.

       "Pork-barrel" policy-making (included in Wilson's client
politics category) is the second type. Because such policies are
generally perceived to be good, in that they involve the politics
of mutual gain, Waste refers to them as "selective goods" at the
local level and "collective goods" at the supra-local level.

       The third type is what Waste calls "routine" policy-mak-
ing. The policies that fit here are more conflictual than most
housekeeping or most pork-barrel policies. Examples include
comparable worth policies — which might be construed as housekeeping in nature, but in practice usually are not — and development projects that are financed locally rather than by higher
levels of government or private sources. These "conflictual matters generally involve interest group lobbying and bargaining
among several community or employee groups lobbying the city
for an increased amount of a limited good ([for example], services,
street lights at intersections, salary or benefit increases) . . .
frequently resulting in a scenario in which at least a few groups
or individuals are willing to resist the cost or the distribution
of the proposed good or policy" (Waste, 1989, p. 87). Because
conventional policies typically involve organized support and
opposition, Waste refers to them as "selective mixed goods"
(meaning mixed goods and bads) at the local level, and "collec-

tive mixed goods" at the supra-local level. For example, conventional policy-making was the initial (and unsuccessful) approach to construction of the Hubert H. Humphrey Metrodome in Minneapolis. The advocates of a domed stadium originally proposed that it be funded by bonds backed by city tax revenues. Downtown businesses, construction workers, and professional sports teams were the most immediate beneficiaries. Large numbers of taxpayers, meanwhile, feared that stadium revenues would not be sufficient to pay off the bonds and that taxpayers would bear the costs. Ultimately, after taxpayer protests defeated the original stadium proposal, the state legislature approved a kind of pork-barrel arrangement whereby construction bonds were issued by an areawide commission and paid off by stadium operating revenues and a narrowly targeted local liquor and lodging tax. Much of the cost of the site was paid by Minneapolis businesses. Although substantial costs connected with developing the site were paid by Minneapolis residents, those costs tended to be hidden from public view.

"Redistributive" policy-making is the fourth type, and usually involves considerable conflict. Redistributive issues "are social welfare measures, or attempts to help the less fortunate in the community, and must, by definition, involve the city in their cost (as opposed to the city administering a welfare program both mandated and funded by the state or federal government)" (Waste, 1989, p. 87). Because of the predictably higher levels of conflict associated with such policies, "and because redistribution usually needs to be organized by nonlocal government in order to be effective, city governments will rarely engage in redistributive policy making" (Waste, 1989, p. 88). Waste calls redistributive policies "selective social welfare" policies at the local level, and "collective social welfare" policies at the supra-local level. For example, the Metropolitan Council developed policies aimed at remedying tax-base disparities among metropolitan communities. The resulting redistribution of tax revenues has generated controversy ever since.

The final type is "intrusive" policy-making, which evokes the highest levels of conflict. Intrusive policies include, for example, the siting of a landfill, hazardous waste disposal facility, or group home for sex offenders. Intrusive policies induce high levels of conflict because they reverse the distribution of costs and benefits found in pork-barrel policies. Pork-barrel policies provide concentrated benefits to some, while the costs are widely dispersed. Intrusive policies, on the other hand, impose highly concentrated costs on some to provide widely diffused benefits to others. The cost-bearers thus have a strong incentive to organize and to make their opposition known. Waste refers to such policies as perceived "selective bads" at the local level and "collective bads" at the supra-local level. For example, liberalized abortion laws benefited the majority of women and men, but those same laws intruded harshly on the people who believed that aborting a fetus was tantamount to killing a human being. Thus, the level of conflict surrounding abortion policy has been extremely high for more than twenty years now.

There are several additional points to be made concerning Waste's typology. First, Waste notes that "issues generally, but do not always, determine conflict levels" (Waste, 1989, p. 90). Second, the same policy can evoke different levels of conflict in different cities, or communities of place or interest. And third, reactions to policies among the same groups of people can change over time; that is, conflict can escalate or de-escalate. For example, the policy type can change, affecting conflict levels; or the policy can move vertically within a policy type from one range of participants to another, with consequent effects on conflict — as happens when "conflicts involving only locals expand to conflicts involving nonlocals" (Waste, 1989, p. 90).

Before leaving the question of issue types, it is worthwhile to explore further how conflicts escalate within communities of place or interest. Coleman (1957) offers a model of community conflict to demonstrate how high levels of conflict are induced and the possibilities for successful conflict resolution, or even reasonable conflict management, sharply reduced. The model shows seven stages of conflict escalation. A conflict begins with (1) a single issue, that (2) disrupts the normal equilibrium of community relations. (3) New and different issues are then introduced that produce higher and higher levels of conflict, as (4) personal antagonisms develop among the various parties and the broad beliefs and world views of the opponents are called into question. (5) The opponents begin to appear totally bad to each other, a situation made even worse when (6) charges are leveled against the opponents as people. Finally, (7) the dispute becomes independent of the initial disagreement as issues are piled on issues, and personal relations among opponents disintegrate into mutual acrimony, derogation, and spite. Waste, who also discusses Coleman's model, points out that "it is the presence of the last three conflict stages—the introduction of new and different issues, the escalation of issue antagonisms into personal antagonisms, and the eventual severing of the conflict from the original issue—that constitutes maximum discord and characterizes high-conflict intrusive policy making" (Waste, 1989, p. 89).

Consider, for example, the shouts of "baby killers" from fetal rights supporters, or perhaps less directly accusatory, the coat hanger symbols brandished by supporters of legal abortion. This atmosphere of strong attacks on personal ethics has polarized the policy battle and may have narrowed the issues in ways that are ultimately harmful to the public. For example, in fighting to legalize abortion, change advocates have tended to lose sight of the fundamental, but broader, issue of women's reproductive health and choice. Similarly, opponents of abortion reform have often become so obsessed with protecting fetal life that they have scarcely worried about the quality of life after birth. These important public concerns remain largely neglected while abortion reform supporters and opponents put their energy into issues where they will meet head-on, such as whether a girl under eighteen must notify her parents before obtaining an abortion and whether hospitals and families can decide to end life-support treatment for terminally ill women who are pregnant.

The leadership advice concerning the management of conflict that emerges from Coleman's model is that if issues can be narrowed and conflicts kept issue centered, rather than person centered, conflicts are likely to be less serious and disruptive. Focusing on interests rather than positions or persons, while maintaining productive social relationships, can allow mutually agreeable answers to issues to emerge (Fisher and Ury, 1981; Susskind and Cruikshank, 1987; Fisher and Brown, 1988; Gray, 1989).

In summary, the way issues are framed, along with the way the costs and benefits of their resolution are perceived to be distributed among stakeholders, strongly affects the politics of issue resolution. Wilson's and Waste's typologies provide very useful ways for public leaders to think about how issues are perceived and what the prospects are for their resolution, based on the politics that are likely to surround them. Coleman's model of community conflict escalation provides an understanding of how issues may move within the typologies, and how interventions may be made to keep excessive conflicts from erupting.

Leadership Guidelines

Public leaders should keep the following guidelines in mind as they construct and communicate alternative solutions for tackling problems. These guidelines are organized under the headings of searching for solutions; report preparation, review, and dissemination; and caveats.

Searching for Solutions

Emphasize Forums, Typically Small Ones. Forums remain important in this phase because the process of issue creation typically requires a great deal of discussion before important problems can be raised in such a way that they are likely to be resolved satisfactorily from the standpoint of most stakeholder groups. These discussions cannot be forced; instead, they must be managed. As in previous phases, such management involves leadership by indirection—that is, by managing the ideas, rules, modes, media, or methods governing the search process and used to publicize its results. Metropolitan governance advocates, for example, did not convene all interested parties and direct them to produce consensus on a metropolitan governance mechanism. The Upper Midwest Research and Development Council, however, did organize a broad-scale seminar to consider proposals for such a mechanism. The council managed the discussion by carefully constructing the invitation list and by using Ted Kolderie's report as a starting point, and the seminar contributed to a consensus that was, as the Citizens League pointed out, already nascent in the collection of reports and statements that had emerged from task forces, committee meetings, and press interviews during the search for solutions.

Consciously Aim at Finding Solutions to Identified Problems. Without a normative thrust, people can be expected to proffer solutions that do not effectively address the problems they are meant to solve. In such unfocused situations, these solutions may even be adopted, but it is not clear that anyone other than the solution advocates will be helped (Kingdon, 1984). Leaders should recall that precisely how solution components are identified is not as important as the fact that they are identified. It is also important to remember that this phase can be overdone as well as underdone. Notwithstanding these observations, it is usually important to design a solution search strategy that will get change advocates to look outside their normal search channels, make efficient use of people's time and existing knowledge sources, and increase the perceived legitimacy of the policy change effort.

Distinguish Between Complex and Simple Situations. In complex situations, the search for solutions may be carried out by one or more planning teams; in simple situations the coordinating group probably will do its own search. In both situations, searchers should remember that they do not have to invent every solution themselves; instead, they should always stay alert for solutions developed by others.

Consider Using a Three-Step Process When Searching for Solutions. We suggest that leaders follow a process based principally on the work of Etzioni (1967, 1968); Delbecq, Van de Ven, and Gustafson (1975); and Bryson and Delbecq (1981). The process consists of (1) a broad scan within and outside normal search channels in order to gain an understanding of the possible territories within which solutions might be found, (2) a narrow-gauge search within the most promising territories to find specific solution components likely to be part of the policy change proposals, and (3) detailed exploration of identified solution components. The components that pass muster in this process will be assembled into a specific proposal in the next phase. Before discussing each of the steps in more detail, however, we must emphasize that in a no-one-in-charge world the possibility of convincing most stakeholders to engage in an organized, potentially time-consuming search process is distinctly limited. Therefore, the three-stage process may be followed only by a limited subset of key players. Nonetheless, the process may still be useful, both for those who do use it and as a model for leaders of how to expand the solution search whenever the opportunity arises.

Step one—the broad scan—has two purposes. The first is to identify potential sources of broad conceptualizers, and then identify the conceptualizers themselves—the cosmopolitans who have a rich and extensive grasp of the knowledge sources likely to yield solutions to identified problems. The second is to find ways to incorporate these cosmopolitans and their knowledge into the solution search. The most effective and inexpensive way to find these people is to solicit nominations of information categories—not people's names just yet—through structured or unstructured individual or group processes. For example, in order to get category suggestions, extensive conversations might be held with several people who seem to be plugged in to relevant networks. After planning team members have engaged in several such conversations, brainstorming or the snow card technique (Bryson, 1988b) can be used to identify specific categories and subcategories to be explored. Information categories might include specific disciplines or skills, organizations similar to the one conducting the search, relevant professional organizations, appropriate technical assistance services, research services, or potential funding sources.

Once the categories have been identified, structured interview procedures can be used to search within categories for further information. Interviews might be conducted in person, over the telephone, or through electronic mail. A standard preprinted interview protocol and record sheet should be followed. Interviewees should be asked to help identify names of authors, names of contact persons, titles, conceptual models, in-process demonstrations, and so forth within each category. Leaders should remember that the search at this point is supposed to be quite broad.

A telephone interview, for example, might include the following steps:

- Assign people who have a high interest in the search process to do the telephoning.
- Send a preliminary letter to those who will be telephoned that explains the purpose of the call, how their name was chosen, and what is needed from them.
- Talk first to the "gatekeepers" for each category — the decision makers, officers, or opinion leaders who are central in their particular network. They can supply the names of the appropriate technical people (Rogers, 1982).
- Give an explicit statement about the policy change project and the sponsors.
- Give an explicit statement about the problem.
- Explain how the interviewee was nominated. Flattery certainly does not hurt!
- Obtain nominations of specific people, authors, titles, conceptual models, and so forth. Start filling in the categories on the record sheet.
- Ask nominees to nominate others, thus creating a "ripple effect" that expands the search ever further into perhaps unknown territories.
- Send a follow-up thank-you letter, so that you can call on the person again should the need arise.

Delbecq, Van de Ven, and Gustafson (1975) find that about one in six calls may result in useful information. That may not seem like much, but the cumulative effect of having several people place numerous calls over the course of several days or a week can be truly astonishing. This rich web of communications and interactions, in which diverse perspectives are

juxtaposed, can produce exactly the kind of environment necessary for significant breakthroughs to occur (de Bono, 1970;
Prince, 1970; Kanter, 1983, 1989; Moore, 1987; Von Oech,
1983).

Step two is the narrow-gauge search. There are three purposes to this search: to decide which areas should be researched
further, to gain a deeper understanding of the chosen areas, and
to identify likely solution components. Leaders can begin targeted, in-depth searches by gaining a reasonable understanding of the narrowed search area through informal discussions
with ten or twelve people who are knowledgeable in that area.
These conversations will provide information about the territory and the tribes; factions; unifiers and dividers; customs, practices, knowledge bases, and world views; and stories to be encountered in the territory. The conversations amount to an
intense orientation prior to undertaking the voyage into the new
territory in earnest. Given that only one in six phone calls is
likely to be useful, it may take seventy-two phone calls to find
these twelve experts.

Once a suitable orientation has occurred, leaders move
to the second step. They should probe the appropriate experts
through structured group processes, such as brainstorming, the
snow card technique, the nominal group technique, or the delphi technique. The purpose of the probe is to create lists of,
first, possible solution components; second, resources already
available to facilitate use of the components, such as technical
assistance services, grant programs, or industry associations;
and third, potential resources—ones that do not yet exist, but
might help, such as new legislation, new coalitions, and funding sources that might change their funding priorities. It is important to remember that an assemblage of high-powered, high-
status experts can be hard to control and that a strong process
facilitator should guide the group of experts as it develops the
three lists. The group meeting should be introduced by a "show
and tell" session that provides an overview of the whole process
and describes how the group meeting fits into that process. The
role of the experts at the meeting should be clarified and should
include the message that the experts are there as part of the supporting cast; they are not the stars.

Even with such guidance, however, it will take time for the experts to settle in and provide the kind of information leaders desire. In our experience, experts will spend the first part of such a meeting simply getting to know one another and trying to feel one another out. Indeed, for most experts, the major benefit of participating in such a meeting — regardless of the size of the honoraria they might be paid — is getting to know the other experts and expanding their professional network and peer learning, not helping the search process. Because of this, it can be extremely productive to build in time for informal socializing among the experts — for example, as part of a cocktail hour and dinner the evening before a daylong meeting.

Our experience has also shown us that experts will spend a major fraction of the front end of such meetings exposing their biases through short — or not so short — normative assertions as they announce and stake out their positions. Experts sometimes seem to be much like high-strung thoroughbred racehorses — emotional, persnickety, nervous, and occasionally fragile. Eventually, however, with strong process facilitation, a group of experts can be expected to get into harness and provide the information leaders seek, often in amazingly short order. Once they do, change advocates will be glad of two things: first, that they obtained the experts' knowledge; and second, that they let prior problem formulation work define which experts should be assembled, rather than let the experts define the problem.

The last step of the three-step search process is a detailed exploration of identified solution components. In this step, the search team decides which solution components to explore in more depth. The team should either visit or import each component, depending on its nature. Structured group processes can then be used to explore the strengths of the component, its weaknesses, and modifications that would improve its applicability or performance in the situation at hand. Useful structured processes might include brainstorming, the snow card technique, nominal group technique, delphi technique, or force field analysis (Johnson and Johnson, 1991, pp. 239-242).

In both the metropolitan governance and the abortion policy cases, the search for solutions was more informal and fragmented than the process outlined above. Nevertheless, it was complete enough to create issues that reached the public agenda. A more formal search might have been difficult in a messy, no-one-in-charge world, but nonetheless, it should have produced a better-articulated and wider range of solutions coupled with a more thorough assessment of stakeholders' pros and cons.

Work for an Issue Framing That Will Increase the Chances That the Issue Can Be Addressed in Politically, Technically, Ethically, and Legally Effective Ways. Leaders should understand that more than one cycle of problem formulation and solution search may be required before a desirable match between problem and solution can be found.

Report Preparation, Review, and Dissemination

Prepare a Report on Possible Solutions. Once solution components have been explored and evaluated, the planning team is ready to prepare a preliminary report for review by the team, coordinating committee, and other involved organizations or persons. The report should include:

- The conceptual framework that links the public problem and its potential solution — that is, the framework that articulates the issue and the ways it might be addressed
- Identification and discussion of solution components
- Existing or potential funding sources
- Recommendations for further action

The recommendations for further action are likely to suggest adaptation of solution ideas that were already known to the planning team, but needed more careful evaluation; the use of solutions that are already available, but were beyond the knowledge of the planning team at the start of the solution search phase; or the development of new, creative, and innovative solutions that have not been used anywhere before (Nutt, 1991).

Review the Report Following the Normative Approach Discussed in Chapter Six. Reviewers should be asked to identify strengths, weaknesses, and modifications (the SWIM analysis) that would improve the report.

Distribute the Reviewed and Modified Report. A public relations and education strategy for dissemination of the report should be prepared in advance of distribution. This strategy is likely to be an important part of the process that gets and keeps the issue on the public agenda. At this stage, the strategy may include using selected media in order to accomplish the following objectives:

- Making various audiences aware that forums will be held to discuss solutions, or reporting the results of those forums.
- Floating "trial balloons" to raise consciousness of the issue and to ascertain what kinds of solutions are likely to garner necessary support (Benveniste, 1989). A trial balloon can also stake out an extreme position in order to see which modifications are most important to stakeholders.
- Emphasizing how solutions would alleviate the problem and help realize a vision of a better society.
- Responding to outcry from opponents who view solutions as threatening or wrongheaded.

Caveats

Think About the Different Kinds of Issues That Are Created by Different Solutions to an Identified Problem. Because the nature of the issue has a profound effect on the politics that will surround the issue's resolution, leaders must think carefully about the issue typologies presented in this chapter in relation to the problem and its potential solutions. They should ask themselves which typology applies to each problem definition and solution combination, and what the implications are for the politics likely to surround such an issue. Is there a way to frame the issue to eliminate unnecessary controversy, yet create a high likelihood that the issue will be addressed constructively and the public problem solved or effectively alleviated?

Keep in Mind That Considerable Controversy Is Likely No Matter How an Issue Is Framed. Controversy is not all bad, since it can be used to focus attention on the issue, to educate key actors and decision makers about the nature of the problem and its potential solutions, and to raise the issue's priority on the public agenda. Leaders' actions in the face of this controversy will show their audiences what the leaders think is important, what interpretation they think should be put on the issue, and what should be done about it. Therefore, leaders should seek what Woodrow Wilson called "action that makes for enlightenment." Franklin Roosevelt's statement that "We have nothing to fear but fear itself" was an action that carried with it the kind of calming, yet also inspiring, influence the United States needed. When coupled with Roosevelt's program, the instruction he conveyed allowed people to see how they could work their way out of an unprecedentedly deep economic depression (Neustadt, 1990, pp. 84–90).

Nonetheless, although controversy is not all bad, public leaders should avoid unnecessary controversy, both because they will have a difficult time controlling controversies that get out of hand, and because dangerous negative spirals of conflict might result. In other words, enough controversy should be sought to place the issue on the public agenda, but not so much controversy that the possibility of compromise and mutual gain is destroyed.

Understand That, as the Situation Becomes More Difficult, The Solution Search Will Become More Extensive. Politically and technically complicated situations may require searches that include:

- a broader scan
- a narrow-gauge search in more areas
- a more detailed exploration of identified solution components
- more care and effort in developing a conceptual framework for understanding the problem and its solutions
- greater assurances to involved parties that the search has been careful and rational
- a more extensive review of the preliminary report

- a more careful exploration of funding options
- a broader distribution and discussion of the final report

Further, in keeping with the first caveat, as the search becomes broader and deeper, it is likely that it will become necessary to revisit, revise, or reduce the problem statement in order to get an effective match between the problem and a solution. Development of an effective match can be extremely difficult, however, as tremendous pressure may develop to disconnect solutions from problems.

Recognize That, in Most Difficult Situations, a Point Is Reached Where More Solution Search Will Neither Increase the Potential Supporting Coalition nor Reduce the Potential Opposition Coalition. Indeed, there may be occasions when leaders are faced with implacable foes, and nothing can be done to alter their opposition. On these occasions, change advocates simply have to decide whether to push ahead to the next phase or not.

When the Situation Is Easy, Pursue the Solution Search, Policy Proposal Development, and Proposal Review and Adoption Phases As One Phase Having Three Parts. In difficult situations, pursue these phases separately as part of a strategy to create sequential major and minor decision points.

Summary

The way a problem is formulated will strongly affect the nature and range of its possible solutions. When a problem and a solution with pros and cons for different stakeholders are joined, an issue is created. The nature of the issue will strongly affect the politics of its resolution — indeed, whether it can be resolved at all. In many policy change processes, these problem-solution-issue-politics connections are made either badly or not at all. We have outlined a conceptual framework and leadership guidelines to help leaders make better connections between problems, solutions, issues, and politics than they would otherwise.

Chapter 8

Developing a Proposal That Can Win in Arenas

History abhors determinism, but cannot tolerate chance.
— Bernard De Voto

Always, always, always have a plan. And always, always change it.

—John Rollwagen
CEO, Cray Research

In the three previous phases of the policy change cycle, change advocates formulated problems and explored solutions to those problems in order to create an issue and place it on the public agenda. In this phase, the focus shifts to developing policies that can be put on the formal agenda of government or other decision-making bodies. Therefore, the purpose of this phase is to develop a proposal that embodies technically workable, politically acceptable, and legally and ethically defensible responses to the issue. This policy proposal may represent an incremental evolution of existing policies; a substantial and far-reaching transformation in the way problems and solutions are viewed; or some combination of evolution and transformation.

216

As historian Bernard De Voto might suggest, trends and circumstances have a powerful, but not deterministic, effect on which issues are placed on the public agenda. Visionary leadership, in particular, is a necessary part of the process as well. Once on the public agenda, there is no guarantee that issues — and specific, desirable proposals to address them — will get on the formal agendas of decision-making bodies; or that useful policies will be decided upon, or adopted, subsequently in the relevant arenas. Political leadership is required, along with visionary leadership, to develop proposals and coalitions of support that will increase the chances that good policies and plans will ultimately be adopted and implemented. Chance clearly plays an important part in human events, but wise public leaders leave as little to chance as they can.

In this phase, forums and informal arenas will again be the principal settings, and the action within these settings must increase the possibilities for successful proposal adoption in the next phase. A conscious strategy, therefore, for linking the forums and informal arenas of this stage with the formal arenas of the next stage is essential. In addition, proposal developers should protect and if possible improve the technical quality and feasibility of the solutions identified in the previous phase, at the same time that they enhance the solutions' political acceptability and, thus, the proposals' chances of being adopted.

A policy proposal's political acceptability increases as the costs of proposal adoption diminish for key stakeholders. As Light (1991) notes in relation to presidential agenda setting, it is primarily the issues with the greatest potential benefit for key stakeholders that get on the agenda, while the responses that are least costly for key stakeholders are the ones that receive prime consideration. Moreover, as noted in Chapter Seven, any proposal likely to be adopted will be a carefully tailored response to specific circumstances, rather than an off-the-shelf solution imported from elsewhere. While the ideas included in the proposal may not be particularly new, their combination into a winning proposal is likely to be a unique creation. Recombination, and occasionally mutation, of existing ideas thus is an important feature of this phase (Kingdon, 1984). Change advocates should be prepared to sculpt the many solution ideas collected in previous phases to fit the specific contours and requirements of both the political landscape and the purposes they pursue.

It is very important to keep in mind that, typically, every member of a winning coalition will not agree on an entire set of policy proposal elements, and that is acceptable. All that is critical is that the coalition's members agree to support the proposal. If leaders have done their initial work well and organized the nucleus of a viable coalition around the idea of doing something about the problem in a certain direction, rather than around specific strategies, the leaders should be able to retain the coalition's support.

Desired Outcomes

Several outcomes may be sought in this phase. First and foremost, of course, is the development of draft policies and plans for review by official decision or policy makers in the next phase. A second desired outcome is proposal drafts incorporating constructive modifications based on careful attention to the goals, concerns, and interests of key stakeholders. Also important, if possible, is the identification or development of necessary resources for implementing the proposal once it is adopted. Too many planners and policy analysts seem to think that good ideas will attract necessary resources on their own, magically. Fourth, successful completion of this phase should result in clear indications that the necessary coalition exists to assure adoption and implementation of the proposal. And finally, successful proposal development should lead to a shared belief among involved parties that the policy change effort represents a joint endeavor. This belief will provide the emotional "glue" that holds the coalition of interest together in support of the proposal.

The metropolitan governance advocates for the Minneapolis–St. Paul area developed several policy proposals in this phase, but the most important was the draft legislation developed by the small group led by Dennis Dunne that included Verne Johnson, Thomas Anding, Ted Kolderie, Clayton LeFevere, and Representative William Frenzel, who would introduce the bill in the state legislature. The bill envisioned a metropolitan council comprising fifteen members elected from equal population districts. In effect a "state-created metropolitan service district" (Wilensky, 1969), the council would have operating control over mass transit, sewage disposal, and mosquito control. It also would have bonding and taxing power. Council advocates completed this phase with a formidable coalition of business groups, civic leaders, local and regional officials, and citizen groups who could be expected to exert effective pressure on legislative, executive, and adminstrative decision makers throughout adoption and implementation of their proposal.

The advocates of legalizing abortion initially concentrated on enacting versions of the American Law Institute's model abortion code. In Minnesota, the Council for the Legal Termination of Pregnancy succeeded in having abortion reform bills introduced in the Minneapolis legislature in 1967 and 1969. One council member, Maynard Pirsig, a former University of Minnesota law school dean, was a particularly important source of advice. By 1969, the bills had garnered support from state feminist groups and the Minnesota Medical Association, but the reformers were never able to build a coalition strong enough to overcome the counterattack from their opponents. The reformers did not have to worry too much about proposal funding, since lifting legal restrictions on abortion would cost very little. If reform succeeded, they would need to raise money to expand abortion services, but public funding would be necessary only to cover costs of serving poor women. The change advocates wisely chose to de-emphasize the public funding issue and simply press for legalization.

Another important proposal development effort involved the preparation of the legal arguments to support Norma McCorvey in *Roe* v. *Wade*. Ultimately, based in part on the legal briefs of both sides and the record of the trial in the state courts, the Supreme Court allowed pregnant women and their physicians to choose abortion during the first trimester of pregnancy. Following this decision, those who wanted to control women's access to abortion advanced numerous proposals for restrictive laws or regulations at the local, state, and national levels. Perhaps their most high-profile proposal was a constitutional amendment declaring that the human fetus embodied life and, thus, was entitled to protection under the U.S. Constitution. However, this amendment failed to be ratified, largely because of the intentionally cumbersome amendment process.

Benefits of the Process

A number of benefits flow from successful policy proposal development efforts (Bryson and Delbecq, 1981). The first important benefit is the creation of draft policies that are technically, politically, and legally and ethically acceptable. A second important benefit is optimizing leaders' ability to communicate and sell draft proposals to key decision makers and opinion leaders in the next phase. And the third important benefit is the creation of a sufficiently powerful, supportive coalition.

These first three benefits are made possible, in part, by the realization of four additional benefits. The first of these is that leaders will have clear indications that the proposed policies, plans, or programs are feasible. Second, the draft policies will be designed to allow flexibility and adaptability during implementation, especially in the face of unforeseen difficulties. Third, the draft proposals will be free of offensive or threatening symbolism, but will incorporate constructive and positively motivating symbols. Finally, successful proposal development in this phase will reduce hostility and embarrassment in the far more formal proposal review and adoption phase, through careful attention to key stakeholder goals and concerns. Realization of all these benefits should make formal proposal review and adoption a far more pleasant and successful experience than it would be otherwise.

Characteristics of "Winning" Proposals

In order to discuss characteristics of winning proposals, we must say what we mean by "winning." Winning, to us, means that the proposed policies, when implemented, address important public problems in ways that effectively serve the public interest, that are just and economically efficient, and that respect the rightful liberties of affected parties.

Further, it is important to keep in mind that there can be a big difference between winning at the adoption stage and winning during implementation. Proposals that may be easily adoptable may not be easily implementable, and that is because there are almost always at least two levels of adopters: those who make the authoritative decision to adopt proposed policies and those who must implement the policies. This fact lies behind a favored tactic of higher-level governments in times of budget stringency, which is to mandate major changes by implementing agencies, but to provide no additional resources or other transitional help. The mandaters then claim victory, while the mandated cry foul (Fix and Kenyon, 1990). Change advocates thus should work hard to make sure their favored proposals are both adoptable *and* implementable. This work is politics of the middle level occurring after the high-level politics of getting an issue on the public agenda.

Proposals are likely to be adopted and implemented when decision makers find them persuasive in light of their own concerns and interests. The characteristics that will be particularly important in a given situation will vary; however, in the following pages, we describe a number of characteristics that can enhance the chances of adoption and implementation of desirable changes (Brief and others, 1976; Kingdon, 1984; Benveniste, 1989).

Formal Linkage of Problems and Solutions

In "organized anarchies" it is likely that problems and solutions will become disconnected. If a proposal puts forth a solution that does not address a real problem, it may be adopted, but is unlikely to succeed during implementation (Bryson, Bromiley, and Jung, 1990). As Kingdon (1984, p. 121) notes, "People in and around government still must be convinced somewhere along the line that they are addressing a real problem."

Congruence with Values Held by Key Decision Makers and Other Stakeholders

Values vary considerably from situation to situation, but equity, efficiency, and congruity with prevailing interpretive schemes are likely to matter. Beyond that, inspiring symbolism, or at least inoffensive and nonthreatening symbolism, can facilitate policy adoption. Reason is important as a motivator of social change, but rarely is enough by itself. Typically, emotion and passion are also needed, and powerful symbolism provides a way of releasing and focusing the emotional energies necessary to create and sustain effective collective action. Similarly, powerful symbolism of the wrong sort can suppress action by discouraging or alienating participants (Edelman, 1964, 1971, 1977). Even worse, certain symbols can inspire and mobilize an opposition that can block potential changes, or even adopt changes that go directly against those desired by the advocate group. As noted earlier, most members of the public are cognitive misers, and symbols are all they are likely to notice. Therefore, constructive and motivating symbolism is crucial.

The proposal for creating the Metropolitan Council was very much in accord with the values evoked by the "regional community" interpretive scheme that was endorsed by key decision makers and other stakeholders in earlier phases. The proposal fit the beliefs that both economic growth and public amenities were desirable and that local government autonomy should be protected. The most powerful symbols associated with the proposals were, on the positive side, a thriving regional community exerting control over its future and, on the negative side, a fragmented political and economic landscape in which cities and suburbs were locked in destructive competition and public services were wastefully duplicated, not provided, or inadequate to keep up with demand. This particular combination of positive and negative symbols was a strong asset for the proposal. Thomas Anding believes that the negative symbols actually were more important to local governments. He commented, "I don't think the argument that metropolitan government was good for the region's general welfare appealed much. Most local government officials were motivated by what was in it for them. The argument that worked was 'we can't continue this insanity.' The have-not communities were already in the soup; they knew they were in deep trouble. Others were initially hostile to the idea of the council, then came around" (personal interview, April 5, 1984).

The proposals advanced by the opposing camps in the

abortion controversy have appealed to very different, but not necessarily exclusive, sets of values. Both groups, however, have tended to focus on the differences among the values rather than on possible common ground. For example, valuing women's liberty and well-being is not incompatible with valuing developing human life as miraculous and sacred. However, by attaching powerful, emotion-ridden symbols to the values they wish to emphasize, the two groups have heightened their sense of divergence. The consequence of this hardened opposition has been the public policy equivalent of trench warfare, producing a series of skirmishes over many years that has chipped away at the main tenets of *Roe* v. *Wade* and made constructive reformulation of the problem nearly impossible.

Anticipated User or Implementer Support and Public Acquiescence

If users or implementers, as well as the public, are likely to balk at proposed changes, decision makers are unlikely to embrace those changes. This is an example of rule by anticipated reactions (Friedrich, 1940), in which decision makers choose courses of action based on the likely responses of others. The proposal for the Metropolitan Council could not have been expected to work without the support of local officials. Thus, it was critical that the proposal generally accorded with the ideas advanced by the majority of local officials in earlier phases. To take another example, federal civil rights legislation was stalled for years because national decision makers believed that governments and white citizens in the deep South would actively resist implementation of the changes, threatening violence against resident African-Americans and undermining federal government sovereignty. Passage of the Civil Rights Acts of 1964 and 1965 was facilitated because constituencies that supported change finally developed among white Southerners (Sherrill, 1969; Oates, 1982; Caro, 1990).

Clear Indications That the Proposal Is Coming from Competent Sources

Decision makers' reputations, prestige, and leadership prospects are linked in part to their abilities to make wise judgments about possible courses of action (Neustadt, 1990). Thus, decision makers are unlikely to embrace proposals put forth by people they perceive to be incompetent or insufficiently skilled. To do so would involve more personal risk than most decision makers will accept. The proposal for creating the Metropolitan Council came from some of the most highly respected civic and political leaders in the Minneapolis–St. Paul area. Proposals for liberalizing abortion laws were often developed or endorsed by respected professionals — lawyers, clergy, and physicians. Similarly, counterproposals by right-to-life groups were developed or endorsed by physicians, ministers, and even U.S. presidents. In the abortion controversy, however, the competence of proposal originators was probably much less important to decision makers than the existence of large constituencies demanding that the proposals be enacted.

Local Adaptation of Key Solution
Components Identified in the Previous Phase

Any off-the-shelf solutions must be designed to fit the problem at hand and the political context. Some elements of the policy proposal developed by the informal coordinating committee in the metropolitan governance case had been tried in other areas or were practiced by the Metropolitan Planning Commission. The committee, however, also had to supply other elements in order to craft a new mechanism that was strong enough to make real improvements in regional services and protect communities from the ill effects of rapid development. Those who sought abortion law reform in the mid 1960s could use the model penal code issued in 1962 by the American Law Institute as a basis for their proposal. The code legalized abortion for specific causes, including severe threats to a pregnant woman's physical or mental health, but it still had to be adapted to the laws and political environments in each state. When the supporters of fetal rights decided to fight back after *Roe* v. *Wade,* they could benefit from the examples of others, such as the suffragettes, who had sought constitutional amendments; they could adapt examples of parental consent ordinances; and they could adapt regulations and funding restrictions for other medical services, but they still had to put together a unique proposal package that would achieve their goals.

High Technical Feasibility and Quality

Decision makers are likely to search for assurances that proposals are technically sound. If changes ultimately fail on technical grounds, decision makers may be able to blame technical specialists involved with development or implementation, but they may also be blamed themselves. To avoid this possibility, decision makers are likely to search for evidence that proposed changes are, at least, technically feasible. The technical features of any proposed solution are not only likely to have a profound effect on the nature of the proposal adoption debate, they may also have a powerful effect on the structuring of coalitions of support and opposition. Therefore, technical feasibility and quality cannot be divorced from questions of political acceptability (Benveniste, 1989). Technical feasibility was more of an issue in the abortion controversy than in the metropolitan governance case. A powerful argument for decriminalizing abortion was precisely that it had become a procedure posing little danger to women when performed by competent physicians in sanitary conditions.

Discussion of a Set of Alternatives Indicating Strengths and Weaknesses. Decision makers are wary of being trapped by planners and technical specialists. Including a set of alternatives in the proposal, along with an outline of their comparative strengths and weaknesses, is a way of indicating to decision makers that they are not being manipulated for some undisclosed end. Inclusion of alternatives also opens the way for decision makers to suggest modifications that improve the proposal.

Indications of a Highly Favorable Cost-Benefit Ratio for One or More of the Alternatives

In times of resource scarcity, decision makers are increasingly attentive to cost-effectiveness. Proposals are more likely to be viewed favorably if decision makers can see that benefits are likely to exceed costs by a substantial margin.

Inclusion of Budgetary Materials and Attention to Budgetary Concerns, Including a Request for More Resources Than Are Thought to Be Absolutely Necessary

Decision makers are likely to wonder exactly how monies devoted to a particular policy, plan, or program change are likely to be spent. Inclusion of budgetary materials addresses these concerns, although there always is the danger that decision makers will insinuate themselves into budgetary detail and ultimately hinder effective implementation. Extra resources should be built in, since decision makers often feel compelled to cut any budget request. Further, implementers will need some budgetary leeway to cover unforeseen contingencies

Recommendations of Administratively Simple Solutions Requiring As Little Skill Readjustment As Possible by Implementers

The more complex the solution is to administer, the more likely it is to fail (Pressman and Wildavsky, 1973). Decision makers know this. Further, if they consult with the likely administrators in advance of proposal adoption, they are likely to be warned about administrative difficulties and advised not to authorize proposed changes. The chances for successful proposal adoption and implementation can be increased to the extent that these concerns can be addressed in advance. Decision makers are also likely to prefer solutions that involve minor skill readjustments by implementers. Solutions that require major readjustments are more likely to fail during implementation, and decision makers know this.

The proposal for creating the Metropolitan Council was not administratively complicated. The council would be governed by an elected board and would subsume most existing regional agencies. Groundwork for the council's regional planning process had already been laid by the Joint Program for

Landuse and Transportation Planning. This proposal was drastically changed by the Minnesota legislature, but because of a desire to diminish council powers rather than because of the proposal's administrative complexity. Reforming U.S. abortion laws in accordance with the American Law Institute's model code did not require a new regulatory or service bureaucracy since the code simply expanded the legal grounds for performing abortions. Repeal of abortion laws was even more administratively simple.

However, there is a caveat to this characteristic of winning proposals, which is exemplified by the efforts of supporters of restrictive abortion laws to pass administratively complicated solutions, such as detailed prescriptions for abortion counseling, because they *want* to complicate matters for abortion seekers and providers; the more difficult abortions are to get, the fewer there will be. Thus, the caveat is that change advocates must determine whether the purposes of the change effort are better served by administratively simple or complex solutions; in some cases, change advocates may actually want administratively difficult solutions.

Indications of Flexibility in Implementation, Including Staged Implementation, If Necessary

Solutions that can be adapted to diverse exigencies that may arise during implementation are likely to be preferred by decision makers. Further, solutions that allow for staged implementation to facilitate learning, minimize risk, and smooth out resource requirements over time are likely to be preferred. The Minnesota legislature, in effect, opted for staged implementation when it established the Metropolitan Council and instructed the council to prepare reports and legislative recommendations for dealing with specific regional issues and service problems.

Guidance for Implementation and Evaluation

Decision makers almost always ask how a solution will be implemented, because the more experienced they are the more likely they are to be familiar with all the ways policies can fail during implementation. Such decision makers want assurances that implementation has been adequately planned. Further, they can be expected to ask how the effectiveness of a solution will be judged in practice; in effect, they are asking for a convincing evaluation plan. In addition, successful implementation of complex projects typically requires a parallel evaluation effort designed to guide midcourse corrections.

Provision of Adequate Resources and Incentives to Ensure Successful Implementation

Proposals are more likely to be adopted and implemented if it is clear that there will be enough resources and incentive to assure implementation. The main concern of many decision makers is whether the proposed changes involve tolerable costs and fit within the decision makers' budget constraints. Absent resources, proposals may still be adopted, but not implemented, as when Congress authorizes a program but does not appropriate funds for it. Sophisticated analysts are usually also attentive to the use of incentives to either facilitate or hinder effective policies during implementation. A winning proposal will provide evidence that it can supply incentives that will promote the desired change (Neustadt and May, 1986; Neustadt, 1990; Hoenack, 1991). For example, the supporters of metropolitan governance for the Minneapolis–St. Paul area could point out that the federal government was giving regional planning agencies review power over federal grants in their areas. Thus, the newly created regional council would have some ability to channel federal grant funds in accordance with its goals.

"Big Wins" and "Small Wins"

Proposal development is likely to present change advocates with a basic choice—namely, whether to go for a solve-the-problem-completely strategy and a "big win," or whether to go for an incremental approach to addressing the problem and a "small win." The choice is important, because of the crucial differences between big and small wins and what it takes to achieve them. Needless to say, small wins are more likely in a shared-power world than big wins. Still, big wins are not unknown. Witness the Civil Rights Acts of 1964 and 1965; Medicare legislation; the first landing of humans on the moon; California's Proposition 13; federally mandated deregulation of the transportation, banking, and savings and loan industries; and the collapse of the Berlin Wall and the subsequent reunification of Germany, and the formal dissolution of the USSR and the establishment of the Commonwealth of Independent States.

A big win is a demonstrable, completed, large-scale victory, usually accomplished in the face of substantial opposition. The creation of the European Economic Community (later the European Community) and the landing of astronauts on the moon were extraordinarily big wins in which big risks were taken and gigantic payoffs were achieved. Taking big risks, however, is perhaps more likely to result in big losses. Barbara Tuchman (1984) has documented some of humankind's more disastrous failures, from the Trojan War to the Vietnam War. History, it turns out, is fairly unforgiving. If you risk all and win, you are a great hero or heroine. If you risk all and lose, you are foolish, knavish, evil, or worse.

The fear of major losses is a key reason why most leaders shy away from attempting big changes. Instead, normal operating procedure for most organizations and organizational networks is "disjointed incrementalism" or "muddling through" (Lindblom, 1959). Incrementalism consists of small marginal adjustments to existing organizational budgets and arrangements. Each adjustment is a small win, or small loss. A small win—"a concrete, completed, implemented outcome of moderate importance" (Weick, 1984, p. 43)—rarely involves substantial risks. Unfortunately, the small adjustments are usually uninformed by any overall sense of direction and, indeed, often cancel one another out, as part of the partisan mutual adjustment among various stakeholder groups (Lindblom, 1965). Incrementalism and partisan mutual adjustment, in other words, form a two-edged sword. While they make big losses less likely, they also typically make big successes unattainable. Change advocates thus are presented with a strategic quandary. How can they work toward major changes without risking everything? Karl Marx offers some important advice with his observation that changes in degree lead to changes in kind. If a series of small wins can be informed by a sense of strategic direction, the small wins can add up to a big win over time. Often, therefore, the trick in achieving fundamental change is to go for it small step by small step (Quinn, 1980; Mintzberg, 1987).

Exhibit 8.1 summarizes the differences between changes in degree — small wins — and changes in kind — big wins. Changes in degree involve smooth, marginal progressions, in which the future is very much like the past. By contrast, changes in kind are abrupt, discontinuous, and transformational (Krieger, 1987). The ascendancy in the United Kingdom of Margaret Thatcher and the Conservative party in 1979, and in the United States of Ronald Reagan and the Republican party in 1981, marked moments of transformation. Though changes had been building up for many years, the assumption of power by conserva-

Exhibit 8.1. Changes in Degree Versus Changes in Kind.

Changes in Degree (Small Wins)	Changes in Kind (Big Wins)
Smooth, marginal, similar to past	Abrupt, discontinuous, transformational
Fixed background	Structural change
Existing coalitions, values	New coalitions, values
Quantitative models, little learning	Qualitative models, new images, new conceptualization
Small resource allocations, commitments	Major resource allocations, commitments
Little impact	Big impact
Management	Leadership, entrepreneurship, heroes and heroines

tives on both sides of the Atlantic marked the beginnings of abrupt transformations — changes in kind — for governmental organizations and other entities in both the United Kingdom and the United States.

Changes in degree assume, and are measured against, a fixed background. By contrast, changes in kind involve fundamental structural changes. The Economic Recovery Act of 1981 installed major changes in U.S. tax and spending policies at both federal and state levels. Changes in degree do not challenge existing coalitions or values, whereas changes in kind are built on new coalitions and values. The landslide victory of Lyndon Johnson and the Democrats in 1964 ushered in major changes in U.S. social policies, ranging from the Civil Rights Acts of 1964 and 1965 to the panoply of Great Society programs. Similarly, the landslide victories of Ronald Reagan in 1980 and 1984 resulted in the turning back of many of those same policies, major increases in defense spending, and a host of privatization moves. Without new coalitions and different values, neither set of changes would have occurred. Changes in degree involve little new learning and, therefore, are amenable to quantitative modeling, forecasting, and projection — activities that employ assumptions and data that are deeply tied to the past. The sheer number of givens that must be assumed makes it unlikely that a future which differs from the past can be created. By contrast, changes in kind involve qualitative models, new images, and new conceptualizations. The future is invented rather than predicted.

The need for new conceptualizations and learning when major changes are involved is highlighted by comparing the French and U.S. efforts to build the Panama Canal (McCullough, 1977). The French thought the construction of a canal through Panama would be a task similar to the one they faced in the Suez; namely, all they had to do was build a sea-level ditch and a few locks and that would be that. Not only were they wrong in that presumption, they didn't figure out how to handle yellow fever. Twenty thousand deaths later, the project, its finances, and the French government were a shambles. The U.S. group succeeded because they realized that a series of step-locks irrigated by the region's heavy rains would minimize the problem of landslides into the canal, one of the problems that had stymied the French effort to build a sea-level canal through a mountain range covered by unstable jungle soils. The U.S. group also succeeded because they learned that mosquitoes carried yellow fever but were unable to survive very long in direct sunlight. By cutting the dense jungle back a few hundred yards, they could keep the mosquitoes away from the construction crews. The Panama Canal could not have been built without this drastically altered view of the problems and their solutions.

Changes in degree typically involve small resource allocations and commitments, whereas changes in kind take major resource allocations and commitments. The Kennedy administration's decision in 1961 to place someone on the moon by the end of the decade would have been meaningless had the administration and the Congress not committed themselves and huge amounts of resources to the decision.

Finally, changes in degree have relatively little impact, and management is charged with promoting and overseeing them. In contrast, big changes typically have a big impact, leadership and entrepreneurship are needed to make them happen, and the change champions and overseers are thought of as heroes and heroines. Managers of small changes are given a pat on the back; leaders of big changes are given a standing ovation. Put differently, structures and systems are usually designed to produce only small changes, never big ones, regardless of the people involved. Therefore, real leadership is required to produce big changes, in large part because the systems and structures themselves must be changed (Selznick, 1957; Burns, 1978).

However, because big wins and changes are much more difficult to achieve than small wins, wise strategists should consider how a series of small wins might be organized around a strategic direction to achieve the same effect as a big win without the concomitant risks of big failure. A small-win strategy is often wise for additional reasons (Kouzes and Posner, 1987; Weick, 1984). Small wins break projects into doable steps, quickly make change "real," and preserve gains. They are cheap and reduce risks. They facilitate learning and adaptation by providing information and allowing for rapid error detection and correction. They release resource flows and human energy. And they involve and empower people, by encouraging participation, providing immediate rewards, and boosting people's confidence and commitment.

Small wins may be promoted in a number of ways (Kouzes and Posner, 1987). The most important element of a small-win strategy, of course, is the vision that guides it. Otherwise, the individual small wins are unlikely to add up to a major accomplishment. The vision does not have to be fully articulated, but it does have to provide enough direction for planning and decision making (Cleveland, 1973; McCaskey, 1974). An overall plan also is important. It should be vision driven, not technique driven, and should empower as many people as possible to improve commitment. It should break the change process down into manageable chunks, so that stakeholders and implementers are not paralyzed by the magnitude of needed changes, and so that interim success is possible. In other words, the planning process and plan should allow people to visualize the journey necessary to achieve the vision, and to break the journey down into short-term goals, objectives, events, and milestones. The achievement of each short-term marker represents a small win.

Continuous experimentation also should be encouraged. This allows leaders to invent the future as they go along, in response to new knowledge and changing circumstances. Pilot and demonstration projects permit frequent feedback and learning (Bryson and Delbecq, 1979; Bryson and Cullen, 1984). At the same time they make the future "real" through clarifying the connections between mental images, behavioral actions, and the consequences of those actions (Boal and Bryson, 1987). People should be encouraged to improvise on a general sense of direction (Cleveland, 1973) so that the likelihood of accomplishments, learning, and rewards is increased.

A small-win strategy works when it helps people say yes. Since small wins represent small gains, the costs of involvement for people are also small. The easiest way to reduce the cost of saying yes is to reduce the personal cost of failure. Rewards, not punishment, improve enrollment and foster commitment. Commitment flows from offering people choices and making those choices visible and relatively binding (Staw and Ross, 1978; Salancik, 1977). Publicizing choices is one way to commit people to them. Small wins then reinforce those choices and make more small wins likely.

Finally, leaders can promote small wins by relying on the natural diffusion of innovations rather than on forcing changes systemwide. Leaders should let the benefits of change sell themselves as much as possible, and allow learning and local adaptation to occur. As changes spread, the more they become the accepted pattern, until relatively complete diffusion is achieved.

Several implications emerge from our discussion of the nature of big wins and small wins. The principal implication, of course, is that often the simplest and most effective way to achieve a big win is to organize a series of small wins informed by a sense of strategic direction. Leaders should consider seriously the advantage of winning small — time after time — instead of trying to win big once. Second, if one accepts the virtues of small-win strategies, one should think big and act small. By itself, such behavior would represent a refreshing change for many public and nonprofit bodies where often the guiding principle seems to be either think small and act small, or else think small and act big. The former approach is pathetic, the latter foolish. Strategically directed small wins can add up to big wins over time and — compared to think-big, act-big strategies — may well be more likely to result in big wins.

Third, small-win strategies allow leadership and management to be linked effectively. High-ranking leaders often charge off in directions that are seriously at odds with what is manageable. They proclaim the need to achieve a big win without any idea of how to achieve it in practice. Sometimes disaster can be avoided, but not always. On the other hand, if a vision can be outlined and a series of small wins imagined that might realize the vision, leadership and management can be joined constructively. Finally, leadership is in part about exercising good judgment when deciding whether to seek a big win or to seek a series of small wins. A big-win strategy may be best when a small-win strategy is unworkable or undesirable for some reason. For example, Britain and France did not first try out a tiny tunnel across the English Channel. Instead they are building the "Chunnel" in what amounts to a single gesture. Big wins might also be pursued when the time is right — for example, when the need is obvious to a large coalition, the proposed solution will effectively address the problem, solution technology is clearly understood and readily available, resources are available, and there is a clear vision to guide the changes.

Twin Cities change advocates went after a big win when they proposed creation of a new level of government that would operate regional services. Incremental solutions had been tried to little avail, the appreciation of the need for a major reform embodying regional solutions to regional problems was widely shared, and a large coalition supported the change. Ultimately, the state legislature approved important elements of the proposal and left the door open to incremental changes that would add up to a big win over time. Those who set out to liberalize abortion laws in the 1960s were seeking a partial win in the overall campaign to give women more control over childbearing, but given the moral, political, and symbolic context in which they operated, this partial win loomed large for them, and for their opponents. Supporters got their big win with *Roe* v. *Wade*, but that victory has been eroded by a series of small defeats engineered by their opponents. These opponents have sought their own big win in the form of a human life amendment or a Supreme Court decision effectively overturning *Roe* v. *Wade*.

Leadership Guidelines

Typically, a great deal of care and attention is necessary to design proposals that stand a chance of adoption. The craft — and it is a craft — involves attention to the technical details and excellence of a proposal; but also, and probably more importantly, attention to the interpretive schemes, goals, concerns, and interests of key stakeholders. Simply being "right" about technical feasibility is not enough. Proposals must also connect with important audiences in ways that are understandable to those audiences and that they perceive to be in their self-interest. Said differently, the key to success in this phase is to focus on helping key decision makers say yes in the next phase when the proposal must be adopted. Leaders must remember that official decision makers must support the proposal or it is unlikely to be placed on the decision agendas and calendars of the relevant arenas.

They must also remember that the dynamics of this phase and the next phase are decidedly different. Usually, there is considerable informality and room for maneuver in this phase, while the opposite may be true in the next phase. Anything "wrong" with a proposal that reaches the proposal review and adoption phase probably will be used to kill it. So leaders are responsible for uncovering and fixing proposal flaws while the proposal is being drafted. Change advocates should consciously design and use forums and informal arenas to craft proposals that are likely to withstand the severe tests to which they will soon be put in formal policy-making arenas. The leadership guidelines for this fourth phase of the policy change cycle fall into the categories of development and review of the draft proposal, "softening up" and media strategies, and caveats.

Development and Review of the Draft Proposal

Decide Whether to Pursue a Big-Win or a Small-Win Strategy. In making this judgment, leaders must remember that a big win is likely to fail unless the need is obvious to a large coalition, there is a clear connection between perceived problems and proposed solutions, solution technology is clearly understood and readily available, resources are available, and there is a clear vision to guide the changes. Absent these conditions, a small-win strategy would appear to be the wiser course of action.

Analyze the Arenas That Will Be Important in the Next Phase. Leaders should ask, Which legislative committees are likely to review the proposal? What are the factions in each arenas and how might they view the proposal? Depending on the arena, will the mayor, the governor, or the president support the proposal? Are elections or appointments for the arena coming up? Can or should they be affected to make the political climate more favorable? Should change advocates attempt to alter hearing procedures or committee structures? The answers to such questions are important for shaping proposal content and for preparing the ground within relevant arenas. Effective leaders seek competent counsel from knowledgeable informants as they evaluate the arenas, recalling the CIA dictum that "one good informant is worth a thousand theories."

Draft a Proposal That Takes Seriously the Results of the Previous Phases. The early phases of the policy change process are designed to provide much of the information necessary to draft a winning policy proposal. The proposal should address the problem as formulated with a tailored set of solution components that are expected to work in the specific situations in which they will be applied. The interpretive schemes of key stakeholders must be kept in mind, along with any guidance leaders have received from the project coordinating committee and other advisors about how to tap into those schemes effectively. The proposal is being prepared for an audience whose capacity to hear and support what is being said must be carefully considered and used to advantage.

Winning proposals can take many different forms. Change advocates should seek advice from key informants about the most desirable form to use in the situation at hand. One possible format is:

- Title page
- Table of contents
- Executive summary
- The process
- Problem statement
- Key solution elements
- Alternative solution designs in more detail
- A summary of strengths and weaknesses of the different solutions

- Recommendations and rationales
- Budget materials
- Appendices, which may include the process in detail, who was involved and how, implementation guidance, and technical reports

The proposal can be drafted by the planning team, the coordinating committee, or a smaller team, which might include members from both groups.

Structure the Proposal Development Process So That Change Advocates Pay Careful Attention to the Goals, Concerns, and Interests of Key Stakeholders. An important way to do this is to provide informal review sessions for involved individuals or organizations. In easy situations, such sessions may be unnecessary, but in difficult ones, they are often crucial. The groups gathered for these sessions may be either homogeneous or heterogeneous. Homogeneous groups will provide a clear picture of their common views, while heterogeneous groups will reveal the views that recur even in disparate groups. In either case, an ideal group size is five to nine members, which allows each person enough "air time" for his or her views and yet also provides the planning team with a sense of the group's view and a sense of where individuals fit within the larger context. Larger groups can be broken down into five- to nine-member groups, whose work can be assembled and discussed in plenary sessions.

A normative process should be used to review and modify the draft proposal. As in the problem formulation phase, drafts are typically reviewed by planning team members; key decision makers—including the coordinating committee, if one is being used; relevant governing boards; and members of arenas that will decide whether or not to adopt the proposal—and other selected stakeholders. The review sessions focus on proposal strengths and the modifications that will improve on those strengths. A focus only on weaknesses helps no one, except those who wish to see no changes adopted. These review sessions can be organized in the same way as those discussed in Chapter Six. Good leaders make sure draft policies and plans are viewed as working documents, so that reviewers feel that the review process is authentic, not a charade. The idea that proposals are in draft form can be emphasized by presenting proposals in outline form; not over-editing the document; avoiding expensive graphics, packaging, and slick desktop publishing approaches; stamping "ROUGH DRAFT," or "DRAFT," on the cover page, the first page of each new chapter or section, or on the top of every page; using cheap paper and reproduction techniques; and verbally telling reviewers that the proposal is a draft and not the final product.

Accept As Many Modifications As Actually Improve the Draft Plan Technically, Politically, Legally, or Ethically. However, do not sacrifice key solution components. They are necessary to address the problem as formulated. If they are sacrificed, there may be little point in going ahead with the policy change process.

Leaders should expect proposal changes that result from unanticipated problems or opportunities brought to light by the review process. Policy change advocates should think of review sessions as helpful sources of new information and not get defensive but be open to proposal improvements. Recall the chapter epigraph from John Rollwagen, chief executive officer of the premier U.S. supercomputer company, Cray Research. Rollwagen stresses the importance of changing plans to fit changing circumstances. In a similar vein, Dwight D. Eisenhower said, "Plans are nothing; planning is everything."

Having said that, however, it is important to emphasize that proposals *do* matter. Constructing a strong political coalition requires persuading people to agree on a specific proposal. Coalition members do not have to agree on an overarching set of goals to be achieved, nor do they need to have many shared interests, nor do they have to agree on every item in the proposal. But they must see that it is in their interest to support adoption of the proposal. Leaders' acceptance of stakeholders' proposed modifications is a way of expanding coalition membership. Again, however, it is important to emphasize that only modifications that actually do improve the proposal should be accepted.

Monitor Opponents' Attempts to Develop Counterproposals, or to Gut the Proposal. If possible, leaders should include any good ideas from opponents' proposals in order to thwart the opponents' opportunities for coalition building and enhance the leaders' opportunities. Also, many interest groups may want to gut the proposal so that, even if it passes, it will have little effect. Interest groups, unlike elected officials, often pay careful attention to the operational details embedded in any proposal, because they know that policy is made as much during implementation as it is in adoption (Moe, 1988). Change advocates must exercise extreme care to assure that the modifications suggested by others do not render the proposal ineffective during implementation.

Additionally, interest groups often try to attach their favored solutions to public problems that others have placed on the public agenda (Kingdon, 1984). Leaders should make sure that the proposal developed with such effort not be replaced on the decision agenda in the next phase by some interest group's favored alternative, if that alternative is at odds with the original proposal. Continual coalition building efforts, and the attendant attentions of sponsors and champions, are the most important ways to prevent such a displacement.

Prepare a More Detailed and Formal Draft for Final Review in the Next Phase. Afer these informal review sessions, leaders must try to develop a draft that has as many characteristics of a winning proposal as are desirable in the context. Any person or group not wishing the proposed changes to be adopted, or wishing them to fail during implementation, will "favor" a proposal without many winning characteristics; and leaders must be on the alert for this tactic. The draft prepared at this stage should be one around which a winning coalition can organize. It should be able to avoid or withstand veto by elected chief executives and overcome other obstacles that may be placed in its path. Also, it should be able to withstand judicial review. It should not violate state or federal constitutions, and its intent and effects should be supported by the relevant courts' interpretations of previous laws.

In preparation for the next phase, the proposal has to be translated into a bill or other formal document for consideration by formal arenas. Arenas typically have legal staff who specialize in the preparation of bills or proposed ordinances. Change advocates should take advantage of this expertise, but they must also be sure to check final drafts to ensure that their formal language will realize the proposal's intent. When advocates of establishing regional governance in the Twin Cities began crafting a proposal — actually draft legislation — they wisely included as one of the drafters state representative William Frenzel, who could advise the proposal drafting team on what was likely to attract or repel his fellow legislators.

Explore Likely Sources for Funding and Other Resources. During this entire phase, leaders should be investigating funding possibilities in detail. A number of clues regarding existing or potential resources will have been identified in the previous phases; here, the resources are pursued in depth. In times of resource abundance, the search is not so crucial, but in times of resource scarcity — probably the typical circumstance — resource development will be a crucial component of this phase (Bryson and others, 1979).

Make Sure Budget Proposals Necessary to Implement Proposed Changes Are Prepared. This is essential if budget review and adoption must proceed through a process separate from policy development. Most policy proposals require at least some resources to implement. Proposal adoption without the authorization and appropriation of necessary resources is a hollow victory, although such a loss might be pursued as part of a strategy that aims to establish a principle that may be given real force later. Moreover, for many governments, budget documents represent their basic policy documents (Wildavsky, 1984; Anderson, 1990). For these governments, it is the inclusion of proposed changes in the budget documents, along with the necessary resources to implement the changes, that signals successful policy adoption.

"Softening Up" and Media Strategies

Use a "Softening-Up" Process to Convince Potential Coalition Members to Support a Big-Win Strategy. Big changes typically require major conceptual adjustments on the part of many stakeholders, and these take time (Sabatier, 1988, 1991). Thus, a strategy designed to open people to the possibility of change must be pursued. In fact, a softening-up process may be necessary for a small-win strategy, also. The general public, the immediate stakeholders, and interested professionals all may need to be softened up. The tools leaders can use in this process are studies, speeches, publicity, draft proposals, and other persuasive materials. In the case of changes at the national level, some observers argue that softening up may take two to six years before legislation implementing changes will be passed (Kingdon, 1984, p. 131).

As the advocates of establishing regional governance for the Twin Cities prepared to submit their proposal to the 1967 Minnesota legislature, they generated a flurry of reports and position papers that again emphasized the regional nature of particular problems and also demonstrated a growing consensus among stakeholder groups in favor of state legislation creating an elected council that would oversee an array of regional services. The major local newspapers gave considerable coverage and endorsement to the campaign. Ted Kolderie, as we already have noted, played an important dual role as a writer for the *Minneapolis Star Tribune* and a participant in strategy and bill-drafting sessions organized by the change advocates. John Finnegan, executive editor of the *St. Paul Dispatch and Pioneer Press,* not only was a former chair of the Metropolitan Planning Commission, but also chair of the MPC task force that developed proposals for commission restructuring during the Joint Program on Landuse and Transportation Planning.

Timing was important in building support for the metropolitan governance proposal. The Citizens League issued a major report in November 1966, and in the same month, the Upper Midwest Research and Development Council convened its metropolitan reorganization seminar accompanied by Ted

Kolderie's background report. Even as the 1967 legislative session got underway, MPC, the Citizens League, and the League of Minnesota Municipalities continued to generate reports and recommendations. This verbal tide, which had been building since the early 1960s, carried decision makers, opinion leaders, and public opinion to the conclusion that a regional governance mechanism must be established to address regional problems.

Abortion reform advocates used an array of softening-up strategies during the 1960s and early 1970s to build public support. They told stories about women who had died or been seriously injured by illegal abortions; they attracted media coverage for flouting restrictive abortion laws; they gave speeches. By the 1970s, women's groups were holding local and national demonstrations to demand abortion reform. They protested at public buildings, medical association conventions, and legislative hearings. Those who backed restrictive abortion laws held counterdemonstrations and used publications, presentations, billboards, films, and exhibits to press their basic contention that fetuses are a form of human life and as such deserve society's protection. Following the *Roe* v. *Wade* decision, March for Life was organized specifically to sponsor mass demonstrations on Capitol Hill each year on the decision's anniversary. Since 1973, right-to-life groups have kept their view of the abortion issue very much in the public eye as they pressed for adoption of their proposals in various arenas.

Develop the Best Media Strategy for This Phase. Leaders who have planned their media strategy well will balance the need to keep public momentum for change alive with the need for candid give-and-take in proposal development and revision sessions. The advocates of regional governance for the Minneapolis-St. Paul area achieved this balance by working on proposals in unpublicized committee meetings, while issuing public reports and organizing a public seminar. However, it may not always be possible to avoid news coverage of proposal development sessions, especially if the proposed policy change is highly controversial. Even this publicity can be helpful, however, particularly if it is provided by a knowledgeable reporter, and change advocates may find it beneficial to provide background sessions for reporters. Awareness that proposal drafting sessions may become public also gives change advocates an incentive to structure the sessions so that acrimony, threats, and rigid position taking are kept to a minimum. The general public also may feel more "in" on the process if at least some proposal development sessions are reported. However, advocates must be prepared to put a positive "spin" on any published reports that threaten successful proposal development.

Caveats

In Difficult Situations, Be Prepared to Create More Opportunity for Informal Review. In order to build a coalition and reach agreement, leaders may have to arrange wider participation, establish additional informal review bodies, allow more revision of draft policies and plans, give more careful attention to funder concerns and provisions, and repeat the review process with some participants.

If the Necessary Coalition Has Not Formed by the End of This Phase, Seriously Consider Cycling Back Through Previous Phases or Dropping the Project. The draft proposal review process should be designed to provide enough information to assess whether key decision makers will favor or oppose policy change. A specific stakeholder position-assessment matrix will be offered in the leadership guidelines in Chapter Nine. Its use in this phase may be advisable as well. The more openly and actively involved groups are solicited to participate in informal review sessions, the more difficult it will be for these groups to raise major objections later. However, leaders should recognize that involving implacable foes is unlikely to be productive. It simply gives them advance warning and more time to organize effective opposition. Wise judgment is called for in deciding when and to what extent various groups should be involved.

Change advocates may also decide at this point that they should press their proposal in the courts rather than in arenas, if it can be justified by principles and mandates that guide the courts. On the other hand, even change advocates who assess the courts as more favorable to their cause than the arenas may still present their proposal in arenas to fan public interest and accumulate gains that may influence the courts. Efforts to overturn restrictive abortion laws, for example, had limited success in state legislatures, but that success was important to the Supreme Court's decision in *Roe* v. *Wade*. The court was able to examine the experience of states that had reformed or repealed their abortion laws and to conclude that legal abortions were relatively safe for women.

Summary

In the fourth phase of the policy change cycle, advocates of change should prepare and review a policy proposal that is ready for formal review and adoption by key decision makers in the fifth phase. The proposal, therefore, should be a technically workable, politically acceptable, and legally and ethically defensible response to the public problem that prompted the policy change effort in the first place. Successful completion of the fourth phase results in a winning coalition that supports the proposed changes. Coalition members do not need to agree with every detail of the proposal, but they must be able to agree to support the proposal.

Chapter 9

Adopting
Public Policy Solutions

*Politics is winning and losing, which depend, mostly, on how
large and strong one side is relative to the other. The actions
of politics consist in making agreements to join people in alli-
ances and coalitions — hardly the stuff to release readers' adrena-
line as do seductions, quarrels, or chases.*

—William Riker

*Greater than the tread of mighty armies is an idea whose time
has come.*

—Victor Hugo

The purpose of the proposal review and adoption phase of the
policy change cycle is to gain an official decision to adopt and
proceed with the policy proposal developed and informally
reviewed in the previous phase. We will concentrate primarily
on legislative decision making, but much of what we have to
say is applicable to interorganizational and administrative decision making in all complex, shared-power situations.

This phase represents a culmination of much of the effort
expended in previous phases. The first four phases of the policy
change cycle, in other words, were designed to achieve an authoritative choice among policy options in this, the fifth phase,
so that the issue at hand can be addressed effectively during the
sixth phase, implementation.

As we have described earlier, the Minnesota legislature was presented with two policy options for metropolitan governance. One envisioned a "strong" Metropolitan Council, essentially a metropolitan service district governed by fifteen elected council members. The bill was introduced by Representative William Frenzel in the house and sponsored by Senator Harmon Ogdahl in the senate. The other policy option was a "weak" council, proposed in bills sponsored by Senator Gordon Rosenmeier and Representative Howard Albertson. This version of the Metropolitan Council would be governed by council members appointed by the governor and would only coordinate metropolitan services; existing regional service agencies would remain intact.

Backing the Frenzel bill was the coalition that had developed the momentum for instituting regional governance, along with Governor Harold LeVander and legislators from Minneapolis, St. Paul, and their first-ring suburbs. Outspoken opposition came from the publisher of a chain of suburban newspapers and a group called the Alliance of Minnesotans to Preserve Local Entities. Rosenmeier's bill tended to be backed by legislators from rural areas and the more far-flung Twin Cities suburbs. The break did not occur along party lines. Frenzel, Ogdahl, Albertson, Rosenmeier, and LeVander were all members of the Conservative party — Minnesota's version of the Republican party, at the time. Since Rosenmeier controlled the senate Civil Administration Committee, to which the council legislation was assigned, it was no surprise that the committee sent his bill to the full senate, which passed it. Supporters of a weak council also triumphed in the house. Both houses narrowly defeated amendments that would have made the council elective, but the final bill did include one feature from the Frenzel-Ogdahl versions — limited taxing power. The bill was signed into law, as the Metropolitan Council Act, by Governor LeVander on May 25, 1967.

Essentially, the act established a reorganized and more powerful Metropolitan Planning Commission, with authority to review long-term comprehensive plans of the various governmental units in the Twin Cities area if the plans had areawide effect, multicommunity effect, or substantial effect on metropolitan development. The new council also had the authority to suspend the plans of metropolitan agencies if those plans were inconsistent with the council's development guide. And the act directed the council to prepare reports and legislative recommendations on a number of recognized metropolitan problems. Although proponents of the strong council had gotten much less than they desired, they hailed the new council as an improvement over MPC and focused on opportunities for strengthening it during implementation. Although by the late 1960s the advocates of liberalizing U.S. abortion law had convinced fifteen state legislatures to enact bills based on the American Law Institute's model code, the new laws did not greatly improve women's access to abortion. Some laws made women go through an onerous approval process, and some physicians were cautious about performing abortions in an atmosphere of public controversy (Tribe, 1990). Dissatisfied with the reformed laws, many change advocates called upon state legislatures to repeal their abortion laws, and four states approved repeal in the early 1970s.

Those who opposed restrictive abortion laws also pressed their case in the courts. Here, their proposals took the form of legal briefs outlining constitutional grounds for overturning the laws. Between 1969 and 1973, the change advocates won several cases. The California Supreme Court ruled that California's law permitting abortions only to save a pregnant woman's life was unconstitutionally vague and violated privacy rights. A U.S. district court exonerated a physician for performing abortions in his office in violation of a Washington, D.C., law that permitted abortions only to preserve the life and health of a pregnant woman. Federal courts also struck down some abortion restrictions in Wisconsin, Texas, Georgia, Illinois, New Jersey, Connecticut, and Maryland. The abortion reformers also lost cases during this period. In Minnesota, Dr. Jane Hodgson, who was active in the reform movement, was convicted of performing a criminal abortion in her St. Paul clinic and sentenced to one year's unsupervised probation. The judge in the case ruled that Minnesota's abortion law was constitutional.

The U.S. Supreme Court took up the abortion issue when

it agreed to hear *Doe* v. *Bolton* and *Roe* v. *Wade.* The court's ruling on both cases, published January 23, 1973, combined elements of the proposals developed by the reform and repeal movements. In *Roe,* the court emphatically endorsed a woman's right
to choose abortion during the first trimester of pregnancy. That
right, the court declared, was an extension of the right to privacy
rooted in the First, Fourth, Fifth, Ninth, and Fourteenth Amendments to the U.S. Constitution. At the same time, a woman's
right to terminate her pregnancy was qualified by the state's (or
government's) interest in protecting both women's health and
potential human life. Thus the court would accept three types
of restrictions on abortion: requirements that abortions be performed only by licensed physicians; during the second trimester
of pregnancy, regulations designed to protect the mother's health;
and during the third trimester, regulations to protect the state's
interest in potential human life. In *Doe* v. *Bolton,* the court indicated it would not tolerate restrictions on abortions that did not
apply to other medical procedures. Justice Harry Blackmun,
writing for the majority in *Roe,* summed up the rationale for
the two decisions when he declared that the *Roe* decision was
"consistent with the relative weights of the respective interests
involved, with the lessons and examples of medical and legal
history, with the lenity of the common law, and with the demands of the profound problems of the present day."

Following the Supreme Court rulings, those who supported restrictive abortion laws sought to have their proposals
adopted by decision makers in legislative, executive, and administrative arenas at the local, state, and national levels. Several
of those proposals—largely aimed at testing the limits of acceptable regulation of abortion under *Roe* v. *Wade*—passed. For
example, the city council of Akron, Ohio, approved a multi-
faceted abortion ordinance in 1978. The law required, among
other things, that abortions after the first trimester be performed
in an acute-care hospital and that doctors inform women seeking abortions about fetal development and the possible consequences of abortion. Throughout the 1970s and into the mid
1980s, the Supreme Court tended to strike down such restrictions; but by the late 1980s, as President Reagan's appointees

assumed control of the court, more restrictions were allowed to stand.

In Congress the advocates of restrictive abortion laws pressed their proposals for a constitutional amendment overturning *Roe* v. *Wade* and for elimination of public funds for abortion services. Within weeks after *Roe* was decided, forty-one members of Congress had signed on as sponsors of constitutional amendments that either conferred "legal personhood" at conception or gave the states the right to regulate abortion (Jaffe, Lindheim, and Lee, 1981). Despite this initial support and despite continued reintroduction of the bills over many years, neither amendment passed. Proposals to eliminate federal funding of abortion services were far more successful. For example, beginning in 1976, Congress regularly approved strict limitations on Medicaid funding of abortions and, during the 1980s, began withholding federal funds from family-planning organizations that presented abortion as an option for women. By the early 1990s, advocates of restrictive abortion laws had had about as many of their proposals adopted as possible in various arenas and courts without the Supreme Court's outright reversal of *Roe* v. *Wade*. Such a reversal, however, seemed increasingly likely since President Bush's two appointments to the court had added to the court's conservative tenor. Only two justices were staunch supporters of women's right to choose abortion. The likeliest prospect for the 1990s was that the fight over current and proposed abortion laws would return to the state legislatures as the Supreme Court demonstrated more tolerance of abortion restrictions.

Desired Outcomes and Benefits of This Phase

In this phase, change advocates seek widely shared agreement with their proposal and a decision to adopt the proposal and proceed with its implementation. Additional desired outcomes are: provision of necessary guidance and resources for implementation; the support of those who can strongly affect implementation success; and a widely shared sense of excitement about the new policy and its implementation.

A number of benefits may result from the proposal review and adoption phase. First, if the coalition is large enough compared to the opposition, there will be widely shared agreement with the policy proposal. Second, a formal decision to adopt and proceed with the policy can be expected to follow. Third, the formal stamp of legitimacy on the proposed changes will give people the permission they need to move ahead with implementation. Further, those who wish to preserve the status quo will find themselves fighting a rearguard action as the burden of proof shifts from the initiators to the opposers of the change (Wilson, 1967). Fourth, once top-level decision makers are on record in favor of the proposed changes, they will find it difficult to change their positions.

A fifth major benefit is that formal proposal adoption proceedings may clarify further the specific change objectives and remove some bothersome uncertainties. On the other hand, because often legislation cannot be passed without deliberate ambiguity concerning change objectives (Lindblom, 1965), this benefit may not be achieved until the implementation phase. As a sixth benefit, change advocates and the coalition they have organized often experience heightened self-esteem and self-confidence based on hope, faith, hard work, and task accomplishment. Proposal adoption is a big victory.

A seventh benefit may result for those who have been involved, perhaps somewhat unwillingly, in the process of change. As support develops for policy changes, a kind of re-norming can be expected—that is, key actors move from an external toward an internal motive for change (Dalton, 1970). Assuming the proposal addresses a real public problem and is technically, politically, legally, and ethically acceptable, people may be expected to come to "own" the problem and solution, thus further assuring adoption and implementation. Such ownership is extremely important if people are to commit to changes and follow through on them (Eden and Sims, 1978; Mangham, 1986; Eden and Huxham, 1986).

A final benefit of this phase should be at best cordial, and at worst civil, relationships among change advocates, their opponents, decision makers, and decision makers' staff. These people are all likely to need to work with each other again on the same or different subjects. This benefit is an important reason for assuring that formal proposal review and adoption sessions proceed with minimal personal embarrassment and acrimony.

Coupling

For a proposal to be adopted, a problem must be recognized, a viable solution must be available, the political climate must be favorable, and the barriers to effective action must be down. There must be a "coupling," in other words, of problems, solutions, and politics (Kingdon, 1984, pp. 93, 173–204). Leaders of many kinds play the crucial role of entrepreneurs in both creating and taking advantage of circumstances to assure that the appropriate couplings occur. By the time the proposal review and adoption phase arrives, savvy policy entrepreneurs or champions already will have organized the nucleus of a strong coalition around the proposal. Gaining additional necessary members in this phase is likely to involve bargaining and negotiation, the gritty work of politics, in which concessions are given or "sweeteners" added in exchange for support. After we look at the ways coupling occurred in the metropolitan governance and abortion cases, we will discuss some specific devices and occasions for coupling solutions, politics, and actions — the bandwagon effect, softening up and signing up, and windows of opportunity.

In the metropolitan governance case, the supporters of a strong Metropolitan Council had organized a strong bipartisan coalition, and the political climate of the legislative arena was more favorable by 1967 than it had been just a few years before. Minnesota's version of both the Democratic and Republican parties supported the strong council, although the Republicans (called Conservatives) definitely took the lead. James Hetland, in his role as chair of the state Conservative platform committee in 1966, was critical to building that party's support. Moreover, as the result of a 1960 lawsuit filed by Twin Cities–area political leaders, the legislature had been forced to reapportion itself to give the Minneapolis–St. Paul suburbs fair representation. The clout of legislators from rural areas and from the central cities of Minneapolis and St. Paul was diminished. Rosenmeier was still considered the most powerful man in the senate, but he had to pay attention to his party's young Turks, such as Frenzel. Ogdahl even tried to undercut Rosenmeier's power further by calling for a new metropolitan affairs committee to handle legislation related to the Twin Cities area, but Rosenmeier forces thwarted the ploy. In sum, the political climate was not perfect for the strong-council advocates, but it was good enough for passage of the Rosenmeier-Albertson bills, which constituted a compromise between a strong council and the status quo.

In the abortion controversy, effective coupling has been more difficult to achieve or sustain. The coalition supporting abortion reform probably reached its peak in the early 1970s, but the political climate in state legislatures tended to remain unfavorable, partly because of all-out resistance by the countervailing coalition and partly because many legislators were unsympathetic to women's demands for increased rights. As we have seen, abortion reformers ultimately were more successful in the federal courts because political coalitions have less impact on judges and because reproductive rights claims resonated with judicial interpretations of the U.S. Constitution as guaranteeing a personal right of privacy.

As fetal rights supporters attempted to undermine women's rights established by *Roe* v. *Wade,* they built a formidable coalition, including the National Committee for a Human Life Amendment (organized by Catholic bishops), March for Life, the National Right to Life Committee, the Prolife Nonviolent Action Project, the Right to Life Crusade, state "right-to-life" organizations, and by the early 1980s, the powerful Moral Majority, itself an alliance of fundamentalist protestants and "New Right" politicians. Despite a strong coalition, however, "right-to-life" groups were fighting a rearguard action in local, state, and national areas. They could win passage of proposals that nibbled at the edges of *Roe* v. *Wade,* and they could reduce public funding for abortion services, but they had to contend with the formidable power of the basic principles enunciated in *Roe* and with a general reluctance to tamper with the Constitution. Moreover, in the post-*Roe* years, the court of public opinion began to shift strongly in favor of women's right to choose abortion.

In order to make the political climate more favorable to their position, those who advocated a return to strict abortion laws set out to elect "pro-life" and "pro-family" politicians wherever possible. The 1980 campaign was their highpoint, bringing Ronald Reagan, a staunch opponent of abortion rights, to the Presidency and producing a Congress far more conservative than its predecessor (Paige, 1983). By the late 1980s and early 1990s, however, the political climate had shifted again. By then, the advocates of liberal abortion laws had also focused their organizational energies on the electoral process, the Moral Majority had dissipated, the public tended to favor retaining the rights granted by *Roe,* and the increasingly conservative tenor of the Supreme Court put supporters of women's rights on battle alert.

The "Bandwagon Effect"

Ultimately, effective policy entrepreneurs may spark a "bandwagon effect," in which people join the coalition out of fear that they will be excluded from the tangible or intangible rewards of participation in a winning coalition (Kingdon, 1984, p. 148; Benveniste, 1989, pp. 130–155). Leaders always should be alert to opportunities for creating this effect, because — to the extent that it designates the proposal as "an idea whose time has come" — it makes proposal adoption easier. A powerful bandwagon effect can make a proposal virtually unstoppable. Creation of a bandwagon effect is particularly important for a major policy change, which is unlikely to occur without strong, and sometimes overwhelming, support. However, the bandwagon effect must be used to advantage promptly, for, as Kingdon (1984, p. 178) notes, "The really big steps are taken quickly or not at all." Since there are so many ways by which crafty opponents can delay adoption of otherwise winning proposals, it is almost always best to push decisions that involve sure victories to a quick conclusion (Riker, 1986). Benveniste (1989) notes that in addition to facilitating proposal adoption, a bandwagon, or multiplier, effect can do the following:

- Provide a bottom-up source of legitimacy, which can make it easier for leaders to say yes to the changes.
- Increase the power that can be used for implementation by increasing the number of committed people. Individuals thus may adapt to change without having to be ordered to do so.
- Decrease the level of uncertainty about the future, because a consensus has been generated about what should be done.
- Reduce conflict, thus increasing the capability of organizations and societies to adapt and change peacefully.

Softening Up and "Signing Up"

The softening-up process described in Chapter Eight prepares the ground for building a substantial coalition and creating the bandwagon effect. Softening up, however, is different from "signing up." Softening up involves opening people to the idea of policy change; signing up involves finding or formulating specific inducements that will gain the support of specific stakeholders. However, both softening-up arguments and signing-up inducements must be geared to their targets' interpretive schemes, values, and interests, because people will choose whether or not to support changes in terms of what is best according to their own lights. As Neustadt (1990, p. 38) observes: "Those who share in governing this country frequently appear to act as though they were in business for themselves. So, in a real though not entire sense, they are and have to be. . . . When they are responsible to many masters and when an event or policy turns loyalty against loyalty—a day-to-day occurrence in the nature of the case—one must assume that those who have the duties to perform will choose the terms of reconciliation. This is the essence of personal responsibility. When their own duties pull in opposite directions, who else but they can choose what they will do?"

The signing-up process often involves an interesting twist on the normal notion of costs and benefits. As the overall cost, or "price," of a proposal goes up, so, too, may support for the proposal. As Kingdon (1984, p. 145) argues, "For a politician the costs are the benefits," because usually the higher the cost to the public of a proposal, the more tangible and intangible benefits a politician can deliver to his or her constituents. In particular, as we showed when describing client politics, if the actual costs can be widely dispersed while the benefits can be concentrated on particular groups, the result is virtually a "no-lose" proposition for the politician.

Development of legislative support for a proposal requires cultivating networks that can effectively push for proposal adoption. As a starting point, leaders should remember that decisions in legislatures are often based on very little information. It is wise to assume that time is short and that legislators have never read *anything* pertaining to any bill other than ones they have introduced. Leaders should also assume that legislators are not interested in any bill unless it relates directly to something they care about — for example, getting reelected, getting their own program through, or setting up a useful relationship. Further, leaders should remember that debate on the legislative floor rarely sways votes. Thus, relationships, including friendships and political connections, are enormously important; legislators look to these relationships and the messages conveyed through them for cues about how to vote. Change advocates must find ways to cultivate these networks and relationships; a supportive elected chief executive, such as a governor or mayor, can help activate these networks.

Solicitation of legislative support can be straightforward or indirect (Beverly Stein, personal communication, 1990). A legislator typically seeks support from another legislator by direct appeal — "Here is a bill I'm supporting, and here is why." Because time is short, simply making the appeal says the support seeker cares about the other legislator. The potential support giver will often say, "Give me more information." The support seeker then can send the information directly or spur the potential support giver's friends and constituents to call or write. In this way, legislators establish or reinforce relationships with one another, however weak, and support seekers have the opportunity to draw on relationships that matter to potential support givers.

If the desired support is gained, so, too, is a debt; the support giver will expect reciprocation. The result is called "logrolling," which is "a way of gaining support from those who are indifferent to or have little interest in a matter, [and which] usually encompasses a straightforward mutual exchange of support on two different topics" (Anderson, 1990, p. 128). Pork-barrel legislation is the classic example, in which legislators vote for each other's home district projects so that everyone can "bring home the bacon."

Explicit vote trading is likely to take place out of the public eye. For one thing, explicit vote trading is often illegal in formal arenas. For another, it is time-consuming and, therefore, unlikely to occur in a full legislature. For yet another, the process of discovery and consideration necessary to find items worth trading involves discussions legislators may not wish their constituents to know about. Thus, in U.S. legislatures, vote trading typically occurs in committees, especially during "markup" sessions, in which final bills are drafted and which, except in Congress, are usually closed to the public. Even in Congress, however, a determined committee chair can find ways to exclude the press and others (Reid, 1980). Riker (1986, p. 90) describes the process of writing final bills as "the successive discovery of themes or formulations that satisfy every element of a winning coalition." He goes on to note: "Naturally some of the themes are contradictory in spirit: What satisfies group A harms group B, and what satisfies B harms A. Yet, in a well-written bill, both A and B are on balance satisfied because each has been satisfied by desired themes more than harmed by undesired ones. This is, of course, what vote-trading consists of; and it is, to a considerable degree, the informality and privacy of the markup that make the literary effort successful."

Vote trading is likely to involve side payments or compromise. Anderson (1990, p. 128) defines "side payments" as "rewards offered to prospective supporters or coalition members that are not directly related to the decision at hand, or at least its main provisions, but are valued for other reasons." Examples include "committee assignments, allocation of office space, campaign assistance, and support for members 'pet' bills as a means of securing their support." "Compromise," on the other hand, involves explicit bargaining over a single issue, in which the bargainers each agree to give up something they value in exchange for support for something else they value. Each agrees, in other words, that "half a loaf is better than none" (Anderson, 1990, p. 29).

As a result of vote trading, the press of time, and the numerous details that must be addressed in major legislation, the actual legislation passed can bear little resemblance to wise public policy. As Otto von Bismarck allegedly said, "There are two things one should never see made — sausage and legislation." Therefore, leaders must be attentive to overall legislative strategy and the details of its execution; otherwise, the solutions developed in the forums of the previous phases can be lost in the legislative arena. Leaders also must not forget the desirability of finding "all-gain" solutions, in which all sides get what they want. Logrolling and side payments can help, which means leaders must find or develop a stock of items that can be traded. Careful attention to the stakeholder analyses that we have emphasized as a means of uncovering and fulfilling key stakeholder hopes and expectations is useful here, and further help can come from an ongoing proposal review process.

In sum, leaders must be both wise and creative in formulating arguments and inducements to give politicians reasons to say yes. They should cultivate relationships with and among legislators or other key decision makers, and then supply the sympathetic ones with research data, public opinion surveys, and moral and practical arguments through written and oral testimony, conversation, and printed materials. Advocates also should be continuously alert to finding, inventing, or trading options for mutual gain. Similarly, when resort to the courts is part of the change strategy, advocates should help judges say yes in light of the judges' interpretive schemes, values, and interests. Much of this argumentation can be included in the briefs submitted to the courts by the main parties to a case, or by "friends of the court," usually experts or groups that support one of the parties. Additionally, the main parties often have the opportunity to present this argumentation orally. Persuasive arguments also might include possible trades for mutual gain among the parties to the dispute.

Windows of Opportunity

A window of opportunity is a time span or occasion when action favoring change is possible. We believe there are three kinds of windows (see also Kingdon, 1984) — those opened by the emergence of pressing problems, those opened by important political shifts, and those opened by reaching decision points — times when official bodies are authorized and empowered to act. In the policy change cycle, all three types are important; problems and solutions must come together at a decision point where the politics are favorable for the desired policy changes.

A coalition organized around a policy proposal will go nowhere unless it finds or creates decision points at which to push, and ultimately adopt, the proposal. Some decision points are predictable, while others are not. Predictable decision points include those tied to regular reports and addresses, such as State of the Union, State of the State, or state of the community or interorganizational network addresses; the annual or biennial budget cycle of governments, organizations, and interorganizational networks; and the renewal of specific pieces of legislation. Unpredictable decision points can arise from crises, sudden changes in official leadership or public opinion, or unexpected opportunities. The coalition and the proposal must be ready in all major respects prior to the decision point. A major purpose of the initial agreement phase was to define the network likely to form the basis of this coalition and to map out likely decision points in advance so that the full-blown coalition and a specific, viable proposal would be ready for adoption at a specific time.

Heresthetics

Even if problems, solutions, and politics are coupled, it is still possible to lose during formal adoption sessions to shrewd opponents who find ways to split the coalition or to use the formal decision-making rules of the relevant arena to defeat what otherwise would be a "sure" winner. This is where a knowledge of "heresthetics" — the name Riker (1986) gives to "the art of political manipulation" — is essential. The roots of the word are Greek and mean "choosing" and "electing." Heresthetics is clearly aimed at winning rather than losing, and "the essential heresthetical skill consists of transforming an unfavorable situation into a favorable one" (p. 94). Opponents can be expected to take advantage of any rules, resources, and transformation relations at their disposal to defeat changes, while change advocates must develop defenses against any likely heresthetic attacks.

According to Riker, there are three components of political manipulation — agenda control, strategic voting, and manipulation of dimensions. Agenda control is a basic design element of arenas. It is the determination of which items, proposals, options, or amendments will come up for consideration by official decision-making bodies at which time, and it is exercised principally by positional leaders such as committee chairs. In its most powerful form, it can defeat what is, on paper, a certain winner, purely for procedural reasons. In the metropolitan governance case, Senator Rosenmeier had considerable control over what would be considered and approved by the Civil Administration Committee, and thereby, he also partially controlled the agenda of the entire legislature. To take just one example from the abortion controversy, in the years just after *Roe* v. *Wade,* the U.S. Senate Judiciary Committee's Subcommittee on the Separation of Powers was chaired by a staunch "right-to-life" senator named John East. East used his control of his subcommittee's agenda and of those invited to testify before the committee to conduct extensive, highly visible, and favorably biased hearings on his bill declaring that human life begins at conception (Paige, 1983).

Strategic voting is, in some ways, the reverse of agenda control. "For the most part, the formal leadership of the decision making body controls the agenda. . . . But individual members, whether leaders or not, control their own votes. Given an agenda, they can sometimes win by appropriate use of their vote resource" (Riker, 1986, p. 149). Strategic voting often takes the form of "voting contrary to one's immediate tastes in order to obtain an advantage in the long run" (p. 78).

Manipulation of the dimensions of an issue is the third major component of heresthetics. Manipulations may include increasing, decreasing, or fixing the dimensions of an issue. Riker uses the example of Abraham Lincoln in the 1958 Lincoln-Douglas debate at Freeport, Illinois, as his premier example of how changing an issue's dimensions can alter the basis of winning coalitions (Riker, 1986). By introducing the question of whether new territories could decide to exclude slavery, Lincoln, in effect, forced Douglas to say that they could, which improved Illinois Senator Douglas's chances of reelection by Northern Democrats in 1858. However, by saying yes, he also alienated himself from Southern Democrats and reduced his chances for the Democratic presidential nomination in 1860.

Lincoln thus increased his own chances of winning the presidency on the Republican ticket in 1860 by splitting the traditional Democratic majority, while furthering the Republican strategy of forging a new majority out of parts of the Whig and Democratic parties. As Riker (1986, p. 6) points out, "the traditional platforms" had been "agrarian expansionism (Democratic and majority) and commercial expansionism (Whig and minority), [therefore,] the Republican combination of commerce and free soil [a principle of allowing new territories to exclude slavery] attracted the Northern Whigs (a large majority of that party) and a substantial proportion of Northern Democrats, so that Republicans had, first, a plurality and, by 1868, a big majority in the nation." The new coalition of commercial expansionism tied to free soil, which was a kind of agrarian expansionism, dominated the American national scene until Franklin Roosevelt forged a new and winning Democratic coalition in 1932.

Riker argues that manipulation of dimensions probably is the most frequently used heresthetical device, because "dimensions can always be used to upset an equilibrium, provided the heresthetician is clever enough to find the correct dimensions to use" (Riker, 1986, p. 150). He goes on to argue, drawing again on the example of the Republican party under Lincoln, that "most of the great shifts in political life result from introducing a new dimension" (p. 151). Like Lincoln's method at Freeport, the heresthetician's method consists primarily of "inventing sentences," and only secondarily of "simple exploitation of the rules" (p. 103).

For example, abortion reform advocates moved from an initial focus on women's health and unwanted pregnancies to the inclusion of abortion under a broader women's rights umbrella that covered a host of efforts to improve women's social and economic status. This heresthetic move broadened the reform coalition but also placed a cap on its potential size, limiting the prospects for a long-lasting victory. The prospects were limited because the opponents of reform made an equally powerful heresthetic move; they expanded the dimensions of the abortion debate to include the state's traditional role in protecting human life. At the same time, they accomplished what Riker calls "fixing" the dimensions of the issue — that is, they accepted no alteration of their definition of the issue. They also transformed politicians' stands on abortion into a litmus test for supporting or opposing the politicians' election. For abortion reformers to achieve a long-lasting victory, they may need to return — as some are now doing — to the initial dimensions of the issue as the basis for their organizing efforts. Organizing along the former lines of preventing unwanted pregnancies and protecting women's health while sustaining legal abortion may neutralize the effectiveness of opponents' organizing strategies.

Dimensions often are manipulated to achieve one of three aims. The first aim is breaking up an otherwise winning coalition, as Lincoln did at Freeport. The other two aims are reducing or expanding the range of conflict. In general, sharply reducing conflicts favors organized interests, because restricted conflicts play out in political subsystems, where the organized are likely to dominate the unorganized, especially those who are not even aware of the conflict. As Kingdon (1984, p. 49) notes, "When the public isn't that involved in [an issue], you have to deal with the vested interests. The lower the partisanship, ideological cast and campaign visibility of the issues in the policy domain, the greater the importance of interest groups." Interest group domination is quite frequent because, as Neustadt (1990, p. 82) observes, "One never should underestimate the public's power to ignore, to acquiesce, and to forget, especially when the proceedings seem incalculable or remote from private life." In contrast, expanding conflicts offers improved prospects for the weak and relatively unorganized, as well as for greater consideration of the broader public interest, because of increased media attention to the circumstances of the affected parties and their advocates (Lipsky, 1968). Further, as Schattschneider (1975, p. 73) notes, "Broad public interests are likely to receive fullest consideration at the macro-political level"—again, because of media attention and because political leaders are wary of the electoral consequences of any public policies that directly hurt the weak and unorganized.

In sum, leaders must be attentive to advocates' and opponents' opportunities for agenda control, strategic voting, and control of issues' dimensions, if they are to obtain passage of their favored policy proposals. The goal of heresthetics "is to structure the decision-making situation to the speaker's advantage and the respondent's disadvantage" (Riker, 1986, p. 8). Change advocates will need to be on guard and they must maintain "the ability to shift from moment to moment, poking and pushing the world until it favors [their] cause" (Riker, 1986 p. 51).

It is important, too, to remember that some arenas can be overruled by arenas higher in the government hierarchy or by arenas such as popular referenda. This may prompt change advocates who lose in local arenas to try a state arena if conditions there are more favorable. Or change advocates may seek congressional help in order to pass new state laws. As we have seen earlier, federal funding incentives helped persuade Minnesota legislators to establish the Metropolitan Council.

The Role of Courts

Action in arenas also can be overruled by courts. Throughout this phase, as in the previous phase, leaders must be sure that changes in the proposal increase its ability to stand up under the court's scrutiny. In some cases, administrative courts are extremely important, since they will oversee and review the development and application of rules and regulations designed to implement the proposed policy. Policy advocates may even go so far as to try to change the composition of the courts, an explicit strategy of presidents as diverse as Franklin Roosevelt, Richard Nixon, Ronald Reagan, and George Bush.

Inaction in arenas likewise can be remedied by courts. Change advocates who are defeated in arenas can win, under certain circumstances, in the courts. The campaign to liberalize abortion laws is a case in point. Reform advocates were stymied in many state legislatures and Congress, but they were able to remedy legislative inaction by successfully challenging existing abortion laws in court. They could do so, however, only because it was possible to couch the challenge in constitutional terms and because the court of public opinion was shifting in favor of reform. Additionally, the reformers' success in some state legislatures gave the courts evidence that access to legal abortion would reduce the numbers of women who were seriously injured or killed by abortions.

Courts can also affect the operation of arenas — for example, by adjudicating the boundaries of new election districts. If change advocates know that redistricting will affect their efforts, they may need to be active in helping shape redistricting plans that will pass both legislative and judicial muster. Alternatively, they may need to decide whether the existing or redistricted arena will be more favorable to their proposal and adjust their timetable for introducing the proposal accordingly.

Courts, however, have their limits for making policy changes. Usually, they do not attempt to implement the changes they have mandated. *Roe* v. *Wade* and *Doe* v. *Bolton,* for example, outlined the framework for women's right to choose abortion and struck down two states' abortion laws. It was then up to state legislatures, Congress, and even local governments whether to repeal their old laws, pass new ones, or simply stop enforcing the existing laws. As it turned out, all of these options were pursued (Tribe, 1990). Meanwhile, Congress fought over whether or not to try to overrule the Supreme Court with a proposed constitutional amendment. State legislatures and Congress also wrangled over whether a woman's right to choose abortion meant that public funds should be used to guarantee that poor women would have access to abortion, or even information about abortion.

Finally, it is important to remember that the formal U.S. court system is hierarchical. Change advocates who win at one level, can lose on appeal to a higher court; conversely they can lose in a lower court and win on appeal. Leaders may have to be prepared to fight their cases all the way to the U.S. Supreme Court, as the abortion reform advocates were.

Leadership Guidelines

The design and use of arenas gains prominence in this phase, as the policy change previously discussed mainly in forums is addressed in formal decision-making arenas. The design and use of courts also may be important. As already noted, one key to success in this phase is careful attention to the informal review process in the previous phase. Development of a proposal that attends to the key stakeholders' interests can help assure the proposal's placement on the formal agenda of government or of a large, complex organization. Finding or creating inducements to be traded for support also can be quite important. But, as this chapter should have made clear, there are any number of ways to defeat good ideas in arenas. Success in this phase can depend as much or more on public leaders' ability to negotiate the intricacies of formal arenas as on the value of the ideas embodied in the proposal.

Leaders ought to reconnoiter the relevant arenas, their rules and resources, and the actors they will encounter there. When entering legislative arenas, they should seek competent advice and counsel ahead of time and from more than one source. The legislative process can be extremely complex, particularly when the arenas are bicameral state legislatures or the U.S. Congress. When an arena comprises two houses, passage of the proposal must be gained in both houses, and then the bill must be signed into law by the governor or president. Competent advisers can suggest which of the committees that could handle the proposal is likely to be most favorable. They might even suggest waiting until a new committee structure is in place or new legislators are elected. When a proposal must clear a large number of committees, along with numerous procedural, technical, and timing hurdles, a determined opposition often can kill it easily. Nonetheless, with a strong policy entrepreneur and the backing of one or more highly placed elected officials, miracles sometimes can be accomplished even in the face of major foes (for example, Reid, 1980). A quick overview of the congressional legislative process can be found in an appendix to each issue of *The Congressional Quarterly Almanac.* Far more detailed and helpful advice can be found in Wise (1991). Many states publish useful guidebooks to their legislatures and executive branches, and chapters of the League of Women Voters often prepare detailed explanations of local and state government structures and processes.

When entering executive and administrative arenas or the courts, it is also important to seek competent advice and counsel — again, from more than one source. Different ideas, rules, modes, media, methods, and resources will be present in each, and advance intelligence gathering improves the prospects for a successful outcome. It is essential for leaders to do their homework. They can use written materials — for example, Perry (1989), Wilson (1989), Rainey (1991), Garner (1991), O'Connell (1985), O'Neill (1987), Houle (1989), Susskind and Cruikshank (1987), and Gray (1989). But they should also talk to knowledgeables with firsthand experience, if at all possible. Again, the CIA's advice pertains — one good informant can be worth a thousand theories.

Political and sometimes judicial leadership are vital in this phase. The following guidelines — aimed at making sure everything comes together at the right time in the right place — will be helpful as leaders move a proposal from more informal settings to formal arenas and possibly courts.

Building Support

Continue to Pay Attention to the Goals, Concerns, and Interests of All Key Stakeholders. Key stakeholders will vary from situation to situation, but in any event, stakeholder categories are likely to include top-level elected or appointed leaders and decision makers; heads and managers of important implementing organizations; technical, professional, and interest group opinion leaders; representatives of key constituent groups; and funding sources. Since many key stakeholders are likely to be "strangers" (Heclo, 1977), leaders must place these individuals and organizations in the appropriate historical and personal contexts. Leaders must create sophisticated stereotypes so that they are better able to attend to stakeholders' interests and construct persuasive arguments to deal with the stakeholders (Neustadt and May, 1986), either directly or through networks important to them.

Use a Simple Matrix to Assess the Nature of Supporting and Opposing Coalitions. Nutt and Backoff (1992, p. 191) have designed an especially useful two-dimensional matrix. One dimension indicates how important the stakeholder is to proposal adoption and implementation; the other dimension indicates how supportive of the proposal the stakeholder is (see Figure 9.1).

The location of each stakeholder is mapped onto the matrix, and lines are drawn around existing or potential coalitions of support and opposition. As a consequence, strategies can be developed to build the coalition in support and to neutralize or break down the coalition in opposition, and arguments and inducements likely to work in favor of adoption can be developed and evaluated. (More detail on how to use this matrix is presented in Resource E.)

Identify One or More Policy Sponsors and Policy Champions to Gain Passage in Legislative and Administrative Arenas. Leaders must find official sponsors of proposed legislation in order to begin the legislative process. But formal sponsorship is not enough. Someone, preferably a legislator, must champion the proposal and do the educating, networking, and bargaining and negotiation likely to be necessary to gain adoption of the policy proposal. Key decision makers or opinion leaders must play similar roles in administrative arenas. Placing the most important stakeholders in their historical and personal contexts, mapping the stakeholders as outlined in Figure 9.1, and simply observing and interviewing stakeholders can indicate likely and effective champions and sponsors.

Figure 9.1. Interpreting the Stakeholder.

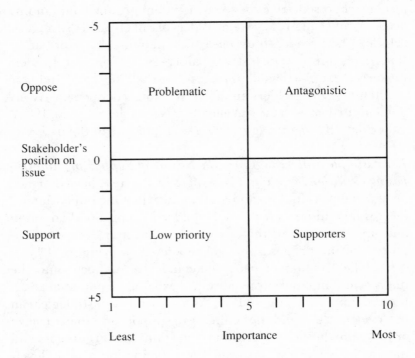

        Source: Adapted from Nutt and Backoff (1992, p. 191). Reprinted by permission.

Reduce Decision-Maker Uncertainty About the Policy Proposal.
Decision makers may not be competent in the area the proposal
addresses and may seek assurances that they are making a good
decision by approving the proposal. Leaders can help decision
makers view a proposal positively by emphasizing the proposal's
compatibility with affected parties' goals, providing persuasive
reassurances about the proposal's technical quality, and providing
reassurances that the proposal comes from competent sources.
Leaders can also ask key supporters — for example, coordinating committee members — to do behind-the-scenes work as well
as make formal presentations. These people are often prominent and influential, with extensive networks and high credibility, and they can effectively marshal support for the proposal.

Develop Arguments and Counterarguments in Support of the Proposal Prior to Formal Review Sessions. While bargaining and negotiation may predominate in this phase, persuasion still matters. Leaders cannot be successful bargainers or negotiators without the ability to develop persuasive arguments. They must be able to articulate the logic of the proposal in ways that are convincing to key decision makers and stakeholders — or that, at least, buy their neutrality — or the proposal will go nowhere (Dunn, 1982; Goldstein, 1984; Throgmorton, 1991). It is particularly important to provide persuasive outlines of the benefits of proposal adoption to various stakeholder groups and to constituencies important to the official decision makers, and to indicate that attendant costs are reasonable. As mentioned earlier, it is also critical to be able to argue against opponents' efforts to change the dimensions of the issue. In the courts, arguments must show how the proposed change accords with, or indeed is required by, judicial principles and previous court decisions.

Seek Agenda Control and Strategic Voting That Favor the Proposal. Agenda control is principally the province of an arena's positional leaders, so they must be "on board" and must give the proposal priority. It also may be possible to end run the agenda-control system. For example, U.S. Representative Henry Hyde knew that most of the committees that would normally consider abortion legislation in the U.S. House of Representatives during the 1970s were chaired by people who opposed restrictive abortion laws. In order to improve the chances of his campaign against Medicaid funding of abortions, he bypassed the committees and introduced proposals as amendments to appropriations bills. Change advocates should also assess the impacts of alternative voting procedures on the proposal's prospects, so they can guard against strategic voting that might defeat an otherwise winning proposal.

Engage Formal Review Bodies in Structured Review Sessions That Focus on Proposal Strengths, Weaknesses, and Modifications. The process is much the same as that described in Chapter Eight.

Again, leaders must be prepared to accept all modifications that actually improve the plan's technical, political, and legal and ethical acceptability, remembering that elected politicians favor proposals and changes that satisfy their constituents, avoid highly controversial issues, enhance their reputations and reelection prospects, and achieve their concept of good public policy (Kingdon, 1984). Further, politicians are likely to vote in a direction consistent with the balance of opinion among their key stakeholders (Kingdon, 1981).

Change advocates can use the formal review process to gain endorsements of the proposed changes prior to the formal adoption session. These endorsements can be added to those gained in the previous phases. This evidence of support can assure decision makers that they are probably on safe ground if they vote for, or sign off on, the proposed changes. For the formal review, change advocates should seek one or more medium-size (five- to nine-member) review bodies, preferably with a history of constructive interaction and open communication patterns. Lacking such a history, the review bodies may require training sessions in effective group communication, problem solving, and conflict management. Larger bodies may experience considerable difficulty in reaching decisions; however, there may be no alternative to a larger group. On the other hand, larger groups such as legislative bodies typically rely on subcommittees to perform much of the work. Except in unusual circumstances, full committees and the full house may be expected to defer to subcommittee judgments (Polsby, 1975).

Remember That Much of the Policy Adoption Process Involves Individuals and Interest Groups Who Explicitly Want the Proposed Policies to Fail (Moe, 1988). These opponents often focus on the details of proposed changes, especially when passage appears likely. They know that policy intentions can be made to fail during implementation through tampering with the details during adoption. Change advocates thus must assess the potential impacts of all suggested modifications, since even small changes can have big impacts. Changes that will limit the proposed policy's effectiveness should be accepted only if absolutely necessary.

For example, effective implementation of the equal employment opportunity provisions of the Civil Rights Act of 1964 was delayed for years through restrictions on the powers of the prime implementing agency, the Equal Employment Opportunity Commission (EEOC). The act had been passed over strong opposition, and only after a number of changes designed to limit its effectiveness were incorporated. The EEOC was required to rely on various voluntary methods to assure compliance, which made it difficult for the EEOC to bring civil suits against alleged discriminators. Further, "the EEOC could not act on complaints from the states in which there was an antidiscrimination law and an agency to enforce it, unless the state agency was unable to complete action within sixty days. Complaints had to be filed 'in writing and under oath,' which is not a customary requirement for a law violation complaint. This stipulation undoubtedly had a chilling effect on many southern blacks as well as others. Whatever the intent behind these provisions, they clearly limited the effectiveness of the law by making the successful completion of cases a slow, tedious process" (Anderson, 1990, p. 195).

Be Prepared to Bargain and Negotiate Over Proposal Features, or Other Issues, in Exchange for Political Support. Even proposals that seem to have no opposition, such as those aimed at the elimination of child abuse, may provoke arguments over resources and the locus of responsibility for implementation. More typical, however, are "position issues," which "do not elicit a single response but instead engender alternative and sometimes highly conflictual responses" (Nelson, 1984, p. 27).

Bargaining and negotiation are particularly likely to predominate if formal adoption must take place in a legislative body. In this setting, there may be many people whose votes are needed who do not particularly care about the proposal. They may be willing, however, to support a proposal they care little about in exchange for support for one they do care about. In addition, more substantive negotiations may be necessary in order to develop a proposal that provides enough benefits to key actors to overcome the costs imposed on those actors. Finding or inventing options that can promote agreement is a key leadership activity (Susskind and Cruikshank, 1987). The price of the last vote necessary for proposal adoption may be the highest, since the voter may know that without this support the entire proposal will go down to defeat (Riker, 1962). Change advocates thus may be willing to offer a great deal in exchange for this support. However, negotiators must make sure that concessions granted in exchange for support do not sacrifice key solution components; otherwise, the proposal may pass, but be gutted of any substance. On the other hand, if a bandwagon effect occurs, relatively costless support may be gained, as latecomers seek to avoid exclusion from the benefits of proposal adoption.

Work to Achieve a Powerful Bandwagon Effect in Favor of the Proposal at Minimum Cost to the Proposal's Substance and to the Public. As noted, the bandwagon effect can make adoption of the policy proposal virtually unstoppable. The effect often arises from the bargaining and negotiation aimed at building support. Once this support reaches a certain threshold, it becomes obvious to participants that policy change is likely. This is when the bandwagon effect takes hold — when a future that is different from the present gains credibility and certainty. As the effect grows, participants often "alter their behavior and responses. They will either pick preferences that have a higher probability of happening or fashion new preferences that fit their image of the future" (Benveniste, 1989, p. 130). A powerful bandwagon effect will create overwhelming support for policy change, and can even overcome hardened opposition.

      The bandwagon effect is likely to result from increased perceptions of the credibility and certainty of policy adoption, and these perceptions, in turn, are likely to increase as a consequence of three kinds of knowledge: knowledge of the technical feasibility of the proposed changes, knowledge of extensive support for the changes among key stakeholders, and knowledge of the degree to which authoritative decision makers specifically support the changes (Benveniste, 1989, p. 141). Change advocates can work to increase and publicize all three kinds of knowledge, and thereby enhance any potential bandwagon effect. Indeed, the policy change cycle phases to this point have been designed to enhance the possibility of a strong bandwagon effect. The effect should be planned to peak at the proposal adoption decision point. If it peaks too soon, enthusiasm may wane, and change opponents will gain an opening. If it peaks too late, the positive impact on proposal adoption may be lost.

Provide a "Public" Announcement of the Reworked Proposal, at Least Within the Affected System. This announcement may occur either before or after formal adoption of the proposal, depending on the circumstances. A public announcement prior to adoption may be a trial balloon to determine whether a sufficiently large supportive coalition has been formed. Or it may be designed to soften up decision makers at the same time that it solidifies or expands the coalition, perhaps triggering a powerful bandwagon effect. A pre-adoption announcement, however, may also allow an opposing coalition time to form. A post-adoption announcement may be a valuable way to inform relevant stakeholders how things have changed and to prepare for implementation.

Use a Two-Pronged Media Strategy in This Phase. First, change advocates may need to keep the issue alive in the pertinent media in order to demonstrate to policy makers that the public is paying attention. Sometimes change advocates organize public rallies or other events to keep the media focused on their issue during this phase. Second, change advocates often need to publicly communicate what is happening to their proposal as it proceeds through the legislative meat grinder. They must maintain good press contacts so that they can immediately signal to the public when their proposal is being advanced, or gutted, in the legislative process. Attention to the media strategy is required in part by the public's capacity for *in*attention.

When the Time Is Right, Press for Formal Adoption of the Proposal by the Appropriate Arena. The time is right when the coalition is as large as it can be; the proposal is politically acceptable, technically workable, and legally and ethically defensible; and a decision point is at hand.

Decide Whether to Ask the Courts to Intervene by Ruling on the Proposal Itself or by Changing the Arena. Generally, the courts can intervene directly in an arena only if the arena's structure or process violates laws or constitutional principles. Change advocates may also decide to test their proposal in court if there are constitutional or other legal grounds for a judicial ruling favoring the proposal.

Guidance and Support for Implementation

Obtain Necessary Resource Commitments, If at All Possible, Prior to the Formal Adoption Session. Gain commitments from formal decision makers and key implementers for, for example, key personnel, additional staff, training costs, conversion costs, technical assistance, and resources to meet unforeseen contingencies.

Remember That Incentives Must Run in the Proper Direction for Effective Implementation. If implementers see that they can benefit from policy implementation, they are more likely to facilitate it than if they see it as a kind of punishment (Hoenack, 1991). Placing potential implementers in their historical context, noting important trajectories, details, and change points, is one way both to choose preferred implementers and to fashion incentives that will be positive motivators rather than punishments (Neustadt and May, 1986).

Know the Six Conditions That Are Likely to Be Sufficient for Effective Implementation of a Policy That Represents a Substantial Departure from the Status Quo. Mazmanian and Sabatier (1983) believe the goals of this kind of policy are more likely to be achieved if:

- The enabling legislation or other legal directive outlines clear and consistent policy objectives or criteria for resolving goal conflicts.
- The legislation incorporates a sound theory of what is needed to achieve the policy objective and gives implementing offi-

cials sufficient jurisdiction over target groups and other factors likely to affect success. (In this regard, see the discussion of forward and backward mapping in Chapter Ten.)

- The legislation structures the implementation process to favor success — for example, by assigning the change to supportive and capable agencies, establishing supportive decision rules, and providing adequate resources.
- Key officials possess the necessary managerial and political skills and are committed to achieving the goals.
- A coalition of key supporters — including important legislators or chief executives — actively supports the implementation process, and the courts are either supportive or neutral.
- New priorities or conflicting policies do not emerge, and underlying social conditions do not change, to weaken the policy's political support or underlying causal theory.

Obviously change advocates cannot control many of these conditions. But they can keep them in mind as guidelines to follow when developing their proposals and shepherding them through the adoption process.

View the Policy Adoption Process as an Exercise in Potential Regime Building. Efforts expended during this phase and the previous phases to construct a regime are likely to pay off in terms of enduring, positive policy changes. The larger the supportive coalition leaders can build, the more widely they can share the interpretive schemes used to frame the problem and its solution, and the more they can design incentives for implementers that actually reward implementation, the more likely it is that a strong and self-sustaining regime of principles, norms, rules, expectations, and decision-making procedures will be established that will *institutionalize* the policy changes during the implementation phase.

In the metropolitan governance case, the underpinnings of a new regime were in place by the end of this phase. The enabling legislation established the Metropolitan Council with specific mandates and authorities in relation to local governments and regional service agencies in the Minneapolis–St. Paul area, it connected the council with the governor and the legislature and both specified and implied their roles and responsibilities, and it established the council's guiding principle as the "orderly and economic development" of the metropolitan area. A large coalition remained not only interested in the council but also intent on making it as strong as possible within the legislated conditions.

Caveats

In Difficult Situations, Consider Using Outside Pressure Groups. The pressure of outside groups may be brought to bear either directly, through lobbying efforts in which third-party concerns and preferences are communicated along with a sense of the size and strength of third-party groups (Ziegler and Baer, 1969; Smucker, 1991), or indirectly, through media reports of third-party concerns and protests (Lipsky, 1968). Recall Kingdon's (1984, p. 49) observation that when the public is not very involved in an issue, vested interests are likely to be particularly prominent. And the public isn't likely to be much involved when an issue's campaign visibility is low because partisanship and ideological clashes are low. The use of outside pressure groups must be approached cautiously, however, as the tactic may backfire. For example, the high-handed ways in which the National Rifle Association has tried to browbeat legislators have begun to backfire in many cities and states and in the Congress. Similarly, the "right-to-life" groups' attacks on politicians who have deviated a whit from the groups' position have aroused resistance among some legislators who had been sympathetic to the "right-to-life" view.

Avoid Unwelcome Surprises at the Formal Adoption Session. The rich network of interactions and effective staff work begun during the initial agreement phase and extended in subsequent phases should provide an effective "early warning system" that eliminates unwelcome news during formal consideration of the proposal. Further, the systematic review process in both this and the previous phase should uncover any troublesome concerns in advance.

Remember That Any System Can Usually Handle Any Number of Specific, Routine Items at a Given Time, but Few Nonroutine Items. If the change advocates' proposal represents a major change, there cannot be too many other items on the formal agenda, or there will not be enough decision-maker attention to go around, and successful policy adoption will become unlikely. Timing matters a great deal when it comes to major changes, and it takes time to prepare a system to consider, adopt, and implement major changes (Kingdon, 1984; Bardach, 1987). An important leadership task may be to keep other items off the agenda or to hold the policy proposal back until a more propitious time.

Be Aware That Some Proposals Must Fail at Least Once Before They Pass. In difficult situations, initial failures are particularly likely — and may be even necessary as part of the social learning process that occurs in all systems. The failures can provide occasions to expand and educate key constituencies about the importance and magnitude of the public problems that are being addressed. In addition, the failures can prepare these constituencies — soften them up — for acceptance of solutions that might initially be distasteful. For example, metropolitan governance proposals failed in the 1961, 1963, and 1965 Minnesota legislatures before the Metropolitan Council was created by the 1967 legislature. By that time, the problems the council was to address had become so pressing, and the coalition in support so strong, that passage was assured. But the need to discuss specific legislative proposals over the course of many years probably was a necessary feature of such a major change in metropolitan governance.

Remember There Are Times When It Is Worthwhile to Lose on the Size and Substance of Changes in Exchange for the Establishment of Some Principle That Will Set a Useful Precedent. New principles may lead to standard operating procedures in the future whose effects will outweigh present losses. For example, by any reasonable cost-benefit calculation, the construction of a new lock and dam on the Mississippi River near Alton, Illinois, in the late 1970s was a loser. Nonetheless, a coalition of supportive barge and river interests made passage of the construction project almost a foregone conclusion. In exchange for support for the project, however, Senator Pete Domenici (R-N.M.) and his allies, who included President Jimmy Carter, were able to extract a new principle designed to govern federal water-traffic projects in the future — namely, that, for the first time, the users of those facilities would be expected to bear a share of the costs in direct proportion to their use of the facilities. Water traffic would no longer be "free," for all intents and purposes, to the barge industry, and a more economically rational and just approach to making decisions on water-traffic projects would be put in place (Reid, 1980). As another example, although advocates of an elected metropolitan council to operate Twin Cities regional services failed to enact key aspects of their proposal, a weaker version of the council was established. However, the council was not as weak as it appeared. Considerable potential for impact was contained in the council's authority to review and suspend long-term comprehensive plans of regional governmental units and to study and make recommendations to the legislature on key regional issues. The council would use these authorized activities to greatly expand its control over metropolitan development and public services.

New principles may also break up some existing coalitions and establish the basis for new ones. In this way, a new principle can change the dimensions of an issue. Recall, for example, the way Lincoln built a winning Republican coalition by introducing the question of territorial choice on whether or not to allow slavery. Whigs and Northern Democrats were able to rally around the issues of commercial expansion and free soil, breaking up the old Democratic majority coalition. New principles may also spill over to adjacent fields. For example, the moves to deregulate the airline, trucking, and railroad industries under President Jimmy Carter built on each other and spread rapidly to banking and telecommunications as well (Hammond and Knott, 1988; Quirk, 1988). Now the deregulation initiative is spreading to public education, as "open enrollment" and "choice" plans are breaking the traditional monopoly public schools had on the education of children within their jurisdiction. Similarly, moves to privatize one kind of service lead to efforts to privatize others (Kolderie, 1986). Thus, leaders may need to decide whether to concede a principle in order to gain the specifics they want; or whether to get a principle established in exchange for giving up the specifics they seek.

When a Policy Change Process Is Well Designed and Pursued and the Policy Still Fails to Be Adopted, Consider the Following Possibilities:

- The time is not yet right.
- The draft policies, plans, or programs are inadequate or inappropriate.
- The problems or needs the proposal purports to address simply are not that "real" or pressing.
- The system cannot handle the magnitude of the proposed changes, and designs need to be scaled back.
- The proposal should be taken to another arena or to a court.

In Difficult Situations, Be Prepared for This Phase to Culminate in the Third Major Decision Point. The first major decision point probably occurred when the initial agreement was forged. The second probably occurred when agreement was reached on what problem should be addressed. In this phase, a solution is formally adopted that addresses the problem and sets the stage for implementation. In the easiest situations, this phase probably will result in the first — and perhaps only — major decision point.

Summary

Formal proposal review and adoption moves the policy change process from forums to arenas and sometimes to courts. However, even when the focus is on arenas, the courts must be kept in mind, because adopted changes are often challenged in the courts. Somehow, the move must be engineered so that official decision makers can say yes to the proposed changes as comfortably as possible. They will be able to do so to the extent they can be assured that the goals, concerns, and interests of all key stakeholders are addressed by a proposal that is technically workable, politically acceptable, and legally and ethically defensible. Such a proposal is likely to be supported by a large and strong coalition that not only can ease adoption of the change, but protect it during implementation. Timing matters in that a public problem and solution must be coupled with supportive politics at a decision point where problems, solutions, and politics can be joined.

A supportive coalition organizes around the idea of doing something about an important public problem with a policy proposal that coalition members can support. Gaining that support will require forging agreements through the standard fare of politics — persuasion, bargaining, negotiation, logrolling, vote trading, and compromise. An apparently winning coalition never is assured victory, however, since agenda control, strategic voting, and manipulation of the issue's dimensions are always options open to shrewd, determined opponents. Public leaders must not only organize and maintain the supportive coalition, they must also always watch out for threats to the coalition's continuation.

Chapter 10

Implementing
New Policies and Plans

You give an order around here and if you can figure out what happens to it after that, you're a better person than I am.
— Harry S. Truman

You can tell how many good ideas the Americans have had because they have built an organization around each one.
— Alexis de Tocqueville

Write the vision and make it plain, that they may run who read it.

— Habakkuk 2:2

The purpose of the implementation phase of the policy change cycle is to incorporate the adopted changes throughout the relevant system. New policies, plans, programs, or projects do not implement themselves automatically, nor necessarily as their authors intend. Instead, implementation, or the operationalization of change, typically is a complex and messy process involving many actors and organizations that have a host of complementary, competing, and often contradictory goals and interests (Goggin and others, 1990). Numerous professionals, technicians, and frontline practitioners will be involved. Thus, the frustration evident in the chapter epigraph from Harry Truman should not be particularly surprising. Indeed, some observers argue that we should *expect* new policies to fail (Pressman and Wildavsky, 1973). While that pessimistic assessment is overdrawn, and there are many successfully implemented policies, successful implementation certainly cannot be assumed (Goggin and others, 1990). Instead, it must be planned, facilitated, and evaluated.

Implementation of major changes requires creation of a new regime to govern decision making and behavior. Earlier we noted that the regime concept is taken from the field of international relations, but clearly applies to development of effective shared-power arrangements in many, if not most, policy fields. In order to develop the shared set of implicit or explicit expectations that regimes embody, public leaders should emphasize several features of regime construction. These include designing and using forums, arenas, and courts and developing supportive coalitions and practices in such a way that implementation outcomes, while not directly controlled, will still effectively address the public problems of concern and satisfy key stakeholders.

The previous stages of the policy change cycle were designed to facilitate development of a new regime. The organization of a winning coalition around a shared sense of public problems and desired solutions, and the development of a specific, agreed-upon and workable, acceptable, and defensible proposal constitute the new regime's basis. The coalition and the new regime are organized—to expand on de Tocqueville's language in the chapter epigraph—around a set of good ideas. It is the worth, application, and institutionalization of these ideas during implementation that mainly will determine the success of adopted policy changes.

Usually the arenas that adopt policy changes mandate their implementation, either by issuing directives to existing organizations or public agencies or by creating new agencies responsible for subsequent implementation actions. The creation of the Metropolitan Council exemplified this mandated approach. In other cases, the formal arenas or courts only remove barriers to policy change, and change advocates are left with the task of implementation. Once *Roe* v. *Wade* was decided, for example, advocates of women's right to choose abortion soon realized that, if the decision was to mean anything in practice, women had to have access to safe, widely available, and affordable abortion procedures across the country. The challenge at one level was to motivate and coordinate people throughout the United States who could organize local services. At a second level, the challenge was to pressure policy makers in formal arenas and courts to provide funding for poor women who sought abortion. The effort at the first level was spearheaded by Planned Parenthood and the National Association for the Repeal of Abortion Laws and was successful, at least in urban areas. The effort to use public funds, however, generally met with failure.

This is a phase in which some change advocates or policy entrepreneurs become implementers, but many simply go on to the next item on their agenda or become political guardians or monitors of the change. In the Metropolitan Council case, several leading advocates of regional governance made the switch from advocate to implementer when they were appointed to the council. One of their number, James Hetland, was even the council's first chair. Some leaders of Minnesota's abortion rights campaign became implementers, but others retained their advocacy role. Robert McCoy, for example, became director of an abortion clinic, but Betty Benjamin stayed with Minnesotans Organized for the Repeal of Abortion Laws, renamed the Minnesota Abortion Rights Council after *Roe* v. *Wade*.

Desired Outcomes

The most important outcome leaders should aim for in this phase is reasonably smooth and rapid introduction of the adopted changes throughout the relevant system. The ease and speed of the introduction, of course, depends on the nature of the changes. Implementing the Metropolitan Council legislation was clearly more complicated than constructing a new building, for example, in that it involved establishing a new regime in a broad geographic and substantive field. The new regime, mostly established between 1967 and the early 1980s, consisted of a new set of forums, arenas, and courts — including the council and its staff, new regional operating commissions and their staffs, legal and political relationships, and a new set of norms and practices throughout the complex shared-power metropolitan area. The implementation process was understandably lengthy. Appropriately, it was viewed as an exercise in institution building by the council's first chair and his key staff people.

Implementation of liberalized abortion policies typically has been even more difficult, because the advocates of change bore the burden of making a woman's right to choose meaningful in the country's numerous political jurisdictions. Moreover, they faced a significant and impassioned opposition that has focused on legislative and judicial processes as well as on direct action such as pickets and sit-ins at abortion clinics and has sometimes resorted to violence. Abortion clinics have been vandalized and firebombed, and their staff and clients harrassed. When "right-to-life" groups succeeded in cutting off federal Medicaid funding for most abortions, they could count on the funds drying up, but only until the next round of congressional budget decisions. They, too, knew that whatever gains they made would continue to be challenged by a determined opposition.

Regardless of the extent and complexity of the actual policy being implemented, a second desired outcome of this phase is the adoption of the changes by all relevant organizations or persons. Typically, a repertoire of strategies and tactics is necessary in order to bring all relevant entities on board (Kaufman, 1986; Elmore, 1982; Chase, 1979). A third outcome is the use of a "debugging" process to identify and fix difficulties that almost inevitably arise as a new solution is put in place. Leaders should recall that well-known administrative adage Murphy's Law: Anything that can go wrong will go wrong. And they should also recall the quip that Murphy was an optimist! The earlier phases were designed to help assure that the proposal as adopted would not contain any major flaws, but it is almost inconceivable that some important difficulties will not arise as big ideas are put into practice. As described earlier, a conscious formative evaluation process is needed to help implementers identify obstacles and steer over, around, under, or through them to achieve policy goals during the early stages of implementation (Scriven, 1967; Bryson and Cullen, 1984; Patton, 1986).

Fourth, successful implementation also includes summative evaluation (Scriven, 1967) — to assure that policy goals actually are achieved. Summative evaluations often differentiate between outputs and outcomes. Outputs are the actual actions, behaviors, products, services, or other direct consequences produced by the policy changes. Outcomes are the larger meanings attached to those outputs. Outputs, in other words, are substantive changes, while outcomes are symbolic interpretations. Both are important in determining whether a policy change has been worth the expenditure of time and effort (Levy, Meltsner, and Wildavsky, 1974). Summative evaluations may be expensive and time-consuming. Further, they are vulnerable to sabotage or attack on political, technical, legal, or ethical grounds. Nonetheless, without such evaluations it is very difficult to know whether, and in precisely what ways, things are "better" as a result of implemented changes.

For example, studies covering the ten years following *Roe* v. *Wade* showed that ten to fifteen million U.S. women had obtained abortions during the period, most of them legal (Hardisty, 1982; Banaszynski, 1983), and that deaths from illegal abortions occurred much less frequently (Hardisty, 1982). On the other hand, studies also revealed that poor or rural women had limited access to abortion services. Moreover, unwanted pregnancies continued unabated. In a report from the Alan Guttmacher Institute, U.S. women reported more than three million unintended pregnancies — about half ending in abortion — each year (Ory, Forrest, and Lincoln, 1983). Such statistics provided evidence that women were gaining access to safe abortions. At the same time, they raised the concern of change advocates for whom an important goal was prevention of unwanted pregnancies.

A fifth desired oucome is the assurance that important features of the policy design are maintained during implementation. The design may have been constructed to address particular problems in desirable ways, but as situations change, implementation can become a kind of "moving target" (Wittrock and deLeon, 1986). It is conceivable that design distortions during implementation can do a better job of addressing the problems than would the design as embodied in the proposal. It is more likely, however, that design distortions will subvert avowed policy aims and gut their intent, as has happened at times with affirmative action policies.

Sixth, the new regime that is established should include the elements that will lead to long-lasting changes: new or redesigned forums, arenas, and courts; the establishment of implicit or explicit principles, norms, rules, decision-making procedures, and incentives; the stabilization of altered patterns of behaviors and attitudes; and the continuation or creation of a coalition of implementers, advocates, and supportive interest groups who favor the changes. The new regime also may feature a widely shared "vision of success" that outlines what the world will look like if the purpose of the adopted changes are achieved and implementation strategies fully effected. Regime construction is not easy and, therefore, will not happen unless the changes clearly are seen to be "worth it" by relevant implementers. A variety of new or redesigned settings that allow the use of a range of tools, techniques, and positive and negative sanctions or incentives may be necessary in order to shape behaviors and attitudes in desired directions.

The last desired outcome is the establishment or anticipation of review points during which policy maintenance, succession, or termination can be considered. The policy change cycle is a series of loops, not a straight line. Politics, problems, and desired solutions often change (Kingdon, 1984). There are no once-and-for-all solutions, only temporary victories. Change advocates must be alert to the nature and sources of possible challenges to implemented solutions, and they should work for maintenance of still-desirable policies; replacement with better ones, when possible or necessary; and termination of completely outmoded ones.

Benefits of the Process

A number of important benefits flow from effective implementation. Obviously, the first is successful goal achievement in which real problems are addressed smoothly and rapidly. The second benefit is in many ways the reverse of the first — namely, the avoidance of the typical causes of failure. These causes are legion, but include the following (Chase, 1979; Wolman, 1981; Elmore, 1982; Kingdon, 1984; Morris and Hough, 1986; Goggin and others, 1990; Hoenack, 1991):

- Resistance based on attitudes and beliefs that are incompatible with desired changes; sometimes these attitudes and beliefs stem simply from the resisters' not having participated in policy development.
- Personnel problems such as inadequate numbers, overcommitment to other activities, inadequate orientation or training, poorly designed incentives, or people's uncertainty that involvement with implementation can help their careers.
- Incentives poorly designed to induce desired behavior on the part of implementing organizations.
- Implementing organizations' preexisting commitment of resources to other priorities, and a consequent absence of uncommitted resources to facilitate new activities; in other words, there is little "slack" (Cyert and March, 1963).
- Communication problems.
- The absence of administrative support services.
- The absence of rules, resources, and settings for resolving implementation problems — that is, the absence of forums, arenas, or courts to facilitate identification and resolution of these problems.
- The emergence of new political, economic, or administrative priorities.

A third significant benefit is increased support for, and legitimacy of, the leaders and organizations that have successfully advocated and implemented the changes (Bryson and Kelley, 1981). Real public problems and needs have been identified and effectively addressed. That is what public leadership is all about. In addition, leaders who advocate and implement desired changes may well become more secure in their leadership positions. Their formal or informal contracts may be extended. They may receive pay raises or other perks. Further, since organizations are externally justified by what they do to address basic social or political problems or needs, the advocating organizations should experience enhanced legitimacy and support (Bryson, 1988b).

Fourth, individuals involved in effective implementation of changes are likely to experience heightened self-esteem and self-confidence (Dalton, 1970). If a person has done a good job of addressing real needs, it is hard for him or her *not* to feel good about it. Professionals, in particular, derive a considerable portion of their work-related self-esteem and self-confidence from doing a good job. Effective implementation thus can produce extremely important "psychic income" for those involved. Recall Winston Churchill's comment, "We make a living by what we earn; we make a life by what we give." Finally, organizations that effectively implement policies are likely to enhance their capacities for action in the future. They acquire an expanded repertoire of knowledge, experience, tools, and techniques and, therefore, are better positioned to undertake and adapt to future changes.

"Forward Mapping" and "Backward Mapping"

There are two contrasting approaches to implementation planning, which Elmore (1982) calls "forward mapping" and "backward mapping." Forward mapping is the rational planning model described in Chapter One. A forward mapping process "begins at the top of the process, with as clear a statement as possible of the policymaker's intent, and proceeds through a sequence of increasingly more specific steps to define what is expected of implementers at each level. At the bottom of the process, one states, again with as much precision as possible, what a satisfactory outcome would be, measured in terms of the original statement of intent" (Elmore, 1982, p. 19).

There is a sound logic to forward mapping, and certainly, there are situations in which it makes sense. However, the major difficulty with forward mapping is "its implicit and unquestioned assumption that *policymakers control the organizational, political, and technological processes that affect implementation*" (Elmore, 1982, p. 20). Clear lines of hierarchical authority and accountability are assumed. Forward mapping thus can be problematic in a shared-power, no-one-in-charge world, where leaders and managers have only influence — not control — over the various implementation processes, and where much of what happens during implementation "cannot be explained by the intentions and directions of policymakers" (Elmore, 1982, p. 20) because it has very little to do with their intentions, and a great deal to do with the implementers' intentions and incentives. Forward mapping is also embodied in the "top-down" approach to implementation research, which focuses on variables controlled by central governments to the exclusion or underemphasis of other factors (for example, Mazmanian and Sabatier, 1981, 1983; Hogwood and Gunn, 1984). The difficulties with this approach are twofold. First, a great deal is left unexplained. And second, advice based on this approach may be impractical, because much of what accounts for implementation outcomes is not controllable by central governments (Goggin and others, 1990).

An alternative approach is backward mapping, which begins not at the "top" of the implementation process but at the very "bottom," with "a statement of the specific behavior at the lowest level of the implementation process that generates the need for a policy" (Elmore, 1982, p. 21). Backward mapping is similar to the "bottom-up" approach to implementation research, which begins at the "street level" and explores the interactions that develop there around a policy problem (for example, Lipsky, 1980; Barrett and Fudge, 1981) — although unfortunately this approach tends to ignore or underemphasize what occurs at higher levels (Goggin and others, 1990). Careful problem formulation efforts — of the sort emphasized in Chapter Six — facilitate preparation of this statement that is focused on specific behavior on the ground that merits policy changes. Next, planners formulate an objective consisting of possible organizational actions at the lowest level that are likely to result in desired changes in behavior, or effects, that would minimize the problem. A careful solution search process should underpin preparation of such an objective. Once the objective is formulated, planners go backward up the actual or possible structure of implementing agencies and ask two questions at each level: what is the ability of this unit to affect the behavior that is the target of policy changes?

What rules, resources, and transformation relations, broadly defined, does this unit need to create the desired effect?

Once these questions are answered, the final stage in the exercise is the formulation of a set of policies that direct or provide the necessary rules and resources to the units that are likely to have the greatest effects. Further, the exercise must involve explicit consideration of the design and use of new or existing forums, arenas, and courts likely to produce and protect desired changes. The source of the greatest effect, in other words, will be actors in forums, arenas, and courts—particularly those closest to the actual behaviors that are the source of the public problems—so those settings and the kind of behavior leaders seek to influence within them must be given careful thought. Effective backward mapping can be seen in the efforts of abortion reform advocates. Women in appalling numbers were suffering severe injury, including death, as a result of illegal abortions performed by unqualified people in unsanitary conditions. Therefore, the most immediate change objective was to assure that abortions were performed by qualified people in sanitary settings. Accomplishing this objective for large numbers of women required the procedure's legalization.

Backward mapping, like forward mapping, is concerned with what policy makers can do to produce desirable change. Backward mapping, however, does not assume that policy makers are the major influence on the behavior of implementers or on the subjects of implementation. Nor does it assume that the appropriate measure of success is the policy makers' intentions; rather, it assumes that the appropriate measure is a reasonable estimate of what can be done in shared-power situations to influence change. The evaluation of public leaders' actions is thus less idealistic and more realistic. The logic of backward mapping should be kept in mind during the earlier problem formulation and search for solution phases. If it is not, and only forward mapping is used, the policies developed and adopted are less likely to alter behavior on the ground in directions that effectively address the public problems that provoked the policy changes in the first place.

We must emphasize, however, that forward mapping and

backward mapping are not antithetical. Indeed, planners should use both. Once they have worked backward, revealing the desired behaviors at the lowest level and the chain of influence linkages that may produce that behavior, the results of the analysis can be written up in a "forward" fashion, as if they had followed that model. This allows them to recheck and elaborate the reasoning behind implementation plans, as they travel back down the influence chain. Planners and leaders must not make the same mistake that an advocate of the bottom-up approach to implementation research and an advocate of the top-down approach make when each downplays the fraction of variance in implementation success accounted for by the other approach, and when each tends to ignore what the two approaches have in common. Both approaches have something to offer and should be considered by change advocates as they attempt to design, facilitate, and institutionalize lasting policy changes (Goggin and others, 1990). Furthermore, the bottom-up approach may be helpful even when the policies to be implemented were developed in an exclusively forward, or otherwise impractical, way. Even in these situations, there often is enough flexibility available to implementers to justify a backward-mapping exercise designed to reveal practical ways to bring about change — often through the creative design and use of forums, arenas, and courts.

Visions of Success

As noted earlier, an important part of a new regime is some shared sense or set of expectations of what the "new order" will be. Such a vision is more likely to emerge as a self-conscious and reflective product of one or more rounds of implementation effort than it is to emerge in advance. As successes build, leaders can weave them into a vision that may include the regime's mission, basic strategies, performance criteria, important decision rules, and ethical standards. At its best, such a statement will be a "vision of success," a description of attainable excellence (see also Bryson, 1988b).

We must emphasize, however, that we are not downplaying

the importance of vision at the beginning of the policy change cycle. Vision at the front end of the process is crucial to inspiring and mobilizing others. What we are talking about in this stage, in contrast, is development of a more detailed vision, tied to adopted policy changes in order to provide useful guidance to implementers. For example, creation of the European Economic Community (EEC) was guided by Jean Monnet's vision of a "United States of Europe," articulated over most of a lifetime (Monnet, 1978). The vision of success for the *actual* EEC — now the European Community (EC) — is an emergent phenomenon derived from, and designed to influence, practical implementation of the idea. As the economic and political integration of Europe proceeds apace, Monnet's early sketch becomes an increasingly detailed portrait.

A vision of success should grow out of past decisions and actions as much as possible. These decisions and actions are often the record of a consensus about what the regime is and what it should do. Basing a vision on this preexisting consensus avoids unnecessary conflict and links the regime effectively to its past. Realization of a new future is easier if it can be shown to be a continuation of the past and present (Weick, 1979; Neustadt and May, 1986). At the same time, a vision of success should not be just an extension of the present. It should be an affirmation in the present of an ideal and inspirational future. However, it should map back to the present to show regime participants how their daily actions can help the regime — and themselves — achieve success. As Wilson (1989, p. 213) notes about governmental organizations, "The decision makers who succeed are those who manage to combine a clear vision of what they want the agency to do with the ability to communicate that vision effectively and to motivate the key civil servants to act on it."

A vision of success offers a number of advantages in shared-power, no-one-in-charge situations. First, a widely accepted vision of success records enough of a consensus on ends and means to channel participants' efforts in desirable directions while at the same time providing a framework for improvisation and innovation in pursuit of regime purposes. Second, conception precedes perception (May, 1969). People must have a conception of what success and desirable behavior look like before they can actually see them. Only when success and desirable behavior are envisioned will they be seen and, therefore, made more likely. A vision of success provides the conception regime participants need to discriminate among preferred and undesirable actions and outcomes, to produce more of what is preferred, and to fashion expectations and reward systems according with what is preferred. Third, a vision of success provides a way to affirm the future in the present. It outlines the future we want to have and motivates us to live it in the present. Therefore, one does not predict the future — a hazardous enterprise at best — one *makes* it (Gabor, 1964).

Fourth, a clear vision of success provides an effective substitute for leadership (Kerr and Jermier, 1978; Manz, 1986). People are able to work more independently if they are given clear guidance about directions and behavioral expectations. They can engage in effective decision making even when they are distant from whatever central or higher authority may exist. And finally, to the extent that a vision of success is widely shared, it takes on a moral quality that can infuse the regime with virtue. Most people want to act in morally justifiable ways in pursuit of morally justifiable ends. A vision of success provides important permission and legitimacy to the actions and decisions that accord with the vision, at the same time that it establishes boundaries of permitted behavior. The normative self-regulation necessary for any moral community to survive and prosper is facilitated (Kanter, 1972). The vision of success, in other words, defines the substance and extent of the court of public opinion within the community subscribing to the vision.

Of course, it may not be possible to construct a vision of success for the new regime, and indeed, it may not be essential to achieving effective regime performance. People do not have to agree on a vision to agree on next steps, as United Nations diplomats, labor-management relations specialists, and used-car buyers and sellers all know (Braybrooke and Lindblom, 1963; Lindblom, 1965; Fisher and Ury, 1981; Cleveland, 1985; Susskind and Cruikshank, 1987). Simply finding ways to frame and deal with a few of the major implementation difficulties is likely to produce important progress on the public problem that prompted the policy change effort in the first place.

Leadership Guidelines

Successful implementation will depend primarily on a regime construction organized around the design and use of various "implementation structures" that coordinate and manage implementation activities (Hjern and Porter, 1981; see also, for example, Friend, Power, and Yewlett, 1974; Friend, Laffin, and Norris, 1981; Rogers, Whetten, and others, 1982; O'Toole and Montjoy, 1984; Goggin and others, 1990; and Whetten and Bozeman, 1991). Formal and informal arenas are likely to be especially important, along with their associated implicit or explicit principles, norms, rules, decision-making procedures, and incentives designed to develop a set of shared expectations among actors about what should happen and why. However, attention also will need to be given to the design and use of formal and informal forums to facilitate communication and to create the symbolic meaning of the regime in practice. Further, formal and informal courts will be necessary for residual conflict management and dispute resolution, along with enforcement of the underlying, and perhaps new, norms in the system. Regime construction also must focus on the stabilization of desired new patterns of behaviors and attitudes, particularly through the use of positive and negative sanctions and incentives; and the continuation or creation of a coalition of implementers, advocates, and supportive interest groups. Because implementation often includes creation of new organizations or transformation of old ones, organizational leadership is especially important in this phase.

The following leadership guidelines should be kept in mind as the adopted policy changes move into the implementation phase, and as a new implementation team in all likelihood takes over from the advocacy group that pushed for and adopted the changes.

General Guidance

Consciously and Deliberately Plan and Manage Implementation.
The implementers of the changes may be very different from
the members of the advocacy coalition that adopted the changes.
This is often the case when changes are "imposed" on implementers by legislative or other decision-making bodies. Implementers
thus may have little interest in making implementation flow
smoothly and effectively. Further, even if implementers are interested in incorporating adopted changes within their respective systems, any numbers of things can go wrong. Implementation, therefore, is hardly ever automatic. It must be explicitly
considered during early phases of the policy change cycle, as
a way of minimizing later implementation difficulties, and it
must be explicitly considered and planned for during the implementation phase itself.

In the case of the Metropolitan Council, implementation
was planned and managed in several stages over fifteen years,
beginning in 1967. In the first stage, the council was appointed,
staff were hired, and citizen advisory groups were organized.
As directed by the legislature, the council began preparing
reports and legislative recommendations on specific regional
problems. It also began preparing a legislatively mandated, comprehensive development guide for the region. The second stage
came as the legislature enacted the council's recommendations
for establishing several regional service agencies overseen by
the council and for otherwise strengthening the council's control over regional development. The third significant stage came
with the legislature's passage of the Metropolitan Land Planning Act, which required local governments and school districts
to develop comprehensive plans within the development framework established by the Metropolitan Council. In effect, the act
mandated an integrated planning system for local governments,
school districts, and the council by requiring each participant
to carry out specific tasks within a given time frame. Although
most local units did not meet the initial 1980 deadline, most
did turn in comprehensive plans by 1983. In this case, therefore,

the legislature, rather than planning the actual implementation, set up structures, processes, and review opportunities to make sure its purposes were accomplished.

In the abortion policy case, both those who support and those who oppose women's access to abortion have worked hard to ensure that their policy victories are implemented. The implementation process, however, has not been as clear-cut as in the metropolitan governance case because it has occurred in so many different forums, arenas, and courts throughout the United States. After the *Roe* v. *Wade* decision, those who supported women's right to choose abortion regeared their national and state organizations to combat their opponents' attempts to place new restrictions on abortion. They also began campaigning for public and charitable funding of abortion services and offered education and training programs to potential implementers. Those who have fought to restore restrictive abortion laws in the post-*Roe* era have understood, perhaps better than the abortion rights advocates, that affecting the composition of arenas and courts is vital for adopting and implementing policy changes. The "pro-life" forces led the way in establishing political action committees, mobilizing supporters to participate in the candidate selection process, and vigorously campaigning for or against candidates, depending on the candidates' abortion stance. By the early 1990s, both sides in the abortion debate had sophisticated networks that could be activated to affect the outcome of elections and appointments to public offices.

Think Strategically About Implementation — That Is, About How to Achieve Important Public Purposes in Practice. We define "implementation strategy" as the *pattern* of purposes, policy statements, plans, programs, actions, decisions, or resource allocations that defines what a policy is in practice, what it does, and why it does it — from the standpoints of various affected publics (see also Bryson, 1988b). Both forward and backward mapping approaches to implementation planning should be tried as a means of finding the strategies most likely to address effectively the public problems that were at or near the heart of the policy change effort. In other words, real effort probably will be needed to find effective connections between the policy makers' intent, on the one hand, and actions on the ground, on the other hand, in order to make desirable headway. Working from the top to the bottom of implementation influence chains and vice versa—and then trying to reconcile the resulting differing views of what will work—is a helpful discipline. This process also should include efforts to understand and accommodate the history and inclinations of key implementing individuals and organizations (Neustadt and May, 1986). Additional detailed advice will be found in Yin (1982), Barry (1986), Friend and Hickling (1987), Bryson (1988b), Rosenhead (1989), Bryant (1989), and Nutt and Backoff (1992).

The Metropolitan Council case again illustrates the need to think strategically about how to proceed. In one instance, which we have described in detail previously, the council responded to the need to deal quickly with sewage disposal problems, and to avoid rekindling old disagreements on this issue, by trying to come to consensus in informal meetings, without resorting to advisory committees. Using this approach, the council was able to develop a sewage disposal plan for submission to the legislature. In another instance, four years after the council's creation, Al Hofstede, a state legislator from Minneapolis, was appointed to succeed James Hetland as chair. Internally, Hofstede faced a staff that was demoralized by the council's mixed record at the legislature. A few council initiatives had been approved by the legislature, but many others had been rejected. Externally, Hofstede had to contend with some local officials who opposed additional powers conferred on the council by the 1971 legislature. Hofstede decided to move strategically and forcefully. He convinced fellow council members that the council should use fully the powers it did have, he reorganized the council staff, and he started a new community services program aimed at mending fences with local officials.

The Metropolitan Council case also offers an example of leaders strategically adapting their decision making to their political culture. Minnesotans have traditionally prized citizen participation in public affairs; therefore, as we showed earlier, the advocates of regional governance developed a highly participatory process for discussing the need for and shape of regional government in a number of forums. This process helped leaders produce the consensus that influenced the legislature to create and then to strengthen the council. The council also followed the participatory model in appointing people from diverse groups — including council opponents — to serve on its many advisory committees. Another aspect of Minnesota's political culture is its pragmatism. For several years after the appointed council's establishment, prominent change advocates kept pushing for an elected council. An elected council certainly seemed "correct" on ideological grounds — how could one argue otherwise in a democracy? the advocates asked. But an elected council was opposed by legislators concerned about disrupting well-established career paths and coalitions by interposing another layer of elected officials between localities and the state. Eventually, the advocates gave up on their pursuit of an elected council, after concluding that the effort was probably futile and that the appointed council was working well anyway.

Develop Implementation Strategy Documents and Action Plans to Guide Implementation and Focus Attention on Necessary Decisions, Actions, and Responsible Parties. Strategies will vary by level. The four basic levels of strategy in a shared-power world are (see also Bryson, 1988b) the grand strategy for the regime as a whole; the strategy statements for the units, typically organizations, that comprise the regime; the program or service strategies that set up reasonable coordination across organizations; and the functional strategies — such as financial, staffing, facilities, or procurement strategies — that also set up coordination across the organizations involved in implementing the policies.

Strategies also may be long-term or short-term. Strategies provide a framework for tactics, the short-term, adaptive actions and reactions used to accomplish fairly limited objectives. However, they also provide the "continuing basis for ordering these adaptations toward more broadly conceived purposes" (Quinn, 1980, p. 9). Action plans are statements about how to implement strategies in the short term (Morrisey, Below, and Acomb, 1987; Randolph and Posner, 1988; Frame,

1987). Typically action plans cover periods of a year or less. They outline specific tasks, the resources necessary to accomplish them, who is responsible, and the target completion date. Without action planning, strategies are likely to remain dreams, not reality. But in a more positive vein, recall our discussion of big wins and small wins in Chapter Eight. There we noted that a whole series of small — short-term — wins organized around a general sense of direction can add up to large gains in the long term. The accumulation of small wins is most likely to grow out of constant attention to managing the stream of small-win opportunities. As Neustadt (1990, p. 192) observes, "Details are of the essence in the exercise of power, day by day, and changes of detail foreshadow institutional development; they cumulate and thus suggest the system's future character."

Try for Changes That Can Be Introduced Easily and Rapidly. Implementers may have little room for maneuver when it comes to the basic design of the proposed changes and the accompanying implementation process. Nonetheless, they should take advantage of whatever discretion they have to improve the ease and rapidity with which changes are put into practice, while still maintaining the basic policy design. Chapter Eight listed a number of common characteristics of winning proposals. Many of these characteristics are designed to gain implementers' support by reducing implementation difficulties. Here we simply highlight some major policy characteristics that facilitate implementation (see also Zaltman, Duncan, and Holbek, 1973; Havelock, 1973; Zaltman and Duncan, 1977; Bryson and Delbecq, 1979; Chase, 1979; Mazmanian and Sabatier, 1983; Wolman, 1981; Morris and Hough, 1986; Bryson, Bromiley, and Jung, 1990; Hoenack, 1991). Implementation will flow more smoothly and speedily if the adopted policy:

- Is conceptually clear.
- Is based on a well-understood theory of cause-effect relations.
- Fits with the values of all key implementers.
- Can be demonstrated and made "real" to the bulk of the implementers prior to implementation; in other words, people

have a chance to see what they are supposed to do before they have to do it.

- Is relatively simple to grasp in practice because the innovation is not only conceptually clear, it also is operationally clear.

- Is administratively simple, with minimal bureaucracy and red tape, minor reorganizations of or impacts on resource allocation patterns, and minimal skill readjustments or retraining.

- Allows a period of start-up time in which people can learn about the adopted changes and engage in any necessary retraining, debugging, and development of new norms and operating routines.

- Includes adequate attention to payoffs and rewards necessary to gain wholehearted acceptance of implementers; in other words, there are clear incentives favoring implementation by relevant organizations and individuals.

Build in Enough People, Time, Attention, Money, Administrative and Support Services, and Other Resources to Assure Successful Implementation. If possible, build in considerable redundancy in places important to program implementation, so that if something goes wrong there is adequate backup capacity. Almost any difficulty can be handled with enough resources — although these days budgets typically are exceedingly tight unless money can be freed from other uses. Think about why cars have seat belts, jetliners have copilots, and bridges are built to handle many times more weight than they are expected to carry: it is to ensure enough built-in capacity to handle almost any unexpected contingency. Tight resources are an additional reason to pay attention to the earlier phases in the policy change cycle. In order to garner sufficient resources, the public problem must be widely viewed as worthy of attention, and the proposed solution as highly likely to produce desirable results at reasonable cost. The supportive coalition should be strong and stable. If these elements are present, the chances of finding or developing the necessary resources for implementation are considerably enhanced. Nonetheless, there still may be resistance from those who must supply the resources, and considerable effort may be needed to overcome it.

Implementation plans should include resources for:

- Key personnel
- "Fixers" — people who know how things work in the complicated world of public policy and how to "fix" things when they go wrong (Bardach, 1977)
- Additional necessary staff
- Conversion costs
- Orientation and training costs
- Technical assistance
- Inside and outside consultants
- Adequate incentives to facilitate adoption of the changes by relevant organizations and individuals
- Formative evaluations to facilitate implementation, and summative evaluations to determine whether or not the changes produced the desired results
- Unforeseen contingencies

The Metropolitan Council benefited from two important funding sources in its formative years: its own taxing authority and federal assistance for regional projects. By the time federal funds became scarcer in the 1980s, the council was well established. In contrast, the advocates of women's right to choose abortion have never obtained adequate funding to make abortion services available to all groups of women. Their opponents have been highly successful in blocking public funds for abortion services, and the "pro-choice" groups have never raised enough money from other sources to compensate for that loss.

Work Quickly, to Avoid Unnecessary or Undesirable Competition with New Priorities. The economy can always go bad and severely damage financial support for proposed changes, whether that support consists of tax revenues, philanthropic contributions, and the markets for products or services that can be sold. Those who remember the deep recession of the early 1980s know this. The recession of the early 1990s may not have been as deep, according to various indicators, but because of its length, tax revolts, tax indexing, and large state and federal deficits, the constriction of public funds for new programs is no less severe, and in many cases is worse. The possibility that the economy can turn sour is yet another reason to build in slack resources for program implementation. A poverty budget can turn out to be a death warrant. So leaders should not make cheapness a major selling point, if they can help it. Instead, they must sell cost-effectiveness — that is, they must sell the idea that the program delivers great benefits in relation to the costs expended and that, therefore, the costs, even if considerable, are worth it.

A change in administration also is likely to bring a change in priorities (Kingdon, 1984). New positional leaders have their own conceptions of the important public problems and viable solutions. Further, the anticipation of a new administration often paralyzes any change efforts. People want to see what will happen before risking their careers by pushing changes that may not be desired by new positional leaders. So, once again, leaders must move quickly to implement new policies before a change in the economy or the political scene undermines the effort.

Focus on Maintaining or Developing a Coalition of Implementers, Advocates, and Interest Groups Intent on Effective Implementation of the Policy Changes and Willing to Protect Them over the Long Haul. One of the clear lessons from the past two decades of implementation research is that successful implementation of programs in shared-power situations depends upon developing and maintaining such a coalition (Sabatier, 1988; Goggin and others, 1990). Coalitions are organized around ideas, interests, and payoffs, so leaders must pay attention to co-aligning these elements in such a way that strong coalitions are created and sustained (Kotter and Lawrence, 1974). Ultimately, leaders should focus on developing a new regime of mutual gain, in which those involved see that their interests are served by the new arrangements.

The coalition that had campaigned for creation of the Metropolitan Council watched closely over the early stages of its implementation. When coalition leaders learned that Governor

LeVander was considering Joseph Maun, a prominent St. Paul attorney and friend of Senator Rosenmeier, as the first chair, they were concerned that whatever potential the council had for acting forcefully was in danger, and they convinced LeVander to give the chairmanship to Hetland instead. In the second year of the council's existence, the coalition organized a major public seminar on tax-base disparities among metropolitan communities and thus laid the groundwork for passage of legislation aimed at remedying the problem. In ensuing years, the coalition continued to issue reports and statements evaluating the council and recommending additional changes to make it more effective.

In the abortion case, a coalition of implementers, advocates and supportive interest groups has attempted to implement the rights to which women were entitled in the wake of *Roe* v. *Wade.* Although the coalition has had periods of somnolence, it has surged impressively in response to significant gains by opponents. The opponents' coalition continued to build during the 1970s and was probably at the height of its powers when it allied with the Moral Majority and New Right political activists to elect conservative candidates in 1980. As early as 1981, however, this alliance was falling apart (Paige, 1983). Some "right-to-life" groups questioned whether abortion was really a priority issue for the New Right, and many of them — particularly the Catholics — found that a large part of the New Right philosophy conflicted with their liberal stands on foreign affairs and some social issues.

Ensure That Legislative, Executive, and Administrative Arenas Facilitate Rather Than Impede Implementation. It is important to maintain liaisons with decision makers in arenas such as state legislatures, governors' offices, and key administrators' offices where future decisions can affect the implementation effort. This means paying attention to agendas, domains, planning and decision-making methods, access rules, and maintenance of desirable asymmetries in the distribution of rules and resources. The supporters of a strong Metropolitan Council knew that the governor of Minnesota would play an important role in council affairs because of the governor's authority to appoint the council chair and other members. Therefore, it was vital to try to influence those appointments and convince the governor to turn to the council for assistance with regional policy-making. State legislators also remained important during council implementation, since additional legislation was needed to flesh out the council's powers. One effective way for supporters to maintain influence in the legislature was by backing the appointment of former legislators as the next three council chairs following Hetland.

Leaders in the implementation phase must also pay attention to the development and use of supplemental policies, regulations, rules, ordinances, articles, or other guidance necessary to implement the policies adopted in the previous phase. Operational details and procedures must be worked out, and many of them will need to pass through specific processes before they can have the force of law. For example, before implementing regulations can become official at the federal level, they must be developed following the procedures outlined in the Administrative Procedures Act (Shapiro, 1982; Cooper, 1989). States have their own administrative procedures acts that must be followed. Change advocates should seek expert advice on how these processes work and attend to the ways in which supplemental policies are developed. Otherwise, the promise of the previous phase may be lost in practice.

Think Carefully About How Residual Disputes Will Be Resolved and Underlying Norms Enforced. This, of course, means paying attention to the design and use of courts, including: norms, in the broad sense; the choice of conflict resolution methods; jurisdictions; access rules; and the deep sources of legitimacy. Leaders may need to use formal courts or court-related offices to clarify implementing authority and fight off challenges to implementation. In the Metropolitan Council case, for example, the Minnesota supreme court declared that the council had the authority to make legislative decisions because the state legislature had specifically granted that authority to the council. The court also made clear that the council had to follow established procedural rules in its administrative decisions. In addition, the council's first chair obtained an opinion from the state attorney general that the council was neither a state agency nor a special form of local government but something in between. And the council itself often served as a court in resolving conflicts between its authority and that of regional service agencies or local governments. Supporters of women's reproductive rights have continually challenged federal, state, and local laws that would prevent women from obtaining abortions. Until 1989, when the Supreme Court handed down its decision in *Webster* v. *Reproductive Health Services,* courts generally struck down these laws. The main exceptions were laws that prohibited the use of public funds for abortion services.

When leaders establish new courts, they must ensure that these courts operate according to basic judicial principles of due process and equal protection — so their decisions won't be overturned by higher courts — and leaders must also ensure that there is an appeal process. In the Metropolitan Council case, for example, the Metropolitan Land Planning Act of 1976 authorized the council to act as a court in overruling local plans that conflicted with council policies. The act, however, also allowed local governments to appeal the council's decision to the state courts. Effective leaders also rely on "alternative dispute resolution" methods wherever possible, in order to keep conflicts out of the formal courts and open up the possibility of all-gain solutions that increase the regime's legitimacy and public acceptance of the outcomes of conflict management efforts (Fisher and Ury, 1981; Susskind and Cruikshank, 1987; Gray, 1989).

Leading implementers ought to remember that the court of public opinion will be important in reinforcing the norms in the new regime. Both of the main opposing camps in the abortion controversy can claim some success in this court. Polls show that the majority of U.S. adults support a woman's right to decide whether or not to have an abortion during the first trimester of pregnancy, but a majority also support restrictions — such as waiting periods and spousal notifications — that are a mainstay of fetal rights proposals (Hugick, 1991).

Finally, maintaining good relations with the police may

be important, especially when opponents are willing to use violence and intimidation to prevent policy implementation. The advocates of women's access to abortion, for example, have had to rely on the police to keep militant fetal rights advocates from shutting down abortion services.

Hang in There! Successful implementation in shared-power settings typically requires large amounts of time, attention, resources, and effort (Kanter, 1983; Kingdon, 1984), and implementers also may need considerable courage to fight the resisters of change. The rewards, however, can be great—namely, effective action against major public problems that affect the lives of many people. The world can be made better only through wise collective thought and action over the long haul. As Woody Allen says, "Eighty percent of success is showing up." So just by sticking with the effort, leaders can accomplish a great deal.

Communication and Education

Invest Heavily in Communication Activities. This means attention to the design and use of communication networks and the messages and messengers that compose them (Goggin and others, 1990). Said differently, leaders must once again pay close attention to the design and use of formal and informal forums. Particularly when large changes are involved, people must be given opportunities to develop shared meanings and appreciations that will further the implementation of policy goals (Trist, 1983; Sabatier, 1988). These meanings will both guide and flow out of implementation activities (Lynn, 1987). People must *hear* about the proposed changes, preferably hearing the same messages across multiple channels many times, to increase the chances that the messages will sink in. Further, people must be able to talk about the changes, in order to understand them, fit them into their own interpretive schemes, adapt them to their own circumstances, and explore implications for action and the consequences of those actions (Trist, 1983; Johnson and Johnson, 1991). Educational programs, information packets, and guidebooks can help establish a desirable frame of reference and common language for addressing implementation issues.

Change advocates may continue the policy change coordinating committee as an important forum at this stage, or they may establish a policy implementation coordinating committee, which ought to include a significant overlap in membership with the old committee. Overlapping membership assures that understanding gained in previous phases is not lost during implementation. In the Metropolitan Council case, the informal group that had coordinated the policy change effort did continue, with some changes in membership, as an implementation coordinating committee in the years immediately following the council's creation. Moreover, as noted, some of the original group members were appointed to the council itself; others — such as leaders of the Citizens League and the Upper Midwest Research and Development Council — continued to convene forums and produce reports on implementation issues.

Supporters of policy changes should maintain their contacts with the reporters, editors, and news directors who followed the earlier policy debates. The news media are usually not interested in the nuts and bolts of implementation, unless the change is a highly visible project, but policy supporters can take advantage of anniversaries or milestones to attract news coverage. Implementers also can begin new media that appeal to both internal and external audiences. The Metropolitan Council, for example, began *Metro Monitor,* a small newspaper that is circulated free around the metropolitan region.

Regime creation in shared-power situations is essentially a process of creating and institutionalizing meaning through the participants' shared discussion and voluntary commitment to new implicit or explicit principles, norms, rules, and decision-making procedures (see also Ostrom, 1990). Typically, formulation of these principles and procedures occurs in forums, before the principles and procedures are used and institutionalized in arenas and courts. People must be able to explore the nature and consequences of regime elements in the relatively safe and nonbinding settings of forums before committing themselves to using these elements in the binding settings of formal arenas and courts. This is the reason the Metropolitan Council often relies on a broadly participatory committee system, which includes citizen advisers, to hammer out new policies and programs before they are adopted.

Moreover, the council is a prime example of implementers' recognizing the need to invest heavily in communication activities. It has hired a sizable public information staff and issued newsletters, press releases, and annual reports. In his four years as chair, James Hetland met with almost all the city councils, chambers of commerce, and Leagues of Women Voters in the metropolitan area. In preparing the document that would guide regional development, the council pulled out all the stops. For the year and a half before the council issued a completed draft of the framework, council members and staff made multiple contacts with the interested public. The goal, said John Boland, the council chair during the period, was to sincerely try "to get as many people involved and aware of our work as possible. We believe we've had a rather unusual process that has included weekly bulletins to interested and affected people, interim public meetings, task forces, preparation of discussion statements, and personal contacts and phone calls" (Center for Urban and Regional Affairs, 1978, p. 177).

Work to Reduce Resistance Based on Divergent Attitudes and Lack of Participation. Actions likely to reduce resistance on the part of implementers include providing those implementers with orientation sessions, training materials and sessions, problem-solving teams, one-to-one interactions, and technical assistance to overcome obstacles to solution use and to support adoption of the solutions, and ceremonies and symbolic rewards to reinforce desired behaviors. After the *Roe* v. *Wade* decision, for example, the American College of Obstetricians and Gynecologists held training sessions and dispensed information on abortion to its members. Planned Parenthood and the National Association for the Repeal of Abortion Laws advised local groups interested in opening abortion clinics. In the Metropolitan Council case, the implementation of the 1976 Land Planning Act probably would have been impossible if council staff had not provided extensive technical assistance to local governments. The staff's efforts included holding numerous workshops, compiling data and resource materials, publishing a series of planning briefs, and providing a capital improvements training exercise.

Consider Developing a Guiding Vision of Success for the New Regime. Developing a vision of success is an exercise in "rhetorical leadership" (Doig and Hargrove, 1987). If such a vision is to provide suitable guidance and motivation, it should include a statement of mission, the basic regime philosophy, the goals, if they are established, the basic strategies, the performance criteria, the important decision rules, and the ethical standards expected of all regime participants. A vision of success should be short, not more than several pages. People are inspired by a clear description of a desirable future backed up by real conviction. Recall the discussion in Chapter Two of the elements of an inspirational vision. Such a vision (Kouzes and Posner, 1987) focuses on a better future; encourages hopes and dreams; appeals to common values; states positive outcomes; emphasizes the strength of a unified group; uses word pictures, images, and metaphors; and communicates enthusiasm and kindles excitement.

To begin constructing a vision of success, the planning team members can prepare individual draft visions, then share and discuss their responses. After the discussion, the task of drafting the actual vision of success should be turned over to an individual. An inspirational document rarely is written by a committee. Wherever there are gaps in the vision, the team may have to arrange special sessions to fill them. For example, performance criteria may need to be developed through stakeholder analyses. A normative process should be used to review the vision. Drafts are usually reviewed by planning team members, key decision makers, governing board members, and other key stakeholder representatives; review meetings are structured so that the strengths of the vision are identified and modifications that would improve on those strengths are listed. These meetings can be structured according to the agenda suggested in Chapter Eight for the review of policy proposals. Consensus on a vision of success is highly desirable but may not be absolutely necessary. It is rarely possible to achieve complete consensus on anything in a regime, so all that can be realistically hoped for is a fairly widespread consensus on the substance and style of the vision statement. Typically, deep-seated commitment to any vision statement emerges only over time (Senge, 1990).

If a vision of success is to help guide regime decisions and actions, it must be widely disseminated and discussed. It probably should be published as a booklet that is given to all key participants and stakeholders, and the statement should be discussed at all orientation and training sessions. The statement should be revisited at any retreats or other major meetings for key regime decision makers and opinion leaders. A vision of success can become a living document only if it is referred to constantly as a basis for discerning and justifying appropriate decisions and actions. If a vision statement does not regularly inform decision making and actions by regime participants, then leaders should consider why it is ineffective. If the vision and the decisions are on two different tracks, leaders should consider why and what can be done about it.

Build in Regular Attention to Appropriate Indicators. This will assure attention to progress — or lack thereof — against the problems that prompted the policy change effort. For example, the U.S. State Department reports regularly on the human rights records of the countries that are actual or potential recipients of U.S. foreign assistance. If a particular country's rights record is not good, it will have a more difficult time acquiring aid (Innes, 1990). The Metropolitan Council prepares a regular "state of the region" report that focuses on indicators presumed to measure the health of the region. The Alan Guttmacher Institute and other researchers issue statistical studies on pregnancy and abortion that help change advocates trace the effect of changes in abortion laws.

Personnel

As Much As Possible, Fill Policy-making and Staff Positions with Highly Qualified People Committed to the Program. As noted, changes do not implement themselves; people make them happen. This is particularly true for major changes. When minor changes are required, systems and structures often can be substitutes for leadership (Kerr and Jermier, 1978; Manz, 1986). But when significant changes are involved, there is no substitute for leadership of many kinds. People — intelligent, creative, skilled, experienced, committed people — are necessary to create the new regime, culture, systems, and structures that will focus and channel efforts toward effective implementation. In order to attract and retain such people, at least three things are necessary:

- People must be adequately compensated for their work. Fortunately, compensation does not always have to mean monetary payments. "Psychic income" — the rewards that come from "doing good" and being part of a new and important adventure — can count as well.
- People must see how their careers can be advanced by involvement in implementation efforts. The most intelligent and able people are likely to take a long view of their careers and will avoid what may be dead-end jobs. Instead, they are likely to choose jobs that can improve their skills, responsibilities, and long-term job prospects (Dalton and Thompson, 1986; Hoenack, 1991).
- People want to have viable "escape routes" if things go bad or if they want to leave on their own. Many mechanisms can achieve this end — for example, an option of returning to prior jobs, outplacement services, or generous severance packages.

Continue the Planning Team or Establish a New Implementation Team That Has a Significant Overlap in Membership. In the Metropolitan Council case, Robert Einsweiler was an important member of the team that planned the consensus building campaign that led to the council's creation. As planning director of the Metropolitan Planning Commission and head of the Joint Program's technical team, he had orchestrated the MPC–Joint Program forums that debated the various proposals for a new regional governing structure. When the Metropolitan

Council was established, he became planning director for the new organization.

Assure Access to, and Liaison with, Top Administrators During Implementation. This task is easy when the change advocates themselves become the top administrators. Even if they do not, they may find that administrators are interested in continued contact with them, either because the administrators want to have, or must have, the advocates' support.

Give Special Attention to the Problem of Easing Out, Working Around, or Avoiding People Who Are Not Likely to Help the Change Effort for Whatever Reason. Standard practice in the public sector, of course, is to start a new agency rather than give implementation responsibilities to an existing agency whose mission, culture, personnel, and history are antagonistic to the intent of the changes. For example, President Lyndon Johnson insisted on a new Office of Economic Opportunity rather than turn over implementation responsibilities for many of his Great Society programs to established agencies such as the departments of Labor or Health, Education, and Welfare. He remarked at one point, "The best way to kill a new idea is to put it in an old-line agency" (Anderson, 1990, p. 180). Or, as management theorist Frederick Herzberg often says, "It is easier to give birth than to resurrect." But even if a new organization is started, leaders still may be stuck with personnel who are detrimental to achievement of the policy goals. There are several options for dealing with such people. First, help them get jobs to which they are more suited. This may take much of a leader's time initially—evaluating people's skills, ascertaining their goals, and writing favorable letters of recommendation—but the resulting increase in the remaining staff's morale and productivity is well worth the effort. Second, award such people merit pay only if they actively implement policy goals. Third, place them in jobs where they cannot damage the change effort. Fourth, buy them off with early retirement. And finally, if all else fails, work around them or ignore them.

Direct Versus Staged Implementation

As we have mentioned, there are two basic approaches to implementation, direct and staged. Direct implementation incorporates changes into all relevant sites essentially simultaneously, while staged implementation incorporates changes sequentially into groups of sites (Bryson and Delbecq, 1981).

Consider Direct Implementation When the Situation Is Technically and Politically Simple, Immediate Action Is Necessary for System Survival in a Crisis, or the Adopted Solutions Entail Some "Lumpiness" That Precludes Staged Implementation. When situations are simple, direct implementation can work if enough resources are built in to cover costs and provide sufficient incentives and if resistance to change is low. Therefore, leaders must try to reduce any resistance to change based on divergent attitudes and lack of earlier participation. A crisis can simplify a situation politically in that people become more willing to defer to top positional leaders and accept centralized decision making (Bryson, 1981). This makes direct implementation feasible, also. However, solutions adopted to address crises must still be technically practical, or at least, practical enough that difficulties can be worked out without weakening people's support for change. Finally, lumpy solutions may demand direct implementation. For example, when the solution to transport between France and Britain is the English Channel tunnel, implementers can't build a little practice tunnel first and a bigger tunnel later. They must carry out the full plan or do nothing.

In Difficult Situations, Consider Staged Implementation. Staged implementation presumes that implementation will occur in "waves," in which initial adopters will be followed by later adopters, and finally, even most of the laggards will adopt the changes. The result is the familiar S-shaped curve associated with the adoptions of most innovations over time. Early on, there are few adopters, so the area under the curve is small. As time progresses, more and more adoptions occur, increasing the area under the curve, which begins to assume an "S" shape. Later, fewer and fewer adoptions occur, partly because there are fewer people or organizations left to adopt the changes, and partly because of deep-seated resistance on the part of the laggards. The curve levels off as the top of the "S" is completed. Ideally, implementation efforts attempt to make the shape of the "S" as steep and smooth as possible (Rogers, 1982).

The exact nature of the staged process will depend on the difficulties faced. When facing technical difficulties, consider beginning with a pilot project designed to discover or to prove the cause-effect relations between particular solutions and particular effects. The more difficult the situation technically, the more necessary pilot projects are to figure out what techniques do and do not work. Once the technical difficulties are resolved, transfer of the implementation process to the remaining potential implementers can be pursued. For example, pilot tests of new U.S. agricultural products and services occur regularly at agricultural experiment stations that involve universities, the U.S. Department of Agriculture, and often business in cooperative partnerships. Another example is the government's funding of a massive investigation of the effects of a guaranteed annual income and varying taxation rates on labor force participation rates, as part of the process of figuring out whether a "negative income tax" made sense as a welfare reform. The experiment demonstrated that a negative income tax had little effect on labor force participation rates (Kershaw and Fair, 1976; Cogan, 1978). The reform initiative, however, stalled for a variety of ideological, political, and financial reasons.

When facing political difficulties, consider beginning staged implementation with demonstration projects to make it clear that solutions known to work in benign and controlled conditions can work in typical implementer settings. Once the generalizability of the changes is demonstrated, transfer to remaining implementers can be pursued. The more organized opposition there is to the proposed changes, the more necessary demonstration projects are likely to be. On the other hand, when the existing or potential opposition is not well organized, direct and massive implementation efforts are probably wisest, because then changes can be put in place before an effective opposition can materialize. However, when the opposition is well organized and also implacable, direct and massive implementation efforts again may be warranted, in order to expand the front and overwhelm opponents, rather than give them a limited number of smaller targets to oppose (Bryson and Delbecq, 1979).

When facing both technical and political difficulties, consider beginning with a pilot project, followed by demonstration projects, followed by transfer to the rest of the implementers. In general, the more difficult the situation, the more important are tactics aimed at education and learning; incentives for desired changes; and the development of a shared sense of commitment to successful implementation and long-term protection of the changes among all the interested parties.

Design Pilot Projects to Be Effective. We suggest that leaders:

- Test for the scientific validity of the proposed changes, probably using experimental or quasi-experimental designs. In other words, test whether the proposed changes actually cause the desired effects. The classic source of advice for such testing is Campbell and Stanley (1966).
- Perform the test in a safe and controlled environment with access to a rich set of resources. The ideal test for causation matches a control group against an experimental group that differs from the control group *only* in experiencing the policy change, or "treatment," being tested. Only with such controlled trials can plausible rival hypotheses be ruled out.
- Test several possible changes and search for their different strengths and weaknesses.
- Use skilled technical specialists to evaluate cause-effect relations. If the specialists' credibility is a concern, consider using outside experts, or an inside-outside team whose objectivity will not be questioned.
- Design tests that are concerned with the effectiveness of the changes, not their efficiency. In other words, tests should measure whether the changes produce the desired effects or not, not whether they do so cheaply. Attention should be on both outputs and outcomes.

*Design Demonstration Projects to Be Effective by Employing the
Following Procedures:*

- Test for the generalizability of proposed changes to typical
  implementer settings, probably through the use of quasi-
  experimental designs. True experiments are rarely possible in the field, but it still is important to have some sort
  of control group, if possible, in order to determine what
  works under what circumstances and why. Quasi-experimental designs can make it possible for such learning to
  occur.
- Test in easy, average, and difficult implementation settings
  in order to gauge the robustness of the changes and the possibilities for handling a range of implementation difficulties.
- Test several possible changes in order to determine their
  comparative strengths and weakness.
- Use a two-cycle process, in which implementers learn how
  to work with the changes in the first cycle, and the effects
  of the changes are monitored in the second cycle.
- Include a qualitative evaluation (Patton, 1990), along with
  quantitative studies, to show different solution strengths and
  weaknesses. Pay attention to outcomes, as well as outputs.
- Remember that what is being tested in the demonstration
  stage is the maintenance of solution design that is already
  known to work in a technical sense; that is, it can produce
  the desired effects.
- Assemble a special monitoring team, if necessary, to carry
  out the monitoring task.
- Provide opportunities for future implementers to witness the
  demonstrations.
- Develop a media strategy to communicate the desirability
  of the changes and the best way they might be implemented.

*When Transferring Tested Changes to Other Implementers, Fol-
low the Steps Below.*

- Commit substantial resources to communication tactics, including cycling in observers likely to influence subsequent

implementer adoptions and to facilitate word-of-mouth information exchanges.

- Promote the visibility of the demonstration projects.
- Produce, emphasize, and disseminate educational materials and operational guides designed to make adoption and implementation easier.
- Develop credible and easily understood models that show clearly how the desired changes work and how they can be implemented.
- Provide additional resources for technical assistance and problem solving.
- Provide incentives for the adoption of the changes.
- Be flexible.

Finally, When the Implementation Process is Staged, Give Special Attention to Those Who Will Implement Changes in the Early Stages. In the early stages, when the practical nature of the changes still needs to be worked out, it is important to attract people with enough experience, skill, and desire to make the changes work. People who are likely to do so will have first-hand experience with the public problem and the need for an adequate response; above-average ability; and experience with prior major change efforts. Further, later adopters will be watching to see whether or not they wish to embrace the changes or resist them. Early implementers thus should be valued and persuasive role models. They are more likely to be effective salespersons for change if they do not mindlessly charge after every new whim and fad that comes over the horizon. Instead, they should be seen as courageous, wise, able, and committed to addressing the public problem in a reasonable way. Further, they should be able to describe their experience to effectively educate the next wave of adopters.

As already noted, the early implementers for the Metropolitan Council included some of the prominent, respected business and civic leaders who had promoted the council's creation. Clayton LeFevere, in particular, might be singled out for his abilities as a fixer. He had considerable influence among local officials, having been president of the Minnesota League of

Municipalities and the attorney in a number of joint-power arrangements among suburban communities. As one who had advised several suburbs in their battles to obtain lower sewer rates, he was well suited to help the council craft a new regional sewage disposal system that would be acceptable to the multiple stakeholders involved. Additionally, the council's first executive director, Robert Jorvig, had previously served as Minneapolis city coordinator and before that had been head of the housing authorities of both Minneapolis and St. Paul. Another crucial early hire and role model was Robert Nethercut, a suburban mayor, to head the council's community services program.

Summary

Implementation must be consciously, deliberately, and strategically planned and managed. Further, successful implementation typically involves creation of a regime to govern decision making and behavior. Elements of the new regime will include new or redesigned forums, arenas, and courts; the establishment of implicit or explicit principles, norms, rules, and decision-making procedures; the development and use of substantive and symbolic incentives promoting the new arrangements; the institutionalization of altered patterns of behaviors and attitudes; and continuation or creation of a supportive coalition of implementers, advocates, and interest groups. The new regime also may incorporate a widely shared vision of success.

Successful implementation introduces desired changes quickly and smoothly, and overcomes the typical causes of implementation failure. A combination of forward and backward mapping facilitates development of implementation strategies and actions likely to promote successful implementation. These strategies may involve either direct or staged implementation. Direct implementation works best when the time is right, the need is clear to a strong coalition of implementers, there is a clear connection between agreed-upon problems and adopted solutions, solution technology is clearly understood, adequate resources are available, and there is a clear vision to guide the changes. (These are the conditions that also favor "big win" strategies.) Staged implementation is advisable when policy makers are faced with technical or political difficulties. It often involves pilot projects, to determine or to prove the cause-effect relations between particular solutions and particular effects; demonstration projects, to show the generalizability of adopted solutions to typical implementer settings; and to diffuse knowledge to later waves of adopters. Staged implementation involves organizing a series of "small wins."

The two cases presented throughout this book have included very different implementation stories. The implementation of the Metropolitan Council was a fifteen-year process in which the council, supported by a strong coalition, was able to establish and expand its authority and power. The implementation story in the abortion controversy, meanwhile, is mainly about the difficulty of implementing changes in the face of a sizable, determined opposition. In both cases, however, implementation is where "the rubber meets the road" in policy change efforts. Policy change is not completed with the adoption of policies by official decision-making bodies. Without effectively implemented solutions, important public problems simply will not be effectively addressed. In that case, implementation will be where "the rubber meets the sky," as the implementation vehicle is upended, its wheels spin uselessly, and its occupants hope they can crawl out unhurt. Implementation must be viewed as a continuation of the policy change process toward its ultimate destination of successful collective action in pursuit of the common good. And effective public leadership should be viewed as a single sweeping gesture pointing from important public problems to desirable solutions, to adopted changes, to implementation of those changes, and to outcomes that indicate the problems have been overcome.

Chapter 11

Reassessing
Policies and Programs

In my end is my beginning.

—T. S. Eliot
Four Quartets

*All organizations by design are the enemies of change, at least
up to a point; government organizations are especially risk averse
because they are caught up in a web of constraints so complex
that any change is likely to rouse the ire of some important
constituency.*

—James Q. Wilson

The policy change cycle is not over once policies are implemented. Times change, situations change, and coalitions of interest change. Policies that work must be maintained and protected through vigilance and adaptability. But not all policies
continue to work as well as they should. These policies must
be bolstered with additional resources; significantly modified or
succeeded by a new policy; or else terminated.

Policies cease to work for four main reasons. First, a basic
policy idea may be good but have insufficient resources devoted
to its implementation, and therefore, insufficient progress is
made against the problem the policy is meant to solve. For example, while many conservative critics of Lyndon Johnson's

Great Society initiatives argue that the policies failed, because they did not eliminate the problems they were designed to address, liberal advocates argue that the policies did make important headway and would have made more had they not been starved for resources by the Vietnam War and other spending priorities (Levitan and Taggart, 1976). Second, problems change, and what was once a solution itself can become a problem. In the early part of this century, automobile use was promoted as a boon to public health, because automobiles didn't defecate on the streets as horses did. Now, automobile exhausts may harm more people's health than horse manure ever did. Third, as substantive problem areas become densely packed with policies, the interaction of all these policies can produce results that no one wants and many wish to change. And fourth, the political environment may shift. As a policy becomes institutionalized, advocates may be less attentive and vocal. Supportive elected officials may be replaced by officials who are uninterested or even hostile to the policy, and they may pass laws or appoint administrators who undermine it. For any one of these reasons, policy can become its own cause — the proximate reason for the initiation of a new round of policy change (Wildavsky, 1979).

The Metropolitan Council showed signs of stress in the early 1980s, mainly because of political shifts and its proliferating policies. When Rudy Perpich became state governor in 1983, he appointed Gerald Isaacs, a St. Paul developer, as council chair, an appointment roundly criticized as a political payoff. Over the following months, Isaacs' actions seriously threatened the policy and programmatic compromises represented by the council, and he ruffled feathers among the council's constituencies by trying to steer the council into new territories such as economic development and by suggesting that the council take over some independent agencies. His integrity also was in doubt after the public learned he had transferred a council account to a bank that had given him personal loans. At the same time, the council was being ignored in debates over major metropolitan facilities, and some regional services were being visibly mismanaged. Only Isaacs' resignation in the spring of 1984 staved off the beginnings of a major policy reform initiative by legislators and civic activists. A *Minneapolis Star Tribune* editorial (June 15, 1984, p. 22A) aptly summarized the council's condition at this time: "With metropolitan services and urban-growth controls largely in place, the council's mission is no longer clear. Its committees are bogged down in detail. It has just gone through a year and a half of turmoil under a controversial chairman. And it seems increasingly vulnerable to attempts by a forgetful Legislature and jealous local governments to erode its authority and effectiveness." When Governor Perpich appointed Sandra Gardebring, a respected administrator who had previously headed the Minnesota Pollution Control Agency, as Isaacs' successor, she had a clear mandate to reform the council's operations.

The abortion policy regime resulting from *Roe* v. *Wade* has operated under stress from the beginning. A determined opposition has helped ensure that there never have been enough resources to provide poor and rural women with access to abortion services. The opposition also has succeeded in enacting numerous restrictions on the rights established in *Roe*. Meanwhile, the problem formulation that led to the new regime may be changing. Some supporters of abortion rights are returning to a focus on unwanted or unintended pregnancies, in part because of technological changes but also because of growing concern about the effects of abortion on women's health. Moreover, the intense social conflict that has surrounded the abortion policy regime for nearly two decades has itself become a problem that cries out for a reframing and re-solving of the abortion issue. The political environment also has shifted. While candidates for elected office are becoming more willing to declare themselves supporters of women's right to abortion, the Supreme Court has been reshaped in the opposite direction as a result of appointments by Presidents Reagan and Bush. In its 1992 decision largely upholding a restrictive Pennsylvania statute, the court both reaffirmed women's right to choose abortion and gave state legislatures more leeway to modify that right.

Desired Outcomes and Benefits of the Process

The purpose of this phase of the policy change cycle is to review implemented policies, plans, or programs and to decide on a course of action. Desired outcomes include maintenance of good policies, modification of less successful policies through appropriate reforms; and elimination of undesirable policies. A further desired outcome is the mobilization of energy and enthusiasm to address the next big public problems that come along.

Several benefits flow from successful action in this phase. First is the assurance that institutionalized capabilities remain responsive to real needs and problems. Institutions often are permanent patterns of response to "old" problem definitions. When the problems change, often the institutions do not and, therefore, become a problem themselves (Wilson, 1989; Schon, 1971). A sort of goal displacement occurs in which the institutions cease to be a means to an end and, instead, become an end in themselves; instrumental values become terminal values (Merton, 1940). Ensuring that institutions remain responsive to real problems and needs takes effort. Periodic studies, reports, conferences, hearings, fact-finding missions and on-site observation, and discussions with stakeholders are necessary to stay in touch with the "real world." The design and use of forums is particularly important for creating and sustaining discussion about the real problems and needs that should be addressed and the appropriate institutional responses.

A second important benefit is the resolution of residual problems that occur during sustained implementation. Even if implemented policies remain generally responsive to the problems that originally prompted them, inevitably there will be a host of specific difficulties that must be addressed if the policies are to be really effective. Attention and appropriate action over the long haul are necessary to assure that policies in practice remain as good as they were in concept. An assortment of advocates and advocacy groups; committed professionals; appropriately designed forums, arenas, and courts (particularly arenas and courts); and suitable incentives is necessary to force an effective response to the difficulties that arise throughout sustained policy implementation.

A third substantial benefit is development of the energy, will, and ideas for significant reform of existing policies. Minor difficulties can be addressed through existing administrative mechanisms, such as "management by exception" routines, administrative law courts, periodic policy review and modification exercises, and routine access channels to key decision makers for advocates and advocacy groups. Major reform, however, will not occur without the development of a substantial coalition in favor of it. And such a coalition will not develop unless there are real problems to be addressed, and the energy, will, and ideas for doing so. However, this is the phase in which the beginnings of such a coalition are most likely to emerge; in other words, this "end" to a policy change cycle is often the "beginning" of a policy change cycle.

Finally, this phase should result in a continuous weeding, pruning, and shaping of crowded policy spaces. While there may be an appropriate "micro-logic" to individual policies, policy-piled-upon-policy often creates a kind of unintended and unwanted "macro-nonsense" (see also Peters and Waterman, 1982; Wildavsky, 1979). Public leaders must discover how to talk about the "system-as-a-whole" in order to figure out what should stay, what should be dropped, and what should be added (Schon, 1971; Senge, 1990). An appropriate set of forums, arenas, and courts — along with a cadre of committed public leaders — should allow this to happen. In Minnesota, Sandra Gardebring was able to guide the Metropolitan Council through a process that bolstered the basics of the council regime, yet shifted policy emphases and actually terminated some programs. Gardebring had a clear mandate from the governor to restore the council's credibility and focus on the critical policy areas of solid waste disposal and water pollution resulting from combined storm and household sewers. She totally reorganized council staff to free resources for priority projects and improve accountability. She introduced a production calendar and expected staff to meet deadlines (Charles Ballentine, personal interview, 1991). She did not, as some council supporters hoped, return the council meetings to a wide-ranging forum on metropolitan issues. Instead, she kept the council focused on the two policy areas of concern to the governor, solid waste and combined-sewer overflow. While she was chair, the council resolved the sewer problem and obtained state legislation giving the council strong planning authority over solid waste disposal. The council also de-emphasized human services planning, in part because federal funds were drying up. By the time the governor gave Gardebring a new assignment in 1986, she had overseen the reestablishment of the council's reputation for providing high-caliber regional planning and for developing workable recommendations on critical metropolitan issues.

Leadership Guidelines

The following guidelines should be kept in mind as public leaders review implemented policies and ponder what to do about them. We first discuss general guidelines. Next, we offer specific suggestions for policy maintenance, succession, and termination (for additional details, see Hogwood and Peters, 1983).

General Guidelines

Stay Focused on What Is Important. Pay attention to the needs and problems that prompted the policy change, and view policies and institutions as a means of responding to them. Public leaders must never let policies and institutions become ends in themselves. Instead, leaders should focus on people and ideals and how best to serve them.

Focus on Indicators of Success and Failure. Attention should be paid to changes in indicators that were used to argue for or against the policy changes in the first place; to new indicators that are important to key stakeholders and that shed light on implementation effectiveness; and to results of any summative evaluations. To the extent that any or all of these indicators provide valid signs of policy progress or failure, they can provide support for deciding to maintain, reform, or terminate a policy. The advocates of safe and legal abortions, for example, have had indicators of both tremendous success and large-scale failure. As noted, reports reveal that millions of women have obtained legal and relatively safe abortions since 1973, but the reports also reveal that access to abortion services has been uneven, and millions of unwanted pregnancies occur each year. These indicators have supported the efforts of legal abortion advocates in their fight to keep abortion legal, but also have raised the concern of those advocates whose ultimate goal is prevention of unwanted pregnancies. This concern is now leading many women's rights advocates to place increased emphasis on pregnancy prevention, while keeping abortion legal. A recent Planned Parenthood advertising campaign in Minnesota proclaimed: "Prevent abortion: support family planning."

Review the Interpretive Schemes and Myths Used to Formulate the Problem and Adopted Solutions. Are they still accurate and useful representations of reality, and do they embody or imply useful solutions to public problems? Or has something changed about the reality — political, economic, social, technological, or otherwise — to make these interpretive schemes and myths distortions that suggest undesirable problem formulations and policy solutions? If so, are there more appropriate myths and interpretive schemes that might be pushed to promote desirable policy changes? For example, as evidence mounted during the 1980s that abortions had harsh emotional effects on women, legal abortion advocates had to ask how well the policy change they had achieved matched up with one of their major interpretive schemes — that legal abortion contributed to personal liberty because it protected women's health and well-being. Additionally, recent technological advances have cast doubt on the Supreme Court's rationale for allowing the state to limit abortion only in the final trimester of pregnancy. The rationale was that the state is compelled to protect the fetus only at the point at which it could survive outside the mother's womb, defined as sometime after the beginning of the third trimester. Now that fetal viability is occurring at increasingly earlier stages, the court and abortion rights advocates may need to rethink this interpretive scheme (Tribe, 1990).

Be Attentive to the Existing or New Forums, Arenas, and Courts in Which Policies Will Be Maintained, Succeeded, or Terminated. These basic settings for action related to policy persistence or change are also the settings through which public leadership is exercised. For example, the advocates of a woman's right to choose abortion — and their opponents — have organized forums such as public demonstrations and seminars each year on the anniversary of the *Roe* v. *Wade* decision. They also have continued to lobby against the passage of new restrictive abortion laws, and they have urged voters to support "pro-choice" candidates for public office. They have fought the appointment of judges who might be expected to undo the *Roe* v. *Wade* guarantees and they have challenged new laws that chip away at women's reproductive rights. Opposition groups, for their part, have taken to staging rallies and sit-ins in front of abortion clinics, to dramatize their commitment to a "pro-life" position and their revulsion against abortion.

Remember That Organizations Often Have Greater Staying Power Than Any Policy (Hogwood and Peters, 1983). Typically, therefore, it is easier to change the latter rather than the former. And typically, it is more productive to call into question or attack the latter than the former. In other words, praising the intentions and goodwill of organizations, while attacking their policies, is more likely to produce change than attacking the motives and goodwill of the organizations themselves. Further, from a strategic standpoint, it is often wise to figure out whether real public problems can be solved with appropriate policies based in existing organizations and interorganizational networks, since policies may be created or changed more easily than organizations and networks. Moreover, it is wise to figure out how existing organizations and their adherents might benefit from possible policy changes, so that allies can be created rather than opponents (Neustadt and May, 1986). But given the distressing inertia of many existing organizations, change advocates may ultimately conclude that new organizations and networks are required to solve real public problems.

Especially in the area of transportation, the Metropolitan Council has found it wise to work around or with existing organizations to make policy changes. The regional agencies responsible for mass transit and airports remained basically independent from the council during the first seventeen years of its existence. Although logic would dictate differently, these agencies had enough political clout to stay outside the council umbrella. At the same time, council planners had to include transportation in their comprehensive regional planning. The council's attempts at developing new policies cooperatively with the transit and airport agencies weren't entirely successful during that period, but they were certainly more productive than attempts to incorporate or ignore the agencies. Finally, in 1984, the state legislature reorganized the transit commission, which was beset by internal disputes and citizen complaints, and gave the Metropolitan Council authority to approve the commission's plans and capital budget.

Use Existing Review Opportunities or Create New Ones. Periodic policy reauthorization sessions and annual or biennial budget review periods provide regular policy review opportunities. Election campaigns and changes in top political or executive leadership also often provide predictable occasions for policy review. For example, shortly after Arne Carlson took over from Rudy Perpich as governor of Minnesota in 1991, he announced that he would give the Metropolitan Council two years to return to his view of its original mission — which was to prepare long-range regional plans, develop a vision for regional growth, and help local governments become more efficient. Saying he would ask the legislature to abolish the council if it did not revitalize itself, Carlson gave council members a powerful mandate to undertake a comprehensive review of policies and programs, as well as stakeholder relations.

However, public leaders can create policy review opportunities almost anytime they wish through the design and use of existing or new forums. The timing and the use of formal arenas and courts are often tightly regulated, but the same is not true of forums. Conferences, hearings, study commissions, media events, investigative reporting, discussion groups, and so on can be arranged whenever public leaders wish to promote policy discussions and critiques.

Convene a Review Group. The composition of this review group may vary considerably depending on the nature of the review.

Legislation and policies requiring scheduled reviews may specify a particular group—for example, a legislative committee, city council, or nonprofit board of directors. Often, however, flexibility is possible in choosing participants, and including outsiders who do not have a vested interest in the status quo often is wise. They can be counted on to focus on important public problems and can offer constructive suggestions for policy change.

Challenge Institutional Rules That Favor Undesirable Inertia. Institutions have an uncanny ability to take on a life of their own, making constructive change extremely difficult (Kouzes and Posner, 1987; Wilson, 1989). There are many routines of politics that challenge anything new but rarely subject what is already in place to a searching critique (Sharkansky, 1970). These routines and other rules embedded in the design and use of existing forums, arenas, and courts often make present arrangements the taken-for-granted "way things are," and make a different, planned future unlikely. If the future is to be what we want it to be, these rules must be confronted and set aside when the need arises (Mangham, 1986). As chair of the Metropolitan Council, Sandra Gardebring shook up several institutional routines. For example, she assigned people to work on projects outside their normal areas of work. Challenging the laissez-faire atmosphere she inherited, she established the expectation that deadlines would be set and met.

Finally, Stay Fresh—Keep from Going Stale! Build energy and enthusiasm for addressing the next big public problem. Public problems will not get formulated and addressed effectively unless public leaders take responsibility for doing so. To paraphrase Edmund Burke, all that is necessary for the powers of evil to triumph is for good people to do nothing.

Policy Maintenance

To Maintain Existing Policies, Seek Little Change in the Design and Use of Forums, Arenas, and Courts. Any significant change is likely to undermine the regime established in the previous phase. It is important, however, to find occasions in forums to recall or reinvigorate the vision that originally inspired and mobilized people to seek the policy changes. As the Metropolitan Council neared its twenty-fifth anniversary, its supporters feared that the original vision had dissipated, making termination a distinct possibility. Therefore, they joined Governor Carlson in urging the council once again to become a forceful voice in shaping the region's future.

To Maintain or Make Marginal Modifications to Existing Policies, Rely on Implementers and Focused Input from Consumers Through Routine Surveys and Discussion, Focus, and Problem-solving Groups, and Involve Supportive Advocates. Broader involvement of policy elites and the public is likely to raise issues and conflicts that may require more fundamental policy changes (Hogwood and Peters, 1983). Mary Anderson, a suburban mayor appointed by Governor Carlson to chair the Metropolitan Council, followed this advice in responding to the governor's demand that the council come up with ways to help local governments work together to cut costs. Instead of convening a new advisory committee, she decided the council staff should survey local governments to find out what cooperative, cost-saving measures already existed. She reasoned that it might be possible to carry out the governor's directive by simply promoting what had already been tested by the local governments themselves.

Policy Change or Succession

To Facilitate a Move to New Policies, Significantly Alter the Design and Use of Forums, Arenas, or Courts. A new set of issues, decisions, conflicts, and policy preferences are then likely to emerge. For example, the opponents of women's right to choose abortion have campaigned for a Human Life Amendment to the U.S. Constitution that would fundamentally alter the constitutional principles applied to abortion laws in Supreme Court cases. They have also strongly supported candidates for the Presidency and for Congress who could be counted on to fill the federal judiciary with people likely to uphold new restrictive abortion laws.

Create or Redesign Forums to Challenge Existing Meanings and Estrange People from Them, and to Create New Meanings and Facilitate Their Enactment. Leaders may wish to estrange people from problem definitions, solution choices, or the political arrangements that support the problems or solutions (Mangham, 1986). New interpretive schemes, myths, or stories supply the seed crystal around which a new coalition can form in support of a different configuration of policies, plans, and programs. For example, a problem reassessment may imply that a different set of categories, value judgments, indicators, comparisons, focusing events, or crises is relevant. Change advocates may articulate a new or revised vision that inspires collective action. This work begins in forums and moves toward arenas and courts. Public leaders use forums first to estrange people from existing meanings, because "estrangement creates a circumstance in which *givenness* becomes *possibility*" (Mangham, 1986, p. 144). Often the estrangement will follow articulation of a changed way of characterizing the dimensions of the issue, one of the heresthetic devices described by Riker (1986).

In 1990, several Minnesota organizations that support women's right to choose abortion decided that the time had come to reframe the abortion debate and return to a problem formulation that had been overshadowed by the "pro-choice" versus "pro-life" battles. The Minnesota Women's Consortium, an association of organizations committed to women's equality, convened a series of brown-bag lunches to discuss abortion as a response to unwanted pregnancy. The discussion leaders argued that an emphasis on preventing unintended pregnancies could be the basis for keeping abortion legal, while also reducing the need for it. "Prevention, not prohibition" was the theme for the discussions, which resulted in a report bearing the theme as its title. The report defined a number of problems, such as the unavailability of birth control for many Minnesotans and the lack of health and sex education for teenagers, and then recommended solutions that could be adopted by the legislature, school boards, parents, adolescents, and social service providers.

Even when change advocates are successful in redefining problems, they should not expect new policies to be adopted without a change in the political circumstances surrounding the policy domain. As Kingdon (1984) notes, these changes may include public opinion swings, election results, administrative changes, ideological or partisan redistribution in legislative bodies, and interest group pressure campaigns. Before new proposals can be adopted, key decision makers in arenas must be receptive, and changes in politics may be necessary before they become receptive. As noted earlier in this chapter, there was evidence in the early 1990s that the political environment of abortion was changing, and in conflicting directions. Many political candidates strongly identified themselves as "pro-choice," not so much as an act of courage — which it definitely would have been in previous election years — but as a strategic decision based on expectations of voter behavior. At the same time, the Supreme Court had become much more sympathetic to arguments for restricting women's access to abortion.

Major reforms may also depend on a successful search for important ideas within the relevant policy communities. Recall that policies usually represent a recombination of already existing ideas, or a mutation of some sort, rather than something totally new (Kingdon, 1984). Still, the right recombination must be put together, one that effectively addresses the new problem definition and is politically salable. Forums again play a crucial role as the settings within which effective solutions to public problems can be developed.

Remember That Policy Succession Typically Is a "Middle-Level" Game. The high-level political elites are unlikely to be involved in policy succession because the legitimacy of the issue area already has been settled. In policy succession, the focus is likely to be on details of program design as they are hashed and rehashed, and this focus belongs to middle-level legislative and administrative arenas (Lynn, 1987). Further, since policy succession is likely to attract the interest of current policy implementers and consumers, these people are likely to exercise more influence on the ultimate outcomes of the new change efforts than they did on initial policy formulation and adoption efforts. Because the high-level elites and major displays of public opinion are unlikely to be involved, and because earlier policies, organizations, clients, and ideologies still exist, Hogwood and Peters (1983) argue that the legislative processing of policy succession is likely to be more difficult than the passage of the initial policy innovation. They add that the concessions and compromises embedded in the existing policy are likely to prevent major reforms and that reformers are likely to be disappointed with the gains achieved in relation to their efforts.

Attempts to reform the abortion policy regime established after *Roe* v. *Wade* have been an obvious exception to the view of policy succession as a middle-level endeavor. The legitimacy of the new regime was never accepted by a well-organized, sizable portion of the public, who have kept pressure on policy elites to dismantle the regime. The Metropolitan Council, on the other hand, does offer examples of the middle-level approach to policy succession. One of these is the fiscal disparities program established in 1971 to equalize tax bases among local governments. Basically, the program pools a portion of the tax base resulting from new development and then redistributes it across the metropolitan area using an equalization formula. In recent years, various local government officials have charged that the program takes too much money from them or gives them too little. They have advocated sweeping reform. Studies of the program, however, indicate it has generally worked as intended, and the governor and state legislators have stayed out of the debate. The most likely scenario is that local government pressure will persuade the council to recommend incremental changes in the program.

Remember That Both Implementers and Beneficiaries of Existing Policies Are More Likely to Be Concerned with Policy Implementation Details Than with Policy Innovation (Hogwood and Peters, 1983; Delbecq, 1977). Policies themselves are often more symbolic than real; what counts is how they are implemented—that is where the real action is for implementers and beneficiaries. There is good news and bad news here. The good news for reformers is that, if the problem they are tackling stems mainly from existing policies, policy changes may be adopted before implementers and beneficiaries of the status quo know what is happening. The bad news is, implementers and beneficiaries may be able to kill any policy they don't like during implementation. More good news for reformers is that, if the problem is not caused by existing policy, only policy implementers and consumers may need to be convinced of the virtues of change. The bad news is, they may not be convinced. The Metropolitan Council, for example, has authority to review and block any major regional construction project that violates the council's development policies. However, the council has hesitated to exercise this authority when powerful political actors have had other ideas. Legislators and governors alike were largely able to ignore the council in debating proposals to provide new or remodeled facilities for professional baseball and football, to build the state's first horse-racing track, and to build a world trade center, all in the metropolitan area. In all three cases, the legislature ultimately assigned the task of choosing sites and designing the projects to new commissions.

To Make Major Policy Reforms, Rely on Key Policy Decision Makers, Along with Policy Implementers and Beneficiaries. In all likelihood, to make substantial changes, leaders will need the support of a coalition that is different from the one that originally adopted and implemented the policy, and a new constellation of ideas, interests, and agreements will need to be worked out (Hogwood and Peters, 1983; Sabatier, 1988, 1991). For example, as advocates of a woman's right to choose abortion endorse new policies and programs that reduce unwanted pregnancies, they may need to recruit educators, children's advocates, and social service groups as prominent participants in the coalition for change. The "prevention, not prohibition" project of the Minnesota Women's Consortium included these types of representatives and three state legislators, in addition to traditional advocates of legal abortion, such as the Abortion Rights Council and Minnesota NOW.

To Achieve Policy Succession, Consider a Move to Either "Split" or "Consolidate" Policies. For example, the Metropolitan Council split off its arts program and the 911 emergency system, both of which are now independent operations. On the other hand, the Nixon administration used policy consolidation when it folded numerous separate programs into "general revenue sharing" and "special revenue sharing" funds, and allowed states and cities to decide how they wished to spend the monies within broad limits. The heresthetic device of changing the dimensions of an issue can facilitate policy splitting or consolidation. Moreover, implementers or consumers will favor consolidation or splitting if it is in their interest. Splitting or consolidation can also resolve conflicts over areas of policy influence through making either separate or combined budgetary allocations and, depending on the circumstances, making ambiguous or clear allocations of jurisdiction. Conflicts over ideas are less easily resolved, although good policy analysis may help. However, there may be strong coalitions in support of each position, and no amount of analysis may convince them to reassess their positions (Lynn, 1987; Sabatier, 1988; Benveniste, 1989; Anderson, 1990).

Consider Building a New System Without Dismantling the Old System. The result is parallel, redundant, or competing systems, but often there are overall net social gains through better market segmentation and the benefits of competition (Bendor, 1985). For example, when Lyndon Johnson favored, and got, an Office of Economic Opportunity to oversee many of his poverty programs, which he thought would be eclipsed or destroyed if they were housed in the departments of Labor or Health, Education, and Welfare, he did not wipe out Labor or HEW; he simply left them to their historic tasks and created a new organization to fill in important gaps in those tasks.

Policy Termination

Think of Policy Termination As an Extreme Version of Policy Reform. Many of the guidelines outlined under policy succession or change are applicable to policy termination as well. In particular, the design and use of forums, arenas, and courts is likely to be crucial. And a new coalition organized around new ideas, interests, and agreements is likely to be necessary. Given the probable resistance of current implementers and beneficiaries, public leadership will be a crucial component of all policy termination efforts. And a fundamental leadership task will be to estrange important stakeholders from the policies to be terminated (Mangham, 1986).

Engage in Cutback Management When Programs Need to Be Eliminated or Severely Reduced. A substantial literature has developed on how to manage cutbacks in general, although this literature is less helpful when it comes to specifics (Cameron, Sutton, and Whetten, 1988; Guy, 1989; Golembiewski, 1990). Behn (1983), for example, argues that there are two stages to cutback efforts in public organizations. In the first stage, the organization typically borrows against the future to cover the gap between current revenues and needed expenditures. Yet if revenues are not increased in the future, this tactic merely makes the adjustments to retrenchment worse by postponing the second stage, or "day of reckoning," when major cuts and redesigns are made. Behn lists the following basic tasks of cutback management:

- Decide what to cut.
- Maintain morale.
- Attract and keep quality people, which may be particularly difficult when people think the ship is sinking.
- Develop the support of key constituencies and legislators.
- Create opportunities for innovation.
- Avoid mistakes.

These are difficult tasks that are unlikely to be executed without effective leaders and managers. According to Behn, managers and leaders must:

- Explain the reality.
- Take a long-term view.
- Develop new strategies for their organizations.

- Develop measures of performance in order to know which units to cut and which to reward.
- Create incentives for cooperation.
- Be compassionate.

During her tenure as Metropolitan Council chair, Sandra Gardebring proved adept at many aspects of cutback management, which was necessitated by her mandate from the governor to refocus the council's efforts. For example, at the staff level, she pruned the number of departments and thus reduced money spent on highly paid department directors. She shifted resources away from human services to environmental issues, partly in response to the realities of federal funding priorities. She also committed resources to the staff-initiated Metropolitan Directions project that suggested long-range strategies for the Twin Cities area. Though not known for her compassion, she did create incentives for cooperation and task completion. She also cultivated the important stakeholders whose support was crucial in making progress on priority environmental issues.

Summary

In the last phase of the policy change cycle, advocates and public policy decision makers review policies that have resulted from previous phases in order to determine whether the new regime should be maintained, significantly altered, or terminated. This chapter has discussed why policies cease to work and outlined the benefits of moving successfully through this review phase. Chief among those benefits are assurance that the new policy regime remains responsive to real needs and problems, that residual implementation difficulties are resolved, that needed energy is generated for policy renewal, and that areas crowded with policies are weeded and pruned.

In this phase leaders should focus on the problems that prompted the policy change being reviewed. They should rely on indicators of policy success or failure to help them decide whether policies should be maintained, reformed, or terminated.

If the policies have not been effective or if the situation has changed, it may be necessary to reformulate the public problems, to reconsider the policies adopted to address the problems, or even to move on to other public problems. Whatever the cause of this changed approach, it may also be necessary to revise the myths or interpretive schemes that underlie the adopted policies. Leaders also must recognize that working with existing organizational structures, rather than trying to change or replace them, may be very productive in this phase. A review group and review opportunities must be established and institutional inertia overcome, however, in order to review and perhaps modify the work of these structures.

The design and use of forums, arenas, and courts in this phase will vary, depending on whether the new regime is to be maintained, reformed, or terminated. In order to maintain the regime, leaders should seek little change in these shared-power settings, and they may be able to involve mainly implementers and consumers in policy review. If significant reform is needed, the design and use of pertinent forums, arenas, and courts will have to be significantly altered. Leaders will especially need to create or redesign forums to challenge existing meanings and to allow the enactment of new meanings. Once again implementers and beneficiaries are the most likely participants in the review, although some key decision makers and probably a new supportive coalition will have to be enlisted as well. Possible approaches to policy succession are policy splitting, policy consolidation, and parallel policy systems. Policy termination is an extreme version of policy succession; leaders will need the strategies and tactics of cutback management to minimize the resulting pain and dislocation. Finally, leaders should renew their own energy for working on public problems.

With this chapter, we complete our detailed consideration of how public leaders and followers can navigate the policy change cycle successfully. The conclusion, which follows, will offer some last words on the two cases used throughout this book and additional guidelines for change advocates who are about to begin the process of tackling public problems in a shared-power, no-one-in-charge world.

Key Lessons and Guidelines for Getting Started

I know only two things for certain. One is that we gain nothing by walking around the difficulties and merely indulging in wishful thinking. The other is that there is always something one can do oneself.

— Alva Myrdal

The most useful and valuable people in the world are those who care most deeply about institutions for making the world better.
— Booker T. Washington

The previous chapters have presented a framework that can guide committed public leaders and followers as they tackle public problems in a no-one-in-charge, shared-power world. Two cases of major policy change have illustrated how public leadership operates in a shared-power world. This chapter revisits those cases to consider the messages they contain about shared power; forums, arenas, and courts; the policy change cycle; and leadership. The chapter also presents a number of guidelines that suggest how individuals, groups, organizations, and communities that are interested in policy change might proceed.

The Cases Revisited

The two cases used to develop and illustrate the framework presented in this book concern two very different policy issues—how to govern the Minneapolis–St. Paul region, and how to reform or repeal U.S. abortion laws. Yet they have important commonalities. Both involve major policy change efforts conducted in shared-power environments. Both reveal how astute change advocates design and use forums, arenas, and courts to achieve their goals, and both further reveal how the design and use of these settings over the course of a policy change cycle reshapes the change effort and the settings themselves. Finally, the cases reinforce Margaret Mead's assertion that a "small group of committed citizens can change the world." The cases remind us that while leadership is and must be widely shared in today's no-one-in-charge world, a few committed people can make the crucial difference as catalysts and nurturers of change.

Metropolitan Council

In the early 1960s, communities in the Minneapolis–St. Paul area were grappling with a number of public problems that spilled beyond the capacity of local governmental units and citizen organizations. Moreover, local governmental responsibility for these problems was shared with regional, state, and federal agencies or with elected bodies. Numerous public leaders began articulating a compelling vision that reframed these problems and suggested solutions. The vision's core interpretive scheme was that Minneapolis and St. Paul and their suburbs constituted a social and economic community with promising potential. The vision suggested that the problems were interconnected and demanded a regional solution, chiefly some form of regional governance.

    In the initial agreement, problem definition, and search for solution phases, leaders like Verne Johnson, James Hetland, Ann Duff, and Robert Einsweiler demonstrated their prowess at redesigning existing forums and organizing new ones with careful attention to building a consensus and to shaping decision making in the most pertinent arena, the Minnesota legislature. They cultivated reporters and editors from the area's daily newspapers, ensured that participants in public discussions and seminars included the main organized stakeholder groups, and assured local officials — one of the most powerful stakeholder groups, as well as the one most fearful of change — that regional governance would not usurp local governments but rather help them. The change advocates did not attempt to include representation from less well-organized groups such as poor and minority people; for one thing, it was clear that unorganized groups would not significantly affect legislative decisions. On the other hand, leaving out these groups meant that the council had a very limited mandate for social development of the Twin Cities region, especially once the federal government became less interested in alleviating poverty and ceased to have much interest in funding regional planning bodies.

The change advocates worked with a legislator to develop a legislative proposal for establishing the Metropolitan Council, which was planned to be essentially a new set of forums, arenas, and courts supported by its own taxing authority. Although the legislature passed a weakened version of the proposal, it left the taxing authority intact, and it left the door open for the council to become more powerful. The legislature adopted a decidedly shared-power solution — in effect, a new regime for metropolitan governance. It gave the Metropolitan Council policy-making authority over planning and coordination of metropolitan development and services, but made council members appointed rather than elected. Although most existing regional boards or agencies were made subordinate to the council, the legislature allowed a few, such as the airports and transit commissions, to remain nearly autonomous. The adopted proposal was less than ideal from the standpoint of the change advocates, but probably was the best possible outcome in light of political realities.

During the implementation phase, the Metropolitan Council faced several court challenges, but in the most important ones, it either obtained a favorable decision or countered an unfavorable decision by obtaining new authority from the legislature.

It also demonstrated organizational leadership by making tough decisions that reinforced its policies. Council members and staff alike cultivated relationships with local officials and legislators at critical junctures when their support was essential to successful implementation. Although the supporters of a strong council persuaded the legislature to expand the council's power over the years, they never succeeded in having council members elected rather than appointed, a change which would have given the council more independence and a more direct link to the citizenry.

The council entered the maintenance, succession, or termination phase in the early 1980s. It no longer had strong support in the legislature or governor's office. The regional agencies responsible for transit and waste water were in a management crisis, and the appointment of Gerald Isaacs as chair was disastrous. Veteran supporters of the council appeared in public forums to call for a return to the council's original vision. Governor Perpich responded by appointing new chairs for the council and other troubled regional agencies. The legislature also restructured transit planning. These changes were sufficient to maintain the council through the 1980s, but in 1991 a new governor, Arne Carlson, threatened to terminate the council, and the regime it represented, if it could not reinvigorate itself. At the same time, several developments augured well for the council's future. Carlson appointed a respected local official as chair, the legislature reestablished metropolitan affairs committees, and veteran supporters offered ideas for council renewal.

Abortion

By the late 1960s, numerous physicians, lawyers, clergy, civil libertarians, and women's rights advocates comprised a loosely connected constituency for the legalization of abortion in the United States. They had decided something could and should be done about state laws that severely restricted women's ability to obtain a safe abortion to end an unwanted pregnancy. Illegal abortionists flourished, while physicians attempting to comply with the laws feared prosecution, even when they judged abortion to be in a woman's best interest. The advocates of change had neither the authority nor the political clout to overturn the laws. Change advocates such as Minnesota's Betty Benjamin or New York's Lawrence Lader began presenting new interpretations of abortion in public forums. They argued that women had a right to control their reproductive capacity, that legal abortion contributed to women's health and safety, and that abortion was a morally defensible choice. In doing so, they challenged, often courageously, the verdict of the court of public opinion that abortion was a socially taboo subject and the resort of women trying to avoid social sanctions for having sexual relations outside marriage. These change advocates were able to attract and retain public attention because the mass media are always interested in controversial issues that verge on the sensational, and because advocates developed mediagenic spokespersons and organized events with media appeal.

Because the campaign to legalize abortion in the United States had to be waged in the legislatures of all fifty states, it was important to organize state-level as well as national forums that could articulate the movement's vision and maximize its resources. National organizations like Planned Parenthood and the American Medical Association offered existing forums, but advocates also formed a new national organization, NARAL, and benefited from the founding of NOW, both of which placed the abortion issue at the top of their agendas. Meanwhile, opponents of legalized abortion formed their own organizations, such as Minnesota Citizens Concerned for Life, to provide forums and pressure state legislators. At this time, the main national organization that forcefully opposed legalized abortion was the Catholic church.

Initially, the proponents of legal abortion attempted to persuade legislators to reform existing abortion laws, rather than demanding their outright repeal. Several legislatures did pass reform legislation aimed at clarifying the conditions under which doctors could legally perform abortions. In practice, however, these laws were often as restrictive as the old ones, a result that led change advocates to change their approach and to call for repeal. But the repeal effort was much less successful because it did not lend itself to traditional methods of legislative compromise. As the abortion battles raged in legislative arenas, some supporters of legalizing abortion challenged old laws in formal courts, and they also continued to present their case in the court of public opinion. Physicians and others were tried for performing abortions or for referring people to abortion clinics. The arguments and verdicts in these cases laid some of the groundwork for the two Supreme Court decisions, *Roe* v. *Wade* and *Doe* v. *Bolton,* that in 1973 effectively accomplished what was impossible in legislative arenas—the repeal of restrictive state abortion laws. An important example of collective public leadership was provided by Norma McCorvey, Sarah Weddington, Linda Coffee, Justice Blackmun, and others who forcefully presented the case for adapting constitutional and legal principles to changing societal and technological conditions.

Opponents—such as Marjory Mecklenburg, who headed the newly formed National Right to Life Committee—did not accept the Supreme Court's word as final, however. Fully recognizing the shared-power nature of the U.S. political system, they returned to state and local arenas, where they pressed for new restrictions that might pass judicial muster. Meanwhile, they also campaigned in Congress for a constitutional amendment that, in effect, would overrule the Supreme Court, and they sought presidential support, especially for appointing new Supreme Court justices who might overturn *Roe* v. *Wade.* Their efforts paid off with a 1989 Supreme Court decision that gave states new leeway in regulating abortion and with the subsequent passage of new state laws that resembled the restrictive laws of old. In 1992, the Supreme Court upheld most of the provisions of Pennsylvania's new law. Supporters of women's right to choose abortion have fought back, however, despite some spells of slackened interest. In the early 1990s, many political candidates, though certainly not all, actually benefited from adopting a "pro-choice" stance, and public opinion polls continue to show that a majority of U.S. adults now believe women should be able to decide whether or not to have an abortion in the early months of pregnancy.

In the 1960s, the advocates of legal abortion were seeking to terminate an old policy regime resulting from policy change initiatives dating from the 1880s and earlier. Although these advocates have been able to establish a new policy regime, that regime has been under constant attack and has never included some elements of its supporters' vision, the most glaring omission being the failure to provide public funds to allow poor women to obtain abortions. Those who want to restore restrictive abortion laws have had some success, but it is unlikely that they can gain public support for directly contravening the rights guaranteed by *Roe* v. *Wade*. Both groups have become skilled in the use of forums, arenas, and courts, yet neither seems so far to have engaged in a well-considered and inclusive issue-creation process focusing on stakeholder analyses, problem formulation, and alternative solutions.

It is entirely possible that the opposing groups in this case will continue to be locked in figurative and sometimes physical combat for some time to come. Perhaps the most promising avenue for moving beyond wars of attrition in this policy area is the recent attempt to focus on family planning as a means of addressing an underlying problem, unwanted pregnancies, that leads to women's need for abortion.

Leadership Lessons About Shared Power; the Design and Use of Forums, Arenas, and Courts; and the Policy Change Cycle

In reflecting on these and other cases used in this book, we identify several lessons about how to raise and address public problems in a shared-power world.

Shared Power

First, in a shared-power world, the advocates of policy change cannot force outcomes. Indeed, pushing too hard for their own aims at the expense of others' aims can produce a vicious spiral of actions designed to get even rather than get ahead. Instead of forcing outcomes, change advocates should seek regimes of mutual gain that are likely to be stable in the long term and to produce widespread benefits at reasonable cost (Axelrod,

1984; Ostrom, 1990). A second lesson is that collective public leadership is vital. In a shared-power world, change efforts can fail in many ways — and they will, without shared public leadership. Systems and structures can be reasonable substitutes for leadership when change isn't required, but when fundamental change is needed, there is no substitute for leadership.

Forums, Arenas, and Courts

The initial lesson here is that forums, arenas, and courts are the basis for both stability and change in a shared-power world, and each setting has different purposes and constituting elements. Forums are the primary setting for creating issues and for exercising visionary leadership. Arenas are the main setting in which policy decisions are made and implemented and political leadership is exercised. Courts are the main setting for resolving residual conflicts, enforcing underlying norms, and exercising judicial leadership. Second, when introducing new ideas, leaders should design and use forums first, because it is here that constructive shared meanings and appreciations are most likely to be developed. These shared meanings and appreciations, in turn, will contribute to the formation of the strong coalitions and citizen support necessary to win in arenas and courts.

Third, when planning for change, it is important for leaders to understand how forums, arenas, and courts are linked. Change advocates should choose their settings carefully, selecting those that are both favorable to their cause and likely to produce desired results. When necessary, change advocates can organize their own forums, arenas, and courts. And the final lesson is that the most effective mode of leadership in forums, arenas, and courts is *indirect* — that is, leaders will be most influential by focusing on the ideas, rules, modes, media, and methods that link action and bedrock structures, rather than focusing on the action or structures themselves. Action, of course, matters a great deal. But the character of the action will be powerfully influenced by the ideas, rules, modes, media, and methods that shape it — and leaders are more likely to be able to affect these carriers of bias than they are to be able to directly control the actions of others.

The Policy Change Cycle

The policy change cycle can start anywhere, but at some point each phase will require leaders' attention. The cycle rarely is linear; more frequently, it consists of a series of repeating loops. In addition, a new cycle often arises from the last phase of a previous cycle. But regardless of the precise way the cycle unfolds in practice, public leaders should keep the purposes, desired outcomes, and benefits of each phase in mind as the leaders try to create desirable proposals supported by winning coalitions. The phases have been organized to assist with the creation of these proposal ideas and coalitions. Another lesson for leaders is that they should make sure that the policy change effort is addressing real problems and is not knocked off course by solutions that do not address the problems. Also, leaders should work to shape or take advantage of political circumstances that favor attention to the problems. There is tremendous pressure, often of a political sort, to grab quickly onto specific solutions that are not particularly helpful (Kingdon, 1984; Nutt, 1984). Public leaders must work to keep attention focused on the public problems that need to be addressed.

A third lesson is that, on the one hand, policy change processes are prone to convolution and disintegration, and often are characterized by disruption and delay; on the other hand, in certain circumstances, they can lead to excessively hasty action (Hickson and others, 1986; McCall and Kaplan, 1990). An important leadership task, therefore, is to influence the flow of action in such a way that problems, solutions, and politics are joined appropriately. It takes real thought, effort, and skill to couple well-understood problems with effective solutions through supportive politics at key decision points. Maintaining an inspiring and animating vision throughout the process can help change advocates stay focused on what is important and realize when they may be off track. Finally, leaders must be available who can fill the roles of policy sponsors, entrepreneurs, and champions in order to keep the proposed policy change moving through forums, arenas, and courts over the policy change cycle. Leaders in positions of power and authority—the sponsors— can help force and legitimize action, as well as provide necessary resources, contacts, and intelligence. Those who are there on a day-to-day basis—the entrepreneurs and champions—can make sure that everything that must happen does happen to keep policy change moving.

In sum, public leaders must recognize that in a shared-power world, things don't always work out "right"—people make mistakes, institutions can be perverse, events can throw everything off course, and the whole can be less than the sum of its parts. All too easily, leaders can have a mess on their hands. This condition, however, does not mean that public leaders should do nothing, nor does it mean they can or should try to be heroic saviors. Instead, they will be most effective by collaborating with others to design regimes of mutual gain that tap and serve people's deepest interests and values, and that continually address important public problems in effective, technically workable, politically acceptable, and legally and ethically defensible ways. As Hubert Humphrey said, "We will have to decide today whether we will design the future or resign ourselves to it."

Getting Started

Our cases indicate that individuals, groups, organizations, and communities of interest or geography can engage in effective policy change processes. The cases also indicate that success is never guaranteed. A number of difficulties or challenges must be overcome if useful policy changes are to be formulated, adopted, and implemented. Let us conclude with some advice on how to get started with policy change.

Focus on the Context and the People Involved

Effective leaders start where they are and where the other affected people are. This is one of the fundamental principles of organizing collective action (Kahn, 1982). They talk to people, read the newspapers and newsmagazines, read public affairs journals, pay attention to opinion polls, and generally keep their eyes open. Also, other involved or affected parties often need some education about the nature of public problems and solutions and about the process, potentialities, and pitfalls of policy change. If they are important to policy formulation or implementation, leaders will have to bring them along so that they can be effective participants.

Leaders need to tailor the policy change process and their own public leadership roles to the community of interest or place. The generic policy change process outlined in this book must be applied with care so that it clearly fits the situation (Bryson and Delbecq, 1979; Hogwood and Peters, 1983; Christensen, 1985). The roles played by public leaders will also be contingent on the situation. Leaders can use the framework and advice offered in this book as a set of orienting concepts and suggestions to consider as they engage in policy change; but they must not allow themselves to become captives of clichés — even ours!

Assess Leadership Capabilities

Leaders must be clear about what animates them as public leaders before they initiate or champion a policy change effort. Also, they should be candid with themselves about their personal strengths and weaknesses. Policy change efforts are not likely to be successful without deep and abiding motivations for change on the part of public leaders, nor are they likely to be successful without the assembly of a team that builds on individuals' strengths and compensates for their weaknesses.

We suggest that potential leaders use two complementary exercises to help them consider exactly how they wish to act as public leaders and what topics should engage them. The first identifies the most satisfying, and the most troublesome, kinds of leadership situations, and helps people draw their own lessons about how they can best act as public leaders. The second exercise explores leadership motives in more depth, along with their wellsprings and sustaining power. The first exercise, "Public Leadership Highs, Lows, and Themes," is loosely patterned after a more elaborate charting exercise described by Kouzes and Posner (1987) and consists of the following ten steps:

1. Take a large sheet of paper (such as a flip-chart sheet), turn it sideways, and draw a horizontal line that divides the paper into top and bottom halves of equal size.

2. At the right-hand end of the line, write in the current year. At the left-hand end, write in the date of your first involvement in public leadership activities.

3. Begin evaluating your public leadership activities. Mark, date, and label your personal public leadership "highs"—broadly conceived—in the appropriate places above the timeline. The height of each mark should represent just how much of a high the "high" was.

4. Mark, date, and label your personal public leadership "lows" in the appropriate places below the timeline. The depth of each mark should represent just how low the "low" was.

5. At the appropriate points on the timeline, fill in as highs or lows any important events that have occurred in your personal life, such as weddings, births, divorces, deaths of relatives or friends, the establishment or breakup of important relationships, graduations, layoffs, and so forth.

6. Identify the themes that are common to the public leadership highs, to the personal highs, and to both.

7. Identify the themes that are common to the public leadership lows, to the personal lows, and to both.

8. Analyze your public leadership abilities and interests by answering these questions:
   a. What works for you?
   b. What does not work for you?
   c. What motivates and inspires you?
   d. What do you really care about?
   e. How do your public and personal lives interact?
   f. What guidance would you give yourself for the future?

9. Share these results with people who know you well and whose friendship, support, and insights you value. Ask for observations and feedback.

10. Reexamine your answers to the questions in step eight in light of the discussion with your friend and prepare a "final" set of answers—final, that is, until you decide to change

them. File these answers in a place where you can review them on occasion as a way of calling you back to your own first principles — what motivates and inspires you, what you really care about, and what you need to do and not to do to stay on track as a public leader.

For the second exercise, we suggest that persons who are considering playing a leading role in a policy change effort take another large sheet of paper, such as a flip-chart sheet, divide it into six vertical columns, and then write their honest answers to the following six questions about their *cares* — the persons, things, or situations that are the objects of their attention, anxiety, or solicitude:

1. *Who* and *what* do I really care about?
2. *Why* do I care about these people, things, or situations?
3. *When* do I care about them?
4. *Where* is the locus of my care — socially, politically, economically, spatially, temporally, or otherwise?
5. *How much* do I care about these people, things, or situations?

Once potential leaders have answered these questions candidly, they may wish to share and discuss their answers with trusted and significant others to gain additional feedback, insight, and advice. The personal learning involved in such an experience can be an invaluable source of wisdom and inspiration, and can help potential leaders make an openhearted and clearheaded assessment of their willingness to invest in a policy change effort (see also Mangham, 1986; Burke, 1945).

Begin Organizing an Effective Team and Laying Groundwork for a Winning Coalition

Unless the policy change process is ultimately, if not initially, sponsored and championed by important and powerful leaders and policy decision makers, it is likely to fail. Authoritative policy decisions will not be forthcoming unless the official decision makers are willing to say yes. Another way of saying this is that

the resource likely to be in shortest supply in policy change efforts
is the attention and commitment of public leaders, especially
official decision makers, so real effort — public leadership — will
be necessary to get the public leaders involved and committed.

Be Aware That Leaders Need Compelling
Reasons to Undertake a Policy Change Effort

The process of change — of building and sustaining a winning
coalition in support of desirable answers to pressing public problems — can be arduous at best. It takes courage, strength, and
endurance to sustain the effort over the long haul. Therefore,
leaders must be able to articulate good reasons for undertaking
the effort if people are to be mobilized and inspired to pursue
collective action for the common good.

Visionary Leadership Requires Thinking
Ahead About the Process of Issue Creation

Recall that issue creation is the process by which a public problem and at least one solution that has advantages and disad-
vantages from stakeholders' standpoints gain a place on the public agenda. Previous chapters have offered detailed guidance for
the issue creation process. Here we simply propose that leaders
engage in a truncated version of that process in small group settings, in order to think ahead about what might occur when
more stakeholders get involved, and to decide whether a policy
change effort in the chosen issue area is likely to be valuable.
In practice, once policy change efforts are under way, they often
turn out differently than expected. Nevertheless, organized and
thorough advance thinking makes leaders and followers more
effective and helps them avoid unwelcome surprises. We recommend that leaders follow this outline:

- Explore various issue formulations to determine whether apparent public problems really need to be addressed. This
  may mean conducting research, gathering data, examining
  the actions and results of the systems already in place, and
  talking with many people.

- Consider the range of possible solutions to the problems. What elements in the various proposals circulating in the "policy community" might address the problems?
- Specify the constellations of stakeholders that might be affected by the causes or consequences of various issue formulations. Develop stakeholder maps (see Resource D) around different issue formulations. Explore the political consequences of the mapped groupings. What is the depth and breadth of support for and of opposition to the various issue formulations? Does it appear possible to create a winning coalition in favor of positive policy change?
- Determine if an issue can be framed so that it can get on the public agenda and, at the same time, be worth all the effort that will be required to have virtuous and effective policy changes adopted and implemented.

Envision the Process Ahead by Developing a "Map," or Set of Maps, of the Formal and Informal Forums, Arenas, and Courts Involved in, or Affected by, the Various Issue Formulations

Blackboards, whiteboards, or flip-chart sheets should be used for this purpose, and again, this will probably be a small group exercise. Once the maps are complete, leaders can ask the following questions of themselves and others:

- How is the issue being talked about now—or not talked about—in existing forums? Who are the main actors in these forums? And what would they think about the various issue formulations?
- What kinds of decisions about the issue are being made now in existing arenas? How do these decisions either alleviate or aggravate public problems? Who are the main actors in these arenas? And what would they think about the various issue formulations?
- How are residual conflicts about the issue being resolved in the existing courts? What underlying norms do those courts enforce? Who are the main actors in these courts? And what would they think about the various issue formulations?

- How would existing forums, arenas, and courts have to be changed to get the issue on the public agenda? Are new forums, arenas, and courts necessary? What would have to occur to place a useful proposal on the formal agenda and get it adopted and implemented? Are new actors necessary?
- In light of the above analyses, what would the general outlines of a strategy for policy change look like?

Issue creation relies on the effective design and use of forums more than anything else, so leaders must be especially thoughtful and creative when it comes to forums. And if leaders are not sure what to do, they should simply discuss that fact with others, following Hubert Humphrey's sage advice: "When in doubt, talk." Forums are the no-one-in-charge settings in which people talk out what they ought to do and what they mean by their statements and actions.

Think About the Costs and Consequences of a Policy Change Effort

How will the changes be beneficial or detrimental to various stakeholders? What are the potential opportunities and rewards of policy change? What are the consequences of doing nothing? And what will be the personal, team, and organizational costs—in terms of time, energy, money, attention, and alternative expenditures forgone—of a policy change effort? In light of the problems and prospects for change, is the effort likely to be worth it? And if it is, how can leaders best sell such an effort?

    Leaders must also think about worst-case scenarios. What are the risks of losing or of ending up with a situation that is worse than the starting point? What do leaders not want to happen? How can they keep it from happening? And leaders must think about whether or not they wish to set any limits on a change effort. Are there things they are unwilling to do, even if those things appear necessary to achieve policy change? Are there personal, financial, political, ethical, legal, or other limits beyond which they are unwilling to go? If so, what are those limits?

Develop an Action Plan for Obtaining an Initial Agreement to Address a Public Problem

The action plan must be based on the ideas and suggestions contained in the preceding lessons and leadership guidelines, and should aim at reaching the kind of initial agreement described in Chapter Five. The plan should embody a strategy for introducing the idea of policy change; developing an understanding of what the changes themselves, and the process of adopting and implementing them, might mean in practice; developing a commitment to the change effort; and reaching an actual agreement.

When the Going Gets Tough, Keep in Mind the Benefits of the Proposed Policy Changes

Leaders must continually recall the visions that motivate and inspire them. As Kanter (1983) indicates, every innovation feels like a failure in the middle. Changes, almost by definition, are failures until they succeed. So if change processes feel bad in the middle, there probably are logical reasons for that feeling. Change advocates must hang in there and be "psychologically hardy" (Kobasa and Maddi, cited in Kouzes and Posner, 1987, pp. 65–69). Those public leaders best able to weather the storms of change are highly committed to all aspects of their lives, believe they are able to make a difference, and see problems as opportunities. They are also optimistic. Pessimists see adversities as permanent, as pervading all aspects of their lives, and as their own fault. They also are likely to have a better grasp than optimists of exactly what they do control—they are the classic realists. Optimists see adversities as temporary, as specific to the situation, and as either someone else's fault or the result of factors beyond the optimists' control. Optimists can be Pollyannas or Panglosses, but they also are more likely to feel empowered, rather than dangerously depressed, when confronted by difficulties (Seligman, 1991). They are the dreamers whose visions and energies can inspire and mobilize others to undertake collective action in pursuit of the common good. Optimism—hope, if you will—is the motivator of positive change.

So good leaders are *flexibly* optimistic; they envision the inspiring and even radical possibilities for change, but also realistically assess the barriers to change and what might be done to overcome them. Flexible optimists learn to dream, in other words, with their feet on the ground.

Finally, Keep in Mind That the Time May Not be Right for the Preferred Policy Changes

The problems may not be big enough or the needs not pressing enough. The potential solutions simply may not be workable. A winning coalition may not be possible. Or there may be too much competition from other existing or potential change efforts. For whatever reason, change advocates' causes may be lost causes, at least for the time being. However, those who are committed to lost causes might benefit from the lessons of those who have championed policy changes that at one time were hopeless, but fully or partially succeeded (Crosby and Bryson, 1990). We have in mind such "lost" causes as a reduction in nuclear weapons, women's suffrage, abolition of slavery, civil rights, and environmental protection. The history of these change efforts emphasizes the importance of a long view and a commitment for the long haul. It reinforces the conviction that no virtuous lost cause is lost forever, as long as some people keep its flame alive.

The examples set by these efforts also remind leaders of the need to promote both a popular sense of crisis and a reason for hope. In the 1980s, groups such as Freeze and Minnesota's Women Against Military Madness helped create a national atmosphere of crisis over nuclear arms buildup and a sense that something could be done. For the 1990s, we need leaders and organizations that can develop a similar sense of crisis and of hope over such major national problems as large-scale homelessness; continued racial cleavages; children in poverty; poorly performing educational and health-care systems; polluted land, groundwater, and seashores; and so on. It also is clear that the way issues are framed makes a difference. The virtuous lost causes of the 1980s tended to be ideas *against* — against repression, against military buildup, against self-indulgence and greed, against environmental destruction. For the 1990s, the world sorely needs ideas *for*—for empowered communities, for reinvigorated public life, for social justice, and for a sustainable global environment (see also Bellah and others, 1991).

Finally, advocates for lost causes need to think about what they would do if they win. The tragedy of the former Soviet Union and Eastern Europe, at present, is that they have won the political battles to promote democracy, freedom, and free enterprise; however, they as yet have nowhere near enough committed leaders and followers who can make those concepts work in practice. If the new policies fail during implementation, the reactionaries and conservative hard-liners may reemerge with force and repressive vigor. The virtue of the economic-conversion movement efforts in the United States is that supporters of the movement have thought about how to bridge the gap from an excessively militarized society to a peaceful society, or the gap from where society is to where they want it to be. Their leadership efforts prompted many communities and governments dependent on defense expenditures to think hard about how to lessen that dependence and move to a different sort of economic base. Now that defense budgets are being scaled back, that advance thinking is proving invaluable.

Summary

Effective public leadership inspires and mobilizes others to undertake collective action to resolve important public problems effectively and ethically, thereby contributing to the common good. Public leadership stimulates vision, hope, courage, and commitment. Public leadership is what makes visions of a better world reasonable and "real"-izable. Acts of public leadership are based on understanding:

- The dynamics of a *shared-power world,* or the context in which leadership occurs
- The people involved, or the essence of *personal leadership*
- Team building, or the essence of *team leadership*
- The nurture of organizations, interorganizational networks, and communities, or the essence of *organizational leadership*

- The design and use of forums, in which *visionary leadership* is crucial
- The design and use of arenas, in which *political leadership* is crucial
- The design and use of courts, in which *ethical leadership* is crucial
- The interplay of leadership and forums, arenas, and courts in the policy change cycle, or *putting it all together*

Public leaders work for the creation of regimes of mutual gain that serve people's deepest interests in safety, justice, economic well-being, environmental saneness, liberty, and community. They help others, in Robert Reich's words, "to create settings in which obligation and trust can take root, supported by stories that focus our attention on discovering possibilities for joint gain and avoiding the likelihood of mutual loss" (1987b, p. 252). They help people to realize the realities and possibilities of the shared-power world. They help people to imagine and create the plausible futures they wish for themselves, their children, and their children's children. They thus help dispel pervasive distrust and cynicism regarding the U.S. political system. They offer an antidote to apathy and pessimism and to the temptation to rely on untested, charismatic leaders. They offer a way to increase the power of the many and reinvigorate the democratic process. They show us—to paraphrase Georgia legislator Mabel Thomas—that we are the leaders we have been looking for.

We hope that we have demonstrated how leadership is central to achieving public purposes in a shared-power, no-one-in-charge world. We believe that public leadership can and must be widely practiced to tackle the long list of public problems that beset society. We also hope that we have mobilized and inspired many public leaders and followers to pursue their visions of a better world by building regimes of mutual gain. This book is dedicated to those people. May their leadership on behalf of the common good inspire and mobilize others.

Using Cause-Effect Diagrams

A cause-effect diagram is a method of identifying and assessing the causes and consequences of some condition, problem or, more generally, situation. It answers two questions: what created this situation, and what are the results, or consequences, if the situation continues? Cause-effect diagrams can be drawn up by either individuals or groups. The steps in the process are describing a situation; brainstorming potential causes and effects of the situation; arraying primary, secondary, and tertiary causes; and arraying primary, secondary, and tertiary effects.

In the first step, the group develops a short statement that describes the problematic situation to be explored. Simple brainstorming followed by group discussion is a useful approach to this task. Ideally, several alternative statements will be written so that a fuller picture of the situation can be developed by the end of the exercise. The second step also typically involves brainstorming. Each participant takes a sheet of scratch paper, draws a vertical line down the middle of the sheet, and labels the left half of the sheet "causes" and the right half "effects."

Then each participant brainstorms silently for a few minutes, writing down all of the causes and effects of the situation that come to mind. In the third step, the group develops a map of primary, secondary, and tertiary causes of the situation. The map can be recorded on a sheet of flip-chart paper, a large black-board or whiteboard, or a wall covered by flip-chart sheets. If a single flip-chart sheet is used, each participant writes her or his own five to seven "best" causes and five to seven "best" effects on 1-by-½-inch white stick-on labels. If the map is to go on a board or a wall, each participant writes her or his five to seven "best" causes and five to seven "best" effects on separate sheets of scratch paper created by cutting 8½-by-11-inch sheets of paper in half.

The map is then developed as follows: The first alternative way to frame the situation is written on a sticker and placed in the center of a sheet of flip-chart paper, or else is written on a half-sheet of paper and placed on the wall. Then, the primary causes are placed in a semicircle to the immediate left of the situation statement. Arrows are drawn from the causes to the situation, and any connections between the causes are also noted. Next, a semicircle of secondary causes is arranged to the left of the primary causes and the arrows indicating causality are inserted. The process is repeated with the tertiary causes, and even more distant causes, if they are important. The same process is followed for effects, except that these are arrayed in semicircles to the right of the situation statement. Direct linkages between causes and consequences—ones that do not go "through" the situation—also may be noted. Once the cause-effect diagram is completed, it should be discussed thoroughly. This conversation will continue and complete the discussion that probably began in earnest as the group began arraying causes and effects.

The usefulness of cause-effect diagrams becomes apparent once several have been constructed. Different causes may imply different solutions, which are likely to show up as ways to address the causes or deal with the effects. Different causes and effects are likely to imply different change effort targets and beneficiaries. Different causes and effects thus also imply that different stakeholders are likely to become activated in different ways and with different intensities, because they will assess the costs and benefits of change in different ways. These different impacts should be noted on the cause-effect diagram using various visual aids. For example, wherever a particular stakeholder is implicated in some way by some cause or effect, a colored stick-on dot representing that stakeholder can be affixed to the cause or effect label. Additional information can be placed on the diagram with the help of Post-Its or stick-on labels. Such information might include notes about the different impacts of the situation on various stakeholders, or the stakeholders' different assessments of costs and benefits of potential solutions.

Once several cause-effect diagrams have been constructed, and supplementary information dots or labels attached, change initiators and champions can begin to identify the most useful ways of framing the issue. In addition, the maps should be saved so that they can be referred to again when needed. Large maps can be copied onto a single flip-chart sheet, and it is wise to take a good 35mm photograph of the large map as a backup record, in case something happens to the paper copy. A Polaroid photograph also may be wise — just to be sure that a copy is in hand before participants leave the room. Maps may also be recorded and reproduced with the aid of various graphics software programs.

Development of cause-effect diagrams in the initial phase of the policy change cycle is not a substitute for careful problem formulation and solution search efforts in the next two phases. Nonetheless, the diagrams can be extremely useful to change initiators and champions who seek insights into potentially winning — and potentially disastrous — policy change strategies. Further, new or revised cause-effect diagrams can be developed at a later date as new problem and solution information becomes available.

Stakeholder
Assessment Process

In Chapter Five we provided an overview of the stakeholder assessment process that answers six questions:

- Who are the individuals, groups, and organizations that are the stakeholders?
- What are the goals, expectations, or criteria different stakeholders use to judge what they should want in the problem area and how they should evaluate any solution?
- How well does the status quo meet each stakeholder's goals, expectations, or criteria?
- How can each stakeholder influence the policy change effort?
- What is needed from each stakeholder to initiate and complete a successful policy change effort?
- How important is each stakeholder to the success of the policy change effort?

The group process methods discussed below are ones we have used many times to facilitate preparation of answers to these questions.

The "snow card" technique (Greenblat and Duke, 1981; Nutt and Backoff, 1992; Bryson, 1988b; Spencer, 1989) is a very simple yet effective method for developing a list of stakeholder categories based on the judgments of the members of a small group. The method combines brainstorming—which produces a long list of possible answers to a specific question—with a synthesizing step, in which the answers are grouped into categories according to common themes. Each of the individual answers is written on a sheet of white paper (for example, a half-sheet of inexpensive photocopying paper) called a "snow card." Individual cards are then taped to a wall in groups according to common themes. The result is a "blizzard" of snow cards—hence, the name. The technique is extremely simple in concept, very easy to use, and extraordinarily productive. It can be used at any point of the policy change cycle when it is important or desirable to draw out many people's ideas and group those ideas into categories. Specifically, the technique can be used to identify stakeholders; to develop elements of alternative problem definitions and proposed solutions; and to identify strengths and modifications that would improve policy proposals.

Here, the specific stakeholder analysis question to be answered through use of the snow card technique is the first of the six listed earlier: who are the stakeholders in the general problem area? And the guidelines for using the snow card technique to answer this question can also be used in any step of the policy change cycle (Bryson, 1988b).

1. Select a facilitator.
2. Form the group that will use the technique. The ideal group is five to nine persons, but the technique can still be effective with as many as twelve to fifteen. Larger groups can be broken down into smaller groups, with each group going through the same exercise and then sharing results.
3. Have the group members seat themselves around a table in a room that has a wall where the snow cards may be taped and then read clearly from where the members sit.
4. Focus on a single question, problem, or issue—in this case, the question of who the stakeholders are.

5. Have the participants silently brainstorm as many ideas as possible in response to the question, and record them on their personal worksheets.

6. Ask the participants to pick out the five — or seven, or nine — "best" items from their worksheets and transcribe them with markers or crayons onto five separate snow cards. Make sure people write so that their items can be read when posted on the wall.

7. Ask the participants to attach a tape roll (drafting tape or masking tape rolled sticky side out into a loop approximately one inch in diameter) to the back of each of their snow cards.

8. Have the members of the group go to the wall and simultaneously tape their cards onto the wall. The group members should then rearrange the cards into thematic clusters. Alternatively, the facilitator collects the cards (shuffling them if anonymity is important) and tapes them one at a time to the wall, clustering cards with similar themes together. The tentative label for each cluster, or category, should be selected by the group.

9. Once the group agrees to a category's name, write it on a separate snow card and place it at the top of the other cards in the category. This label card should be differentiated in some way, perhaps through use of a different colored paper, marker, or crayon, or by drawing a box around the category name.

10. Once all items are on the wall and categorized, ask the group to rearrange the categories, and perhaps the items within categories, into some useful order. For example, items might be arranged in a logical, priority, or temporal order. New items can be added and old items deleted as necessary. Subcategories can be added.

11. When group members are satisfied with the categories and their contents, ask them to discuss, compare, and contrast the results. If more than one group has been doing the exercise, sharing of results among groups should occur.

12. When the session is over, have the cards collected in order and typed up in outline or spreadsheet form. Then, distribute the outlines to the group members so they have a record of their work.

Once the basic list of stakeholders is established through the snow card technique, we have found that it is often useful to solicit the group members' judgments about the relative importance of the various stakeholders while the snow cards are still on the wall. In order to solicit and pool the separate judgments of individual group members, we usually ask each member, first, simply to look at the stakeholder categories and then mark down on a sheet of scratch paper who they think the five — or seven, or nine — most important stakeholders are. We ask group members not to discuss the relative importance of stakeholders among themselves prior to making their individual judgments because we are interested in what each individual thinks, and we do not want any of them to be influenced by their peers' opinions. We then give each member five self-adhesive colored dots and ask the members to put a single dot on each of the five stakeholder category labels they think are the most important. We prefer ¾-inch dots; they are large enough to be clearly visible from a distance, but not so large that they block out important information when many are applied. As members are placing their dots on the stakeholder category labels, we again emphasize that we are interested in each member's individual judgments and, therefore, do not want members to be swayed by their peers' judgments. The resulting scatter of colored dots represents a "straw poll," or measurement of group opinion, regarding the relative importance of the various stakeholders.

The next part of a stakeholder analysis exercise is the development of the list of goals, expectations, or criteria the planning team thinks each individual stakeholder and each stakeholder group uses to make judgments about what they want in both the problem and solution areas. Guidelines for this step are as follows:

1. Select a facilitator.
2. Form the group or groups that will develop the lists. Again, groups of five to nine members are ideal.
3. Decide on the stakeholder categories for which lists of goals, expectations, or criteria will be developed. Typically, a list will be developed for each of the most important stakehold-

ers, as determined by the "dots" exercise discussed above. If more than one group has been formed, assign different stakeholder categories to each group.

4. Begin with the first stakeholder category, placing the stakeholder's name at the top of a sheet of flip-chart paper. Draw a vertical line down the right side of the sheet approximately three inches from the edge.

5. Have the group brainstorm possible goals, expectations, or criteria out loud. Record the items to the left of the vertical line with a "bullet" in front of each item. Stop after the group thinks it has listed the most important items.

6. Once a list of items has been listed for each stakeholder, have the group make a judgment about how well the status quo serves each stakeholder according to the stakeholder's goals, expectations, or criteria. In the right-hand column next to each item, place a green dot if the status quo serves the group very well, a yellow dot if the group is served only adequately, and a red dot if the group is served poorly.

7. Discuss, compare, and contrast results for insights into the stakeholders' perceived need for policy change and the prospects for successful policy change.

8. When the session is over, have the results typed and distributed to the group members.

These activities should result in answers to the first three questions in a stakeholder analysis. The final three questions can be answered through guided — or, perhaps, facilitated — discussion based on the lists and opinions developed in answer to the first three questions. The information developed so far can help a group discuss how each stakeholder can influence the policy change process, where the possible coalitions for and against policy change might be, what would be needed from each stakeholder in order to initiate and complete a successful policy change effort, and how important each stakeholder is to the success of the change effort.

Initial Policy Retreats

An initial retreat to consider a policy change effort should begin with an introduction to the nature, purpose, and process of policy change. Key decision makers may need such an introduction — and the development of the shared understanding that comes with it — before they are willing to fully endorse a policy change effort that will require collective leadership and involve groups or organizations other than their own. Such an introduction will be particularly important if the change will be initiated primarily by outsiders who are unfamiliar with the machinery of organizational or governmental policy-making. Orientation and training methods can include lecture-discussions, case presentations by leaders who have been involved in successful and unsuccessful policy change efforts, analyses by key decision makers of written case study materials followed by group discussions, analyses of policy change documentary films, and circulation and discussion of reading materials.

Many different retreat formats are possible. The initiators of change should carefully think through the strengths and weaknesses of alternative formats in light of their particular situations. One possible format for the first day of a policy retreat is as follows — this format assumes that many of those present are not seasoned veterans of successful policy change efforts:

> *Morning:* Lecture-discussion about the nature, purpose, and process of policy change. Presentation of possible "visions of success" as a consequence of policy change. Presentation of supporting studies, reports, and so forth.

> *Lunch:* Presentation from a decision maker involved in a previous policy change effort; the presentation should highlight lessons learned about how to create success and avoid failure.

> *Afternoon:* Analysis and discussion of a written policy change case study, plus instruction in any special techniques likely to facilitate movement through the change process, such as brainstorming, the nominal group technique (Delbecq, Van de Ven, and Gustafson, 1975), the snow card technique (see Resource B), cause-effect diagrams (see Resource A), or conflict resolution methods (Filley, 1975; Fisher and Ury, 1981; Susskind and Cruikshank, 1987). The case analysis should highlight the different stakeholders involved, their views about appropriate problem definitions and solutions, the exercise of leadership, and the design and use of forums, arenas, and courts in the successful pursuit of change.

> *Evening:* Discussion of possible next steps in undertaking a policy change effort, including finalizing the agenda for the retreat's second day.

By the end of the first day it should be clear whether or not the key decision makers wish to proceed. If so, the second day might be organized as follows:

Morning: A stakeholder analysis, followed by tentative definition(s) of the problem(s) to be addressed.

Lunch: A speaker who can present another case example; or a high-status, nonvested speaker who can emphasize the importance of collective action in the problem area; or a personal "call to mission" from someone with a special message relevant to the problem area.

Afternoon: Development of an initial agreement among participants that states the need to respond to the problem(s) raised and that outlines the basic initial response strategy. It is important that the session not end until agreement is reached on the immediate next steps in the process' and the people responsible for each step.

If a group can reach quick agreement at each point, less than two days may be necessary. If quick agreement is not possible, more time may be necessary, and sessions may have to be spread out over several weeks or even months. The more problematic the problem area for those involved or affected, the more groundwork is likely to be required to reach agreement on the purposes, timing, and length of the retreat, as well as the subsequent next steps.

A retreat, or series of retreats, provides a valuable forum for discussion, as well as an informal arena for initial decisions about the purpose, nature, scope, and timing of a policy change effort. A retreat can also provide an important signal and symbol that a community of place or interest is about to address one of its most important concerns, it can prompt desirable media coverage, and it can prompt other stakeholders, who might have been lukewarm about the process, to participate. Additional advice on initial retreats, as well as gatherings for later phases in the policy change cycle, may be found in G. Morgan (1988), Gray (1989), Nadler and Nadler (1987), and Cogan (1992).

Linking Stakeholders to Alternative Problem Definitions

Effective problem formulation involves not just the definition of a problem, but the definition of a problem that can be solved. The preferred problem definitions are those that can lead to a winning coalition. Careful analysis is usually necessary in order to find desirable problem definitions that can motivate action by a coalition of stakeholders large enough to secure adoption of preferred solutions and to protect them during implementation. This analysis can be made by linking stakeholders to alternative problem definitions through problem-definition stakeholder maps. The most useful problem-definition stakeholder map typically will be developed by a group in the following manner:

1. Gather the planning team in a room that has a large blank wall to which pieces of paper may be taped. Typically, the sheets of paper will be snow cards — half-sheets of 8½-by-11-inch inexpensive plain white paper. Alternatively, find a room that has a whiteboard that covers all or most of a

wall and use whiteboard markers to write entries on the board. Or, as another alternative, use a single flip-chart sheet and 1-by-½-inch stick-on labels.

2. Ask members of the group to take a blank sheet of scratch paper and to brainstorm silently, writing down as many problem definitions as they can that relate to the general problem area. Be sure definitions likely to be favored by current or potential opponents are included.

3. Have group members individually identify the "best" problem definition, or definitions, on lists. Then ask them to fill out a snow card for each of their "best" definitions. Once this has been done, each member of the group tapes his or her snow cards to the wall, and then the group organizes these cards into useful categories.

4. Ask the group members to discuss the categories and to decide which ones appear to hold the most promise for developing a winning coalition. Be sure that opponents' definitions are considered during this discussion. The resulting list of definitions will provide the focus for further analysis and the development of problem-definition stakeholder maps.

5. Place a snow card containing the first problem definition in the middle of the wall. Write out the interpretive scheme(s) from which the problem definition flows on another sheet of paper, and place that sheet above the problem definition. Considerable group discussion may be necessary before agreement can be reached on the interpretive scheme. Such discussion is important, however, because it is the interpretive scheme that will tap into the world views, experiences, and motivations of potential coalition members and opponents.

6. Next, ask each member of the planning team to take a sheet of scratch paper, draw a vertical line down the middle of the paper that divides it into two columns, and engage in silent brainstorming for several minutes in order to write out two lists — one list of stakeholders who would support action on the problem as defined, and one of those who would not.

7. Ask planning team members to "star" the "most important" five to nine stakeholders on their lists. Importance is judged by the stakeholder's ability to either promote or block action on the problem as defined.

8. Have each team member fill out a separate snow card for each of the "most important" stakeholders on his or her list, and attach a one-inch tape roll to the back of each card.

9. Ask the team members to tape their snow cards to the wall and then group them into categories. Cards representing stakeholders who would support action on the problem are placed to the left of the problem definition. Cards representing stakeholders who would oppose action on the problem are placed to the right. Cards for stakeholders who are expected to be ambivalent are placed above or below the problem definition.

Once these nine steps are completed and the snow cards are up and grouped into useful categories, steps ten through fifteen may be taken to develop further understanding of the politics surrounding the problem area.

10. Ask team members to group stakeholders around the problem definition according to the intensity of each stakeholder's interest in the problem. Those whose interests are most at stake should be placed closest to the problem definition, while those whose interests are least at stake should be placed farthest away.

11. Have the group determine patterns of influence among stakeholders. Arrows that indicate the directions of influence can be drawn with colored sticky tape or with colored yarn and masking tape between stakeholders. Notes outlining the nature of the influence may be placed on the arrows. Alternatively, sheets of yard-wide clear acetate may be hung across the stakeholder map and arrows of influence may be drawn on the acetate with erasable marking pens. Or, if the stakeholder map has been placed on a whiteboard, influence arrows may be drawn directly on the board.

12. Once the map is completed, ask the team members to prepare an additional set of snow cards for each stakeholder category, indicating in general what solutions might be acceptable to the stakeholder.

13. Have the team discuss similarities and differences among stakeholders; the possibilities for effective coalition formation in support of, and in opposition to, action on the problem as temporarily defined; and any possible shifts in the nature of the coalitions if different problem definitions were used.

14. Record the map. It can be reduced, for example, to a matrix like the one depicted in Figure 9.1 in Chapter Nine. Simple maps can be reproduced on a large sheet of flip-chart paper. A laptop computer with a spreadsheet program is useful here, since a computer-generated version of the map will lend itself to inclusion in working papers (although arrows will still have to be placed on the map by hand). The map also can be recorded using a computer graphics software program. Or the map can be photographed with a high-quality 35mm camera so that the arrows are clearly recorded. For safety's sake, however, a Polaroid snapshot also is handy, because it shows right away whether a legible photographic record has been made.

15. Repeat the exercise with alternative problem definitions and their associated interpretive schemes.

This activity is vital if the politics surrounding the problem area and the possibilities for meaningful change are to be explored carefully. The way a problem is formulated will have an incredibly powerful impact on how—and how successfully—it is resolved. Therefore, time spent on problem formulation is time very well spent.

Stakeholder Mapping and Management

Nutt and Backoff (1992), drawing on the work of Freeman (1984), argue that different strategies will be needed for different stakeholders depending on the importance of the stakeholders and their positions with respect to any given course of action. Nutt and Backoff focus on an organization and how it might assess its stakeholders in relation to proposed changes. Here we are concerned with issue stakeholders and their relation to the adoption and implementation of a particular policy proposal.

Nutt and Backoff propose using the two-by-two matrix, which appears in slightly modified form in Figure 9.1. One dimension represents the stakeholder's importance to the passage or implementation of the proposal. The other dimension indicates whether the stakeholder supports or opposes the proposal. For each proposal, the planning team locates stakeholders on the matrix in order to determine whether a winning coalition is possible, to predict the likely size of the opposing coalition, and to identify neutral or "swing" stakeholders who might be targeted for special lobbying or influence efforts. One effective way to involve the planning team in use of the matrix is to reproduce the matrix on two large sheets of flip-chart paper taped together. Stakeholder names then can be written on adhesive labels, such as Post-It notes, and attached to the matrix in the proper place. A notation can be placed on each label to indicate whether the stakeholder is important to the adoption or to the implementation—or to both—of the proposal. The labels can be moved around based on the ensuing discussion.

Nutt and Backoff (1992) propose a set of tactics to deal with the different categories of stakeholders. The following recommendations are a somewhat modified version of Nutt and Backoff's tactics.

Potential supporters are stakeholders who are very important to either the passage or the implementation of a proposal, and who will support the proposal. Tactics that may be used with them to reinforce their support include:

- Providing information to reinforce beliefs about potential benefits and costs
- Co-opting them by involving them in some or all of the planning team's deliberations
- Asking them to sell the strategy to those who are neutral
- Inviting potential supporters who are at present neutral to react to proposed strategies, so that changes can be incorporated that will turn these stakeholders' potential support into actual support

Potentially antagonistic stakeholders are those who will oppose the proposal, and who will exert considerable influence on the attempts to pass or implement it. Tactics that may be used to lessen the impact of this group include:

- Finding potential supportive coalition members by identifying currently neutral stakeholders in the problematic and low-priority categories who are closely aligned or related to the antagonistic stakeholders

- Taking steps to block formation of coalitions among antagonistic and neutral stakeholders
- Preventing antagonistic stakeholders from undermining the support of potential supporters
- Determining which antagonistic supporters must be surprised (kept in the dark) to delay or prevent the mobilization of their opposition
- Anticipating the nature of the antagonists' opposition and developing counterarguments in advance
- Engaging selected antagonists in negotiations to identify and perhaps adopt changes in the proposal, or to find or invent other options to be traded with antagonists in order to change them into neutrals or even supporters

Problematic stakeholders are those who oppose the proposal, but who are relatively unimportant to its adoption and implementation. These stakeholders present fewer problems than antagonists and supporters, but nonetheless precautions should be taken to prevent problematics from becoming antagonists. Possible tactics include:

- Preparing defensive tactics to be used if a coalition that unites problematic stakeholders with antagonists becomes possible, or if a problematic stakeholder appears likely to take a public position in opposition to the proposal
- Targeting moderately problematic stakeholders for education and lobbying efforts
- Modifying the proposal to assuage the concerns of strongly negative stakeholders

Finally, there are low-priority stakeholders, who are relatively unimportant to the proposal's passage or implementation, but who do support the proposal. Possible tactics for maintaining this group's support include:

- Using low-cost education with those stakeholders who almost fall into the high-importance category

- Finding ways to involve low-priority stakeholders with other supporters in order to expand the size of the supportive coalition

Obviously many more tactics might be used with each group of stakeholders. The main importance of Nutt and Backoff's scheme, however, is that it prompts change advocates to think of the formulation, adoption, and implementation of any proposal in stakeholder terms.

References

Ackoff, R. L. "The Systems Revolution." *Long Range Planning,* 1974, *7*(6), 2–19.

Ackoff, R. L. *The Art of Problem Solving.* New York: Wiley, 1979.

Ackoff, R. L. "The Art and Science of Mess Management." *Interfaces,* 1981a, *11*(1), 20–26.

Ackoff, R. L. *Creating the Corporate Future.* New York: Wiley, 1981b.

Agre, G. P. "The Concept of Problem." *Educational Studies,* 1982, *13*, 121–142.

Alexander, E. A. "Design in the Decision-Making Process." *Policy Studies,* 1982, *14*(3), 279–292.

Alexander, E. A. "From Idea to Action: Notes for a Contingency Theory of the Policy Implementation Process." *Administration & Society,* 1985, *16*(4), 403–426.

Alexander, E. A. "A Transaction Cost Theory of Planning." Paper presented at the annual conference of the Association of Collegiate Schools of Planning, Austin, Texas, Nov. 1990.

Allison, G. "Conceptual Models and the Cuban Missile Crisis." *American Political Science Review,* 1969, *63*(3), 689–718.

Allison, G. *Essence of Decision: Explaining the Cuban Missile Crisis.* Boston: Little, Brown, 1971.

Anderson, J. E. *Public Policymaking.* Boston: Houghton Mifflin, 1990.

Anton, T. J. *American Federalism and Public Policy.* New York: Random House, 1989.

Argyris, C. "The Executive Mind and Double-Loop Learning." *Organizational Dynamics,* Autumn, 1982, 5–22.

Arkes, H. *First Things.* Princeton, N.J.: Princeton University Press, 1986.

Axelrod, R. *The Evolution of Cooperation.* New York: Basic Books, 1984.

"Back to What the Metro Council Is All About." *Minneapolis Star Tribune,* June 15, 1984, p. 22A.

Bachrach, P., and Baratz, M. S. "Two Faces of Power." *American Political Science Review,* 1962, *56,* 947–952.

Bachrach, P., and Baratz, M. S. "Decisions and Non-Decisions: An Analytical Framework." *American Political Science Review,* 1963, *57,* 632–642.

Bachrach, P., and Baratz, M. S. *Power and Poverty.* New York: Oxford University Press, 1970.

Backoff, R. W., and Nutt, P. C. "A Process for Strategic Management with Specific Application for the Nonprofit Organization." In J. M. Bryson and R. C. Einsweiler (eds.), *Strategic Planning: Threats and Opportunities for Planners.* Chicago: Planners Press, 1988.

Bailey, F. G. *Humbuggery and Manipulation: The Art of Leadership.* Ithaca, N.Y.: Cornell University Press, 1988.

Banaszynski, J. "Unbending Abortion-Issue Foes Face Each Other Again at Capitol." *Minneapolis Star Tribune,* Jan. 23, 1983, p. 4A.

Banfield, E. C. *The Unheavenly City.* Boston: Little, Brown, 1970.

Banfield, E. C. *The Unheavenly City Revisited.* Boston: Little, Brown, 1974.

Bardach, E. *The Implementation Game: What Happens After a Bill Becomes a Law.* Cambridge, Mass.: MIT Press, 1977.

Bardach, E. "The Political Entrepreneur Amidst the Flux." Paper presented at the annual research conference of the Association for Public Policy Analysis and Management, Washington, D.C., Oct. 1987.

Baron, D. P. "An Introduction to Political Analysis for Business." Unpublished course material, Graduate School of Business, Stanford University, 1987.

Barrett, S., and Fudge, C. (eds.). *Policy and Action: Essays on the Implementation of Public Policy.* London: Metheun, 1981.

Barry, B. W. *Strategic Planning Workbook for Nonprofit Organizations.* St. Paul, Minn.: Amherst H. Wilder Foundation, 1986.

Bartunek, J. "The Dynamics of Personal and Organizational Reframing." In R. Quinn and K. Cameron (eds.), *Paradox and Transformation.* New York: HarperBusiness, 1988.

Bartunek, J., and Moch, M. "First-Order, Second-Order, and Third-Order Change and Organizational Development Interventions: A Cognitive Approach." *Journal of Applied Behavioral Science,* 1987, *23*(4), 483–500.

Bass, B. M. *Bass and Stogdill's Handbook of Leadership.* (3d ed.) New York: Free Press, 1990.

Behn, R. D. "The Fundamentals of Cutback Management." In R. J. Zeckhauser and D. Leebaert (eds.), *What Role for Government?* Duke Press Policy Studies. Durham, N.C.: Duke University Press, 1983.

Behn, R. D. "The Nature of Knowledge About Public Management: Lessons for Research and Teaching from Our Knowledge About Chess and Warfare." *Journal of Policy Analysis and Management,* 1987, *7*(1), 200–212.

Behn, R. D. *Leadership Counts: Lessons for Public Managers from the Massachusetts Welfare, Training, and Employment Program.* Cambridge, Mass.: Harvard University Press, 1991.

Belenky, M. F., Clinchy, B. M., Goldberger, N. R., and Tarule, J. M. *Women's Ways of Knowing.* New York: Basic Books, 1986.

Bell, R. *The Culture of Policy Deliberations.* New Brunswick, N.J.: Rutgers University Press, 1985.

Bellah, R. N., and others. *The Good Society.* New York: Knopf, 1991.

Bendor, J. B. *Parallel Systems: Redundancy in Government.* Berkeley: University of California Press, 1985.

Bennis, W. "Leadership Transforms Vision into Action." In A. D. Timpe (ed.), *Leadership.* New York: Facts on File, 1987.

Bennis, W., and Nanus, B. *Leaders: The Strategies of Taking Charge.* New York: HarperCollins, 1985.

Benveniste, G. *Mastering the Politics of Planning: Crafting Credible Plans and Policies That Make a Difference.* San Francisco: Jossey-Bass, 1989.

Bernstein, R. J. *The Restructuring of Social and Political Theory.* Philadelphia: University of Pennsylvania Press, 1976.

Bly, R. *Iron John.* Reading, Mass.: Addison-Wesley, 1990.

Boal, K. B., and Bryson, J. M. "Charismatic Leadership: A Phenomenological and Structural Approach." In J. G. Hunt, B. R. Balinga, H. P. Dachler, and C. A. Schriescheim (eds.), *Emerging Leadership Vistas.* Elsmford, N.Y.: Pergamon, 1987.

Bobrow, D. B., and Dryzek, J. S. *Policy Analysis by Design.* Pittsburgh: University of Pittsburgh Press, 1987.

Bok, S. *Lying: Moral Choice in Public and Private Life.* New York: Vantage, 1978.

Bolan, R. S. "The Practitioner as Theorist: The Phenomenology of the Professional Episode." *Journal of the American Planning Association,* 1980, *46,* 261–274.

Bolan, R. S. "Planning and Institutional Design: Notes Toward a Theory." Working paper, Hubert H. Humphrey Institute of Public Affairs. Minneapolis: University of Minnesota, 1991.

Bolen, J. S. *Goddesses in Everywoman.* New York: HarperCollins, 1984.

Bolen, J. S. *Gods in Everyman.* San Francisco: HarperSan Francisco, 1989.

Boyd, W. L. "The Politics of Declining Enrollments and School Closings." In N. H. Cambron and A. Odden (eds.), *The Changing Politics of School Finance.* New York: HarperBusiness, 1982.

Boyte, H. C. *Backyard Revolution.* Philadelphia: Temple University Press, 1980.

Boyte, H. C. *Community Is Possible.* New York: HarperCollins, 1984.

Boyte, H. C. *Commonwealth: A Return to Citizen Politics.* New York: Free Press, 1989.

Bozeman, B. "The Credibility of Policy Analysis: Between Method and Use." *Policy Studies Journal,* 1986, *14,* 419–439.

Bozeman, B. *All Organizations Are Public: Bridging Public and Private Organizational Theories.* San Francisco: Jossey-Bass, 1987.

Bozeman, B., and Landsbergen, D. "Truth and Credibility in Sincere Policy Analysis: Alternative Approaches for the Production of Policy-Relevant Knowledge." *Evaluation Review,* 1989, *13*(4), 355–379.

Bradley, R. T. *Charisma and Social Structure.* New York: Paragon House, 1987.

Braybrooke, D., and Lindblom, C. E. *A Strategy of Decision: Policy Evaluation as a Social Process.* New York: Free Press, 1963.

Brickman, P. "Is It Real?" In J. H. Harvey, W. Ickes, and R. F. Kidd (eds.), *New Directions in Attribution Research.* Vol. 2. Hillsdale, N.J.: Lawrence Erlbaum, 1978.

Brief, A., Delbecq, A. L., Filley, A. C., and Huber, G. P. "Elite Structure and Attitudes: An Empirical Analysis of Adoption Behavior." *Administration and Society,* 1976, *8*(2), 227–248.

Briggs, K. C., and Myers, I. B. "Myers-Briggs Personality Type Indicator." Palo Alto, Calif.: Consulting Psychologists Press, 1977.

Bromiley, P., and Marcus, A. "Deadlines, Routines, and Change." *Policy Sciences,* 1987, *20,* 85–103.

Bryant, J. *Problem Management.* New York: Wiley, 1989.

Bryson, J. M. "A Perspective on Planning and Crises in the Public Sector." *Strategic Management Journal,* 1981, *2,* 181–196.

Bryson, J. M. "The Policy Process and Organizational Form." *Policy Studies Journal,* 1984, *12,* 445–463.

Bryson, J. M. "Strategic Planning: Big Wins and Small Wins." *Public Money and Management,* 1988a, *8*(3), 11–15.

Bryson, J. M. *Strategic Planning for Public and Nonprofit Organizations: A Guide to Strengthening and Sustaining Organizational Achievement.* San Francisco: Jossey-Bass, 1988b.

Bryson, J. M. "The Role of Forums, Arenas, and Courts in Organizational Design and Change." Paper presented at the Graduate School of Public Affairs, University of Colorado, Denver, 1989a.

Bryson, J. M. "You Are as Good, or as Bad, as Your Calendar." *Government Executive,* 1989b, *21*(10), 67.

Bryson, J. M. *Getting Started on Strategic Planning—What It's All About and How It Can Strengthen Public and Nonprofit Organizations.* San Francisco: Jossey-Bass, 1991. Audiocassette.

Bryson, J. M., Boal, K. B., Poole, S., and Terrell, C. "A Contingent Planning Model for Programs and Projects." *Project Management Quarterly,* 1979, *10*(1), 19-29.

Bryson, J. M., Bromiley, P., and Jung, Y. S. "Influences of Context and Process on Project Planning Success." *Journal of Planning Education and Research,* 1990, *9*(3), 183-195.

Bryson, J. M., and Crosby, B. C. "The Design and Use of Strategic Planning Arenas." *Planning Outlook,* 1989, *32*(1), 5-13.

Bryson, J. M., and Cullen, J. W. "A Contingent Approach to Strategy and Tactics in Formative and Summative Evaluations." *Evaluation and Program Planning,* 1984, *7,* 267-290.

Bryson, J. M., and Delbecq, A. L. "A Contingent Approach to Strategy and Tactics in Project Planning." *Journal of the American Planning Association,* 1979, *45,* 167-179.

Bryson, J. M., and Delbecq, A. L. "A Contingent Program Planning Model." Working paper, Hubert H. Humphrey Institute of Public Affairs. Minneapolis: University of Minnesota, 1981.

Bryson, J. M., and Einsweiler, R. C. "Planning as the Design and Use of Forums, Arenas, and Courts." A paper presented at the Conference of the Association of Collegiate Schools of Planning, Chicago, October 22-24, 1982.

Bryson, J. M., and Einsweiler, R. C. (eds.). *Strategic Planning—Threats and Opportunities for Planners.* Chicago: Planners Press, 1988.

Bryson, J. M., and Einsweiler, R. C. (eds.). *Shared Power.* Lanham, Md.: University Press of America, 1991.

Bryson, J. M., and Kelley, G. "A Political Perspective on Leadership Emergence, Stability, and Change in Organizational Networks." *Academy of Management Review,* 1978, *3,* 113-123.

Bryson, J. M., and Kelley, G. "Leadership, Politics, and the Functioning of Complex Organizations and Interorganizational Networks." In A. Negandhi, G. England, and B. Wilpert (eds.), *The Functioning of Complex Organizations.* Cambridge, Mass.: Oelgeschlager, Gunn and Hain, 1981.

Bryson, J. M., and Roering, W. D. "Initiation of Strategic Planning by Governments." *Public Administration Review,* 1988, *48,* 995–1004.

Bryson, J. M., and Roering, W. D. "Mobilizing Innovation Efforts: The Case of Government Strategic Planning." In A. H. Van de Ven, H. Angle, and M. S. Poole (eds.), *Research on the Management of Innovation.* New York: HarperCollins, 1989.

Bryson, J. M., Van de Ven, A. H., and Roering, W. D. "Strategic Planning and the Revitalization of the Public Service." In R. C. Denhardt (ed.), *The Revitalization of the Public Service.* Columbia, Mo.: University of Missouri, Extension Publications, 1987.

Bunch, C. *Passionate Politics.* New York: St. Martin's Press, 1987.

Burke, K. *A Grammar of Motives.* Englewood Cliffs, N.J.: Prentice-Hall, 1945.

Burns, J. M. *Leadership.* New York: HarperCollins, 1978.

Cameron, K. S., Sutton, R. I., and Whetten, D. A. (eds.). *Readings in Organizational Behavior.* New York: HarperBusiness, 1988.

Campbell, D. T., and Stanley, J. C. *Experimental and Quasi-Experimental Designs for Research.* Skokie, Ill.: Rand McNally, 1966.

Carnoy, M. *The State and Political Theory.* Princeton, N.J.: Princeton University Press, 1984.

Caro, R. A. *The Years of Lyndon Johnson: Means of Ascent.* New York: Knopf, 1990.

Carpenter, S. L., and Kennedy, W.J.D. *Managing Public Disputes: A Practical Guide to Handling Conflict and Reaching Agreements.* San Francisco: Jossey-Bass, 1988.

Carson, R. *Silent Spring.* Boston: Houghton Mifflin, 1962.

Cartwright, T. J. "Problems, Solutions and Strategies: A Contribution to the Theory and Practice of Planning." *Journal of the American Institute of Planning,* May 1973, 179–187.

Carver, J. *Boards That Make a Difference: A New Design for Leadership in Nonprofit and Public Organizations.* San Francisco: Jossey-Bass, 1990.

Center for Urban and Regional Affairs. *Managed Growth: Proceedings from Five Community Workshops on the Issue of Managed Growth of the Twin Cities Metropolitan Area.* Minneapolis: University of Minnesota, 1978.

Chaffee, E. E. "Three Models of Strategy." *Academy of Management Review,* 1985, *10,* 89–98.

Chase, G. "Implementing a Human Services Program: How Hard Will It Be?" *Public Policy,* 1979, *27,* 385–435.

Chisholm, D. *Coordination Without Hierarchy.* Berkeley: University of California Press, 1989.

Christensen, K. S. "Coping with Uncertainty in Planning." *Journal of the American Planning Association,* 1985, *51,* 63–73.

Citizens League. *Summary of Comments and Proposals on Areawide Governmental Problems of the Twin Cities Metropolitan Area.* Minneapolis: Citizens League, 1966.

Citizens League. *A Metropolitan Council for the Twin Cities Area.* Minneapolis: Citizens League, 1967.

Clegg, S. *Power, Rule and Domination.* New York: Routledge & Kegan Paul, 1975.

Clegg, S. *The Theory of Power and Organization.* New York: Routledge & Kegan Paul, 1979.

Clegg, S. "Organization and Control." *Administrative Science Quarterly, 26,* 1981, 545–562.

Clegg, S. *Frameworks of Power.* Newbury Park, Calif.: Sage, 1989.

Cleveland, H. *The Future Executive.* New York: HarperCollins, 1973.

Cleveland, H. *The Knowledge Executive.* New York: Dutton, 1985.

Cobb, R. W., and Elder, C. D. *Participation in American Politics: The Dynamics of Agenda-Building.* Baltimore, Md.: Johns Hopkins University Press, 1972.

Cobb, R. W., and Elder, C. D. *Participation in American Politics: The Dynamics of Agenda-Building.* (2d ed.) Baltimore, Md.: Johns Hopkins University Press, 1983.

Cogan, E. *Successful Public Meetings: A Practical Guide for Managers in Government.* San Francisco: Jossey-Bass, 1992.

Cogan, J. F. *Negative Income Taxation and Labor Supply: New Evidence from the New Jersey-Pennsylvania Experiment.* Santa Monica, Calif: RAND Corporation, 1978.

Cohen, M. D., and March, J. G. *Leadership and Ambiguity: The American College President.* New York: McGraw-Hill, 1974.

Cohen, M. D., March, J. G., and Olsen, J. P. "A Garbage Can Model of Organization and Choice." *Administrative Science Quarterly*, 1972, *17*, 1–25.

Coleman, J. S. *Community Conflict.* New York: Free Press, 1957.

Collins, R. "On the Microfoundations of Macrosociology." *American Journal of Sociology*, 1981, *86*, 948–1014.

Cooper, P. J. "Legal Tools for Accomplishing Administrative Responsibilities." In J. L. Perry (ed.), *Handbook of Public Administration.* San Francisco: Jossey-Bass, 1989.

Coplin, W., and O'Leary, M. *Everyman's Prince: A Guide to Understanding Your Political Problem.* Boston: Duxbury Press, 1976.

Crenson, M. *The Unpolitics of Air Pollution.* Baltimore, Md.: Johns Hopkins University Press, 1971.

Crosby, B. C. "Women: New Images of Leadership." *Social Policy*, 1988, *19*(2), 40–44.

Crosby, B. C., and Bryson, J. M. "Converting Lost Causes into Triumphs." *Minneapolis Star Tribune*, Jan. 6, 1990, p. 15A.

Cyert, R., and March, J. *The Behavioral Theory of the Firm.* Englewood Cliffs, N.J.: Prentice Hall, 1963.

Dahl, R. A. "The Concept of Power." *Behavioral Science*, 1957, *2*, 201–215.

Dahl, R. A. *Who Governs?* New Haven, Conn.: Yale University Press, 1961.

Dahl, R. A. *Modern Political Analysis.* (3d ed.) Englewood Cliffs, N.J.: Prentice Hall, 1976.

Dalton, G. W. "Influence and Organizational Change." In G. Dalton, P. Lawrence, and L. Greiner (eds.), *Organization Change and Development.* Homewood, Ill.: Dow Jones–Irwin, 1970.

Dalton, G. W., and Thompson, P. H. *Novations — Strategies for Career Management.* Glenview, Ill.: ScottForesman, 1986.

Daneke, G. A. "Why Sam Can't Plan: Industrial Policy and the Perils of a Nonadaptive Political Economy." *Business Horizons*, Nov.–Dec. 1984, 50–56.

de Bono, E. *Lateral Thinking.* New York: HarperCollins, 1970.

Delbecq, A. L. "Negotiating Mandates Which Increase the Acceptance of Evaluation Findings Concerning Demonstration Findings in Human Services." A paper presented at the Annual Conference of the Academy of Management, Orlando, Fla., 1977.

Delbecq, A. L., Van de Ven, A. H., and Gustafson, D. *Group Techniques for Program Planning.* Glenview, Ill.: ScottForesman, 1975.

deLeon, P. "A Theory of Policy Termination." In J. May and A. Wildavsky (eds.), *The Policy Cycle.* Newbury Park, Calif.: Sage, 1978.

deLeon, P. "Policy Evaluation and Program Termination." *Policy Studies Review, 2*(4), 1983, 631–647.

deLeon, P. *Advice and Consent: The Development of the Policy Sciences.* New York: Russell Sage Foundation, 1988.

deLeon, P. "The Contextual Burdens of Policy Design." *Policy Studies Journal, 17*(2), 1988–89, 297–309.

DeLong, J. V. "How to Convince an Agency." *Regulation,* Sept.–Oct. 1982, 27–36.

de Neufville, J. I. "Human Rights Reporting as a Policy Tool: An Examination of the State Department Country Reports." *Human Rights Quarterly,* 1986, *8,* 681–699.

de Neufville, J. I., and Barton, S. E. "Myths and the Definition of Policy Problems: An Exploration of Home Ownership and Public-Private Partnerships." *Policy Sciences,* 1987, *20,* 181–206.

Doig, J. W., and Hargrove, E. C. (eds.). *Leadership and Innovation: A Biographical Perspective on Entrepreneurs in Government.* Baltimore, Md.: Johns Hopkins University Press, 1987.

Downs, A. *Inside Bureaucracy.* Boston: Little, Brown, 1967.

Downs, A. "Up and Down with Ecology — The Issue Attention Cycle." *Public Interest,* Summer 1972, *28,* 38–50.

Drake, R. "Leadership: It's a Rare Blend of Traits." In A. D. Timpe (ed.), *Leadership.* New York: Facts on File, 1987.

Dror, Y. "Planning as a Mode of Policy-Reasoning." In L. Guelke and R. Preston (eds.), *Abstract Thoughts, Concrete Solutions: Essays in Honor of Peter Nash.* Department of Geography Publications Series. Waterloo, Canada: University of Waterloo, 1987.

Dunn, W. N. *Public Policy Analysis: An Introduction.* Englewood Cliffs, N.J.: Prentice Hall, 1981.

Dunn, W. N. "Reforms as Arguments." *Knowledge: Creation, Diffusion, Utilization,* 1982, *3*(2), 293–326.

Dunn, W. N., and Holzner, B. "Knowledge in Society: Anatomy of an Emergent Field." *Knowledge in Society,* 1988, *1,* 3–26.

Dutton, J. E. "The Making of Organizational Opportunities." Prepublication draft, 1990.

Dye, T. R. *Politics in States and Communities.* (7th ed.) Englewood Cliffs, N.J.: Prentice-Hall, 1991.

Easton, D. *A Systems Analysis of Political Life.* New York: Wiley, 1965.

Edelman, M. *The Symbolic Uses of Politics.* Urbana: University of Illinois Press, 1964.

Edelman, M. *Politics as Symbolic Action.* New York: Academic Press, 1971.

Edelman, M. *Political Language.* New York: Academic Press, 1977.

Eden, C. "Problem-solving or Problem-finishing." In M. C. Jackson and P. Keys (eds.), *New Directions in Management Science.* Aldershot, England: Gower, 1987.

Eden, C., and Huxham, C. "Action-Oriented Strategic Management." *Journal of the Operational Research Society,* 1986, *39*(10), 889–899.

Eden, C., and Radford, J. *Tackling Strategic Problems.* Newbury Park, Calif.: Sage, 1990.

Eden, C., and Sims, D. "On the Nature of Problems in Consulting Practice." *Omega,* 1978, *7*(2), 119–127.

Elmore, R. F. "Backward Mapping: Implementation Research and Policy Decisions." In W. Williams (ed.), *Studying Implementation.* Chatham, N.J.: Chatham House, 1982.

Emery, M., and Emery, F. E. "Searching for New Directions: In New Ways . . . for New Times." In J. W. Sutherland (ed.), *Management Handbook for Public Administration.* New York: Van Nostrand Reinhold, 1978.

Etzioni, A. "Mixed Scanning: A 'Third' Approach to Decision Making." *Public Administration Review,* 1967, *27,* 385–392.

Etzioni, A. *The Active Society: A Theory of Societal and Political Processes.* London: Collier, 1968.

Evans, P. B., Rueschemeyer, D., and Skocpol, T. (eds.). *Bringing the State Back In.* New York: Cambridge University Press, 1985.

Evans, S. M., and Boyte, H. C. *Free Spaces.* New York: Harper-Collins, 1986.

Feinstein, D., and Krippner, S. "Bringing a Mythological Perspective to Social Change." *ReVISION,* 1988, *11*(1), 23–34.

Filley, A. *Interpersonal Conflict Resolution.* Glenview, Ill.: Scott-Foresman, 1975.

Fink, A., and Kosecoff, J. *How to Conduct Surveys.* Newbury Park, Calif.: Sage, 1985.

Fisher, R., and Brown, S. *Getting Together: Building a Relationship That Gets to Yes.* Boston: Houghton Mifflin, 1988.

Fisher, R., and Ury, W. *Getting to Yes: Negotiating Agreement Without Giving In.* New York: Penguin Books, 1981.

Fix, M., and Kenyon, D. A. (eds.). *Coping with Mandates: What Are the Alternatives?* Washington, D.C.: Urban Institute, 1990.

Forester, J. "Critical Theory and Planning Practices." *Journal of the American Planning Association,* 1980, *46,* 275–286.

Forester, J. "Planning in the Face of Conflict: Negotiation and Mediation Strategies in Local Land Use Regulation." *Journal of the American Planning Association,* 1987, *53,* 303–314.

Forester, J. *Planning in the Face of Power.* Berkeley: University of California Press, 1989.

Fowler, F. J. *Survey Research Methods.* (Rev. ed.) Newbury Park, Calif.: Sage, 1988.

Frame, J. D. *Managing Projects in Organizations: How to Make the Best Use of Time, Techniques, and People.* San Francisco: Jossey-Bass, 1987.

Freeley, A. J. *Argumentation and Debate: Rational Decision Making.* (4th ed.) Belmont, Calif.: Wadsworth, 1976.

Freeman, R. E. *Strategic Management: A Stakeholder Approach.* Boston: Pitman, 1984.

French, J.R.P., Jr., and Raven, B. "The Bases of Social Power." In D. Cartwright and A. Zander (eds.), *Group Dynamics.* (3d ed.) New York: HarperCollins, 1968.

Frey, J. H. *Survey Research by Telephone.* (2d ed.) Newbury Park, Calif.: Sage, 1989.

Frieden, B. J., and Sagalyn, L. B. "Downtown Shopping Malls and the New Public-Private Strategy." In J. M. Bryson and R. C. Einsweiler (eds.), *Shared Power.* Lanham, Md.: University Press of America, 1991.

Friedmann, J. *The Good Society.* Cambridge, Mass.: MIT Press, 1979.

Friedmann, J. *Planning in the Public Domain: From Knowledge to Action.* Princeton, N.J.: Princeton University Press, 1987.

Friedrich, C. J. "Public Policy and the Nature of Administrative Responsibility." *Public Policy,* 1940, *1,* 3–24.

Friend, J. K., and Hickling, A. *Planning Under Pressure: The Strategic Choice Approach.* Oxford, England: Pergamon, 1987.

Friend, J., Laffin, M. J., and Norris, M. E. "Competition in Public Policy: The Structure Plan as Arena." *Public Administration,* 1981, *59,* 441–463.

Friend, J. K., Power, J. M., and Yewlett, C.J.L. *Public Planning: The Intercorporate Dimension.* London: Tavistock, 1974.

Fritschler, A. L., and Ross, B. H. *How Washington Works: The Executive Guide to Government.* New York: HarperBusiness, 1987.

Gabor, D. *Inventing the Future.* New York: Knopf, 1964.

Gandhi, M. K. *An Autobiography: The Story of My Experiment with Truth.* Boston: Beacon Press, 1957.

Gardner, J. W. *The Antileadership Vaccine.* Carnegie Foundation Report. Princeton, N.J.: Carnegie Foundation, 1965.

Gardner, J. W. *The Heart of the Matter: Leader-Constituent Interaction.* Leadership Papers/3. Washington, D.C.: INDEPENDENT SECTOR, 1968.

Gardner, J. W. *Attributes and Context.* Leadership Papers/6. Washington, D.C.: INDEPENDENT SECTOR, 1987.

Garner, C. W. *Accounting and Budgeting in Public and Nonprofit Organizations: A Manager's Guide.* San Francisco: Jossey-Bass, 1991.

Garud, R., and Van de Ven, A. H. "Technological Innovation and Industry Emergence: The Case of Cochlear Implants." In A. H. Van de Ven, H. L. Angle, and M. S. Poole (eds.), *Research on the Management of Innovation.* New York: HarperCollins, 1989.

Gaventa, J. *Power and Powerlessness: Quiescence and Rebellion in an Appalachian Valley.* Urbana: University of Illinois Press, 1980.

Gerston, L. N. *Making Public Policy: From Conflict to Resolution.* Boston: Little, Brown, 1983.

Giddens, A. *Central Problems in Social Theory: Action, Structure and Contradiction in Social Analysis.* Berkeley: University of California Press, 1979.

Giddens, A. *The Constitution of Society.* Berkeley: University of California Press, 1984.

Gilligan, C. *In a Different Voice.* Cambridge, Mass.: Harvard University Press, 1982.

Glick, H. R. (ed.). *Courts in American Politics: Readings and Introductory Essays.* New York: McGraw-Hill, 1980.

Goggin, M. L., Bowman, A. O., Lester, J. P., and O'Toole, L. J., Jr. *Implementation Theory and Practice: Toward a Third Generation.* Glenview, Ill.: ScottForesman, 1990.

Goldstein, H. "Planning as Argumentation." *Environment and Planning B: Planning and Design,* 1984, *11,* 297–312.

Golembiewski, R. T. "The Boom in the Decline Literature: Surveying the Field and Detailing One Metaphor." *Public Administration Review,* 1990, *50,* 108–110.

Gray, B. *Collaborating: Finding Common Ground for Multiparty Problems.* San Francisco: Jossey-Bass, 1989.

Greenblat, C., and Duke, R. *Gaming-Simulation: Rationale, Design, and Applications.* New York: Wiley, 1975.

Greenblat, C., and Duke, R. D. *Principles and Practices of Gaming Simulation.* Newbury Park, Calif.: Sage, 1981.

Greenleaf, R. K. *Servant Leadership.* New York: Paulist Press, 1977.

Griffith, E. *In Her Own Right: The Life of Elizabeth Cady Stanton.* New York: Oxford University Press, 1984.

Gutmann, A., and Thompson, D. *Ethics and Politics.* (2d ed.) Chicago: Nelson-Hall Publishers, 1990.

Guy, M. E. *Organizational Decline to Organizational Renewal.* New York: Quorum Books, 1989.

Habermas, J. *Legitimation Crisis.* Boston: Beacon Press, 1973.

Habermas, J. *Communication and the Evolution of Society.* Boston: Beacon Press, 1979.

Hage, J., and Dewar, R. "Elite Values Versus Organizational Structure in Predicting Innovation." *Administrative Science Quarterly,* 1973, *18,* 279–290.

Hall, B. P., and Thompson, H. *Leadership Through Values, a Study in Personal and Organizational Development.* New York: Paulist Press, 1980.

Hammond, T., and Knott, J. "The Deregulation in the Financial Industry." *Journal of Politics,* 1988, *50,* 2–30.

Hardisty, J. V. *ACLU Speaker's Manual on Abortion.* Chicago: The Roger Baldwin Foundation of ACLU, Inc., 1982.

Havelock, R. *The Change Agent's Guide to Innovation in Education.* Englewood Cliffs, N.J.: Educational Technology Publications, 1973.

Healey, P., McNamara, P., Elson, M., and Doak, A. *Land Use Planning and the Mediation of Urban Change.* New York: Cambridge University Press, 1988.

Heclo, H. *A Government of Strangers: Executive Politics in Washington.* Washington, D.C.: The Brookings Institution, 1977.

Heclo, H. "Issue Networks and the Executive Establishment." In A. King (ed.), *The New Political System.* Washington, D.C.: American Enterprise Institute, 1978.

Heifetz, R. A., and Sinder, R. M. "Political Leadership: Managing the Public's Problem Solving." In R. B. Reich (ed.), *The Power of Public Ideas.* New York: HarperBusiness, 1985.

Hersey, P., and Blanchard, K. H. *Management of Organizational Behavior: Utilizing Human Resources.* (5th ed.) Englewood Cliffs, N.J.: Prentice Hall, 1988.

Heydebrand, W. "Organizational Contradictions in Public Bureaucracies." *Sociological Quarterly,* 1977a, *18,* 83–107.

Heydebrand, W. "Context and Resources of Public Bureaucracies: An Organizational Analysis of Federal District Courts." *Law and Society Review,* 1977b, *11,* 759–821.

Heydebrand, W., and Seron, C. "The Double Bind of the Capitalist Judicial System." *International Journal of the Sociology of Law,* 1981, *9,* 407–437.

Hickson, D. J., Astley, W. G., Butler, R. J., and Wilson, D. C. "Organization as Power." In L. L. Cummings and B. M. Staw (eds.), *Research in Organizational Behavior.* Vol. 3. Greenwich, Conn.: JAI Press, 1981.

Hickson, D. J., and others. *Top Decisions—Strategic Decision Making in Organizations.* Oxford, England: Basil Blackwell, 1986.

Higham, J. (ed.). *Ethnic Leadership in America.* Baltimore, Md.: Johns Hopkins University Press, 1978.

Hilgartner, S., and Bosk, C. L. "The Rise and Fall of Social Problems: A Public Arenas Model." *American Journal of Sociology,* 1988, *94*(1), 53–78.

Hirschman, A. O. *Exit, Voice and Loyalty.* Cambridge, Mass.: Harvard University Press, 1970.

Hjern, B., and Porter, D. O. "Implementation Structures: A New Unit of Administrative Analysis." *Organization Studies,* 1981, *2*(3), 211–227.

Hobbes, T. *Leviathan.* (Michael Oakeshott, ed.) London: Collier, 1962.

Hoenack, S. A. "The Domain of Policy Analysis and the Implementation of Efficiency-Enhancing Policies." Working paper, Hubert H. Humphrey Institute of Public Affairs. Minneapolis: University of Minnesota, 1991.

Hogwood, B. W., and Gunn, L. A. *Policy Analysis for the Real World.* New York: Oxford University Press, 1984.

Hogwood, B. W., and Peters, B. G. "The Dynamics of Policy Change: Policy Succession." *Policy Sciences,* 1982, *14,* 225–245.

Hogwood, B. W., and Peters, B. G. *Policy Dynamics.* New York: St. Martin's Press, 1983.

Holder, R. J. "Visioning: An Energizing Tool." *Journal for Quality and Participation, 11*(3), 18–22.

Houle, C. O. *Governing Boards: Their Nature and Nurture.* San Francisco: Jossey-Bass, 1989.

Howe, E. "Role Choices of Urban Planners." *Journal of the American Planning Association,* 1980, *46,* 398–409.

Howe, E., and Kaufman, J. "The Ethics of Contemporary American Planners." *Journal of the American Planning Association,* 1979, *45,* 243–255.

Hugick, L. "'Pro-Life' Wichita Demonstrations Fail to Change Opinion on Abortion." *Gallup Poll Monthly,* Sept. 1991, 49–53.

Hunsaker, J., and Hunsaker, P. *Strategies and Skills for Managerial Women.* Cincinnati, Ohio: South-Western Publishing, 1986.

Hunt, J. G. "Organizational Leadership: The Contingency Paradigm and Its Challenges." In B. Kellerman (ed.), *Leadership: Multidisciplinary Perspectives.* Englewood Cliffs, N.J.: Prentice Hall, 1984.

Hunt, J. G. *Leadership: A New Synthesis.* Newbury Park, Calif.: Sage, 1991.

Hunt, S. M. "The Role of Leadership in the Construction of

Reality." In B. Kellerman (ed.), *Leadership: Multidisciplinary Perspectives*. Englewood Cliffs, N.J.: Prentice Hall, 1984.

Hunter, F. A. *Community Power Structure*. Chapel Hill: University of North Carolina Press, 1953.

Huntington, S. P. *American Politics: The Promise of Disharmony*. Cambridge, Mass.: Belknap Press, 1981.

Innes, J. "The Power of Data Requirements." *Journal of the American Planning Association*, 1986, *52*, 275–278.

Innes, J. "Effects of Data Requirements on Planning: Case Studies of Environmental Impact Assessment and Community Development Block Grants." *Computers, Environment and Urban Systems*, 1988, *12*, 77–78.

Innes, J. *Knowledge and Public Policy: The Search for Meaningful Indicators*. New Brunswick, N.J.: Transaction, 1990.

Jackson, S. E., and Dutton, J. E. "Discerning Threats and Opportunities." *Administrative Science Quarterly*, 1988, *33*, 370–387.

Jaffe, F. S., Lindheim, B. L., and Lee, P. R. *Abortion Politics: Private Morality and Public Policy*. New York: McGraw-Hill, 1981.

Jago, A. G. "Leadership: Perspectives in Theory and Research." *Management Science*, 1982, *28*(3), 315–336.

Janeway, E. *Powers of the Weak*. New York: Morrow, 1981.

Janowitz, M. *The Last Half-Century: Societal Change and Politics in America*. Chicago: University of Chicago Press, 1978.

Jantsch, E. *Technological Planning and Social Futures*. New York: Wiley, 1972.

Jantsch, E. *Design for Evolution*. New York: George Braziller, 1975.

Johnson, D. W., and Johnson, F. P. *Joining Together*. (4th ed.) Englewood Cliffs, N.J.: Prentice Hall, 1991.

Jones, B. *Governing Urban America: A Policy Focus*. Boston: Little, Brown, 1982.

Jones, C. O. "Why Congress Can't Do Policy Analysis (or Words to That Effect)." *Policy Analysis*, 1976, *2*(2), 251–264.

Jorgensen, D. L. *Participant Observation*. Vol 15: *Applied Social Research Methods*. Newbury Park, Calif.: Sage, 1989.

Kahn, S. *Organizing*. New York: McGraw-Hill, 1982.

Kammen, M. *A Machine That Would Go of Itself.* New York: Vintage, 1986.

Kanter, R. M. *Commitment and Community: Communes and Utopias in Sociological Perspective.* Cambridge, Mass.: Harvard University Press, 1972.

Kanter, R. M. *The Changemasters.* New York: Simon & Schuster, 1983.

Kanter, R. M. *When Giants Learn to Dance, Mastering the Challenge of Strategy, Management and Careers in the 1990s.* New York: Simon & Schuster, 1989.

Karpik, L. "Technological Capitalism." In S. Clegg and D. Dunkerley (eds.), *Critical Issues in Organizations.* New York: Routledge & Kegan Paul, 1977.

Kartez, J. D. "Rational Arguments and Irrational Audiences." *Journal of the American Planning Association,* 1989, *55,* 445–456.

Kaufman, J. L. "Making Planners More Effective Strategists." In B. Checkoway (ed.), *Strategic Perspectives on Planning Practice.* Lexington, Mass.: Lexington Books, 1986.

Keirsey, D., and Bates, M. *Please Understand Me.* Del Mar, Calif.: Prometheus Nemesis Books, 1978.

Kellerman, B. *Leadership: Multidisciplinary Perspectives.* Englewood Cliffs, N.J.: Prentice Hall, 1984.

Kelman, S. "'Public Choice' and Public Spirit." *Public Interest,* Spring 1987, 80–94.

Kerr, S. "On the Folly of Rewarding A, While Hoping for B." *Academy of Management Journal,* 1975, *19,* 769–783.

Kerr, S., and Jermier, J. "Substitutes for Leadership: Their Meaning and Measurement." *Organizational Behavior and Human Performance,* 1978, *22,* 375–403.

Kershaw, D., and Fair, J. *The New Jersey Income Maintenance Experiment.* New York: Academic Press, 1976.

King, A. "The American Polity in the Late 1970s: Building Coalitions in the Sand." In A. King (ed.), *The New American Political System.* Washington, D.C.: American Enterprise Institute, 1978.

Kingdon, J. W. *Congressmen's Voting Decisions.* (2d ed.) New York: HarperCollins, 1981.

Kingdon, J. W. *Agendas, Alternatives, and Public Policies.* Boston: Little, Brown, 1984.

Kiser, L., and Ostrom, E. "The Three Worlds of Action." In E. Ostrom (ed.), *Strategies of Political Inquiry.* Newbury Park, Calif.: Sage, 1982.

Koestenbaum, P. *The Heart of Business: Ethics, Power and Philosophy.* San Francisco: Saybrook, 1987.

Kokopeli, B., and Lakey, G. "Leadership and Leaders: What's the Difference?" *Win Magazine,* Nov. 2, 1978.

Kolderie, T. "Area Views Governmental Change Constructively." *Minneapolis Star Tribune,* Oct. 27, 1965, p. 12A.

Kolderie, T. "Two Different Concepts of Privatization." *Public Administration Review,* 1986, *46,* 285–291.

Kotter, J., and Lawrence, P. *Mayors in Action.* New York: Wiley, 1974.

Kouzes, J. M., and Posner, B. Z. *The Leadership Challenge: How to Get Extraordinary Things Done in Organizations.* San Francisco: Jossey-Bass, 1987.

Kraemer, K. *Policy Analysis in Local Government.* Washington, D.C.: International City Management Association, 1973.

Krasner, S. D. "Structural Causes and Regime Consequences: Regimes as Intervening Variables." In S. D. Krasner (ed.), *International Regimes.* Ithaca, N.Y.: Cornell University Press, 1983.

Krieger, M. H. *Advice and Planning.* Philadelphia: Temple University Press, 1981.

Krieger, M. H. "Planning and Design as Theological and Religious Activities." *Environment and Planning B: Planning and Design,* 1987, *14,* 5–13.

Krueger, R. A. *Focus Groups.* Newbury Park, Calif.: Sage, 1988.

Lader, L. *Abortion II: Making the Revolution.* Boston: Beacon Press, 1973.

Landsbergen, D., and Bozeman, B. "Credibility Logic and Policy Analysis." *Knowledge, Diffusion, Utilization,* 1987, *8*(4), 625–648.

Laszlo, E. *Introduction to Systems Philosophy.* New York: HarperCollins, 1972.

Lavrakas, P. J. *Telephone Survey Methods.* Vol. 7. Newbury Park, Calif.: Sage, 1987.

Levinthal, D. "A Survey of Agency Models of Organizations." *Journal of Economic Behavior and Organization,* 1988, *9,* 153–185.

Levitan, S., and Taggart, R. *The Promise of Greatness.* Cambridge, Mass.: Harvard University Press, 1976.

Levy, F., Meltsner, A., and Wildavsky, A. *Urban Outcomes.* Berkeley: University of California Press, 1974.

Light, P. C. *The President's Agenda.* (Rev. ed.) Baltimore, Md.: Johns Hopkins University Press, 1991.

Lindblom, C. E. "The Science of Muddling Through." *Public Administration Review,* 1959, *19,* 79–88.

Lindblom, C. E. *The Intelligence of Democracy.* New York: Free Press, 1965.

Lindblom, C. E. *Politics and Markets.* New York: Free Press, 1977.

Lindblom, C. E. *The Policy-making Process.* (2d ed.) Englewood Cliffs, N.J.: Prentice Hall, 1980.

Linder, S. H., and Peters, B. G. "Implementation as a Guide to Policy Formulation: A Question of 'When' Rather Than 'Whether.'" *International Review of Administrative Sciences,* 1989, *55,* 631–652.

Lipsky, M. "Protest as Political Resource." *American Political Science Review,* 1968, *62*(4), 1144–1158.

Lipsky, M. *Street-Level Bureaucracy: Dilemmas of the Individual in Public Services.* New York: Russell Sage Foundation, 1980.

Lodahl, T., and Mitchell, S. "Drift in the Development of Innovative Organizations." In J. Kimberly and R. Miles (eds.), *The Organizational Life Cycle: Issues in the Creation, Transformation, and Decline of Organizations.* San Francisco: Jossey-Bass, 1980.

Long, N. "The Local Community as an Ecology of Games." *American Journal of Sociology,* 1958, *64,* 251–261.

Lowi, T. "American Business, Public Policy and Political Theory." *World Politics,* 1964, *16,* 677–715.

Lowi, T. "Four Systems of Policy, Politics, and Choice." *Public Administration Review,* 1972, *32,* 298–310.

Lowi, T., and Ginsberg, B. *American Government.* (2d ed.) New York: Norton, 1992.

Lukas, A. J. *Common Ground.* New York: Vintage, 1985.

Luke, J. S. "Managing Interconnectedness." In J. B. Bryson and R. C. Einsweiler (eds.), *Shared Power.* Lanham, Md.: University Press of America, 1991.

Luke, J. S., and Caiden, G. E. "Coping with Global Interdependence." In J. L. Perry (ed.), *Handbook of Public Administration*. San Francisco: Jossey-Bass, 1989.

Lukes, S. *Power: A Radical View*. New York: Macmillan, 1974.

Lyles, M. A., and Thomas, H. "Strategic Problem Formulation: Biases and Assumptions Embedded in Alternative Decision-making Models." *Journal of Management*, 1988, *25*(2), 131–145.

Lynn, L. E., Jr. *Managing Public Policy*. Boston: Little, Brown, 1987.

McCall, M. W., and Kaplan, R. E. *Whatever It Takes: Decision Makers at Work*. (Rev. ed.) Englewood Cliffs, N.J.: Prentice Hall, 1990.

McCaskey, M. "A Contingency Approach to Planning: Planning with Goals and Planning Without Goals." *Academy of Management Review*, 1974, *17*, 281–291.

Maccoby, M. *The Leader*. New York: Ballantine, 1983.

McCracken, G. *The Long Interview*. Vol. 13: *Qualitative Research Methods*. Newbury Park, Calif.: Sage, 1988.

McCullough, D. *The Path Between the Seas*. New York: Simon & Schuster, 1977.

McKillip, J. *Need Analysis*. Vol. 10: *Applied Social Research Methods*. Newbury Park, Calif.: Sage, 1987.

McNeil, K. "Understanding Organizational Power: Building on the Weberian Legacy." In M. Zey-Ferrell and M. Aiken (eds.), *Complex Organizations: Critical Perspectives*. Glenview, Ill.: ScottForesman, 1981.

Mandelbaum, S. J. "Telling Stories." *Journal of Planning Education and Research*, 1991, *10*(3), 209–214.

Mangham, I. L. *Power and Performance in Organizations*. Oxford, England: Basil Blackwell, 1986.

Mangham, I. L., and Overington, M. A. *Organizations as Theatre: A Social Psychology of Dramatic Appearances*. New York: Wiley, 1987.

Manz, C. C. "Self-Leadership: Toward an Expanded Theory of Self-Influence Processes in Organizations." *Academy of Management Review*, 1986, *11*, 585–600.

Manz, C. C., and Sims, H. P. *SuperLeadership*. New York: Prentice Hall, 1989.

March, J. G. "Decisions in Organizations and Theories of Choice." In A. H. Van de Ven and W. F. Joyce (eds.), *Perspectives on Organization Design and Behavior.* New York: Wiley, 1981.

March, J. G., and Olsen, J. P. *Ambiguity and Choice in Organizations.* (2d ed.) Bergen: Universitetsforlaget, 1979.

March, J., and Simon, H. *Organizations.* New York: Wiley, 1958.

May, J. V., and Wildavsky, A. B. *The Policy Cycle.* Newbury Park, Calif.: Sage, 1978.

May, R. *Love and Will.* New York: Norton, 1969.

Mayhew, D. R. *Congress: The Electoral Connection.* New Haven, Conn.: Yale University Press, 1974.

Maynard-Moody, S. "Stories Public Managers Tell: Making Sense out of the Defunct Dichotomy." Paper presented at the National Public Management Research Conference, Maxwell School, Syracuse University, Syracuse, N.Y., Sept. 1991.

Mazmanian, D. A., and Sabatier, P. A. (eds.). *Effective Policy Implementation.* Lexington, Mass.: Heath, 1981.

Mazmanian, D. A., and Sabatier, P. A. *Implementation and Public Policy.* Glenview, Ill.: ScottForesman, 1983.

Meltsner, A. J. *Rules for Rulers: The Politics of Advice.* Philadelphia: Temple University Press, 1990.

Merton, R. K. "Bureaucratic Structures and Personality. *Journal of Social Forces,* 1940, *17,* 560–568.

Meyers, M. "GNP Is Out; GDP Is In." *Minneapolis Star Tribune,* Dec. 4, 1991, p. D1.

Miles, M. B., and Huberman, A. M. *Qualitative Data Analysis.* Newbury Park, Calif.: Sage, 1984.

Milhone, K. "A Justification for the Study of Followership." Minneapolis: Student Organizational Development Center, University of Minnesota, 1987.

Milward, H. B. "Interorganizational Policy Systems and Research on Public Organizations." *Administration and Society,* 1982, *13*(4), 457–478.

Milward, H. B. "Current Institutional Arrangements That Create or Require Shared Power." In J. M. Bryson and R. C. Einsweiler (eds.), *Shared Power.* Lanham, Md.: University Press of America, 1991.

Milward, H. B., and Laird, W. "Where Does Policy Come From?" Paper presented at the Western Political Science Association Meeting, Newport Beach, Calif., Mar. 1990.

Mintzberg, H. *The Nature of Managerial Work.* New York: Harper-Collins, 1973.

Mintzberg, H. "Crafting Strategy." *Harvard Business Review,* July–Aug. 1987, 66–75.

Mintzberg, H., and Waters, J. A. "Of Strategies, Deliberate and Emergent." *Strategic Management Journal,* 1985, *6,* 257–272.

Mitnick, B. *The Political Economy of Regulation: Creating, Designing and Removing Regulatory Forms.* New York: Columbia University Press, 1980.

Mitroff, I., and Featheringham, D. "On Systematic Problem Solving and Errors of the Third Kind." *Behavioral Science,* 1984, *19,* 383–393.

Moe, T. M. *The Organization of Interests: Incentives and the Internal Dynamics of Political Interest Groups.* Chicago: University of Chicago Press, 1980.

Moe, T. M. "The Politics of Structural Choice: Toward a Theory of Public Bureaucracy." Paper presented at the annual meeting of the American Political Science Association, Washington, D.C., Sept. 1988.

Monnet, J. *Memoirs.* New York: Doubleday, 1978.

Moore, C. M. *Group Techniques for Idea Building.* Vol. 9: *Applied Social Research Methods.* Newbury Park, Calif.: Sage, 1987.

Morgan, D. L. *Focus Groups as Qualitative Research.* Vol. 16: *Qualitative Research Methods.* Newbury Park, Calif.: Sage, 1988.

Morgan, G. *Images of Organization.* Newbury Park, Calif.: Sage, 1986.

Morgan, G. *Riding the Waves of Change: Developing Managerial Competencies for a Turbulent World.* San Francisco: Jossey-Bass, 1988.

Morris, P., and Hough, G. *Preconditions of Success and Failure in Major Projects.* Major Projects Association Technical Paper, No. 3. Oxford, England: Templeton College, Oxford University, 1986.

Morrisey, G. L., Below, P. J., and Acomb, B. L. *The Executive Guide to Operational Planning.* San Francisco: Jossey-Bass, 1987.

Munter, M. "How to Conduct a Successful Media Interview." *California Management Review,* 1983, *25*(4), 143–150.

Murdock, M. *The Heroine's Journey.* Boston: Shambhala, 1990.

Myers, I. B., with Myers, P. B. *Gifts Differing.* Palo Alto, Calif.: Consulting Psychologists Press, 1980.

Nadler, N., and Nadler, Z. *The Comprehensive Guide to Successful Conferences and Meetings: Detailed Instructions and Step-by-Step Checklists.* San Francisco: Jossey-Bass, 1987.

Neely, R. *How the Courts Govern America.* New Haven, Conn.: Yale University Press, 1981.

Nelson, B. J. *Making an Issue of Child Abuse.* Chicago: University of Chicago Press, 1981.

Neustadt, R. E. *Presidential Power and the Modern Presidents.* New York: Free Press, 1990.

Neustadt, R. E., and May, E. R. *Thinking in Time: The Uses of History for Decision Makers.* New York: Free Press, 1986.

Nicoll, D. "Leadership and Followership: Fresh Views on an Old Subject." In J. D. Adams (ed.), *Transforming Leadership: From Visions to Results.* Alexandria, Va.: Miles River, 1984.

Nordlinger, E. *On the Autonomy of the Democratic State.* Cambridge, Mass.: Harvard University Press, 1981.

Nutt, P. C. "Types of Organizational Decision Processes." *Administrative Science Quarterly,* 1984, *29,* 414–450.

Nutt, P. C. "Idea Development in Decision Making." Unpublished paper, Department of Management Sciences, School of Business, Ohio State University, Columbus, 1991.

Nutt, P. C. "Formulation Processes and Tactics." *Organization Science,* 1992 (forthcoming).

Nutt, P. C., and Backoff, R. W. *Strategic Management of Public and Third Sector Organizations: A Handbook for Leaders.* San Francisco: Jossey-Bass, 1992.

Oates, S. B. *Let the Trumpet Sound: The Life of Martin Luther King, Jr.* New York: New American Library, 1982.

O'Connell, B. *The Board Member's Book: Making a Difference in Voluntary Organizations.* New York: Foundation Center, 1985.

O'Neill, M. *The Third America: The Emergence of the Nonprofit Sector in the United States.* San Francisco: Jossey-Bass, 1989.

Ory, H. W., Forrest, J. D., and Lincoln, R. *Making Choices: Evaluating the Health Risks and Benefits of Birth Control Methods.* New York: Alan Guttmacher Institute, 1983.

Ostrom, E. *Governing the Commons.* New York: Cambridge University Press, 1990.

O'Toole, L. J., and Montjoy, R. S. "Interorganizational Policy Implementation: A Theoretical Perspective." *Public Administration Review,* 1984, *44*(6), 491–503.

Ouchi, W. "M-Form: Making Decisions and Building Consensus." *Challenge,* July–Aug. 1984, 31–37.

Ozbekhan, H. "Toward a General Theory of Planning." In E. Jantsch (ed.), *Perspectives of Planning.* Paris: Organization for Economic Cooperation and Development, 1969.

Paige, C. *The Right to Lifers.* New York: Summit Books, 1983.

Palmer, P. J. *The Active Life: A Spirituality of Work, Creativity, and Courage.* New York: HarperCollins, 1990.

Patton, M. Q. *Practical Evaluation.* Newbury Park, Calif.: Sage, 1982.

Patton, M. Q. *Utilization-Focused Evaluation.* (2d ed.) Newbury Park, Calif.: Sage, 1986.

Patton, M. Q. *Creative Evaluation.* (2d ed.) Newbury Park, Calif.: Sage, 1987.

Patton, M. Q. *Qualitative Evaluation and Research Methods.* Newbury Park, Calif.: Sage, 1990.

Pearson, C. *The Hero Within: Six Archetypes We Live By.* San Francisco: HarperSan Francisco, 1986.

Perry, J. L. (ed.). *Handbook of Public Administration.* San Francisco: Jossey-Bass, 1989.

Peters, B. G., and Hogwood, B. W. "In Search of the Issue-Attention Cycle." *Journal of Politics,* 1985, *47,* 238–253.

Peters, T. J., and Waterman, R. H., Jr. *In Search of Excellence: Lessons from America's Best-Run Companies.* New York: HarperCollins, 1982.

Peterson, P. *City Limits.* Chicago: University of Chicago Press, 1981.

Pfeffer, J. *Power in Organizations.* Marshfield, Mass.: Pitman, 1981.

Pfeffer, J., and Salancik, G. R. *The External Control of Organizations.* New York: HarperCollins, 1978.

Polsby, N. "Legislatures." In F. I. Greenstein and N. Polsby (eds.), *Handbook of Political Science.* Vol. 5: *Governmental Institutions and Processes.* Reading, Mass.: Addison-Wesley, 1975.

Posner, R. A. *The Federal Courts: Crisis and Reform.* Cambridge, Mass.: Harvard University Press, 1985.

Pressman, J., and Wildavsky, A. *Implementation.* Berkeley: University of California Press, 1973.

Prince, G. M. *The Practice of Creativity.* New York: Collier, 1970.

Provan, K. G. "The Federation as an Interorganizational Linkage Network." *Academy of Management Review,* 1983, *8,* 79–89.

Quinn, J. B. *Strategies for Change: Logical Incrementalism.* Homewood, Ill.: Dow Jones–Irwin, 1980.

Quinn, R. E. *Beyond Rational Management: Mastering the Paradoxes and Competing Demands of High Performance.* San Francisco: Jossey-Bass, 1988.

Quirk, P. J. "In Defense of the Politics of Ideas." *Journal of Politics,* 1988, *50,* 31–41.

Rainey, H. *Understanding and Managing Public Organizations.* San Francisco: Jossey-Bass, 1991.

Randolph, W. A., and Posner, B. Z. *Effective Project Planning and Management.* Englewood Cliffs, N.J.: Prentice Hall, 1988.

Reich, R. B. "Entrepreneurship Reconsidered: The Team as Hero." *Harvard Business Review,* 1987a, *65*(3), 77–83.

Reich, R. B. *Tales of a New America.* New York: Times Books, 1987b.

Reich, R. B. *The Power of Public Ideas.* New York: HarperBusiness, 1988.

Reid, T. R. *Congressional Odyssey: The Saga of a Senate Bill.* San Francisco: W.H. Freeman, 1980.

Rein, M., and White, S. H. "Policy Research: Belief and Doubt." *Policy Analysis,* 1976, *3*(2), 239–271.

Riker, W. H. *The Theory of Political Coalitions.* New Haven, Conn.: Yale University Press, 1962.

Riker, W. H. *The Art of Political Manipulation.* New Haven, Conn.: Yale University Press, 1986.

Rittel, H.W.J., and Webber, M. M. "Dilemmas in a General Theory of Planning." *Policy Sciences,* 1973, *4,* 155–169.

Roberts, N. C. "Towards a Synergistic Model of Power." In J. M. Bryson and R. C. Einsweiler (eds.), *Shared Power.* Lanham, Md.: University Press of America, 1991.

Roberts, N. C., and King, P. J. "Public Entrepreneurship: A Typology." Paper presented to the Public Sector Division of the Academy of Management, Washington, D.C., Aug. 1989.

Roberts, N. C., and King, P. J. "Policy Entrepreneurs: Their Activity Structure and Function in the Policy Process." *Journal of Public Administration Research and Theory,* 1991, *1*(2), 147–175.

Rogers, D. L., Whetten, D. A., and others. *Interorganizational Coordination.* Ames: Iowa State University Press, 1982.

Rogers, E. *Diffusion of Innovations.* (3d ed.) New York: Free Press, 1982.

Rosen, D. M. "Leadership in World Cultures." In B. Kellerman (ed.), *Leadership: Multidisciplinary Perspectives.* Englewood Cliffs, N. J.: Prentice Hall, 1984.

Rosenhead, J. (ed.). *Rational Analysis for a Problematic World.* New York: Wiley, 1989.

Sabatier, P. A. "An Advocacy Coalition Framework of Policy Change and the Role of Policy-Oriented Learning Therein." *Policy Sciences,* 1988, *21,* 129–168.

Sabatier, P. A. "Toward Better Theories of the Policy Process." *PS: Political Science & Politics,* 1991, *24*(2), 144–156.

Salancik, G. R. "Commitment and the Control of Organizational Behavior and Belief." In B. M. Shaw and G. R. Salancik (eds.), *New Directions in Organizational Behavior.* Chicago: St. Clair Press, 1977.

Schaef, A. W. *Women's Reality.* San Francisco: HarperCollins, 1985.

Schattschneider, E. E. *The Semisovereign People: A Realist's View of Democracy in America.* (Reissued with an introduction by David Adamany.) Hinsdale, Ill.: Dryden Press, 1975.

Schein, E. H. *Organizational Culture and Leadership: A Dynamic View.* San Francisco: Jossey-Bass, 1985.

Schneeweis, J. "The Building of Castles: Leadership, Professional Practice and Storytelling." Unpublished paper, University of Minnesota, 1986.

Schneider, A., and Ingram, H. "Behavioral Assumptions of Policy Tools." *Journal of Politics,* 1990, *52,* 510–529.

Schon, D. A. *Beyond the Stable State.* London: Temple Smith, 1971.

Schon, D. A. *The Reflective Practitioner.* New York: Basic Books, 1983.

Schorr, L. B., with Schorr, D. *Within Our Reach.* New York: Anchor Press, 1988.

Schriesheim, C. A., Tolliver, J. M., and Behling, O. C. "Leadership Theory: Some Implications for Managers." In A. D. Timpe (ed.), *Leadership*. New York: Facts on File, 1987.

Schultze, C. L. *The Politics and Economics of Public Spending*. Washington, D.C.: Brookings Institution, 1968.

Schultze, C. L. *The Public Use of Private Interest*. Washington, D.C.: Brookings Institution, 1977.

Schutz, A. *The Phenomenology of the Social World*. Evanston, Ill.: Northwestern University Press, 1967.

Schwenk, C. R. "Cognitive Simplification Processes in Strategic Decision-making." *Strategic Management Journal*, 1984, *5*, 111–128.

Scriven, M. S. "The Methodology of Evaluation." In R. E. Stake (ed.), *Curriculum Evaluation*. Vol. 1: *AERA Monograph Series on Curriculum Evaluation*. Skokie, Ill.: Rand McNally, 1967.

Seligman, M.E.P. *Learned Optimism*. New York: Knopf, 1991.

Selznick, P. *TVA and the Grassroots*. Berkeley: University of California Press, 1949.

Selznick, P. *Leadership in Administration*. Berkeley: University of California Press, 1957.

Senge, P. M. *The Fifth Discipline: The Art and Practice of the Learning Organization*. New York: Doubleday, 1990.

Sennett, R. *Authority*. New York: Knopf, 1980.

Shapiro, M. *Law and Politics in the Supreme Court*. New York: Free Press, 1964.

Shapiro, M. "Courts." In F. I. Greenstein and N. Polsby (eds.), *Handbook of Political Science*. Vol. 5: *Governmental Institutions and Processes*. Reading, Mass.: Addison-Wesley, 1975.

Shapiro, M. *Courts: A Comparative and Political Analysis*. Chicago: University of Chicago Press, 1981.

Shapiro, M. "On Predicting the Future of Administrative Law." *Regulation*, 1982, *6*(3), 18–25.

Sharkansky, I. *The Routines of Politics*. New York: Van Nostrand Reinhold, 1970.

Sherrill, R. *Gothic Politics in the Deep South*. New York: Ballantine, 1969.

Simon, H. A. *Administrative Behavior*. New York: Macmillan, 1947.

Simon, H. A. *Administrative Behavior.* (2d ed.) New York: Macmillan, 1957.

Smircich, L., and Morgan, G. "Leadership: The Management of Meaning." *Journal of Applied Behavioral Science,* 1989, *18,* 257–273.

Smucker, B. *The Nonprofit Lobbying Guide: Advocating Your Cause — And Getting Results.* San Francisco: Jossey-Bass, 1991.

Spencer, L. *Winning Through Participation.* Dubuque, Iowa: Kendall/Hunt, 1989.

Staw, B. M., and Ross, J. "Commitment to a Policy Decision: A Multi-Theoretical Perspective." *Administrative Science Quarterly,* 1978, *23,* 40–64.

Stewart, D. *Secondary Research.* Vol. 4: *Applied Social Research Methods.* Newbury Park, Calif.: Sage, 1984.

Stewart, D., and Shamdasani, P. N. *Focus Groups.* Vol. 20: *Applied Social Research Methods.* Newbury Park, Calif.: Sage, 1990.

Stewart, R. *Choices for the Manager.* Englewood Cliffs, N.J.: Prentice Hall, 1982a.

Stewart, R. "The Relevance of Some Studies of Managerial Work and Behavior to Leadership Research." In J. G. Hunt, U. Sekaran, and C. Schriescheim (eds.), *Leadership: Beyond Establishment Views.* Carbondale: Southern Illinois University Press, 1982b.

Stogdill, R. M. "Personal Factors Associated with Leadership." *Journal of Psychology,* 1948, *25,* 35–71.

Stone, D. A. *Policy Paradox and Political Reason.* Glenview, Ill.: ScottForesman, 1988.

Straus, M. "Cultural Leadership and the Avant-Garde." In B. Kellerman (ed.), *Leadership: Multidisciplinary Perspectives.* Englewood Cliffs, N.J.: Prentice Hall, 1984.

Strunk, W., and White, E. B. *The Elements of Style.* (3d ed.) New York: Macmillan, 1982.

Stuart, D. G. "Rational Urban Planning: Problems and Prospects." *Urban Affairs Quarterly,* 1969, *5*(2), 151–182.

Sturdevant, L. "Catholic Church Closely Tied to State Pro-Life Group." *Minneapolis Star Tribune,* July 16, 1978, p. 11.

Suchman, E. A. *Evaluative Research.* New York: Russell Sage Foundation, 1967.

Susskind, L., and Cruikshank, J. *Breaking the Impasse: Consensual Approaches to Resolving Public Disputes.* New York: Basic Books, 1987.

Swidler, A. "Culture in Action: Symbols and Strategies." *American Sociological Review,* April 1986, *51,* 273–286.

Tan, A. *The Joy Luck Club.* New York: Ivy Books, 1989.

Taylor, H. R. "Power at Work." In A. D. Timpe (ed.), *Leadership.* New York: Facts on File, 1987.

Terry, R. *Action Leadership.* Unpublished manuscript, Hubert H. Humphrey Institute of Public Affairs. Minneapolis: University of Minnesota, 1988.

Terry, R. *Rethinking Leadership: Building a Framework for Authentic Action.* San Francisco: Jossey-Bass, forthcoming.

Thompson, J. D. *Organizations in Action.* New York: McGraw-Hill, 1967.

Thompson, J. D., and Tuden, A. "Strategies, Structures, and Processes of Organizational Decision." In J. D. Thompson and others (eds.), *Comparative Studies in Administration.* Pittsburgh, Pa.: University of Pittsburgh Press, 1959.

Throgmorton, J. A. "The Rhetoric of Policy Analysis." *Policy Sciences,* 1991, *24,* 153–179.

Timpe, A. D. *Leadership.* New York: Facts on File, 1987.

Toulmin, S. *The Uses of Argument.* New York: Cambridge University Press, 1958.

Tribe, L. H. *God Save This Honorable Court.* Cambridge, Mass.: Harvard University Press, 1985.

Tribe, L. H. *Abortion: The Clash of Absolutes.* New York: Norton, 1990.

Trist, E. "Referent Organizations and the Development of Interorganizational Domains." *Human Relations,* 1983, *36*(3), 269–284.

Tuchman, B. *The March of Folly: From Troy to Vietnam.* New York: Knopf, 1984.

U.S. Department of Education. *America 2000: An Education Strategy.* Washington, D.C.: U.S. Department of Education, 1991.

Utterback, J. "Innovation in Industry and the Diffusion of Technology." *Science,* 1974, *183,* 620–626.

Van de Ven, A. H. "In Search of Excellence: Lessons from America's Best-Run Companies." Book review. *Administrative Quarterly*, 1983, *28*(4), 621–624.

Van de Ven, A. H. "Findings on Innovation Development from the Minnesota Innovation Research Program." Discussion Paper, no. 151. Minneapolis: Strategic Management Research Center, University of Minnesota, 1990a.

Van de Ven, A. H. "Managing the Process of Novel Organizational Change." Discussion Paper, no. 148. Minneapolis: Strategic Management Research Center, University of Minnesota, 1990b.

Van de Ven, A. H., Angle, H. L., and Poole, M. S. *Research on the Management of Innovation*. New York: HarperCollins, 1989.

Van de Ven, A. H., Emmett, D., and Koenig, R., Jr. "Frameworks for Inter-organizational Analysis." *Organization and Administrative Sciences Journal*, 1974, *5*(1), 113–129.

Vance, J. *Inside the Minnesota Experiment: A Personal Recollection of Experimental Planning and Development in the Twin Cities Metropolitan Area*. Minneapolis: Center for Urban and Regional Affairs, University of Minnesota, 1977.

VanDoren, P. "Should Congress Listen to Economists?" *Journal of Politics*, 1989, *51*, 319–336.

VanHorn, C. E., Baumer, D. C., and Gormley, W. T. *Politics and Public Policy*. Washington, D.C.: CQ Press, 1992.

Verdier, J. M. "Advising Congressional Decision-Makers." *Journal of Policy Analysis and Management*, 1984, *3*(3), 421–438.

Vickers, G. *The Art of Judgment: A Study of Policy Making*. New York: Basic Books, 1965.

Volkema, R. J. "Problem Formulation in Planning and Design." *Management Science*, 1983, *29*(6), 639–652.

Volkema, R. J. "Problem Formulation as a Purposive Activity." *Strategic Management Journal*, 1986, *7*, 267–279.

Volkema, R. J. "Problem Formulation in Planning and Design: What We Know and What We'd Like to Know." Proceedings of the Conference on Planning and Design in Management of Business and Organization, International Congress on Planning and Design Theory, Boston, Aug. 1987, 91–95.

Von Oech, R. *A Whack on the Side of the Head: How to Unlock Your Mind for Innovation.* New York: Basic Books, 1983.

Vroom, V. H., and Yetton, P. W. *Leadership and Decision Making.* Pittsburgh, Pa.: University of Pittsburgh Press, 1973.

Wallace, D., and White, J. B. "Building Integrity in Organizations." *New Management,* 1988, *6*(1), 30–35.

Wallerstein, I. *The Modern World System.* (Text ed.) New York: Academic Press, 1974.

Wallerstein, I. *The Modern World–System II.* New York: Academic Press, 1980.

Waste, R. J. *The Ecology of City Policymaking.* New York: Oxford University Press, 1989.

Weber, M. *The Theory of Social and Economic Organization.* (A. M. Henderson and T. Parsons, trans.) New York: Free Press, 1947.

Weber, M. *On Charisma and Institution Building: Selected Papers.* S. N. Eisenstadt, ed. Chicago: University of Chicago Press, 1952.

Weick, K. *The Social Psychology of Organizing.* (2nd ed.) Reading, Mass.: Addison-Wesley, 1979.

Weick, K. E. "Small Wins: Redefining the Scale of Social Problems." *American Psychologist,* 1984, *39*(1), 40–49.

Weimer, D. L., and Vining, A. R. *Policy Analysis: Concepts and Practice.* Englewood Cliffs, N.J.: Prentice Hall, 1989.

Whetten, D. A. "Sources, Responses, and Effects of Organizational Decline." In J. R. Kimberly, R. H. Miles, and Associates, *The Organizational Life Cycle: Issues in the Creation, Transformation, and Decline of Organizations.* San Francisco: Jossey-Bass, 1980.

Whetten, D. A., and Bozeman, B. "Policy Coordination." In J. M. Bryson and R. C. Einsweiler (eds.) *Shared Power.* Lanham, Md.: University Press of America, 1991.

Wildavsky, A. *Speaking Truth to Power: The Art and Craft of Policy Analysis.* Boston: Little, Brown, 1979.

Wildavsky, A. *The Politics of the Budgetary Process.* (4th ed.) Boston: Little, Brown, 1984.

Wildavsky, A. "Choosing Preferences by Constructing Institutions: A Cultural Theory of Preference Formation." *American Political Science Review,* 1987, *81*(1), 3–21.

Wildavsky, A. *The New Politics of the Budgetary Process.* Glenview, Ill.: ScottForesman, 1988.

Wilensky, A. J. *The Twin Cities Metropolitan Council: A Case Study in the Politics of Metropolitan Cooperation.* Unpublished senior thesis, Woodrow Wilson School of Public and International Affairs, Princeton University, 1969.

Williamson, O. E. *The Economic Institutions of Capitalism: Firms, Markets, Relational Contracting.* New York: Free Press, 1985.

Wilson, J. Q. "Innovation in Organizations: Notes Toward a Theory." In J. D. Thompson (ed.), *Approaches to Organizational Design.* Pittsburgh: University of Pittsburgh Press, 1967.

Wilson, J. Q. *Political Organizations.* New York: Basic Books, 1973.

Wilson, J. Q. "The Politics of Regulation." In J. Q. Wilson (ed.), *The Politics of Regulation.* New York: Basic Books, 1980.

Wilson, J. Q. *American Government: Institutions and Policies.* Lexington, Mass.: D. C. Heath, 1986.

Wilson, J. Q. *Bureaucracy.* New York: Basic Books, 1989.

Wise, C. R. *The Dynamics of Legislation: Leadership and Policy Change in the Congressional Process.* San Francisco: Jossey-Bass, 1991.

Wittrock, B., and deLeon, P. "Policy as a Moving Target: A Call for Conceptual Realism." *Policy Studies Review,* 1986, *6*(1), 44–60.

Wolman, H. "The Determinants of Program Success and Failure." *Journal of Public Policy,* 1981, *1*(4), 433–464.

Women's Equity Action League. "Equity for Wives Under Social Security." *WEAL Washington Report,* July 1976, pp. 1, 4.

Yin, R. K. "Life Histories of Innovations: How New Practices Become Routinized." *Public Administration Review,* Jan.-Feb. 1982, 21–28.

Young, O. R. "Regime Dynamics: The Rise and Fall of International Regimes." *International Organization,* 1982, *36*(2), 277–297.

Young, O. R. "International Regimes: Toward a New Theory of Institutions." *World Politics,* 1986, *34,* 104–122.

Young, O. R. *International Cooperation: Building Regimes for Natural Resources and the Environment.* Ithaca, N.Y.: Cornell University Press, 1989.

Zaleznik, A. "Charismatic and Consensus Leaders: A Psychological Comparison." In M.F.R. Kets de Vries (ed.), *The Irrational Executive: Psychoanalytic Explorations in Management*. New York: International Universities Press, 1984.

Zaltman, G., and Duncan, R. *Strategies for Planned Change*. New York: Wiley-Interscience, 1977.

Zaltman, G., Duncan, R., and Holbek, J. *Innovations and Organizations*. New York: Wiley-Interscience, 1973.

Zeckhauser, R. J., and Leebaert, D. (eds.). *What Role for Government?* Duke Press Policy Studies. Durham, N.C.: Duke University Press, 1983.

Ziegler, H., and Baer, M. A. *Lobbying: Interaction and Influence in American State Legislatures*. Belmont, Calif.: Wadsworth, 1969.

Name Index

Subject Index

A

Abortion policies case: and adoption phase, 248–250, 253–254, 260, 262, 264–265; arenas for, 101, 105–108; in assessment phase, 322, 325–327, 330–334; courts for, 110, 112–114; forums for, 93–100; and implementation, 282–285, 290, 296, 301, 303, 305, 306, 308, 310, 319; and initial agreement, 126–127, 129, 131, 134–136, 138, 139, 145, 150, 151; and leadership tasks, 32, 34, 40, 46, 50, 54–55; and policy change cycle, 60, 67–69, 71, 72, 75, 77–79; and problem formulation, 163, 165–167, 169–174, 177–180, 182; and proposal development, 219–220, 223–225, 227, 235, 243; and settings of power, 89, 131; and

shared power, 22, 26–29, 342–345; and solution search, 193–195, 199, 204, 205

Abortion Rights Council, 334

Access: to arenas, 104–105, 106; to courts, 113–114; to forums, 100–101

Action plan: for implementation, 298–299; for shared power, 355

Administrative Procedures Act, 304

Adoption phase: announcements in, 273; aspects of, 72–73, 246–280; bandwagon effect in, 254–255, 272–273; cases of, 247–250; caveats on, 276–279; coupling in, 252–259; and courts, 248–250, 258, 263–265, 274; desired outcomes and benefits of, 250–252; failures at, 277, 279; formal session for, 273–274, 276–277; heresthetics in, 259–263; implementation guidance at,

423